Expedition into Empire

Expeditionary journeys have shaped our world, but the expedition as a cultural form is rarely scrutinized. This book is the first major investigation of the conventions and social practices embedded in team-based exploration. In probing the politics of expedition making, this volume is itself a pioneering journey through the cultures of empire. With contributions from established and emerging scholars, *Expedition into Empire* plots the rise and transformation of expeditionary journeys from the eighteenth century until the present. Conceived as a series of spotlights on imperial travel and colonial expansion, it roves widely: from the metropolitan centers to the ends of the earth. This collection is both rigorous and accessible, containing lively case studies from writers long immersed in exploration, travel literature, and the dynamics of cross-cultural encounter.

Martin Thomas is Associate Professor in the Research School of Social Sciences at the Australian National University. He is the author of *The Artificial Horizon: Imagining the Blue Mountains* (2003) and *The Many Worlds of R. H. Mathews: In Search of an Australian Anthropologist* (2011), winner of the National Biography Award of Australia.

Routledge Studies in Cultural History

For a full list of titles in this series, please visit www.routledge.com

3 Film, History, and Cultural Citizenship
Sites of Production
Edited by Tina Mai Chen and David S. Churchill

4 Genre and Cinema
Ireland and Transnationalism
Edited by Brian McIlroy

5 Histories of Postmodernism
Edited by Mark Bevir, Jill Hargis, and Sara Rushing

6 Africa after Modernism
Transitions in Literature, Media, and Philosophy
Michael Janis

7 Rethinking Race, Politics, and Poetics
C.L.R. James' Critique of Modernity
Brett St Louis

8 Making British Culture
English Readers and the Scottish Enlightenment, 1740–1830
David Allan

9 Empires and Boundaries
Rethinking Race, Class, and Gender in Colonial Settings
Edited by Harald Fischer-Tiné and Susanne Gehrmann

10 Tobacco in Russian History and Culture
From the Seventeenth Century to the Present
Edited by Matthew P. Romaniello and Tricia Starks

11 History of Islam in German Thought
From Leibniz to Nietzsche
Ian Almond

12 Israeli-Palestinian Conflict in the Francophone World
Edited by Nathalie Debrauwere-Miller

13 History of Participatory Media
Politics and Publics, 1750–2000
Edited by Anders Ekström Solveig Jülich, Frans Lundgren, and Per Wisselgren

14 Living in the City
Urban Institutions in the Low Countries, 1200–2010
Leo Lucassen and Wim Willems

15 Historical Disasters in Context
Science, Religion, and Politics
Edited by Andrea Janku, Gerrit J. Schenk, and Franz Mauelshagen

16 **Migration, Ethnicity, and Mental Health**
International Perspectives, 1840–2010
Edited by Angela McCarthy and Catharine Coleborne

17 **Politics of Memory: Making Slavery Visible in the Public Space**
Edited by Ana Lucia Araujo

18 **Neutrality in Twentieth-Century Europe**
Intersections of Science, Culture, and Politics after the First World War
Edited by Rebecka Lettevall, Geert Somsen, and Sven Widmalm

19 **Americans Experience Russia**
Encountering the Enigma, 1917 to the Present
Edited by Choi Chatterjee and Beth Holmgren

20 **A Social History of Disability in the Middle Ages**
Cultural Considerations of Physical Impairment
Irina Metzler

21 **Race, Science, and the Nation**
Reconstructing the Ancient Past in Britain, France and Germany
Chris Manias

22 **Identity, Aesthetics, and Sound in the Fin de Siècle**
Redesigning Perception
Dariusz Gafijczuk

23 **Disease and Crime**
A History of Social Pathologies and the New Politics of Health
Edited by Robert Peckham

24 **Critical Perspectives on Colonialism**
Writing the Empire from Below
Edited by Fiona Paisley and Kirsty Reid

25 **Old World Empires**
Cultures of Power and Governance in Eurasia
Ilhan Niaz

26 **The Afterlife of Used Things**
Recycling in the Long Eighteenth Century
Edited by Ariane Fennetaux, Amélie Junqua, and Sophie Vasset

27 **Holocaust Consciousness in Contemporary Britain**
Andy Pearce

28 **The Invention of Race**
Scientific and Popular Representations
Edited by Nicolas Bancel, Thomas David, and Dominic Thomas

29 **Indigenous Networks**
Mobility, Connections and Exchange
Edited by Jane Carey and Jane Lydon

30 **Shadows of the Slave Past**
Memory, Heritage, and Slavery
Ana Lucia Araujo

31 **Expedition into Empire**
Exploratory Journeys and the Making of the Modern World
Edited by Martin Thomas

Expedition into Empire
Exploratory Journeys and the Making of the Modern World

Edited by Martin Thomas

LONDON AND NEW YORK

First published 2015 by Routledge

2 Park Square, Milton Park, Abingdon, Oxfordshire OX14 4RN
52 Vanderbilt Avenue, New York, NY 10017

Routledge is an imprint of the Taylor & Francis Group, an informa business

First issued in paperback 2018

Copyright © 2015 Taylor & Francis

The right of Martin Edward Thomas to be identified as the author of the editorial material, and of the authors for their individual chapters, has been asserted in accordance with sections 77 and 78 of the Copyright, Designs and Patents Act 1988.

All rights reserved. No part of this book may be reprinted or reproduced or utilised in any form or by any electronic, mechanical, or other means, now known or hereafter invented, including photocopying and recording, or in any information storage or retrieval system, without permission in writing from the publishers.

Notice:
Product or corporate names may be trademarks or registered trademarks, and are used only for identification and explanation without intent to infringe.

Library of Congress Cataloging-in-Publication Data

Expedition into empire : exploratory journeys and the making of the modern world / edited by Martin Thomas.
    pages cm. — (Routledge studies in cultural history ; 31)
    Includes bibliographical references and index.
  1. Discoveries in geography—History.   2. Discoveries in geography—
Social aspects.   3. Voyages and travels—History.   I. Thomas, Martin, 1964–
    G80.E88 2014
    910.9—dc23
    2014018418

ISBN: 978-1-138-79068-1 (hbk)
ISBN: 978-0-367-20883-7 (pbk)

Typeset in Sabon
by Apex CoVantage, LLC

Contents

List of Figures		ix
Acknowledgments		xi
1	What Is an Expedition? An Introduction	1
	MARTIN THOMAS	
2	What Is an Explorer?	25
	ADRIANA CRACIUN	
3	Settler Colonial Expeditions	51
	LORENZO VERACINI	
4	The Expedition as a Cultural Form: On the Structure of Exploratory Journeys as Revealed by the Australian Explorations of Ludwig Leichhardt	65
	MARTIN THOMAS	
5	The Theatre of Contact: Aborigines and Exploring Expeditions	88
	PHILIP JONES	
6	Expeditions, Encounters, and the Praxis of Seaborne Ethnography: The French Voyages of La Pérouse and Freycinet	108
	BRONWEN DOUGLAS	
7	Armchair Expeditionaries: Voyages Into the French Musée de la Marine, 1828–78	127
	RALPH KINGSTON	

viii *Contents*

8 On Slippery Ice: Discovery, Imperium, and the
Austro-Hungarian North Polar Expedition (1872–4)   148
STEPHEN A. WALSH

9 A Polar Drama: The Australasian Antarctic
Expedition of 1911–14   171
TOM GRIFFITHS

10 The 1928 MacRobertson Round Australia Expedition:
Colonial Adventuring in the Twentieth Century   194
GEORGINE CLARSEN

11 The Expedition's Afterlives: Echoes of Empire in Travel to Asia   214
AGNIESZKA SOBOCINSKA

Contributors   233
Index   237

Figures

1.1	Expedition leader Charles Mountford photographing a family group at Yirrkala during the American-Australian Scientific Expedition to Arnhem Land, 1948	2
1.2	Mammalogist David H. Johnson performing taxidermy during the American-Australian Scientific Expedition to Arnhem Land, 1948	3
1.3	Biochemist Brian Billington using a microscope during the American-Australian Scientific Expedition to Arnhem Land, 1948	15
1.4	A View of a bridge over the Ba-Fing or Black River, 1799	18
2.1	S. Koenig and Frederick Christian Lewis, *Luminous Phenomenon*, 1818	31
2.2	Vicente de la Fuente, *Natural Phenomena*, 1748	33
2.3	William Scoresby Jr., 'Anthelion and Coronae', 1823	37
4.1	John F. Mann, Map showing progress of Ludwig Leichhardt's Swan River Expedition, 1847	66
4.2	John F. Mann, 'Dinner for Nine', 1846–7	82
4.3	John F. Mann, 'Leichhardt catching a mule', 1846–7	83
5.1	G. Barnard and T. Mitchell, frontispiece of *Three Expeditions Into the Interior of Eastern Australia*, vol. 1, 1839	91
5.2	G. Barnard and T. Mitchell, 'First Meeting with the Chief of the Bogan Tribe,' 1839	95
5.3	G. Barnard and T. Mitchell, 'Natives Robbing the Blacksmith, While the Old Men Chanted a Hymn or Song,' 1839	100
6.1	Pierre-François Tardieu, *Carte du grand océan ou mer du Sud dressée pour la Relation du voyage de découvertes faites par les frégates françaises la Boussole et l'Astrolabe dans les années 1785, 86, 87 et 88*, 1797	111
6.2	François Godefroy after Gaspard Duché de Vancy, *Insulaires et monumens de l'île de Pâque*, 1797	113

x *Figures*

6.3 François-Nicolas-Barthelemy Dequevauviller after
Nicolas-Marie Ozanne, *Massacre de MM. de Langle,
Lamanon et de dix autres individus des deux équipages*, 1797   114

6.4 Jacques Arago, *Première entrevue avec les sauvages*, 1927   119

7.1 View of the salle La Pérouse in the Musée de la Marine
au Louvre, *Magasin pittoresque*, 1847   128

7.2 View of salle La Pérouse in the Musée de la Marine au
Louvre, *Magasin pittoresque*, 1847   130

7.3 Ambroise Louis Garneray, *Iles des Papous, vue du mouillage
de l'Uranie sur l'île Rawak, dessiné par Garneray d'après
A. Pellion*, 1822   137

8.1 'Nord Polar Moden,' *Der Floh*, 1874   151

8.2 'Payer und Weyprecht,' *Die Bombe*, 1874   154

8.3 Julius Payer, 'Zweite Provisorische Karte von Franz
Josef Land,' 1874   160

9.1 Frank Hurley, 'A turreted berg' as seen from the *Aurora*,
circa 1913   174

9.2 Tom Griffiths, *Aurora Australis* off Commonwealth
Bay, 2012   177

9.3 Tom Griffiths, Mawson's Huts, Commonwealth Bay, 2012   180

9.4 Karen Barlow, Mawson's Huts, January 2012, overlaid
with photo of the proclamation ceremony, February 1912   181

9.5 Frank Hurley, 'Midwinter Dinner, Adélie Land', 1911   184

10.1 Postcard of the Round Australia Expedition, 1928   195

10.2 *Night Camp Outside Port Augusta, South Australia*, 1928   197

10.3 *Crossing the Naam (Jur) River, South Sudan*, 1926   206

11.1 Antony Barrington-Brown, Oxford-Cambridge Far
Eastern Expedition crew, 1955   219

Acknowledgments

Most chapters in this volume were first workshopped in 2012 as papers at 'What is an Expedition?' This conference at the Kioloa Coastal Campus of the Australian National University was generously funded by the university's College of Arts and Social Sciences. Thanks to all workshop participants, especially Tom Griffiths for feedback on the manuscript and Amanda Harris for editorial input. For her administration of the conference, research assistance, and proofing, thanks to Margo Daly. Roy MacLeod has been a generous reader and critic. Béatrice Bijon has been all that and more. The professionalism of Max Novick and Jennifer E. Morrow have made working with Routledge a pleasure. For financial support of my own investigations into matters expeditionary, I gratefully acknowledge the Australian Research Council (FT0992291 and DP1096897).

1 What Is an Expedition?
An Introduction

Martin Thomas

SETTING THE SCENE

As preliminary forays into foreign territory, expeditions were integral to the making of the modern empires. They connected Europeans with indigenous trade routes and laid the groundwork for the foundation of colonies. Once settlements were established in 'new' territories, the young colonies launched their own expeditions that further advanced the process of imperial expansion. So it is no exaggeration to observe that exploratory expeditions have shaped our world. The momentous histories of human migration and dispossession, dating from the early modern era, were seeded by expeditionary voyages and the inland explorations that followed.

Expeditions involve more than travel. Systemized collection and dissemination of data lie at their essence. Being indelibly associated with the growth and diffusion of science, they affect not only *what* we know but *how* we know it. In addressing this subject, the historian Roy MacLeod suggests that the nineteenth century saw a shift in which the metropolitan centres ceased to be the exclusive locales for the advancement of science. For the Victorians, 'the instrument by which the world was to be known was the expedition,' which 'became a major agent of Western influence, creating new disciplines, exploring new ideas, and establishing new forms of cultural appropriation.' Science as both a practice and a metaphor was defined by its relationship with expeditions. That is why, according to MacLeod, science presents itself 'as a symbolic act of perpetual exploration.'[1] Yet despite the profound impact of expeditions on diverse peoples throughout the world, there remains a considerable gulf between the effects of expeditions and what we know about them as cultural entities. This disparity was the motivation for *Expedition into Empire*, which emerged as a multi-author project—as befits a study of team-based travel.[2] And like many an expedition, there were personal inspirations for why, as editor, I initiated the journey. This background illuminates some major themes of the volume.

Several years ago, I began to study a large-scale research venture known as the American-Australian Scientific Expedition to Arnhem Land. A collaboration involving the National Geographic Society, the Smithsonian

Institution, and the Australian Government, during 1948, it travelled widely through the extensive Aboriginal reserve of Arnhem Land in northern Australia. As a twentieth-century journey, sponsored by the publisher of *National Geographic Magazine*, the Arnhem Land Expedition (to use its abbreviated title) resulted in a vast cache of media including many hours of colour film footage, thousands of photographs, and audio documentation of Aboriginal music and ceremony made on electronic wire recorders. Aboriginal men and women displayed aspects of their lives and culture to the camera, as did the expeditionaries themselves. Naturalists and anthropologists enacted their own esoteric rituals as they gathered data or collected and preserved specimens in front of the camera. News of the expedition was communicated around the world.[3]

For some observers—and some of the participating scientists, too—the media archive produced by the expedition was mere populist ephemera. The scientific world had its 'serious' if specialist outcomes: four large volumes of reports, extensive collections of flora and fauna, and superb examples of Aboriginal art and material culture, now held by Australian and American museums.[4] But 60-plus years after the expedition, the enduring value of the photographic and other 'ephemera' has been demonstrated in ways that the expedition and its backers did not anticipate. Aboriginal people have found their own uses for the expedition's documentation of their culture

Figure 1.1 Expedition leader Charles Mountford photographing a family group at Yirrkala during the American-Australian Scientific Expedition to Arnhem Land, 1948. Photograph by Frank M. Setzler. By Permission of the National Anthropological Archives, Smithsonian Institution (Photo lot 36, Yirrkala 48).

Figure 1.2 Mammalogist David H. Johnson performing taxidermy during the American-Australian Scientific Expedition to Arnhem Land, 1948. Photograph by Howell Walker. By Permission of the State Library of South Australia (Bessie Mountford Papers PRG 487/1/2/204/2).

and society, which they regard as their intellectual property. To research the place of archival media in contemporary Aboriginal society, I began to visit Arnhem Land to work with local experts in interpreting digitized copies of the audio and photographic documentation.[5] This developed into a larger study of the Arnhem Land Expedition and of expeditions more generally.

Some of the Arnhem Land people with whom I have studied were children when the expedition visited. To spend time with them, watching film from 1948, or hearing recordings of songs performed by their forbears, is an experience both poignant and intellectually challenging, for it complicates any simplistic assumption that the relationships between expeditions and indigenous societies can be nothing but exploitative. I have sat with old men as they tearfully review footage of an initiation ceremony, now defunct although still remembered with great affection. Film of a painter reveals his deft workmanship as he paints a kangaroo on a piece of bark. Archaeologist Denis Byrne suggests in a paper titled 'Archaeology in Reverse' that the backward movement of objects and data from repositories to communities

4 Martin Thomas

expresses an essential aspect of our zeitgeist.[6] In the work of ethnomusicologist colleagues with whom I collaborate, I have seen how song recordings documented by expeditions and independent ethnographers provide an enduring source of pleasure and fascination for many indigenous musicians today. Such material can inform contemporary cultures in productive ways.[7]

Acknowledging the contemporary relevance of these expeditionary outputs does not deny that imperial agendas were embedded in the original venture. Especially troubling to Aboriginal audiences is film footage of Frank Setzler, a Smithsonian curator, who can be seen toiling away at an ossuary site—a cave within a sandstone massif, familiar to all locals in the West Arnhem Land region—removing human crania and other bones from crevices. At the end of the expedition, these bones were exported to the United States where they found a new 'home' in the Smithsonian Institution's United States National Museum (now known as the National Museum of Natural History).[8] By the time a film archivist at the National Geographic Society unearthed this footage and showed it to me, the bones taken by Setzler were the subject of a repatriation claim, lodged by the Australian Government on behalf of communities affected by the theft. After years of disagreement and procrastination, the National Museum of Natural History eventually agreed to return them to their owners—another example of archaeology in reverse.[9] More than six decades after their removal, a ceremony held in the West Arnhem Land settlement of Gunbalanya welcomed the stolen ancestors back to their homeland.

This particular example of how the impacts of an expedition have reverberated through time and across cultures is a sign of the multivalency of expeditions. Whenever they intrude on inhabited terrain, expeditionary journeys are intercultural phenomena. As vehicles for cultural display and inquiry, they probe the human interface. Of course, the tenor of their interpersonal encounters varies enormously, covering the full spectrum from empathy to murder. The history of expeditions is accordingly complex and their relevance is not confined to the societies or cultures that launched them. A well-established historiography, much of it indebted to Margaret Connell Szasz's pioneering book on cultural brokerage, has drawn attention to the diverse roles played by indigenous people in mediating between indigenes and visitors during the age of empire.[10] Fortunately, much of the triumphalism traditionally accorded to expeditionary projects has diminished, and more nuanced assessments of their activities, reportage, and relations with indigenous people have developed. These changing perspectives are inflected by the technological transformations we are witnessing in our own era. As my own research in Arnhem Land shows, digitization of archival data allows indigenous communities newfound access to the findings of expeditions past. This development only adds to the urgency of better understanding the phenomenon of the expedition.

Later in the book, I argue that expeditions are 'cultural formations, as distinctive to their epoch as the novel or the photograph' (Thomas, Chapter 4, this volume). Significantly, the dearth of attention usually afforded to them is not due to lack of public interest in expeditions or exploration. On the contrary, a veritable industry is devoted to the recounting and reprocessing of exploratory journeys. Old journals get reprinted, documentaries made for television, anniversaries celebrated, discoveries re-enacted, novels written, and history books published by the wagonload. Whether they are revered, reviled, lampooned, or surgically dissected with every instrument in the postcolonial toolbox, expeditionary journeys are etched ever more deeply into the cultural imaginary.

So exploratory expeditions continue to speak to large audiences, as they have done since their inception. Yet the great outpouring of cultural product concerning them is something of a hindrance to understanding the traits of the expedition itself. Popular accounts do not encourage the identification of cultural patterns, preferring instead to proclaim the exceptionalism of each adventure. Somewhat strangely, this limitation often extends to more scholarly treatments of exploration. 'Biography has been its leading genre and hagiography its main mode of representation,' complains Dane Kennedy in *The Last Blank Spaces* (2013), a comparative study of Australia and Africa as sites of imperial discovery.[11] Kennedy, like many of us who contributed to the present volume, is indebted to the seminal work of the geographer Felix Driver, who in *Geography Militant* (2001) writes at length about the codes, conventions, and networks that regulated the business of nineteenth-century exploration.[12] Driver's study was largely researched in the archives of the Royal Geographical Society, which in the nineteenth century was the preeminent organization for sponsoring and in other ways encouraging scientific exploration within the British Empire.

Informed by these sources, Driver necessarily concentrates on the role of metropolitan London in setting and controlling the geographical agenda. He discusses imperial practices that influenced the business of scientific travel: the issue of formal instructions to explorers, the standardization of requirements for keeping journals and recording data, the loan of scientific instruments to expeditions, and 'expert' evaluation of the findings of returned travellers to ensure that the rules of engagement had been observed. That interest in imperial control is evident also in the work of Kennedy, although he, like several contributors to this volume, places greater emphasis on the role played by colonies in launching exploratory expeditions. To understand this history, he argues, we need to 'decenter our understanding of exploration as an imperial enterprise.'[13] Just as importantly, we need to understand how imperialism lingers, even when the age of empire has supposedly ended. The history of the expedition provides insight into that process.

QUESTIONS OF FORM

That the Arnhem Land Expedition is historically recent, sitting somewhere at the limit of living memory, allows access to eyewitness accounts. In 2007,

6 Martin Thomas

I recorded an interview with Gerald Blitner (now deceased), who as a young man worked as an interpreter and guide for the expedition. Blitner had an Aboriginal mother and a European father. Like many so-called 'half-castes' in northern Australia, he was taken from his family and brought up in a Christian mission where he learned English. He went on to become the classic cultural broker, mediating between the visiting researchers and older Aboriginal people who spoke little or no English. Blitner provided an extraordinary perspective on the expedition's sojourn on Groote Eylandt, a sizable landmass off the Arnhem Land coast, where the party was stationed for some months. He explained how he came to dislike its leader, the Australian photographer-ethnologist Charles Mountford, whom he regarded as intrusive and tactless. Blitner told me how he did all in his power to assist the scientific work of other expedition members in preference to Mountford.[14] Here was evidence of how the processes of investigation that a scientific expedition had set in train could be affected by the decisions of indigenous people. Undoubtedly, this is true of countless expeditions through the centuries, but it is acknowledged only obliquely—if at all—in the majority of official expeditionary records.

Blitner was not the only witness whom I interviewed. The late Peter Bassett-Smith, the expedition's cine-photographer, recorded his recollections in oral-history sessions, as did the botanist Raymond Specht, now the sole surviving veteran.[15] As I learnt fairly early in my practice as an oral historian, interviews are revealing not only for the wealth of data they throw up, but for their silences and omissions. These became obvious when I compared the oral-history interviews with other streams of evidence concerning the 1948 adventure, of which there are plenty. After all, expeditions are machines for producing discourse. Letters, diaries, and administrative records are part of a great cache of documentary evidence concerning Arnhem Land in 1948. The journal of another participant, the Sydney archaeologist Frederick McCarthy, unequivocally reveals that he, like Blitner, had no fondness for Mountford.[16] Internal dissent began to threaten the expedition's research agenda and its propagandist message of bilateral friendliness between Australia and the United States. That there were problems with the management of the expedition is hardly a secret. Even Mountford's authorized biography—as pure an exercise in hagiography as one could find—is forced to concede that by mid-1948 dissatisfaction with his leadership was so strong that his superiors in Canberra attempted to dismiss him from the top post.[17] On most subjects, Specht and Bassett-Smith were loquacious interviewees. But it was clear that they were far from comfortable when asked about the internal ructions. An earlier oral history with another expedition member, *National Geographic* photographer Howell Walker, reveals extraordinary obfuscation and feigned misunderstanding when questions concerning interpersonal relations were raised.[18] These men's reticence reveals much about the group ethos and codes of propriety observed by the expedition. By the time these interviews were recorded, Mountford and other protagonists were long in

What Is an Expedition? 7

the grave. But the corporate memory of the expedition was still something to be revered and protected by the few survivors.

In addressing the history of an expedition, one is grappling with more than a tour by individuals travelling in parallel. An expedition is a distinct socio-cultural formation. This inevitably affects members' perception of the land and its inhabitants, and their relations with one another. Equally, it affects the way they observe and report. To understand an expedition's activities and output we need to think about how it operates as a social unit, branded with its own sense of identity. For all the agony caused by the internal politics, the Arnhem Land Expedition had its core values and understandings. The expedition had its own folklore; its repertoire of funny stories and embarrassments. While in the field, members wrote comic ditties about their exploits, set to familiar tunes of the day, and sang them around the campfire. In later years, when veterans mustered for reunions (usually on prominent anniversaries), the lyrics were distributed in roneoed song-books and sung again. This is but one example of how an expedition generated its own microculture. Despite the lack of any apparent rulebook, the 1948 expedition had conventions and a code of conduct. Thinking about the origins of these mores raises deeper questions about the historical roots of exploratory and scientific travel.

THE JOURNEY AHEAD

This volume examines the emergence and proliferation of expeditions during the age of the modern empires and it throws light on why expeditions continue even today, their diminished prestige notwithstanding. A work such as this cannot provide a comprehensive history of the expedition. That would be a different book and a longer one, more extensive in its periodization and more systematic in tracing the course of imperial expansion. Here, the aim is less panoptic and more interventionist: we hope to encourage a new and more critical dialogue around the concept of the expedition that will see it recognized as a cultural and, more specifically, as an imperial formation. The chapters can be thought of as a succession of spotlights on expeditionary history. The earliest journeys discussed are voyages dating from the Enlightenment; the most recent—if a centennial pilgrimage to Douglas Mawson's Antarctic base camp is counted as an expedition—dates from 2012. While the scope is international, there is something of an Oceanic bias to the content, a reflection of the Australian origins of the project. Books, like expeditions, emerge from networks. A spotlight approach cannot represent all oceans, continents, or empires, even from the modern period. Similarly, it cannot cover with any thoroughness 'the Greats' of exploration—an approach to expeditionary history that we are writing against. The fame of an expedition or its members was not a criterion when commissioning the volume. The journey ahead will I think persuade the reader that an obscure

8 Martin Thomas

tour of discovery can illuminate the phenomenon of the expedition as readily as one of international renown. As the first extended study of the expedition as a cultural form, this is a narrative told by 10 writers, each with an individual perspective on what makes an expedition. There are themes that resonate across all chapters, and just as importantly there are juxtapositions. The contents are not grouped into named sections, but their sequencing brings a narrative trajectory, just as it puts chapters with a particular affinity into conversation.

This introductory chapter, which will soon turn to the task of defining the expedition culturally and etymologically, is the first of four overviews that argue for the reconceptualization of expeditionary modalities. Despite variations in style and approach, these four texts offer a corrective to the lack of attention usually given to the collective properties of expeditionary travel. Debates about authorship and the role of the printing press in enabling the mythos of exploration to blossom are at the heart of Chapter 2 by Adriana Craciun, titled 'What Is an Explorer?' Addressing Michel Foucault's 1969 lecture on authorship as a historical construction, Craciun historicizes the emergence of the explorer by comparing early nineteenth-century Arctic voyages to geodetic expeditions from the 1730s. Explorers, she argues, emerged as 'a distinct species in the nineteenth century, with their own private clubs, costumes, props, and professional organizations.' She reveals the British explorer as a proprietorial figure, originally empowered by naval conventions that required the confiscation of any notes kept by officers and crew. Publication and the kudos it brought was the exclusive right of those captains whom the Admiralty 'authorized to affix their names to a particular kind of object: expensive, illustrated, beautifully produced quarto volumes representing the collective shipboard work.'

Whereas Craciun's contribution reveals the eclipsing of the expeditionary party by the heroic leader, Lorenzo Veracini in Chapter 3 illuminates the expedition by stepping around the question of exploration. He is interested in expeditions that were intended for the purpose of founding settlements, rather than making discoveries and reporting back. Think of covered wagons with families and livestock advancing across prairies, and you have an image of the settler colonial expedition examined in this chapter. Veracini argues that the structures of feeling, modes of perception, and the core narratives that underpin this type of expedition are structurally different from those of other expeditions into empire. He dissects the assumptions underlying the settler expedition, which is predicated on *occupying* the territory on which it intrudes and remaining there indefinitely. He compares this ethos to the standard trajectory of an exploratory journey that, as Beau Riffenburgh argued in *The Myth of the Explorer* (1994), conforms to tropes ingrained in the mythology of many cultures, where the archetypal hero experiences a tripartite life cycle involving 'the departure, the initiation, and the return.'[19]

What Is an Expedition? 9

Veracini emphasizes that expeditions have ingrained attributes, although they manifest themselves in very different ways according to their purpose: settling or discovering. He reads the expedition for what it reveals about how a colonial society expands the polity and acquires new living space, and how it justifies the dispossession of indigenous people. Both Craciun and Veracini help set the context for my own examination in Chapter 4 of how exploratory expeditions are structured and how they are empowered as political entities. My case study is the mid-nineteenth-century Australian explorer, Ludwig Leichhardt, who promoted his journeys as independent 'squatting expeditions': embodiments of the same independence of spirit that colonists identified in their own pioneering ventures. Leichhardt successfully appealed to such persons in his fundraising, a necessity resulting from his lack of personal income or official sponsors. His chequered career, which culminated in his disappearance and presumed death after embarking on his second attempt at an east-west crossing of Australia, provides a window on the economy of expeditions and their affinity with other capitalist initiatives that use models of subscription to float projects. Leichhardt's tours of discovery represent socioeconomic microcosms of the colony that supported them.

Chapters 5, 6, and 7 are concerned with processes of encounter. Leichhardt reappears in Chapter 5, 'The Theatre of Contact,' as do many of the major figures in Australian inland exploration. Drawing on his long experience as an ethnographic curator and historian, Philip Jones combs the records of a vast array of exploring expeditions for what they reveal about protocols of encounter between explorers and Aboriginal people. This reading of inland expeditions argues that they reveal patterns sufficiently distinct for the encounter narrative to be analysed afresh. Jones is attentive to the roles played by the traffic in objects as well as the gestural exchange set in train by the arrival of an expedition. Apparently fickle and irrational actions can be understood in the light of shared if sometimes misunderstood codes of behaviour. From these insights, Jones is able to chart the morphology of these 'first contact' experiences.

Chapter 6 by Bronwen Douglas is similarly interested in narratives of encounter between indigenous societies and expeditionary travellers, although French rather than British journeys provide the source material. Like Jones, Douglas grapples with generic features of expeditions in her comparative reading of the voyages of La Pérouse (1785–8) and Freycinet (1817–20). These include the issue of 'official instructions,' intended to guide and regulate the expeditionary traveller. Douglas shows the significance of maritime expeditions in producing scientific and practical knowledge about indigenous populations in Oceania, arguing that whereas human encounters were a minor concern in official instructions to voyagers, they loomed large in travellers' experiences. In consequence, their journals and other accounts were profoundly affected by the agency of indigenous people whom they met along the way.

10 *Martin Thomas*

Chapter 7 by Ralph Kingston complements Douglas's account of how Pacific voyagers dealt with the complexity of intercultural encounter, for he deals with a later phase in the train of events resulting from expeditions. 'Armchair Expeditionaries' is set not in 'the field' but in Paris, where in the late 1820s native weapons and other artefacts collected during exploratory voyages were installed as the Musée de la Marine, a specialist collection within the Louvre. Kingston's chapter assesses the ways in which the expeditionary imaginary manifested itself in the metropole. As well as housing artefacts from the Pacific and elsewhere, the Musée de la Marine included models of French naval vessels and a monument to La Pérouse, whose fate was still unknown when the museum opened. The collection was much frequented by naval officers who handled and rearranged objects as they inspected and compared them to each other. Kingston explores connections between expeditionary and intellectual history, examining how the museum functioned as an interactive theatre that spoke to, and at times contradicted, the scientific and racial theories developing in France through the nineteenth century.

Accounts of polar journeys are presented in Chapters 8 and 9. Both the explorations discussed were motivated by the loftiest of scientific ideals, and both establish that science is seldom detachable from national or imperial ambitions. Stephen A. Walsh's aptly named 'On Slippery Ice' tells one of the stranger stories in this volume. He investigates the First Austro-Hungarian North Polar Expedition (1872–4), led by Carl Weyprecht and Julius Payer. For much of its two-year duration, the expedition's ship, the *Tegetthoff*, was trapped in ice. After an almost miraculous escape, they returned to civilization to report the magnificent 'discovery' of Franz Josef Land, an allegedly vast terrain, and reputedly the northernmost landmass in Eurasia. Initially a publicity boon to the struggling Habsburg Monarchy, these happy tidings from the far North proved multivalent and transitory. In ensuing decades, as other voyagers reached the land that Payer and his party had glimpsed through the fog, the great discovery fragmented into the modest archipelago, still called Franz Josef Land, that appears on maps today. Walsh's chapter is a forensic investigation of the propagandist use of the expedition and its 'discovery' by the Habsburgs, the Nazis, and many others along the way. It is also a tale of pathos, in that it charts the pressures experienced by the expedition leader Payer: to deliver a significant discovery when he was out in the field, and his defence of it as the years passed and his great Arctic territory began to melt away.

The hostility of polar environments increases the co-dependence of expeditionary parties, bringing both the strengths and limits of the expedition to the surface. Fatigue, boredom, and internal friction often test the limits of leaders and personnel. In Chapter 9, Tom Griffiths writes about the Australasian Antarctic Expedition of 1911–14, led by Douglas Mawson. This was the most comprehensively scientific expedition of the 'heroic era' of Antarctic exploration. While Walsh's case study looks at the propagandist value of polar journeying to a European empire already in a state of atrophy,

What Is an Expedition? 11

Griffiths's narrative is attuned to the temper of an ascendant nation, amalgamated from the six Australian colonies only 10 years earlier, and determined to establish its presence on the world stage. Mawson's expedition became crucial to Australia's eventual claim to 42 percent of Antarctic territory. Titled 'A Polar Drama,' this chapter investigates the daily experiences of expeditioners through close readings of their diaries, presented in six 'acts.' Expeditions are 'theatre,' writes Griffiths, 'plays of power and possession.' Along the way, he gives account of his own visit to the expedition's base camp for an official centennial celebration, and he takes us through the Antarctic winter of 1913 when Mawson and the remainder of his party were trapped in their hut, sitting out the long months of relentless blizzard, while wireless operator Sidney Jeffryes careered into madness.

By the time the Australasian Antarctic Expedition set out, the blank spaces left uncharted by Western cartographers—the classic drivers for expeditionary discovery—were no longer. Expeditions continued, although their goals had shifted. Roy MacLeod argues that as the rush for territory lost momentum, science increased its already considerable stake in the expedition. Hence the proliferation of university and museum expeditions that began in the 1880s and flourished through the early decades of the twentieth century.[20] Mawson can be seen as the living embodiment of this ethos. He famously declined the invitation of Captain R. F. Scott to join his second attempt to reach the South Pole because he deemed the journey insufficiently scientific. The last two chapters in this volume examine the fate of expeditions as the twentieth century progressed. Although scientific credibility remained important, it was, by the interwar period, no longer an essential ingredient. Other aspects of the expedition, including showmanship and the generation of media product, became more prominent.

In Chapter 10 Georgine Clarsen tells the little-known story of the Mac-Robertson Round Australia Expedition of 1928, the brainchild of Melbourne confectionary magnate MacPherson Robertson, widely known by the moniker 'MacRobertson.' An Australia-wide truck journey, it was essentially a publicity stunt that generated media as it toured the outback, filming locals and distributing the sponsor's candy. The MacRobertson expedition could be readily dismissed as a protracted advertisement—which it certainly was! Yet this does not diminish its significance as a cultural event, as Clarsen demonstrates in her meticulous interpretation. This journey, she argues, provides vivid evidence of how the colonial expedition enjoyed 'a dynamic afterlife' in an emerging national culture. The two trucks that performed the Round Australia journey were named 'Burke' and 'Wills' in homage to Robert O'Hara Burke and William John Wills, the famed leaders of a disastrous attempt at a north-south crossing of Australia in 1860–1. The MacRobertson journey mobilized vehicular technology in its reprocessing of a failed colonial expedition. In its new, revitalized iteration, the Burke and Wills narrative emerged triumphantly 'as a new form of settler expedition that drew on familiar colonial tropes of land being won through arduous feats of exploration and travel.'

12 *Martin Thomas*

In Chapter 11, Agnieszka Sobocinska leads the expeditionary journey into the post-Second World War era. 'The Expedition's Afterlives' concerns a Land Rover journey from England to Singapore, known as the Oxford and Cambridge Far Eastern Expedition of 1955–6. The title of the expedition was extravagant, given that it had no official connection with either of the universities namedropped. Similarly, its claim to be the 'first overland' journey (a phrase immortalized in the title of Tim Slessor's widely read book on the expedition) was dubious, given that Francis Birtles had driven much the same route and more in his London to Melbourne journey of 1928. Sobocinska's purpose is to track a genealogy of influence by examining how the imperial model of expeditionary travel provided inspiration for this latter-day adventure. Like Clarsen, she is interested in national re-imaginings of imperial gestures, although the postcolonial context makes the Far Eastern Expedition radically different from the MacRobertson journey. With a portfolio of sponsors that included the Mobil Corporation, provider of fuel throughout the journey, the expedition's pair of Land Rovers rattled their way through the Middle East to East Asia, 'discovering' a British Empire that was in the process of being dismantled. Colonial clubs were still dispensing the gin slings, but the Oxford and Cambridge men had arrived at a 'last drinks' moment. The accomplishments of this expedition were slight indeed, but its 'afterlife' was powerful. Sobocinska shows how in the wake of the journey substantial parts of the route became the 'Hippie Trail' between Europe and Asia. Lonely Planet guidebooks and a new form of backpacking tourism drew inspiration from the 'first overland' journey, which provided 'a vehicle (both literal and symbolic) into postcolonial Asia at a key historical juncture: a moment when international tourism was booming and metropolitan attitudes towards the decolonizing world were in the process of renegotiation.'

From this perspective, it might seem that the journey ahead leads *out* of empire (at least in the formal sense of that term). But the title is appropriate if we acknowledge that imperialism in various guises continues to prosper, even if it disavows that name. Having charted the trajectory of the book from the eighteenth to the twentieth century, my purpose now is to pick up at the point where Clarsen and Sobocinska finish. As their contributions, like my own delving into the Arnhem Land Expedition in the present chapter, establish, the more recent history reveals traits of the expedition that help illuminate the period when Europe's empires were at their height.

TRAITS OF THE EXPEDITION

Historians of exploration mostly agree that the end of the nineteenth century brought the terminus of the great epoch of geographical discovery. As Simon Naylor and James R. Ryan gloss this position, the 'completion' of the cartographic project coincided with 'the professionalization and

What Is an Expedition? 13

institutionalization of science at that time,' which was instrumental in consolidating the scientific turn of expeditionary endeavours.[21]

This did not in itself dispel the romance of exploration, just as it did not quell the widespread nostalgia for imperial glory, symbolized by expeditionary heroics. Like the proverbial ocean liner losing momentum, it was not until the empires of Europe were manifestly unraveling that the end-of-discovery was widely and deeply felt. An emblematic moment was the ascent of Everest in 1953—an event that marked the death knell and the apotheosis of the exploratory expedition. In the triumphalism that greeted this long-anticipated victory, which happily coincided with the coronation of Elizabeth II, the New Zealander Edmund Hillary and his Sherpa companion Tenzing Norgay shared equal credit for the first ascent. With this occurrence, the mythos of the explorer collided with the geo-political reality of decolonization—with explosive effect.[22] For if the input of the local guide, the indigenous knowledge-holder, was now to be put on equal footing with the heroics of the white discoverer, what was the status of all those 'explorations' that had shaped world history in previous centuries; those triumphs of 'discovery' in which the input of innumerable persons such as Tenzing had been obscured, diminished, or ignored?

Several books have already been published on the tantalizing subject of how residual echoes of exploration persisted through the twentieth century, despite the absence of those seductive blank spaces on maps.[23] Bathyspheres plumbed the depths of oceans, while rockets ventured into the upper atmosphere and beyond. Expeditionary ventures, directed at the remaining pockets of humanity who lived beyond the zone of 'contact,' continued. Curiously, the imperial associations of expeditionary adventure, and the draining of its scientific import, made the term 'expedition' less attractive to publicists of space travel. In their quest for the heavens, astronauts are said to go on *missions* not expeditions. At one level, this choice of terminology can be seen as endowing a religious significance to the skyward trajectory. Yet the term 'mission' is also replete with military connotations, which makes it such an apposite descriptor for this form of travel.

Like the Everest ascent, the Arnhem Land Expedition postdated the 'über-project' of geographical exploration and discovery. Yet as I think I have shown, it reveals aspects of the structure and social makeup of expeditions that are survivals from the imperial age—the epoch when geography was still 'militant' (to use Conrad's phrase).[24] In this vein, I will go a little further in probing some recent expeditionary history, in which key characteristics of expeditions are revealed, often with remarkable clarity. Four key traits strike me as especially pertinent.

Trait 1: Man versus Nature

In expeditions of the twentieth and twenty-first centuries, we find that the spectacle of 'man versus nature' is heightened, sometimes to the point of

14   *Martin Thomas*

absurdity. My choice of language reflects the gendered nature of expeditionary activity. As I note in relation to Leichhardt's journeys, the masculine culture of exploratory expeditions reflected—and indeed accentuated—the gender politics of the societies they represented (see Chapter 4, this volume). Certainly, this began to shift in the late nineteenth century when, as Kennedy observes, 'the boundaries between explorers and other travellers began to blur.'[25] Figures such as May French Sheldon, Mary Kingsley, Gertrude Bell, and Marianne North ventured into the field and won renown in their own right as exploratory travellers. Yet the celebrity of these women did not result in a general opening of doors to female expeditionaries. As late as 1948, the admission of two women to the Arnhem Land Expedition was deemed inappropriate by some participants and at least one sponsor.[26]

Physical hardship and preparedness to sacrifice oneself in the service of science or empire were always endemic features of the expeditionary journey and its construction of masculinity. When these conventions first became manifest, it was recognized that physical and psychological sufferings were necessary trials on the road to discovery: a means to an end. When the rubric of discovery was stripped away, expeditionary hardship became an end unto itself. Hence the advent of kayak assaults on stormy seas, runs across deserts, and sledge-dragging marches across Arctic wastes. In this newly individuated iteration of the heroic adventure, the body and its limits become the site of discovery, and the 'expedition' begins to merge with other forms of extreme sport.

Trait 2: Technology

Questions of technology are central to expeditions. The deployment of advanced technology, especially precision-navigational instruments, has lain at the essence of expeditionary endeavour since the Enlightenment, if not before. Cook's testing of the Harrison chronometre and other new inventions is paradigmatic, and it fuelled a tradition in which the recording of instrumentally derived data would differentiate the scientific explorer from the common herd of mere travellers.[27] Throughout their history, exploratory expeditions have been used to test, display, and eventually advertise a vast array of products and technologies. When the candy manufacturer MacRobertson utilized his expedition as a form of advertising (see Clarsen, this volume), he did not vulgarize or corrupt the concept. He merely accentuated—almost to the point of parody—a long tradition in which commercial interests used expeditions to promote commodities that might include scientific instruments and gadgetry, generations of weaponry, communicational and media devices (especially cameras), all forms of mechanized transport, pharmaceuticals, and sundry brands of food, clothing, and tobacco.

In expeditionary travel, technology performs multiple roles. While enabling the party's trajectory through space, it also facilitates the documentation of the journey. Moreover, technology serves as a framing mechanism

What Is an Expedition? 15

Figure 1.3 Biochemist Brian Billington using a microscope during the American-Australian Scientific Expedition to Arnhem Land, 1948. Photograph by Howell Walker. By Permission of National Geographic Creative (Image 1270982). Howell Walker/National Geographic Creative.

for intercultural encounter. Displaying the marvels of 'advanced' technology to those who are technologically 'backward' is a pervasive ritual in the history of Western expeditions. Since the Second World War, the tradition of technological display has continued. Yet there has been a distinctive deviation from it, in which the explorer purposefully adopts the mantle of technological backwardness. Thor Heyerdahl's *Kon-Tiki* Voyage (1947) and Tim Severin's *Brendan* Voyage (1976–7) are prominent examples.[28] These voyages were retro-expeditionary gestures that inverted the customary 'rules of the game' by re-enacting mythic or historic journeys in vessels purportedly constructed according to the outmoded methods of bygone eras. Although proudly atavistic, such voyages do not eschew technology. On the contrary, they fetishize it. In a process analogous to the way the human body gained prominence as the mythos of discovery became increasingly redundant, expeditions have maintained their relevance by enriching the smorgasbord of technological display. At times they disavow (and thereby emphasize) the high-tech by valorizing the antiquated and the redundant in an effort to validate the expeditionary achievements of earlier epochs. In this way, the theatre of technological difference is both perpetuated and reinvented.

16 Martin Thomas

Trait 3: Machines for Producing Discourse

The whispering of ghosts from expeditions past is often heard in expeditions present. The protagonists are gone, but the relics of historic expeditions survive to form a discursive quarry; an increasingly self-referential domain that contemporary expeditions routinely exploit. Exploration's connection with textual production, emerging as it did conjointly with the diffusion of the printing press, suggests analogies between expeditionary history as a discursive phenomenon and the construction of a literary canon, with its hierarchy of authors: major, middling, and minor. The relative status of these heroes is of course fervently contested. Forgotten figures, exhumed from the archives, are presented as worthy candidates for admission to the explorers' pantheon. Exploratory journeys are passionately debated and disputed, resulting in arguments that are expressions of difference, but only superficially. By contesting the detail of the canon, the disputants affirm its overall sanctity.

Expeditions are written in ink, but kept alive through performance. Recreation, re-enactment, return to localities where 're-discoveries' are made: these are examples of the great buzz of activity around expeditions today, ranging from costume dramas performed by schoolchildren to the planting of memorials.[29] Tom Griffiths's account of the on-site theatrics of expeditionary memorialization is but one example of the sway anniversaries have on the expeditionary imaginary (Griffiths, this volume). On occasion they induce high-budget, high-risk enterprises, such as the centennial re-enactment of Ernest Shackleton's perilous boat ride from Elephant Island to South Georgia (another expedition that uses the 'original' technology of a century ago).[30] Today's penchant for re-enactment could be seen as typically postmodern, a hollow theatre of mimicry. Yet it reveals a trait of expeditions that was engrained in the eighteenth century. Douglas's discussion of the fallout from the search for La Pérouse and my own discussion of Leichhardt make the point that expeditions are self-replicating phenomena. New expeditions build on the successes of earlier travellers or, almost as frequently, use the disappearance or failure of their predecessors as the stimulus for new journeys.

Trait 4: Media

The relationship with media I have by now touched upon, for of course all these aspects of the expedition are entangled. In lieu of 'new territory' on which to report, the report itself has become territory for the expedition of today. Gathering content for a book, film, television program, broadcast, website, or, quite often, all of the above, becomes *the object* of the expedition. Once again, this involves a tilt in emphasis rather than any substantive revision of how expeditions are constituted. The Enlightenment traveller was expected to make diaries, maps, sketches, and other types of representation that would be published or in other ways disseminated. In the

What Is an Expedition? 17

same vein, the traveller collected talismans from the landscapes traversed and called them 'specimens.' The image-making function of expeditions has now gone into *over*production—a reminder that semiosis lies at the heart of explorations. The signs they generate acquire legitimacy through association with the codes and gestures inherent to the cultural form that is the expedition.

THE EXPEDITION AND THE EXPLORER

Further traits of the expedition are identified in the pages ahead, but those listed above are fundamental. Considered together, they prime the canvas for one of the key arguments of *Expedition into Empire*: that exploration as an imperial project can only be understood if we acknowledge the clear distinction between explorers and the enterprises they lead. To return to the most axiomatic of differences, explorers are *individuals* while expeditions are *collectives*. Individualism is the value most slavishly enshrined in the cult of the explorer—a remarkable thing when you think about it, for solo explorers, while they certainly existed, are only a small minority of those who travelled under that descriptor. Co-operative enterprise is the dream that unites an expedition; anomy is its nightmare—and often the seed of its destruction.

Plurality is in fact fundamental to an expedition, which involves a bringing together of a range of skills and types of knowledge. Yet it tends to be understated—and is often actively obscured—in the published expeditionary narrative, a literary genre in which it is admissible and even desirable for the author-cum-leader to downplay the contribution of his party (see Craciun, this volume). The reduction of the ensemble and the valorization of the leader are recurrent features in the history of exploration. Expeditions are seemingly designed to obscure the collectivity upon which their ability to travel and produce discourse depends.

This subsumption of the greater party is connected with another trait of the expedition that differentiates it from other, less formalized, modes of journeying. Expeditions have titles. Sometimes it is the leader, and sometimes a publisher or other progenitor of the journey, who generates the proper noun by which an expedition is known. That title is usually determined well before the expedition sets out, and it is often used to recruit participants, garner finance, or generate publicity. The title might include the name of a nation, ship, military unit, university, museum, society, company, or other sponsor with an interest in the journey, but in the majority of cases an expedition is identified by the name of its leader. Exploration and cartography are inextricably linked with nomenclatural practices, as Paul Carter discussed in *The Road to Botany Bay* (1987), a study that investigates and interprets the toponyms recorded by a range of travellers.[31] Despite the influence of Carter's book, little has been said about the way the expedition, a vehicle for recording established toponyms and/or imposing new ones, is *itself* a site of nomenclature. The attachment of the leader's name to the journey, and the diminution of his companions resulting from that act of naming, should be recognized as a further, significant trait of the expedition—one that reveals much about the political structure of these journeys and the empowerment of those who lead them.

The figure of the author-explorer represents a modern iteration of a hero-archetype, handed down from the mythology of earlier eras. Championed in various forms of print-based media, they were imperial heroes, calibrated to the aspirations of a scientific age.[32] Notably, the figure of the expeditionary explorer is historically recent. The first usage of 'explorer,' in a sense that could include a scientific or imperial traveller, occurred in 1812, according to the *Oxford English Dictionary* (OED).[33] In the hothouse of the nineteenth century, the term grew with astonishing rapidity, fertilized in no small part by the long-term impact of travellers such as Mungo Park, whose *Travels in the Interior Districts of Africa* proved a publishing sensation when released in 1799. The immortality of Park's name was further guaranteed when he returned to Africa in 1805 to lead a military-style expedition that would navigate the Niger. In contrast to his first, modestly funded journey,

Figure 1.4 A View of a bridge over the Ba-Fing or Black River. Engraving by W. C. Wilson in Mungo Park's *Travels in the Interior Districts of Africa*, 1799. By Permission of the State Library of New South Wales (Call no. DL 79/73).

What Is an Expedition? 19

the second expedition was a fiasco, resulting in the deaths of Park, all his party, and countless Africans whom they slaughtered.[34]

Mungo Park would occupy a prominent position in any dictionary of explorers, but that term—explorer—makes no appearance in his *Travels*. In contrast, the word 'expedition' appears often. His published journal uses the term in at least three different ways. The first—consistent with today's usage—occurs in the preface, where he refers to discoveries made 'previous to my expedition.'[35] Clearly, therefore, he saw his own journey as part of a larger expeditionary tradition. The second usage refers not to his own journey, or those of other Europeans, but to raids of plunder made by Africans on local enemies (for example, 'the success of this expedition encouraged the governor of Bangassi . . . to make a second inroad upon another part of the same country').[36] The third—and for Park the most common—usage of 'expedition' is rather different, since it involves qualitative assessment of his own mode of journeying. With variations, he describes moments when his party travelled 'with uncommon expedition.'[37]

Although unorthodox by today's standards, that third usage was a standard expression of swiftness or efficiency for Park. In it we can discern the persistence of a meaning, first recorded in the late medieval period, in which *expedition* might include, although it was not restricted to, a form of travel. The 'action of expediting, helping forward or accomplishing; speedy performance or prompt execution (of justice, a journey); prompt supply (of anything), dispatch' is the first definition of the word given by the OED. This general, and now largely obsolete, notion of 'expedition' existed contemporaneously with another, more specific meaning, recorded in English in 1430. John Lydgate, the Benedictine poet, employed it in a long verse on the Trojan Wars: a usage that the OED defines as a 'sending or setting forth with martial intentions; a warlike enterprise.'[38] Here we touch on its most ancient roots, for 'expedition' is derived from the Latin *expeditio*, 'a voyage of war.' As Bronwen Douglas notes, this usage of 'expedition' had roughly parallel histories in French and English, being applicable to both ocean voyages and terrestrial travel (Douglas, this volume). While the notion of an exploratory foray into foreign territory is hardly incongruent with a 'voyage of war,' the specific and *modern* concept of an expedition, defined in the OED as a 'journey, voyage, or excursion made for some definite purpose,' is an innovation of the early seventeenth century. The timing is not surprising, for it indicates that that the notion of an exploring expedition emerged in tandem with the great stirrings of European expansion, coming in the wake of the Columbus voyages.

Within the noun 'expedition' lies the verb 'expedite': 'To clear of difficulties; to clear up (confusion); to facilitate (action or movement); to disentangle,' '[t]o help forward, hasten the progress of.'[39] These definitions are likely to be familiar to contemporary readers. 'Expedite,' like its antonym 'impede,' is part of that great Latinate family of *ped* words, all to do with 'foot.' The English 'impede' comes from the Latin *impedire*, meaning to

20 Martin Thomas

shackle the feet; *expedire*, the origin of 'expedite,' means 'to free (a person's) feet from fetters.' Here are hints of the origins of a term that would come to refer to exploratory footwork in foreign territory.

LAST WORDS

In 1831, when Major Thomas Mitchell set forth on his first expedition into inland Australia, his mind went back 20 years to his service in the Peninsula War. As he rode through bushland north of Sydney, it occurred to him

> that even war and victory, with all their glory, were far less alluring than the pursuit of researches such as these; the objects of which were to spread the light of civilization over a portion of creation . . . where science might accomplish new and unthought-of discoveries.[40]

Perhaps it is not surprising that war should be the natural point of reference for a man schooled in the military. As a young officer, he acquired the knowledge of cartography that would take him to New South Wales where he became Surveyor General and made his name as an explorer. Inculcated in the knowledge and traditions of the military, Mitchell, like so many of his contemporaries in the field of discovery, went on to lead journeys that in many ways resembled 'warlike enterprises.' The affiliation between military and scientific journeying is consistent with other aspects of imperial administration.[41] C. A. Bayly, in a reassessment of the economic foundations of the modern empires, draws attention to the structural effect of military organization on the spread of capitalism as an invasive force. Bayly argues that 'military attitudes, military finance, intentions, and structures tied together the fabric' of the Western empires.[42]

The investigations in this book are limited to the modern European empires and their aftermath—though that is hardly a small canvas. But we acknowledge that empires and expeditions have a deep provenance in world history. Lorenzo Veracini cites *Anabasis*, the expeditionary account of the Athenian soldier and historian, Xenophon, with its vision of a 'marching republic.' Veracini suggests that Xenephon's great journey encapsulates the logic of settler colonial expeditions in North America and elsewhere (see Veracini, this volume). To this I would add that just as the word 'expedition' is an inheritance from the Latin, the concept was greatly developed by the Romans. In his study of geographical knowledge in the early Roman Empire, Claude Nicolet identifies at least 20 exploratory expeditions from the period 29 BC to AD 93 that resulted in 'an "opening up" between the world of the empire or the *orbis Romanus* . . . and the rest of the world.'[43]

In *The Artificial Horizon* (2003), a study of landscape and colonization, I argued that maritime models of charting space and recording movement had a profound effect upon the methods, perceptions, and fantasies of imperial

What Is an Expedition? 21

travellers.[44] Mitchell was among the explorers who carted boats into the interior of Australia, expecting that at some point he would have to navigate an inland sea. If the oceans represented a great imaginary for a culture in migration, ships—specifically *naval* ships—served as models for expeditions of all sorts. As Greg Dening detailed at length in his wonderful exposition of the mutiny against William Bligh on the *Bounty*, ships were enclosed social environments with strict hierarchies, rituals, disciplinary codes, and conventions for dealing with the exotic.[45] Europe's navies provided organizational models for terrestrial travellers, just as they developed the precise navigational systems that nineteenth-century explorers exploited as they journeyed into the interior. Dane Kennedy says of these maritime precedents that they permitted explorers 'to conceive of continents, like oceans, as vast and seemingly empty spaces that could be truly known only after they had been made unknown.'[46] Consistent with the defining influence of naval models, the military, or vestiges of it, surface constantly in the expeditions described in the chapters that follow. There are the codified voyages, described by Bronwen Douglas and the publishing conventions determined by the Royal Navy, discussed by Adriana Craciun. Ralph Kingston looks at naval collections in the Louvre, while many of the explorers described by Philip Jones (including Mitchell) had military training. Agnieszka Sobocinska tells us that experience of the Second World War was fresh in the minds of some members of the Oxford and Cambridge Far Eastern Expedition. This was the case, also, for many of the scientists and support staff who participated in the Arnhem Land Expedition of 1948.

For these reasons, we should acknowledge that despite their variety and multivalency, the infrastructure of violence lies buried in the DNA of the expedition, a cultural form with many faces, as this volume establishes. Expeditions are analysed as political structures and as vehicles for intercultural contact. We see them as spectacle, as theatre, and as roving hothouses for the growth of culture. They are mechanisms for expanding polities and seizing land. They are sites of nostalgia and repositories of memories. This is a book that investigates what expeditions are. This is a necessary task, for it is the stepping-stone to understanding what they do.

NOTES

1. Roy MacLeod, 'Discovery and Exploration,' in *The Cambridge History of Science*, vol. 6, *The Modern Biological and Earth Sciences*, eds. Peter J. Bowler and John V. Pickstone (Cambridge: Cambridge University Press, 2009), 38.
2. The book was developed from a conference titled 'What Is an Expedition?' at the Australian National University in 2012. See http://historynet.anu.edu.au/what-is-an-expedition. Accessed 1 October 2013.
3. See Martin Thomas and Margo Neale, eds., *Exploring the Legacy of the 1948 Arnhem Land Expedition* (Canberra, AU: ANU E Press, 2011).
4. Charles P. Mountford, ed., *Records of the American-Australian Scientific Expedition to Arnhem Land* (Melbourne, AU: Melbourne University Press, 1956–64).

5. Martin Thomas, 'Taking Them Back: Archival Media in Arnhem Land Today,' *Cultural Studies Review* 13:2 (2007): 20–37.
6. Denis Byrne, 'Archaeology in Reverse,' in *Public Archaeology*, eds. N. Merriman and T. Schadla-Hall (New York: Routledge, 2000), 240–54.
7. See Allan Marett, *Songs, Dreamings, and Ghosts: The Wangga of North Australia* (Middletown, CT: Wesleyan University Press, 2005) and Allan Marett and Linda Barwick, 'Aural Snapshots of Musical Life: The 1948 Recordings,' in *Exploring the Legacy*, Thomas and Neale, 355–75. On the significance of digital archiving to many indigenous cultures, see Linda Barwick, 'Turning It All Upside Down . . . : Imagining a Distributed Digital Audiovisual Archive,' *Literary and Linguistic Computing* 19:3 (2004): 253–63.
8. Howell Walker (cine-photographer), *Aboriginal Australia*, National Geographic Society, 1950. Lecture Film.
9. Martin Thomas, 'Bones as a Bridge Between Worlds: Responding with Ceremony to the Repatriation of Aboriginal Human Remains from the United States to Australia,' in *Conciliation on Colonial Frontiers: Conflict, Performance, and Commemoration in Australia and the Pacific Rim*, eds. Kate Darian-Smith and Penelope Edmonds (New York: Routledge, 2015).
10. Margaret Connell Szasz, ed., *Between Indian and White Worlds: The Cultural Broker* (Norman, OK: University of Oklahoma Press, 1994).
11. Dane Kennedy, *The Last Blank Spaces: Exploring Africa and Australia* (Cambridge, MA: Harvard University Press, 2013), 64.
12. Felix Driver, *Geography Militant: Cultures of Exploration and Empire* (Oxford: Blackwell, 2001).
13. Kennedy, *The Last Blank Spaces*, 100.
14. Martin Thomas, 'Unpacking the Testimony of Gerald Blitner: Cross-Cultural Brokerage and the Arnhem Land Expedition,' in *Exploring the Legacy*, Thomas and Neale, 377–41.
15. Peter Bassett-Smith, interview by Sally K. May and Martin Thomas, 12 February 2006, Kangaroo Ground, Vic, ORAL TRC 5655, National Library of Australia Oral History Collection (NLAOHC), Canberra, AU; Raymond Louis Specht, interview by Sally K. May and Martin Thomas, 2–4 May 2006, St Lucia, Qld, ORAL TRC 5662, NLAOHC.
16. F. D. McCarthy, 'Diary 1: Field Notes Groote Eylandt 1,' in Papers of Frederick David McCarthy, MS 3513/14/1, Australian Institute of Torres Strait Islander Studies, Canberra, AU.
17. Max Lamshed, *'Monty': The Biography of C. P. Mountford* (Adelaide, AU: Rigby, 1972). For more recent analysis see Martin Thomas, 'A Short History of the 1948 Arnhem Land Expedition,' *Aboriginal History* 34 (2010): 143–69 and Philip Jones, 'Inside Mountford's Tent: Paint, Politics and Paperwork,' in *Exploring the Legacy*, Thomas and Neale, 33–54.
18. Howell Walker was the National Geographic Society writer-photographer assigned to the expedition. He was interviewed by Barbara Blackman on 1 September 1987 at Port Piper, NSW, ORAL TRC 2316, NLAOHC.
19. Beau Riffenburgh, *The Myth of the Explorer: The Press, Sensationalism, and Geographical Discovery* (Oxford: Oxford University Press, 1994), 5.
20. MacLeod, 'Discovery and Exploration,' 38.
21. Simon Naylor and James R. Ryan, 'Exploration and the Twentieth Century,' in *New Spaces of Exploration: Geographies of Discovery in the Twentieth Century*, eds. Simon Naylor and James R. Ryan (London: I. B. Tauris, 2010), 11.
22. For his readings of the postcolonial context to the Everest ascent see Peter H. Hansen, 'Confetti of Empire: The Conquest of Everest in Nepal, India, Britain, and New Zealand,' *Comparative Studies in Society and History* 42:2 (2000): 307–32 and Peter H. Hansen, 'Tenzing's Two Wrist-Watches: The

Conquest of Everest and Late Imperial Culture in Britain 1921–1953,' *Past and Present* 157 (1997): 159–77.

23. Naylor and Ryan, *New Spaces of Exploration*. For examples of how expeditionary anthropology kept alive the ethos of 'discovery' see Joshua A. Bell, Alison K. Brown, and Robert. J Gordon, eds., *Recreating First Contact: Expeditions, Anthropology, and Popular Culture* (Washington, DC: Smithsonian Institution Scholarly Press, 2013) and Thomas and Neale, *Exploring the Legacy*.

24. Joseph Conrad, 'Geography and Some Explorers,' *National Geographic*, March 1924, 243.

25. Kennedy, *The Last Blank Spaces*, 265.

26. Martin Thomas, 'Expedition as Time Capsule: Introducing the American–Australian Scientific Expedition to Arnhem Land,' in *Exploring the Legacy*, Thomas and Neale, 377–41; Martin Thomas, 'A Short History of the 1948 Arnhem Land Expedition;' Amanda Harris, 'Food, Feeding and Consumption (or the Cook, the Wife and the Nutritionist): The Politics of Gender and Class in a 1948 Australian Expedition,' *History and Anthropology* 24:3 (2013): 363–79.

27. Rupert T. Gould, *The Marine Chronometer: Its History and Development* (London: The Holland Press, 1960) and Dava Sobel, *Longitude: The True Story of a Lone Genius Who Solved the Greatest Scientific Problem of His Time* (London: Fourth Estate, 1996).

28. Thor Heyerdahl, *The Kon-Tiki Expedition: By Raft Across the South Seas*, trans. F. H. Lyon (London: George Allen & Unwin, 1950); Tim Severin, *The Brendan Voyage* (London: Hutchinson, 1978).

29. Christy Collis, 'Walking in Your Footsteps: "Footsteps of the Explorers" Expeditions and the Contest for Australian Desert Space,' in *New Spaces of Exploration*, Naylor and Ryan, 222–40. For a range of views on re-enactment see *Extreme and Sentimental History*, a special issue of *Criticism* devoted to historical re-enactment, eds. Vanessa Agnew and Jonathan Lamb, 46:3 (2004), 323–523.

30. 'Shackleton Epic,' http://shackletonepic.com, accessed 12 November 2013.

31. Paul Carter, *The Road to Botany Bay: An Essay in Spatial History* (London: Faber and Faber, 1987).

32. See Riffenburgh, *The Myth of the Explorer*.

33. Sir Robert Wilson, an army officer and colonial governor, is credited with this first modern usage when he wrote, 'the explorers enter, and immediately find themselves in a marble cave.' See 'explorer, n.,' OED Online, www.oed.com. rp.nla.gov.au/view/Entry/66670?redirectedFrom=explorer, accessed 8 October 2013.

34. See Kenneth Lupton, *Mungo Park the African Traveller* (Oxford: Oxford University Press, 1979).

35. Mungo Park, *Travels in the Interior Districts of Africa: Performed under the Direction and Patronage of the African Association, in the Years 1795, 1796, and 1797* (London: W. Bulmer & Co., 1799), viii.

36. Ibid., 293.

37. Ibid., 330–1.

38. See 'expedition, n.,' OED Online, www.oed.com.rp.nla.gov.au/view/Entry/664 87?redirectedFrom=expedition&, accessed 8 October 2013.

39. See 'expedite, v.,' OED Online, www.oed.com.rp.nla.gov.au/view/Entry/664 86?isAdvanced=false&result=2&rskey=nsCeNs&, accessed 8 October 2013.

40. T. L. Mitchell, *Three Expeditions into the Interior of Eastern Australia, with Descriptions of the Recently Explored Region of Australia Felix, and of the Present Colony of New South Wales* (London: T. & W. Boone, 1838), 5.

24 Martin Thomas

41. Felix Driver, 'Modern Explorers,' in *New Spaces of Exploration*, Naylor and Ryan, 243.
42. C. A. Bayly, 'The First Age of Global Imperialism, C. 1760–1830,' *Journal of Imperial and Commonwealth History* 26:2 (1998), 41.
43. Claude Nicolet, *Space, Geography, and Politics in the Early Roman Empire* (Ann Arbor: University of Michigan Press, 1991), 88.
44. Martin Thomas, *The Artificial Horizon: Imagining the Blue Mountains* (Carlton, AU-VIC: Melbourne University Press, 2003), 114–21.
45. Greg Dening, *Mr Bligh's Bad Language: Passion, Power and Theatre on the Bounty* (Cambridge: Cambridge University Press, 1992).
46. Kennedy, *The Last Blank Spaces*, 20.

2 What Is an Explorer?

Adriana Craciun

Le précurseur c'est l'homme de savoir dont on sait seulement bien après lui qu'il a couru devant tous ses contemporains et avant celui qu'on tient pour le vainqueur de la course.

(A precursor is a man of knowledge who, one knows only much later, ran ahead of all his contemporaries and before the one taken to be the winner of the race.)

Georges Canguilhem[1]

What is an Explorer? 'In proposing this slightly odd question,' I am inspired by Michel Foucault's 1969 lecture and will argue that we are overdue for an interdisciplinary reassessment of the discursive practices cohered under the sign of 'Explorer.'[2] This under-theorized term continues to circulate widely in scholarship, obscuring the heterogeneous traditions of natural and human sciences, and visual and literary aesthetic practices, of earlier eras with what is a nineteenth-century 'false historical object.'[3] The case I will focus on—of an author and would-be Arctic Explorer in 1818 and his controversial exploration narrative—offers an unusually clear glimpse of how the Explorer became visible in the early nineteenth century, and why any discussion of exploration and Explorers should acknowledge what Simon Schaffer describes as 'the indisciplined character [of] systems of knowledge established in the early nineteenth century.'[4]

The 1818 author-Explorer in question is located during the so-called second scientific revolution in Britain, when, according to narratives of disciplinary formation, increasingly formal institutional controls over scientific practices and sites introduced new restrictions on already exclusive patronage networks, even as scientific practice continued to expand its shared terrain with popular culture and public spectacle. According to literary periodization, this particular author-Explorer is situated in the Romantic period, when, according to traditional studies, the modern proprietary author was enshrined as an original and expressive genius. The domain of 'literature,' its periodization of writing and of reading, its generic

26   Adriana Craciun

and national taxonomies, and its juridical regulation (in Anglo-America) through copyright, has preoccupied authorship studies of the long eighteenth and nineteenth centuries, in which the Romantic author remains a central figure. A number of more recent histories of intellectual property and authorship have imported into their accounts a 1980s model of this so-called Romantic author, which in the last two decades has been subject to intensive critiques in literary studies, but continues to flourish beyond the field's temporal and disciplinary boundaries.[5] Juxtaposing authorship models from literary histories and histories of science at the turn of the nineteenth century thus remains both immensely fruitful and risky, as we refashion our modern genealogies of knowledge. While pursuing converging lines of inquiry into shared but incommensurate authorship practices, I am thus cognizant of the need to avoid reifying the master narratives long abandoned in our extra-disciplinary companion traditions.

To these ends, my goal is not to bridge the supposed gap between what we now distinguish as literature and science, but to side-step it. I want instead to consider an under-theorized third category, exploration, and with it a third subject position alongside those of the author and the savant: the Explorer. Given that the Explorer as a distinct identity did not yet exist at the turn of the nineteenth century, what are we doing when we look at narratives and images of exploration from that historical moment, and from earlier ones? What criteria do we rely on in recognizing exploration and Explorers as such, what are the mechanisms through which an Explorer is visible, memorable, discoverable? What can we gain by not becoming distracted by the mirage of the Explorer, looking instead at the multifarious practices, professions, and textual artefacts that brought this identity into being, and which were then in turn obscured?

Explorers became a distinct species in the nineteenth century, with their own private clubs, costumes, props, and professional organizations. As such, the Explorer is not a disciplinary formation, as is his near contemporary the Scientist; he is a consumer product of the early tourism and travel industries developing in the nineteenth-century age of empire. The Raleigh Club (1827), the Royal Geographical Society (1830), the Hakluyt Society (1846), the American Geographic Society (1851), and The Explorers' Club (1904) all made possible what Mary Fuller has described as the Victorian rediscovery of Elizabethan exploration, a nationalist project in which Victorians created their own precursors.[6] These precursors include such Enlightenment figures as James Cook, Charles Marie de La Condamine, and William Dampier, whose retroactive amalgamation as 'Explorers' continues today.

In the supposed golden age of Elizabethan discovery idealized by the Victorian exploration industry, Richard Hakluyt had been careful to distinguish between diverse practices in his landmark second collection, *The Principal Navigations, Voyages, Traffiques, and Discoveries of the English Nation* (1599–1600). Neither Hakluyt nor Samuel Purchas used the term 'explorer' in the sense in which scholars use it today: Hakluyt distinguished

What Is an Explorer? 27

between 'Navigations by sea, voyages by land, and traffiques of merchandise by both,' enumerating the 'discoveries' of renown and the 'pilots' and 'knights' who accomplished them.[7] Purchas praised the travellers, pilgrims, labourers, and 'Authours who voyaged.'[8] In the early Enlightenment era, we see in Dampier's ambitious illustrated publications the growing interests of distinct parties in transforming buccaneering and coasting voyages into something new—in Dampier's case, an early model for Enlightenment voyage narratives aspiring to a predisciplinary comprehensiveness, a form that would reach its zenith in the volumes devoted to the voyages of Cook, Constantine Phipps, and La Pérouse. None of these four was described as an Explorer/*explorateur*, nor were they authors of the narratives that appeared under their names. They were understood to rely on ghostwriters, compilers, and collaborators—Dampier unabashedly, Cook controversially, La Pérouse posthumously.

To the Enlightenment scientific practices of these diverse voyagers, we owe a new taxonomy of 'types,' according to Mary Louise Pratt: 'frontier figures of the seafarer, the conqueror, the captive, the diplomat,' and the 'herborizer.'[9] But as in the so-called Age of Discovery, during the Enlightenment the Explorer was not one of these types and should not continue to overwrite the diverse hierarchies of occupations through which Enlightenment-era voyagers were employed to undertake their '*Navigations, Voyages, Traffiques, and Discoveries*': that is, savant, *voyageur, navigateur, philosophe*, herborizer, mathematician, mariner, privateer, whaler, traveller, adventurer, surveyor, factor, trapper, agent, and interpreter. These diverse occupations always included indigenous people along a spectrum of association and autonomy: for example, the high-ranking Polynesian Tupaia, who chose to travel with Cook; the extraordinary, enslaved Dene woman known as Thanadelthur, employed as an agent by the Hudson's Bay Company in the early eighteenth century; or such indigenous leaders as the Chipewyan Matonabbee, on whom Samuel Hearne and other legendary English surveyors completely depended. In fact, the *Oxford English Dictionary* records only one pre-Victorian use of the noun 'explorer' in the sense of a person 'who explores a country or place'; and in the small additional number of instances I have located, 'explorer' carried a universally negative connotation of espionage or cowardly wandering, alien to the heroic Victorian sense we have inherited.[10] This is consistent with the Enlightenment French usage of *explorateur* as a synonym for spy/*espion*.[11] Diverse men on voyages of geographical discovery, themselves a small subset of voyage types, may have been charged with the activity of seeking out or exploring specific places, but this did not transform them into Explorers: not until this identity became dependent on a form of proprietary, solitary authorship that was in fact alien to the corporate and military domains in which the business of exploration was typically carried out.

Foucault's identification of the author as 'a privileged moment of individualization,' one lacking in rigorous analysis in 1969, applies today to the

28   Adriana Craciun

Explorer, a term still deployed in histories of empire, travel, postcolonialism, and science as if it refers to a specific identity or profession. The Explorer often remains beneath the threshold of critical interest, I suggest, because it obscures its reliance on that over-studied 'privileged moment of individualization,' the proprietary author. The Explorer is a nebulous, transhistorical figure to which we erroneously assign the origin of exploration, when we should be asking the questions we have learned from Foucault to ask of discursive practices: 'What are the modes of existence of this discourse? Where does it come from, how is it circulated, who controls it? What placements are determined for possible subjects?'[12]

Long-range networks, collective agency, indigenous knowledge, commercial secrecy, local modernities: these are the models of circulation and agency drawn from current historical geography, history of science, and historical anthropology, in which the Explorer as a meaningful eighteenth-century type does not play a useful function. While 'recovering collectivity'[13] has long been the order of the day in social authorship models like those pioneered by Jerome McGann and D. F. McKenzie, as in the multidisciplinary approaches to European empire and exploration described above, we await a critique of 'the explorer' that simultaneously resists both the back-formation of an identity—originally (in the Victorian era) a hero, today a villain—and the notion of autonomy obscuring the near identity of Explorer and author.

AUTHOR EFFECTS IN THE ARCTIC

European voyages in (and writings about) the Arctic at the turn of the nine-teenth century offer a unique theatre in which to consider the intersection of exploration and authorship, and the individualization of both. In the British context, interest in the Northwest Passage was at fever pitch in 1818, in part because of an innovative publication nexus centred on the Tory publisher John Murray, designated in 1813 as 'Official Bookseller to the Admiralty' and authorized to publish the accounts of state-sponsored Arctic exploration. From 1818, when the Admiralty restarted its Arctic program, to 1848, Murray published a total of 18 first editions by nine authors on the Arctic alone.[14] Attempting to monopolize the authorship of discoveries in an entire geo-imaginary region, this highly regulated nexus included the publisher, his journal the *Quarterly Review*, and its editor John Wilson Croker and reviewer John Barrow, who were also First and Second Secretaries of the Admiralty, respectively. Arctic publication was thus a domain distinct from that of commercial, proprietary authorship with which histories of authorship and copyright are chiefly concerned. Those whom we designate as Explorers in this respect were often naval captains—for example, Cook and Phipps—associated with long-range scientific networks, who were authorized to affix their names to a particular kind of object: expensive, illustrated,

What Is an Explorer? 29

beautifully produced quarto volumes representing the collective shipboard work of numerous officers and crew, the knowledge of indigenous people encountered en route, and the metropolitan authorities who authorized and financed the expeditions. Obeying shipboard hierarchy and corporate authority within the Admiralty and Colonial Office, the confiscation of all journals, and prepublication censorship were all necessary conditions of authoring a book on Arctic exploration in 1818.

In other words, early nineteenth-century author-Explorers operated in a domain radically different from that described by most studies of eighteenth-century authorship. Only when we consider in tandem the developments in Enlightenment-era scientific authorship and literary commercial authorship up to the turn of the nineteenth century, can we see the emergence of the hybrid figure of the Explorer as a distinct subject position, one outside our prevailing evolutionary models of print and authorship. Whether drawn from literary, legal, or sociological disciplines, histories of authorship are typically dependent on competing but consistently linear lines of descent: from prepublication censorship and state licensing prior to 1695; to the eighteenth century's commercial monopoly of print and copyright; and the subsequent rise of proprietary authorship, ending in that much-maligned mythical creature, the 'Romantic author' as solitary genius.

Rather than fitting such a progressive model of increasing individualization and print modernity, exploration writings reveal the persistence of aggregate institutional authorship models along with a thriving corporate manuscript and archival culture, thoroughly documented by early modern scholars but actually continuing well into the nineteenth century. In 1818, exploration writing was thus more regulated, more collective, and more dependent on co-present scribal and oral networks than was commercial print culture, the domain of the charismatic Romantic author. Gone were the loose, informal controls and gentlemanly networks of exploration relied upon by Joseph Banks and Lord Sandwich in the 1770s, which had allowed the embarrassing revelations in John Hawkesworth's authorized narrative of the first Cook expedition. Also gone by 1818 were the numerous competing accounts surrounding the disastrous losses of life on George Anson's circumnavigation (1740s), which the Admiralty had allowed into print a generation earlier. How and why would-be authors and diverse voyagers, excluded from the official and increasingly narrow ranks of state-sponsored Explorers, struggled to inhabit this category of Explorer in print reveals the migration of proprietary author effects into historically collective and corporate domains.

With these broad stakes in mind, I will narrow my focus to the example of a single book, and within that a single page, with an uncanny ability to visualize the multiple registers and disciplines that exploration narratives inhabited. The book is *Greenland, the Adjacent Seas, and the Northwest Passage*, published with Baldwin, Cradock, & Joy in 1818 by the Irish ship's surgeon Bernard O'Reilly, following one summer he spent aboard a

30 *Adriana Craciun*

Davis Strait whaler. O'Reilly's *Greenland* circulated amid controversy, violating the Admiralty's attempted monopoly on expensive illustrated Arctic accounts and accumulating accusations of plagiarism and inauthenticity that persist today.

O'Reilly's book offered a comprehensive account of Greenland, with chapters devoted to history, geography, ethnography, ice, and zoology, accompanied by maps and illustrations, a voyage log, and speculative chapters on the Northwest Passage. O'Reilly dismissed the Admiralty's current 1818 voyages—four ships searching for the North Pole and Northwest Passage—as a 'utopian paper-built plan of sailing to the North Pole' in 'absolute futility.' Instead, he advocated the annexation of Greenland's Disco Island from Denmark to allow for further exploration and exploitation of Baffin Bay.[15] Its large quarto size, respected publisher, and high cost meant that the book's intended readers would have been the same social and scientific elites as those of the Admiralty's authorized publications of the 1818 voyages, which did not appear until John Ross's controversial *Voyage of Discovery* in 1819, itself engulfed in controversies of plagiarism and incompetence. O'Reilly deliberately avoided the small, inexpensive format of such works as John Laing's *A Voyage to Spitzbergen* (1818), typically printed by provincial presses, and designated as travel narrative.[16] Laing's account (which Barrow praised as 'unpretending') identified its author on the title page as 'John Laing, surgeon,' and the entire book consists of a descriptive narrative, summarizing the existing state of knowledge on Spitzbergen, but making no claims for original discovery. By flamboyantly displaying the material 'authenticity effects' of quartos monopolized by naval voyages, and preemptively critiquing the priorities of the state-authorized expeditions, O'Reilly's book attracted a particularly vicious attack by Barrow in the *Quarterly Review*, for presuming to publish a 'pompous and frothy quarto,' instead of the 'small duodecimo' to which his station entitled him.[17]

In 1818, what distinguished a voyage of discovery from a commercial venture? A naturalist from an author? And either from an Explorer? For Barrow of the Admiralty, establishing these distinctions was increasingly important: 'A voyage of discovery implies danger,' he wrote of John Ross's abortive 1818 attempt to traverse the Northwest Passage, 'but a mere voyage, like his, round the shores of Baffin's Bay, in the three summer months, may be considered as a voyage of pleasure.'[18] O'Reilly and Ross's three-month stints in the Arctic in fact mirrored Barrow's own Arctic experience, which consisted of one summer aboard a whaling ship. But, infuriatingly, both men had returned and produced the kind of object signalling a voyage of danger and discovery.

O'Reilly's *Greenland* allows us to see what Explorers looked like in 1818: one of his illustrations of atmospheric phenomena offers an unusual silhouette of 'the author' delineated by a complex atmospheric effect (Figure 2.1). The aquatint engraving, based on O'Reilly's own 'on the spot' illustration in Davis Strait, is accompanied by a lengthy verbal description of its occasion.[19]

What Is an Explorer? 31

Figure 2.1 S. Koenig and Frederick Christian Lewis, *Luminous Phenomenon*, in Bernard O'Reilly, *Greenland, the Adjacent Seas, and the Northwest Passage* (London: Baldwin, Cradock, & Joy, 1818), plate 18, 202. Based on 'on the spot' drawing by Bernard O'Reilly. Courtesy of the John Carter Brown Library at Brown University.

The rare atmospheric phenomenon that O'Reilly observed was a fogbow accompanied by a glory, encircling the projected shadow of the observer—that of O'Reilly himself, according to the narrative. The looming shadow of the observer, focused at the antisolar point (anthelion), could have been described as a simple Brocken Spectre had it appeared over mountains, but O'Reilly's far rarer phenomenon occurred at sea and required both fog and ice crystals.

32 Adriana Craciun

The Brocken Spectre is familiar to scholars of Romanticism: Goethe's *Faust*, Coleridge's 'Constancy to an Ideal Object,' De Quincey's *Suspiria De Profundis*, and Hogg's *Private Memoirs and Confessions of a Justified Sinner* all include examples of Brocken Spectres, with or without encircling glories but lacking the rare fogbow. Brocken Spectres illustrated a wide range of Romantic associations, from the diabolical supernaturalism of Goethe and Hogg, to the 'dark symbolic mirror' of hidden suffering for De Quincey, and the 'coronation of one's own desire' in Coleridge.[20] As such a 'Dark Interpreter' of Romantic consciousness, the Brocken Spectre is a familiar apparition, but one whose visual resemblance to O'Reilly's 'Luminous Phenomenon' is deceptive.

The immediate difference between these literary spectres and O'Reilly's phenomenon is that O'Reilly's is a composite image-text. The visual and discursive accounts of this Luminous Phenomenon together place O'Reilly and his book in a tradition very different from that of his gothic contemporaries. O'Reilly's composite Luminous Phenomenon produced a unique 'author effect' in an attempt to situate the author of *Greenland* within an exclusive and increasingly regulated discursive tradition: that of the naturalist and 'explorer' in Britain's expanding second empire.

Although he claimed this Luminous Phenomenon as an original discovery, as a trained naturalist who had worked for the Royal Dublin Society, O'Reilly would have known of the most famous recorded instance of this phenomenon, described visually and verbally by survivors of the French geodetic expedition to South America led by La Condamine in the 1730s. European interest in South American exploration was at a new all-time high when O'Reilly was writing, as publishers and state authorities sought to capitalize on Alexander von Humboldt's recent publications, which in Britain included Helen Maria Williams's influential 1814 translation of his *Personal Narrative*. Thanks to Humboldt, La Condamine's earlier expedition had recently found a new English-language audience in John Pinkerton's popular 14-volume series, *General Collection of the Best and Most Interesting Voyages and Travels in all Parts of the World*. Pinkerton's edition replaced the original illustrations from the various La Condamine publications with engravings lifted from Humboldt's more recent voyage narratives, effectively resolving the expeditions' notorious priority disputes via the formidable authority of Humboldt's synthetic approach.

One of the Spanish captains of the ill-fated La Condamine expedition, Antonio de Ulloa, had described this same complex phenomenon of concentric glories, fogbow, and shadow as encountered at sunrise on a mountain in Pambamarca, Peru. Ulloa highlighted the individualizing force of this phenomenon, particularly significant in Enlightenment exploration because of the priority disputes that imploded expeditions like La Condamine's. Ulloa wrote that 'what was most remarkable, tho' we were six or seven together, every one saw the phenomenon with regard to himself, and not that relating to others.'[21] Ulloa's account and the accompanying illustration of the phenomenon (Figure 2.2) in the original eighteenth-century editions

What Is an Explorer? 33

Figure 2.2 Vicente de la Fuente, *Natural Phenomena*, in Antonio Ulloa, *Relación histórica del viage a la América meridional*, vol. 3, pt. 2 (Madrid: Antonio Marin, 1748), fold-out plate 14, following p. 598. Courtesy of the John Carter Brown Library at Brown University.

continue to interest atmospheric scientists today, when the phenomenon is often referred to as 'Ulloa's Rings.'[22] But Ulloa's original discovery was a shared one, as he admitted: 'we were six or seven together.'

The phenomenon itself, in fact, generates questions of individuation by its dramatic differentiation of observers, being uniquely visible to, and making visible, each one. Ulloa's fellow observers included La Condamine and the mathematician Pierre Bouguer; the latter was one of the few survivors of the disastrous expedition, which by this point was hopelessly fissured by rivalries. Bouguer, the first to return to Paris, read a paper in which he described the expedition's discovery of the fogbow and glory phenomenon in revealing terms:

> There is an extraordinary phenomenon visible almost every day upon these mountains, and which must necessarily be as old as the world, yet there is much probability we have been the first to notice it.
> This was a sort of apotheosis of each spectator; and I must not neglect to apprise you, each every day calmly enjoyed the exquisite pleasure of viewing himself decorated with all these glories, and saw no trace of those of his neighbour's. It is true it is precisely the same thing with regard to the rain-bow, although it has not always been attended to. Each spectator views a distinct rain-bow, since the arch has a different

34   *Adriana Craciun*

centre for each person; but as the coronets which are seen upon the mountains of Peru are very small, and seem to belong to the shadow of the spectator, each has a right to appropriate what he discovers to himself.[23]

Like his fellow spectator Ulloa, Bouguer is interested in the individualizing illusion of this specific phenomenon, though like Ulloa he, too, fails to name his 'neighbours' in discovery. Moreover, Bouguer sets the scene for his discovery by noting that the phenomenon occurs daily and is 'as old as the world.'[24] What allows Bouguer to appropriate this discovery is his claim to describe it first, and he can do that because he is a self-described *philosophe*—and more importantly, the first *philosophe* back to Paris.

Bouguer's account is also noteworthy because it considers this localized phenomenon's relationship to the indigenous inhabitants for whom this 'discovery' may have been a quotidian event:

The time proper to view this phenomenon [i.e., sunrise] . . . is a sufficient excuse for the Peruvians never having beheld it, and why they should not be blamed for it. It is an hour not usual for any but a philosopher to be found upon the summit of a high mountain. [25]

Thus the Luminous Phenomenon is akin to other riches of the New World, which indigenous people either fail to see the true value of, or fail to see at all. The rival names of Ulloa and Bouguer became attached to this complex phenomenon on Pambamarca, their observations and the Ulloa illustration reverberating throughout popular British accounts of natural science by Erasmus Darwin, Joseph Priestley, and Oliver Goldsmith, who alternatively referred to the phenomenon as either Ulloa's Rings or Bouguer's Halo.[26]

O'Reilly's Luminous Phenomenon was designed to affix his name to this 'original' discovery of an atmospheric phenomenon, as was the case with Ulloa and Bouguer (and William Parry for a different phenomenon)—individual authors of identical discoveries, open to infinite re-authoring.[27] What is intriguing and I think original in O'Reilly's visual presentation of this particular phenomenon, however, is the extraordinary vantage point he assumed, allowing the spectator to share the observer's unique perspective of fogbow, glories, and shadow aligned. After all, what distinguishes this phenomenon, according to its serial discoverers, is its illusion of exclusive possession. O'Reilly's Luminous Phenomenon, then, does mark an innovation from his Enlightenment predecessors, and from the longer tradition of picturing rainbows and other optical phenomena, in that he made visible this individualizing effect itself.

Philip Fisher has noted how traditional Aristotelean and Cartesian illustrations of rainbows, which triangulate rainbow, observer, and the sun, are seen from a point that cannot exist in nature, and the same applies to the fogbow in Ulloa's image: 'The rainbow cannot be seen unless we are standing

What Is an Explorer? 35

at the point represented by the observer, but from that point neither the sun nor the observer could be seen. The very thing represented by the diagram cannot exist as a visual state of affairs.'[28] In allowing us the innovation of seeing observer and object simultaneously, O'Reilly is not projecting a spectral double or a deep self. Neither is he inviting us into the 'thoroughly subjectivized aesthetic' of Friedrich's landscape paintings, for example the *Wanderer Above the Sea of Mist* (also dating from 1818).[29] In that painting, according to Joseph Koerner, the autoscopic *Rückenfigur* contemplates the 'full presence of landscape' as part of the 'subjectively constituted nature of the visible.'[30] Yet O'Reilly's autoscopic phenomenon obliterates all landscape, resisting also the popular pleasure of exoticizing Greenland ice for the more rarefied delight of projecting himself as an Explorer in the act of (self-)discovery.

While displaying a striking affinity with the spectral Romantic idealism of his contemporaries in visual art and literary Gothic, this self-image of the (re)discovery of a Luminous Phenomenon inserts O'Reilly's book in a larger field of Enlightenment exploration. While his prose text struggled to convey the shifting atmospheric light, the relative distance and mobility of the glories and fogbow, the iridescent colours and the subtle diffusion of light in distance, the image is dominated by an expanse of negative space and within this, the projected shadow of the author/observer, a clearly delineated and static void. Projected shadow has been since Plato the 'bearer of imperfect knowledge of the object that projects it,' but it could also provide eighteenth-century thinkers with different kinds of knowledge: it could enlighten, argues Michael Baxandall, as an 'image of the makings of any actual experience at all.'[31] In O'Reilly's Luminous Phenomenon we see the makings of an author-centred ideal of exploration. A projected shadow in an empty void, a plagiarized text in an unauthorized format, a renegade theory from a self-promoting colonial impostor: the Luminous Phenomenon enlightens as a 'hole in light'[32] does, making visible the making of an Explorer.

When considered as a more specific form of author effect, a self-portrait, the Luminous Phenomenon again evokes not the psychological depths of literary Brocken Spectres, but the self-fashioning necessary to the careers of such Enlightenment Arctic savants as Linnaeus and Pierre Louis Maupertuis. O'Reilly's reviewers had accused him of self-promotion, and they were right to do so, because his self-portrait as Luminous Phenomenon placed him in the company of fellow self-promoters like Maupertuis and Linnaeus (whose apostle he belatedly was): men who by 1818 were successfully consolidated as heroic national figures, and solitary Arctic savants, after similarly brief sojourns near the Arctic Circle.

The French mathematician Maupertuis had led the Arctic geodetic expedition co-ordinated with La Condamine's voyage to the equator, and like the South American voyagers, he was engulfed in a series of controversies upon returning to Europe. In a famous portrait exhibited in the Salon of 1741, Maupertuis appeared wearing an ostensibly Sami (Lapp) costume,

36 Adriana Craciun

surrounded by carefully composed signs of his arduous voyage to Samiland (Lapland). Via this 'flamboyant act of self-advertisement,' Maupertuis crafted an individualized identity of the man of science, visually 'remaking . . . collaborative effort into the triumph of one individual,' according to Mary Terrall.[33] The Sami portrait of Maupertuis also elevated a brief sojourn near the Arctic Circle to what the mathematician would frequently describe in later years as 'my voyage to the pole.'[34]

Linnaeus affords the best-known example of how an exotic Arctic portrait functioned to elevate a brief Arctic visit into a national iconic identity. As Lisbet Koerner has shown, in his frontispiece portrait to *Flora Lapponica* (1737), Linnaeus 'posed as a lone innovator and as a founder of a new science,' transforming his 18-day journey in Samiland into a career and identity as consummate Arctic traveller and Sami expert. Linnaeus oversaw the design of his widely reproduced portrait, in which he wears a contrived Sami costume and clutches his botanical 'discovery,' his 'floral talisman, *Linnaea borealis*.'[35] Like Maupertuis, Linnaeus leveraged a brief Arctic foray into an enduring identity as solitary man of science, in significant part through an iconic portrait in an ambitious publication. O'Reilly's portrait as Luminous Phenomenon thus places him squarely in the company of fellow self-promoters, who by O'Reilly's day had been successfully rehabilitated as the heroic, solitary Arctic savants their portraits and ambitious publications had helped to invent.

Two years after the publication of *Greenland*, the Luminous Phenomenon appeared in the work of O'Reilly's contemporaries with a radically different author effect. In *The Climate of London* (1818–20), the Quaker meteorologist Luke Howard had classified and illustrated a new taxonomy of clouds, and in the catalog of meteorological phenomena presented to Britons as locally accessible, he included a specimen of '*Iris Gloria*,' his name for Bouguer's Halo/Ulloa's Rings/O'Reilly's Luminous Phenomenon. Howard described how he and his family experienced this phenomenon together in Kent in 1820:

> The whole phenomenon was highly curious and interesting; and the facility with which each of the party could either appropriate the *glory* to himself or share it with the company present, suggested to me some reflexions of a *moral* nature. [36]

A Quaker minister committed to demonstrating the providential regularity of Britain's weather, Howard used this phenomenon's extraordinary ability to visualize self-aggrandizement as an occasion for self-fashioning as a humble Christian, not a solitary Explorer or *philosophe*. Howard's popularizing meteorological practice was possible because, as Jan Golinski argues, 'the weather constituted a common domain in which elite and popular discourse intersected,' a form of 'public property.'[37] But this particular meteorological effect, because it made visible the apotheosis of the individual within a social setting, in fact embodied the illusion of private property within this public sphere of science, specifically the illusion of original discovery as the hallmark of an Explorer and man of science. By resisting the likes of Bouguer and O'Reilly, who had effaced the shared and local nature of this phenomenon, Howard deferred his scientific authority and the glory of discovery to his god, the author of all natural knowledge.

The autodidact man of science and Arctic whaler William Scoresby Jr. described a similar Greenland phenomenon in *Journal of a Voyage to the Northern Whale-Fishery* (1823), citing only Bouguer's precedent but offering a strikingly depersonalized account and illustration (Figure 2.3). In the centre of Scoresby's concentric glories we see the shadow of the observer's head, but this is dwarfed by the integrated image of the round top-gallant crow's nest, mast, and sails.[38] This apparitional observer is completely absorbed into the fabric of the ship: the narrative description tells us it is Scoresby himself at the centre; but both the prose, with its nod to Bouguer, and the image, with its integration of the observer into the larger workings of the ship, set apart Scoresby, a devout evangelical, as reluctant to use exploration as a means of self-glorification.

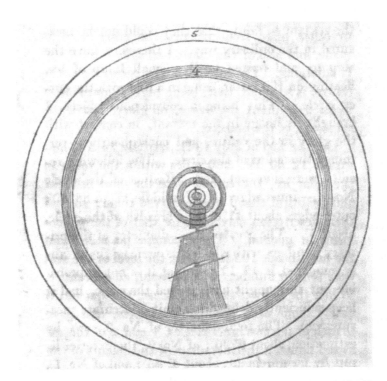

Figure 2.3 William Scoresby Jr., 'Anthelion and Coronae', in *Journal of a Voyage to the Northern Whale-Fishery* (Edinburgh: Archibald Constable and London; Hurst, Robinson, and Co., 1823), 276.

38 *Adriana Craciun*

Perhaps the best-known authority on Arctic maritime science in his day, Scoresby was twice rebuffed by a vindictive Barrow in his efforts to command state-funded Arctic voyages of discovery. Michael Bravo argues that Scoresby's struggle to gain access to the rank of Explorer invites us to ask, 'how wide was the gap between the aspirations and skills of a successful early nineteenth-century English whaling captain and the credibility of a would-be explorer licensed by the state to represent the nation?'[39] Scoresby used his unparalleled Arctic maritime experience and knowledge, circulated in his influential books on the Greenland seas, to demonstrate an entitlement to both of these regimes, revealing not a gap between them but a set of shared knowledge increasingly subject to authorities' enclosure and discipline, and made manifest in the distinct kinds of printed objects each produced.

Devout Christians and respected authors, Howard and Scoresby subordinated the glory of discovery to a higher social and spiritual purpose than that claimed by Bouguer or Ulloa, or their ambitious contemporary O'Reilly. The Luminous Phenomenon thus provided a recurring occasion for a range of speculations on the exclusive possession of discovery claimed by its serial authors. The relationship of authorship's absence, and of its occultation and illicit usurpation, to the appearance of the Explorer at this moment is the subject of the second half of this essay.

LOST BOOKS OF GREENLAND

The Luminous Phenomenon was actually only one of four types of original discoveries that O'Reilly claimed and illustrated in his book. First, he designed a Linnaean binomial system for classifying wind force at sea into seven genera, effectively merging the Beaufort wind scale recently adopted by the navy with Luke Howard and Thomas Forster's studies of clouds.[40] Second, he sighted, named, and charted a new Arctic archipelago off the west coast of Greenland, naming these the Linnaean Isles 'in honour of the prince of natural historians,'[41] and thereby alienating himself further from the nationalist project of the 1818 naval voyages. Third, he identified and named three new species of birds. And fourth, he described another new atmospheric phenomenon, a type of aurora he named 'cirrus radiation.'

With each new discovery, the belated Linnaean apostle O'Reilly attempted to inscribe a lasting mark in the history of science and of exploration, while making it clear that he was an outsider to (and thus independent of the regulation imposed by) both the naval and the whaling networks through which all previous Arctic science and exploration had been conducted. Not trusting 'for support to documents placed in custom-houses, nor [relying] on the uncertain information which might be coaxed from the master of a whale ship,' O'Reilly relied on a higher authority, that of empirical observation 'on the spot.'[42] Nevertheless, O'Reilly could claim to be the author of these four original

What Is an Explorer? 39

discoveries because he presented them as a set of immutable mobiles—objects, specimens, observations, maps, and drawings—indistinguishable from those of the authorized state expeditions, like those of Ross and Parry, that would begin to appear in quarto editions after 1818.

Barrow's review had ungenerously accused O'Reilly of 'pilfering' prior research, but more serious accusations were to follow. O'Reilly was alleged to have plagiarized the unpublished works of Karl Ludwig Giesecke, a Prussian Wernerian mineralogist who spent seven winters marooned in Greenland (1806–13). The charge of plagiarism is complex and probably inaccurate; what is interesting for our purpose of understanding the relationship of Explorer and author is that Giesecke himself never published his three-volume account of his 'Voyage to Greenland.' Almost as obscure as O'Reilly today, the polymath Giesecke cut a figure as remarkable as Humboldt's across cosmopolitan European society (he is rumoured to have been the librettist for Mozart's *Magic Flute*), and at the turn of the nineteenth century was the greatest European expert on Greenland. But his manuscripts remain unpublished in the National Library of Ireland and the Royal Dublin Society, his name largely forgotten as an Explorer because he declined proprietary authorship of his 'discoveries.'[43]

Giesecke circulated his work in public lectures[44] at the Royal Dublin Society (the site of O'Reilly's alleged plagiarisms), in a small number of individual scientific essays published in Britain and Ireland, and in the archived maps and manuscripts to which the authorities in Britain, Ireland, and Denmark had access—he did not publish in the elegant quarto format required of authors who would be Explorers.[45] Moreover, Giesecke's published essays were unusual in crediting native Greenlanders with discoveries, including the indigenous names of minerals, places, and animals, which he claimed merely to report and translate: most importantly, the location of the large cryolite deposit at Ivittuut, the source of Denmark's profitable mining industry in Greenland, lasting until the 1980s.[46]

Giesecke was appointed professor of mineralogy at the Royal Dublin Society in December 1813 through the efforts of Robert Jameson, the central figure in Edinburgh's scientific circles. He was placed in charge of the society's large Leskean natural history collection, which Bernard O'Reilly was arranging and cataloguing at that time. O'Reilly published the catalogue, the only other known work under his name, and sent it to the Principal Librarian of the British Museum, Henry Ellis.[47] January 1814 marked O'Reilly's expulsion from the institution around which every Explorer's club was built, the library. In January 1814, the same month in which Giesecke took up his professorship, the society voted to revoke O'Reilly's access to their library, for unknown reasons.[48] Banished from the metropolitan circles of calculation, excluded from the circles of patronage, O'Reilly continued his attempts to enter the rank of Explorer through that of author. By presuming to situate his *Greenland* book in the archive of Arctic science, he tried to join the exclusive ranks of Explorers, at a time and place when the

40   *Adriana Craciun*

public designation of exploration as an idealized pursuit of disinterested knowledge was closely policed by a man whose Arctic experience also consisted of a summer whaling voyage.

Giesecke's absence from our histories of science and of exploration is as extraordinary as O'Reilly's controversial presence in them, and both anomalies can be explained through the same mechanisms of original authorship. After presenting his 1816 Greenland lectures (which reportedly only had 12 attendees),[49] Giesecke left Jameson to decide whether or not to publish his account of Greenland mineralogy[50] and embarked on a continental tour until 1819. In 1818 he was publicly expected to publish a three-volume illustrated quarto work on Greenland in both English and German, but never did.[51] Via his long post-1818 career in the Royal Dublin Society and his extensive links to Edinburgh, London, and the Continent, Giesecke's archived research added considerably to European knowledge of Greenlandic geography, geology, and ethnography. After Giesecke's death in 1833, O'Reilly was identified as the usurper of his true destiny as author of the object all Explorers needed to produce (the expensive quarto), but there is no evidence of plagiarism to support this persistent charge. The more likely explanation, offered by Giesecke's friend Friederike Brun, is that the expense of independently publishing a three-volume book with an estimated 50 engraved plates proved too great, willing subscribers too few, and the risk of cross-border reprinting too high. What we see instead is more evidence of the widely held expectation in 1818 that proprietary authorship anoints solitary Explorers. O'Reilly's *Greenland* quarto only appears to have supplanted Giesecke's: the one a public simulacrum of spectacular authenticity effects, the other a substantial body of research which remained confined to restricted manuscript, archive, and lecture networks.

Giesecke's Greenland researches, even more so than Scoresby's autodidactic Arctic researches, remain largely unknown because the identity of author and Explorer remains unchallenged in traditional histories of the latter. It is instead John Ross's brief visit to Greenland in 1818 that looms large in our accounts via the public dispute in print between Barrow, Ross, Sabine, and others following Ross's publication of his *Voyage of Discovery* with Murray (1819). Giesecke's and O'Reilly's star-crossed paths in Greenland and Dublin, their shared invisibility as Explorers, and their heterodox approaches to authoring exploration, are more enlightening than is Ross's actual voyage.

Lacking in state authorization and funding as an Explorer, or the artisanal experience of a whaler like Scoresby, O'Reilly had entered the fray of 1818 Arctic speculation by assembling his own authority from such esteemed Enlightenment figures as Carl Linnaeus, Bouguer, and Ulloa. But O'Reilly was not a failed would-be Explorer, a straggler in a dying Enlightenment tradition. Rather, he was an early example of what the nineteenth-century Explorer would become. We can see how O'Reilly's book and career chart this new course by following the surprising afterlife of one of his discoveries.

Of all O'Reilly's over-stated claims to original discovery in *Greenland*, one has remained on the books and carries his name still: *Procellaria gravis,* the Greater Shearwater, identified and named as a distinct species for the first time in O'Reilly's book.[52] He noted in *Greenland* that his bird specimens were now in William Bullock's Egyptian Hall museum in London. This is one of several visible intersections of O'Reilly's practice of Explorer and author with popular spectacle and exhibition. Bullock was a collector and museum entrepreneur whose major exhibitions of Sami and Mexican artefacts (and people) in the 1820s drew tens of thousands of spectators to his Piccadilly museum. Bullock's passion was ornithology, and by 1818 his museum contained 3,000 specimens, which were auctioned along with the entire natural history collection for £12,000 in 1819.[53] Many of Bullock's specimens went into the British Museum collections, probably O'Reilly's birds among them.[54] His discredited and allegedly plagiarized book, *Greenland*, remains today the authoritative source first identifying the Greater Shearwater in such international references as the Integrated Taxonomic Information System.

O'Reilly experienced this minimal success in placing his work within the orbit of established London scientific networks because of the shared territory between these networks, popular spectacle, and his ambitious approach to authorship. Britain's Arctic fever was significantly fuelled by the ability of showmen, entrepreneurs, and men of science to exploit the Arctic's unique visual properties through such new media as moving panoramas and stereoscopes. The 1818 Arctic naval voyages of discovery that O'Reilly had set out to displace had discovered nothing and produced only one official publication (Ross's *Voyage*, ridiculed for discovering a refraction mirage as compelling as the Linnaean Isles, the 'Croker Mountains'), but they did result in a successful panorama designed by Henry Barker (1818–19).[55] The Admiralty's 'paper-built plan' and O'Reilly's simulacrum of it were equally indebted to this new visual culture of Arctic spectacle. In fact, we owe to Barrow's crushing review an early recognition of how O'Reilly fashioned a new kind of author-Explorer. Ridiculing O'Reilly's 'power of vision,' Barrow wrote that his atmospheric observations '[produce] over the more misty pages of his quarto, as numerous and as various transformations as may be seen in the tube of a kaleidoscope.'[56] Invented by David Brewster in 1815, the kaleidoscope swept across Europe and its colonies, and was instrumental in the revolutionary 'remaking of the visual field'[57] in the early nineteenth century. The 'promiscuous range of effects' created by the kaleidoscope in fact suited O'Reilly's approach to Greenland wonders, which combined the expensive authenticity effects of enlightened exploration with the individualized showmanship of an idealized identity, enjoying affinities both with Friedrich's high art and the vulgar materiality of kaleidoscopism. *Greenland*'s kaleidoscopic effects were thus particularly noisome to authorities like Barrow who were eager to replace 'delighted curiosity' with the 'diligent curiosity'[58] characteristic of naval field sciences.

While he may have missed the boat as a Linnaean disciple, in the end O'Reilly is not a straggler in a dying Enlightenment tradition. The Luminous

42 Adriana Craciun

Phenomenon forecasts the appearance of the Explorer, a deceptively static figure in which there remained at play numerous disciplines, professions, and aesthetic codes, many of them with 'exotic genealogies'[59]—in this case, an Irish subject's bold intervention in the British and Danish competition for Arctic resources, territories, and waterways. The 'Explorer' as a distinctive identity remained empty until later nineteenth-century institutions reconfigured these exotic genealogies into the linear narratives of direct precursors, from the Elizabethan Age to their own age of empire. They could do this because the proprietary author under whose name Explorer cohered had become naturalized, though it remained a construction alien to the naval and corporate cultures inhabited by the most lauded state-funded and commercial 'Explorers' well into the nineteenth century.

O'Reilly's peripheral status in the circles of science and collecting, his expulsion from the rank of naturalist by the Royal Dublin Society, and from that of Explorer by the Admiralty's publishing nexus, situate him at the forefront of a new authorship regime central to exploration as we recognize it. After his fugitive appearance as author and Explorer, he was again submerged into the fiercely competitive networks of medical practice— registering as an apothecary in Ireland, serving aboard merchant vessels as a surgeon, tutoring medical students.[60] O'Reilly was found dead in a rented room above a London pub in 1827, indigent and possibly a suicide, leaving behind pitiful notes he had been using to beg for assistance from prominent men of science. 'I have voyaged much and published many works,' he wrote:

> In 1817 . . . I proceeded to explore the Arctic regions; my observations on which were published in quarto, and led, I presume to say, to the recent expeditions in quest of a north-west passage. Subsequently, I traversed the Southern Ocean, visited Van-Diemen's Land, New South Wales, Java, Bengal, and St Helena; the national productions of which I examined with care, with a view to publication.[61]

He published several volumes based on his global travels, but these 'not being in my own name, are unproductive,' he wrote. According to O'Reilly's deathbed note, these grandiose achievements—his circumnavigations and seminal role in Arctic exploration—are delusive because of his failure to author them. Indeed, they repeat as farce Linnaeus and Maupertuis's efforts (by 1818 no longer visible because successful) to leverage brief Arctic forays into lasting identities, in O'Reilly's case as one who 'explore[s] . . . in quest of a north-west passage.'

O'Reilly insisted that his failure was one of proprietary authorship, a view of exploration echoed by Michel de Certeau:

> The name pays. The publication contract seems to duplicate—as its shadow, as the condition of its production—the book in which heroic explorers go about filling the great empty expanses of the map of the world with names.[62]

In the nineteenth century it would no longer be the authorization of state or commercial institutions that seemed to propel would-be Explorers into the unknown, but rather the power of commercial authorship, visual spectacle, and costumed public performance, which drew a heterogeneous group of voyagers toward the profitable display of autonomy, discovery, and identity. The voyagers retrospectively referred to as Explorers, from Dampier to Cook, Mungo Park to Bernard O'Reilly, continued to engage in a diverse range of professions and practices, but by the early nineteenth century a narrow understanding of authorship had eclipsed authorization as the public nexus of these discourses and agents, one newly cohered under the sign of the Explorer. O'Reilly, his book *Greenland*, and his author effect as Luminous Phenomenon beautifully illustrate the ephemeral and material channels through which the Explorer first became visible.

ACKNOWLEDGMENTS

Copyright © 2011 The Johns Hopkins University Press. This article first appeared in *Eighteenth-Century Studies*, Volume 45, Issue 1, Fall 2011, pages 29–51. This essay is dedicated to the memory of Marc Blanchard.

NOTES

1. Georges Canguilhem, 'Introduction: L'objet d'histoire des sciences,' in *Études d'histoire et de philosophie de sciences*, 7th ed. (Paris: Vrin, 2002), 22.
2. Michel Foucault, 'What Is an Author?,' in *Language, Counter-Memory, Practice*, ed. Donald Bouchard, trans. Donald Bouchard and Sherry Simon (Ithaca, NY: Cornell University Press, 1977), 113–38. On the vagaries of translations of Foucault's essay, see the relevant note in Luisa Calè and Adriana Craciun, 'The Disorder of Things,' *Eighteenth-Century Studies* 45:1 (2011), 1–13. For an important challenge to Foucault's essay, see Roger Chartier, 'Foucault's Chiasmus,' in *Scientific Authorship: Credit and Intellectual Property in Science*, eds. Mario Biagioli and Peter Galison (London: Routledge, 2003), 13–32.
3. Canguilhem, 'Introduction,' 23.
4. Simon Schaffer, 'How Disciplines Look,' in *Interdisciplinarity: Reconfigurations of the Social and Natural Sciences*, eds. Andrew Barry and Georgina Born (London: Routledge, 2013), 57–81. I am grateful to Simon Schaffer for sharing an advance copy of this essay.
5. A key text is the collection edited by Martha Woodmansee and Peter Jaszi, *The Construction of Authorship: Textual Appropriation in Law and Literature* (Durham, NC: Duke University Press, 1994), particularly the editors' two essays, both titled 'On the Author Effect.' An important and excellent volume, it also had the effect of disseminating a static 'romantic author' (as expressive, original genius) that still flourishes in histories of intellectual property, although it has been widely challenged in literary studies. See, for example, James Boyle, *Shamans, Software, and Spleen: Law and the Construction of the Information Society* (Cambridge, MA: Harvard University Press, 1996). A better approach is found in the legal analysis of David

44 *Adriana Craciun*

Saunders and Ian Hunter, who estrange expressive literature and literary approaches on the whole without relying on a limiting notion of 'romantic authorship': see their 'Lessons from the "Literatory": How to Historicise Authorship,' *Critical Inquiry* 17:3 (1991): 479–509. For an overview of authorship practices in relation to exploration, see Adriana Craciun, 'Writing the Disaster: Franklin and *Frankenstein*,' *Nineteenth-Century Literature* 65:4 (2011): 433–81.

6. Mary Fuller, *Voyages in Print: English Travel to America 1576–1624* (Cambridge: Cambridge University Press, 1995). Canguilhem's critique of the notion of precursors significantly influenced Foucault's archaeology of ideas as a departure from the history of ideas. On writers creating precursors, see Jorge Luis Borges, 'Kafka and His Precursors,' in *Labyrinths: Selected Stories & Other Writings* (New York: New Directions, 1964), 199–201.

7. Richard Hakluyt, 'Preface to the Reader,' in *The Principal Navigations, Voyages, Traffiques, and Discoveries of the English Nation*, eds. Richard Hakluyt and Edmund Goldsmid (London: G. Bishop, R. Newberie, and R. Barker, 1599–1600).

8. Samuel Purchas, 'To the Reader,' in *Purchas his Pilgrimage* (London: Printed by W. Stansby for H. Fetherstone, 1626).

9. Mary Louise Pratt, *Imperial Eyes: Travel Writing and Transculturation*, (London: Routledge, 2008), 26.

10. The OED's only pre-Victorian usage of 'explorer' as a noun ('one who explores a country or place') is in William Warburton's 1740 description of the wandering Israelites as 'cowardly Explorers' who doubted their god's promise to Moses (*OED, Warburton Div. Legat.iv. vi. II. 288*). Other pre-1800 usages exist, also connoting aimless wandering, espionage, and disorder. For example, William Cecil's anti-Papist *The Execution of Justice in England* (London: Christopher Barker, 1583): 'Shal no subiect, that is a spial and an explorer for the rebell or enemie, against his naturall Prince, be taken and punished as a traitour, because he is not found wt armour or weapon, but yet is taken in his disguised apparell, with writings, or other manifest tokens, to proue him a spie for traitors, after he hath wandered secretly in his soueraigns campe, region, court or citie?,' in *Early English Books Online*, http://eebo.chadwyck.com/, accessed 19 March 2011. Similarly, in Raphael Holinshed's *The Third Volume of Chronicles, Beginning at Duke William the Norman* (1586), 'explorer' is a synonym for 'Catholic spy:' 'for these disguised persons (called scholers or priests) hauing beene first conuersant of long time with the traitors beyond the sea in all their conspiracies, came hither by stealth in time of war and rebellion by commandement of the capitall enimie the pope or his legats, to be secret espials and explorers in the realme for the pope, to deliuer by secret, Romish tokens, as it were an earnest or prest, to them that should be in readines to ioine with rebels or open enimies' (1368), in *Early English Books Online*, http://eebo.chadwyck.com/, accessed 19 March 2011.

11. See Marie-Noëlle Bourguet, 'The Explorer,' in *Enlightenment Portraits*, ed. Michel Vovelle, trans. Lydia Cochrane (Chicago: University of Chicago Press, 1997), 257–315. Bourguet notes the absence of 'explorer' as descriptive noun aboard expeditions like La Pérouse's, despite the noun's existence in the 1718 *Dictionnaire de l'Académie française*, and focuses on the 'gap between the usage and the dictionaries' in order to produce a 'semantic analysis of the term' (257, 259). I did not see Bourguet's essay until completing my own, but given that her work is devoted to an overview of numerous Enlightenment explorers' *avant la lettre*, our approaches to the problem signalled by the Explorer's semantic absence are very different.

12. Foucault, 'What Is an Author?,' 138.

What Is an Explorer? 45

13. Martha Woodmansee, 'On the Author Effect: Recovering Collectivity,' in *The Construction of Authorship*, eds. Martha Woodmansee and Peter Jaszi (Durham, NC and London: Duke University Press, 1994), 15–28.

14. On the Murray nexus of publication and exploration, see Craciun, 'Writing the Disaster'.

15. Bernard O'Reilly, *Greenland, the Adjacent Seas, and the Northwest Passage* (London: Baldwin, Cradock, & Joy, 1818).

16. John Laing, *A Voyage to Spitzbergen* (Edinburgh: printed for Adam Black, 1818).

17. John Barrow, review of *Greenland, the Adjacent Seas, and the Northwest Passage*, by Bernard O'Reilly, *Quarterly Review* 19 (1818): 208. The *Monthly Review* gave a positive extended review of O'Reilly, including a long excerpt of the Luminous Phenomenon text, which must have incensed Barrow further because his own *Chronological History* was part of the same review essay (*Monthly Review* 88 (1819): 62–82). In 1818 a range of different Arctic accounts were in print, including inexpensive recent travel narratives from provincial presses, accounts in popular and elite periodicals, large collected voyages like John Pinkerton's 14-volume *General Collection of the Best and Most Interesting Voyages and Travels* (London: Longman, Hurst, Rees, Orme, and Brown, 1813), and reprints of foundational European accounts of Arctic peoples and places (particularly regarding the lost Greenland colonies), all attempting to capitalize on the 1818 expeditions. None of these accounts attempted to replicate Murray's authorized objects of exploration as O'Reilly's did. Arctic accounts from rival presses to which Barrow and Murray had no objection included Laing's *A Voyage to Spitzbergen* and reprints of such influential texts as those of the Lutheran missionary Hans Egede and the Moravian chronicler David Crantz: see Hans Egede, *A Description of Greenland. A New Edition* (London: Printed for T. and J. Allman, and Baldwin, Craddock, & Joy, 1818); and David Crantz, *The History of Greenland* (London: Longman, Hurst, Rees, Orme, and Brown, 1820). O'Reilly's models would have included the recent quarto *Travels in the Island of Iceland, During the Summer of the Year 1810. By Sir George Steuart Mackenzie, Fellow of Royal Society of Edinburgh* (Edinburgh: Printed for Thomas Allan and Co.; . . . and John Murray, 1811), based on a summer voyage to Iceland and including beautiful hand-coloured plates as well as appendices by different naturalists. In 1818, the most lauded precedent for an authorized Arctic scientific voyage publication remained Constantine Phipps's ghostwritten, illustrated quarto, *A Voyage Towards the North Pole* (London: printed by W. Bowyer and J. Nichols, for J. Nourse, Bookseller to His Majesty, 1774).

18. John Barrow, review of *A Voyage of Discovery*, by John Ross, *Quarterly Review* 21 (1819): 213–62. Actually, all Arctic whaling voyages were dangerous; in summer 1817, when O'Reilly sailed, four whaling ships were lost (*Times* [London], 17 August 1817).

19. O'Reilly observed the phenomenon on 15 July 1817 near Sugar Loaf Bay in Davis Strait: 'The atmosphere, at noon, being obscured by a fog, which advanced from the eastward, presented an observation. The mist in the afternoon appearing rather shallow, the upper atmosphere appearing mostly clear, I was induced to ascend to the hurricane house, in hopes of seeing the land more satisfactorily, when a phenomenon of novel character presented itself to view. As the reader may desire to have an account of this experience, the figure in Plate XVIII will give a good idea of it, taken from a sketch drawn at the moment. The sun-light falling on the mist formed an ellipsis strongly illuminated, apparently rising from the surface of the sea to the upper edge of the mist, at an angle of about twenty degrees from the horizon. In this ellipsis

46 *Adriana Craciun*

the iridescent colours were not distinguishable. The inner edge was pearly white, with the faintest tinge of blue; the middle, yellowish, deepening into brown and purple; the outer edge a blackish blue; beyond that, a brighter line; outside of which again lay the cirrostratus mist in its peculiar brown. Within, the ellipsis was bounded by a deep blue line, and the inner space filled with mist of the same colour and illumination as the exterior. In one centre of the ellipsis my shadow appeared depicted, the head surrounded with a circle of the liveliest iridescence. Beyond this was another with similar iridescence; but the colours were reversed in order, and more faint; the belts were also broader. One circumstance surprised me much: whilst the ellipsis rose at an angle from the horizon, the iris circle appeared depicted on the surface of the sea. No account of such a phenomenon having in my recollection been recorded, I thought it might be worthy of consideration' (*Greenland*, 203–5). I am grateful to Les Cowley for his help in identifying this complex phenomenon.

20. Tillotama Rajan, *Dark Interpreter: The Discourse of Romanticism* (Ithaca, NY: Cornell University Press, 1980), 244; Sebastian Mitchell, 'Dark Interpreter: Literary Uses of the Brocken Spectre from Coleridge to Pynchon,' *Dalhousie Review* 87 (2007): 167–87.

21. Antonio Ulloa, *Voyage to South-America* (London: printed for L. Davis and C. Reymers, 1758), 473.

22. David K. Lynch and Susan N. Futterman, 'Ulloa's Observations of the Glory, Fogbow, and an Unidentified Phenomenon,' *Applied Optics* 30:24 (1991): 3538–41.

23. Pierre Bouguer, 'An Abridged Relation of a Voyage to Peru,' in *General Collection of the Best and Most Interesting Voyages and Travels*, ed. John Pinkerton (London: Longman, Hurst, Rees, Orme, and Brown, 1813), 270–313. Bouguer's original publication was *La Figure de la Terre* (1749), which launched a pamphlet war with La Condamine; see Michael Rand Hoare, *The Quest for the True Figure of the Earth* (Aldershot, UK: Ashgate, 2005), 204–8.

24. The quotidian nature of this phenomenon may have been an invention of the English translation, which added 'every day' to the original French in Bouguer's 'Relation Abrégée du Voyage Fait au Perou' in his *La Figure de la Terre* (Paris: Charles-Antoine Jombert, 1749), 'C'est comme une espèce d'apothéose pour chaque spectateur; et je ne dois pas manquer d'avertir que chacun jouit tranquillement du plaisir sensible de se voir orné de toutes ses couronnes, sans rien appercevoir de celles de ses voisins' (xliv). Pinkerton's 1814 edition omits the final ethnographic section of Bouguer's 'Relation' and the entirety of the geodetic treatise.

25. Bouguer, 'Abridged Relation,' 291.

26. Erasmus Darwin, 'The Economy of Vegetation,' Canto III, in *The Botanic Garden, A Poem. In Two Parts*, 4th ed. (London: printed for J. Johnson, St Paul's Churchyard, 1799), 133; Joseph Priestley, *The History and Present State of Discoveries relating to Vision, Light, and Colours*, vol. 2 (London: printed for J. Johnson, St Paul's Churchyard, 1772), 599; Oliver Goldsmith, *An History of the Earth, and Animated Nature*, vol. 1 (London: printed for J. Nourse, 1774), 383.

27. On his celebrated attempt to find the Northwest Passage, William Parry described seeing a rare optical phenomenon in April 1820, a 22° halo combined with parhelia and tangent arc, known to this day as a Parry Arc; see Parry, *Journal of a Voyage for the Discovery of a North-West Passage* (London: John Murray, 1821), 162–3.

28. Philip Fisher, *Wonder, the Rainbow, and the Aesthetics of Rare Experiences* (Cambridge, MA: Harvard University Press, 1998), 123.

29. Joseph Leo Koerner, *Caspar David Friedrich and the Subject of Landscape* (Chicago: University of Chicago Press, 1990), 181.

What Is an Explorer? 47

30. Ibid., 164, 181.
31. Michael Baxandall, *Shadows and Enlightenment* (New Haven, CT: Yale University Press, 1995), 144.
32. Ibid., 144.
33. Mary Terrall, *The Man Who Flattened the Earth: Maupertuis and the Sciences in the Enlightenment* (Chicago: University of Chicago Press, 2002), 161.
34. Ibid., 163–4, 247.
35. Lisbet Koerner, *Linnaeus: Nature and Nation* (Cambridge, MA: Harvard University Press, 1999), 17, 65.
36. Luke Howard, *The Climate of London*, vol. 2 (London: W. Phillips, 1820), 346, original emphasis.
37. Jan Golinski, *British Weather and the Climate of Enlightenment* (Chicago: University of Chicago Press, 2007), 76.
38. William Scoresby Sr. is credited with developing this new kind of 'round top-gallant's nest' in 1806, hereafter used extensively on British Arctic whaling and naval vessels. See William Scoresby Jr., *Memorials of the Sea: My Father* (London: Longmans, 1850), 135.
39. Michael Bravo, 'Geographies of Exploration and Improvement: William Scoresby and Arctic Whaling, 1782–1822,' *Journal of Historical Geography* 32 (2006): 512–38.
40. See Thomas Forster, *Researches about Atmospheric Phenomena* (London: Baldwin, Cradock, & Joy, 1815); Luke Howard, *On the Modifications of Clouds* (London: J. Taylor, 1804); and Scott Huler, *Defining the Wind: The Beaufort Scale* (New York: Crown, 2004).
41. O'Reilly, *Greenland*, 203.
42. Ibid.
43. Giesecke's manuscripts are now difficult to locate because they are not in the main manuscript catalogue, but they are listed in the *Report of the Trustees of the National Library of Ireland 1967–1977* (Dublin, Stationer's Office): MS 262, 263, 264–5, 266. MS 264–5 appears to be the complete three-volume autograph fair copy prepared for press, with marginal gloss and index. According to Gunni Jørgensen, there also exist papers at the Danish Record Office ('Charles Lewis Giesecke, Professor of Mineralogy in Dublin,' *Irish Journal of Earth Sciences* 15 (1996): 155–60).
44. We have some idea of the content of Giesecke's lectures because the Royal Dublin Society published a catalogue of them in 1824: Charles Lewis Giesecke, *Lectures on the Natural History of Greenland* (Dublin: R. Graisberry, 1824). On 4 July 1816 Giesecke had written to the RDS offering to start a series of 'lectures on the natural history of Greenland in general, and its mineralogy in particular,' *The Proceedings of the Dublin Society, from Nov. 2, 1815 to Oct. 17, 1816* 3 (Dublin: R. Graisberry, 1816), 212. This is the lecture series O'Reilly was later accused of plagiarizing; the earliest source of this accusation which I have located is 'Biographical Sketch of Sir Charles Lewis Metzler von Giesecke,' pt. 2 of 2, *Dublin University Magazine* 3 (March 1834): 296–306. According to this biographer, while on his continental tour in 1818, 'Giesecke fully intended publishing his Greenland travels and discoveries, and even had his manuscript ready for press in Vienna,' but did not publish because of the 'very extensive and unjustifiable plagiarism committed on the original materials of our traveller by Mr. Bernard O'Reilly. This gentleman sedulously attended the course [of lectures] delivered by Sir Charles on the natural history of Greenland, and took notes of all the discoveries enumerated by the lecturer . . . which he afterwards modestly published to the world as "Journals of Travels and Discoveries in Greenland" [*sic*]. . . . This gentleman [O'Reilly] did not long survive his unsuccessful attempt at original authorship' (300). This accusation is probably inaccurate (as is the title of O'Reilly's

48   *Adriana Craciun*

book), because O'Reilly's *Greenland* exhibits no obvious specific plagiarisms in structure or content from either Giesecke's *Description of Greenland* (1816, published as pamphlet and in the *Edinburgh Encyclopedia*) or of the structure of his lecture notes (as described in the 1824 catalog), though as there are no extant lecture texts this is impossible to confirm either way. But clearly a ship's surgeon on a whaling voyage could not produce the amounts of original research (especially in Greenlandic language and customs) that O'Reilly laid claim to. Unfortunately, histories of the RDS repeat the plagiarism charges (Terence de Vere White, *The Story of the Royal Dublin Society* (Tralee: The Kerryman, 1955), 90).

45. Giesecke's published accounts include the pamphlet *Description of Greenland* (Scotland: Andrew Balfour, 1816), reprinted from Brewster's *Edinburgh Encyclopedia* (1816); the British Library's copy is inscribed by Giesecke to Joseph Banks (BL B.471.(18)). Giesecke also published a pamphlet on his theory of the cause (natural disaster) of the disappearance of the Greenland colonies, *On the Norwegian Settlements on the Eastern Coast of Greenland* (Dublin: R. Graisberry, 1824).

46. Giesecke insisted 'that we owe the first discovery of cryolite to the Greenlanders,' and that 'it was of course incorrectly stated in some periodical papers, that the cryolite was discovered by me; I only found its geological situation, and I dare say by a mere accident' (1822). Cryolite was an extremely rare mineral even in 1806, and the Ivittuut deposit was essentially the only mineable source on the planet. The story of Giesecke's arrival in Scotland with a large collection of cryolite after his Greenland adventure is a remarkable one; see Jessie Sweet, 'Robert Jameson and the Explorers: The Search for the North-West Passage. Part I,' *Annals of Science* 31:1 (1974): 21–47. Contemporary history of science has completely ignored Giesecke, so for overviews of his remarkable career one must read traditional accounts in mineralogical and geological circles; see Alfred Whittaker, 'Karl Ludwig Giesecke: His Life, Performance and Achievements,' *Mitteilungen der Österreichischen Mineralogischen Gesellschaft* 146 (2001): 451–79; and Patrick Wyse Jackson, 'Sir Charles Lewis Giesecke and Greenland: A Recently Discovered Mineral Collection,' *Irish Journal of Earth Sciences* 15 (1996): 161–8. Giesecke enjoyed substantial links with European cosmopolitan culture before and after his Greenland sojourn, during which time he compiled beautiful illustrated autograph albums; see Gilbert Waterhouse's essays, 'Sir Charles Giesecke's Autograph Albums,' *Proceedings of the Royal Irish Academy* 43 (1936): 291–306, and 'Goethe, Giesecke, and Dublin,' *Proceedings of the Royal Irish Academy* 41 (1933): 210–18. I have examined all of Giesecke's manuscripts and albums at the National Library of Ireland (the latter MS 3533–34), and they merit further study and reproduction, chronicling his interactions in Greenland, Scotland, Ireland, the Faroes, Norway, and Denmark—an exceptional geographic range in which to consider the interactions of diverse knowledge and aesthetic communities.

47. Bernard O'Reilly, *A Catalogue of the Subjects of Natural History, in the Museum of . . . The Dublin Society* (Dublin: Gaisberry & Campbell, 1813). Henry Ellis, 24 November 1813 (British Library, Add. 38,626 f.9). In 1818 he also wrote to Thomas Moore, telling him about *Greenland*; see *Memoirs, Journals and Correspondence of Thomas Moore*, vol. 2 (London: Longman, Brown, Green, and Longmans, 1853), 165.

48. O'Reilly does not appear in the RDS List of Members for 1800–50 (my thanks to RDS archivist Mary Kelleher for this confirmation). Neither was he on the short list of candidates for Giesecke's job (Henry Berry, *A History of the Royal Dublin Society* (London: Longmans, Green, & Co., 1915), 163).

49. James Ogilby wrote to Robert Jameson that Giesecke's audience was only twelve strong, 'three of them ladies'; 12 January 1816 (Edinburgh University Library, Pollock-Morris Correspondence, Jameson Correspondence, [Gen. 1996/16]). This was the course of lectures O'Reilly was later rumored to have plagiarized, as discussed above. I have searched Edinburgh University's extensive Jameson papers, including those on the sale of Bullock's collections, and they contain correspondence from and about Giesecke but nothing on O'Reilly. Likewise, the records of the Wernerian Natural History Society, also at Edinburgh, show no mention of any plagiarism dispute at the time.

50. Giesecke to Jameson, 1 October 1816 (Edinburgh University Library, [Gen. 129/61–102 D-G]). John Fleming met with Giesecke at this time and also noted that he deferred the decision to publish to Jameson, noting that he (Fleming) thought Giesecke probably 'wished for their publication'; Fleming to Jameson, 30 October 1816 (Edinburgh University Library, [Gen. 1996/16 (A-H, folder 1 of 2)]).

51. *Annals of Philosophy* printed a 'Notice of the Chevalier Giescke's [*sic*] Travels in Greenland,' summarizing his account of Greenland's mineralogy and the Inuit, and noting that Giesecke 'is at present preparing to publish an account of his travels both in English and German' in 'three large volumes, and will contain many engravings' (*Annals of Philosophy* 12 (August 1818): 150). *Annals of Philosophy* was published by the same publisher as O'Reilly's *Greenland*. An intriguing detail is provided in a letter by Friederike Brun, whom Giesecke visited on his tour, regarding his publishing plans: 'He takes the path of subscription in order to cover himself in such a costly enterprise and to protect himself to some extent from the thievery of the reprinters.' Brun went on to say that he had already completed the English version, and that both would have 50 engravings; she personally saw the plate for Disco Island based on Giesecke's drawing and it had a 'wild and imposing' beauty (Brun, quoted in K.J.V. Steenstrup, 'Einleitung und biographische Mitteilungen,' *Meddelelser om Gronland* 35 (1910): 1–37, on 27); my thanks to Kari Lokke for translating Brun.

52. The Greater Shearwater's genus has been reclassified as *Puffinus gravis* (evidently the taxonomy of *Procellaria* is complex), but the species retains O'Reilly's authorship. The Greater Shearwater was not among the birds identified in Edward Sabine's 'A Memoir on the Birds of Greenland, . . . Read April 6, 1819,' *Transactions of the Linnaean Society* 12 (1818) [sic]: 527–59.

53. On the sale of Bullock's collections see J. M. Chalmers, comp., *Natural History Auctions 1700–1972* (London: Sotheby Parke Bernet, 1976); Susan Pearce, 'William Bullock: Collections and Exhibitions in the Egyptian Hall, 1816–25,' *Journal of the History of Collections* 20:1 (2008): 17–35. Jameson was particularly interested in purchasing Bullock's petrels (which are in the same family as *Procellaria*) and his correspondence with his London agent at the auction, in the Edinburgh University Library, provides fascinating details into this event.

54. See J. P. O'Connor, 'Bernard O'Reilly—Genius or Rogue?' *Irish Naturalist's Journal* 21:9 (1985): 379–84. I am grateful to O'Connor's essay for the information on O'Reilly's work in the RDS collection (for which he was paid £100) and his exclusion from the RDS Library.

55. On Barker's panorama, see Russell A. Potter, *Arctic Spectacles: The Frozen North in Visual Culture, 1818–1875* (Seattle: University of Washington Press, 2007), 41–6.

56. Barrow, review of *Greenland*, 212.

57. Jonathan Crary, *Techniques of the Observer: On Vision and Modernity in the Nineteenth Century* (Cambridge, MA: MIT Press, 1990), 133. See also Helen

50 *Adriana Craciun*

Groth, 'Kaleidoscopic Vision and Literary Invention in an "Age of Things": David Brewster, Don Juan and "A Lady's Kaleidoscope",' *ELH* 74:1 (2007): 217–37.

58. Lorraine Daston and Katharine Park, *Wonders and the Order of Nature, 1150–1750* (New York: Zone, 1998), 355.

59. Schaffer, 'How Disciplines Look'.

60. Upon returning from the Arctic, O'Reilly evidently was instrumental in the building of Dunleary Harbor near Dublin; see Thomas Reid, *Travels in Ireland, in the Year 1822* (London: Longman, Hurst, Rees, Orme, and Brown, 1823), 331.

61. 'Coroner's Inquest,' *Times* [London], 11 August 1827. The lengthy inquest provides fascinating details about O'Reilly's life on the periphery of London, Dublin, and Edinburgh medical culture, and details about his extraordinary last day; he died the day after hearing of Prime Minister George Canning's imminent death. Witnesses at the pub described how O'Reilly had hoped for an appointment from Canning and suspected he committed suicide when his plans were doomed.

62. Michel de Certeau, 'Writing the Sea,' in *Heterologies: Discourse on the Other,* trans. Brian Massumi (Manchester: Manchester University Press, 1986), 137.

3 Settler Colonial Expeditions

Lorenzo Veracini

This chapter hypothesises the existence of a specifically *settler colonial* mode of conceiving, organising, and conducting expeditions.[1] Emphasising structurally dissimilar 'expeditions into empire,' even if only for heuristic purposes, requires an enhanced degree of abstraction. I acknowledge that in reality colonial and settler colonial forms are inevitably mixed and routinely interpenetrate (and indeed co-define) each other. But the fact that two distinct phenomena regularly overlap is no reason for not seeing them as analytically distinct. While this chapter focuses on the distinction separating colonial and settler colonial phenomena, it does not assume that settler colonial polities are necessarily linked to foundational expeditions, or that typically colonial expeditions cannot be followed by—and indeed be conducive to—subsequent settler ones. At times the settler polity is unable to refer to specific foundational moments (the 'founding' voyages of the 'pioneering' generation), and the suggestions outlined in this chapter only refer to settler colonial situations where it does. However, the fact that settler colonialism is inherently premised on a foundational displacement contributes to making settler expeditions structurally specific undertakings. As Patrick Wolfe has remarked, 'settler colonisers come to stay,' they are not colonial 'sojourners.'[2]

Two elements structuring this distinction should be emphasised. First, unlike other explorers, who are often charged with the task of establishing diplomatic or trade relations with the sovereigns they encounter, and with the explicit task of mapping or in other ways recording the physical and human landscapes they traverse, the settlers travel with an implicit determination to disavow indigenous sovereigns that is linked to the need to focus on a putative 'final' destination. Besides, the settlers aim to establish their own sovereign polities in their destination locales, thereby *replacing* the indigenous collectives they encounter. Thus, while both types of expedition traverse previously 'unknown' territories, one movement is premised on a resolve to recognise alien sovereigns, if only to *subjugate* them; the other is premised on a determination to disavow and (immediately or eventually) replace them.

52 *Lorenzo Veracini*

Second, and most importantly, settlers 'remove' from their original locations to permanently settle; they do not expect to return. If returning to the starting point, no matter how hard the journey, is what generally defines a successful colonial expedition, *not returning* is what defines a successful settler colonial one. One gets worried when an explorer that should have returned doesn't show up. In contrast, the proof of failure in a settler expedition is when the settlers start trickling back. I suggest that these structuring distinctions, and the narrative structures that underpin these very different undertakings, can be seen 'typologically': the settler colonial expeditions and the mobility narratives that underpin them reproduce Xenophon's 'marching republic,' the *Anabasis*, while those defining colonial expeditions resemble Homer's *Odyssey*. The ability to traverse uni-directionally an alien and hostile expanse—rather than connecting two specified locations and reporting back—is a crucial defining trait of settler colonial expeditions.

CROSSINGS

Explorer, politician, land speculator, writer, firm believer in Manifest Destiny, and first governor of Colorado William Gilpin describes a typical settler *Anabasis*:

> Upon the western edge of our Union, at the confluence of the Kansas and Missouri rivers, there assembled during May, 1843, American citizens with their families to the number of one thousand, each one on himself alone dependant [sic], and animated by impulses driving him irresistibly towards the west. Surrounded by his wife and children, equipped with wagon, ox-team, and provisions, such as the chase does not furnish, accompanied by his rifle and slender outfit of worldly goods, did these hard men embark upon the unmeasured waste before them. Plunged into the immense plains which slope up to the Rocky Mountains, contending with great rivers, and surrounded by the uncertain dangers of an Indian foe, a government and a discipline, at once republican and military, was created for the common safety, and implicitly obeyed by this moving people.[3]

This expedition is generic; its constituent ingredients are well known. The oxen-pulled wagon is indeed one of the foundational images of the settler colonial imagination.[4] Like the Greek army in Xenophon's *Anabasis*, the 'government and a discipline' of a moving people, the bare bones of a pre-constituted sovereign polity, equally defined by a self-defensive capacity and by mobility, would finally get to the ocean. They would establish the Oregon settlement on behalf of a vigorously expanding republic and, more importantly, on behalf of its constituent members: the men who joined in a collective endeavour. (From that moment onward, the story of settlement

Settler Colonial Expeditions   53

becomes more like Virgil's *Aeneid*, but that is another story.)[5] A sovereign displacement of this type, however, is not unique to North America. As a consistent body of literature has now established, settler colonialism is indeed a global phenomenon.

A *collective* foundational crossing—a settler expedition—is indeed an indispensable settler colonial trait. (Don't get distracted by 'each one on himself alone dependant': the individual self-reliance Gilpin describes is premised on the desire to transfer a specific *political*—that is, collective—regime.) The land beyond the 'unmeasured expanse' is promised to a people already constituted and finds itself in a locale of origin that in a way has become alien, hence the need to depart. (On the subject of 'promised lands' and settler colonialism: imagine God appearing to a bunch of indigenous peoples and endowing land they already own—it wouldn't really impress.) And if the founding Puritans crossed the water, like, for example, the New Zealand Company settlers, other settler collectives crossed the plains, or crossed mountain chains. The 'promised land' is necessarily beyond a 'desert' (a term that originally could refer to any empty space) and a crossing remains a foundational experience of all settler orders. This is very different from colonial expeditions, which produce 'encounters'—a succession of relationships—rather than distinct and exclusive socio-political entities.

The notion of the crossing is crucial because settler projects are premised on a necessary degree of geographical and psychological distantiation.[6] The new polity is simultaneously similar to and different from the old one, hence, the inherent 'ambivalence' of settler colonial circumstances.[7] But while settler colonialism is about making a 'new' land—literally about bringing it into existence—this new land has to be an *improved* copy of the original.[8] This is a most crucial element of the global 'settler revolution': everything is reproduced but contradictions.[9] Thus, for example, even the future 'New Britannia in another world!' that Australian-born explorer-cum-statesman William Charles Wentworth prophesied in 1823 had to excel over the old one, despite being expressed timidly at that stage. Note that in Australia's case, the foundational crossing of the Blue Mountains, which is celebrated for opening access to the interior of the continent, was an especially fraught affair, as the colonial authorities were explicitly forbidding unsupervised expansion. Other crossings would eventually establish 'Australia' out of 'Botany Bay.'[10]

Even if they 'come to stay,' settlers do not necessarily stop, and the new place can in due course become an 'old new' place. In 1854 the *Herald of Freedom*, a newspaper published in Lawrence, Kansas, carried a poem titled 'The Kansas Emigrant,' a true settler manifesto identifying a *succession* of successful crossings.

> We cross the prairies as of old
> The Pilgrims crossed the sea
> To make the West as they the East

54 Lorenzo Veracini

> The homestead of the free
> The homestead of the free, my boys
> The homestead of the free
> To make the West as they the East
> The homestead of the free.[11]

'As,' and the double identity it sustains, is key here: the equivalence in the crossing from one place to another and the equivalence in the process of making one place into another are crucially linked. Indeed, they are equivalent. This is the power of settler crossings and the expeditions that constitute them.

That 'old' New England had once been 'new' should be emphasised (and indeed, despite the best efforts of the local boosterists, Kansas was often merely a base for further settler expeditions along the Oregon and California trails). The idea that the new place has to be a distant one is inherent to the logic of these expeditions. The settlers that colonise near home enlarge the polity, they do not build a better one. On the contrary, the settler colonial 'method' of social transformation is premised on isolation; it is this that enables a putative model of social regeneration to be set up *away* from supposedly corrupting influences in the first place, and it is isolation that allows the settler collective to imagine itself as being *seen* from the outside.[12] Settlers change the world by moving to another one by way of settler expeditions, and by providing a *visible* model of social regeneration that can then be emulated by the old land. What Puritan leader John Winthrop's 'city on the hill,' Theodor Herzl's 'light unto the nations,' and a variety of 'God's Own countries' scattered over a few continents have in common is an enhanced degree of visibility that can only be imagined through distance. In contrast to colonial explorers who typically see themselves seeing, settlers prefer to see themselves being seen.[13] The settler colonial expedition, and thus the settler colonial project, is dependent on the notions of crossing, isolation, distantiation, and visibility.

The settlers typically carry with them their 'worldly possessions'—and much more. True, they have to abandon everything behind, and the settlers who refuse to shed at least part of their socio-cultural baggage and associated material implements fail to successfully indigenise—as good a definition of a failed settler expedition as any. We know what happens to stuck-up Victorians who fail to adapt to the informality of frontier settings. However, settlers travel with an uncanny capacity to establish permanent institutions. As settler expeditions envisage a permanent move, settler collectives are proverbial founders of political orders, and for this you need what Niall Ferguson would call a 'killer app': institution building.[14] Settler colonial migrations are *systematic*. The terminology is Edwin Gibbon Wakefield's, and even if settlers do not always adopt Wakefield's 'system,' they proceed systematically nonetheless. That is, they *preemptively* establish the political institutions of settler colonial life. In other words, settler migration aims to immediately supersede the 'unsettled' circumstances that characterise other migrations. John Stuart Mill, for example, was especially impressed with the systematic colonisers' promise of immediately establishing progressive political communities that 'could play a catalytic role in the global "improvement" of humanity.'[15] Another 1850s contribution to the *Herald of Freedom* made this point in the North American setting, when a correspondent pointed out that

> there are no other public lands [in Kansas] where I can locate myself and enjoy the institutions I left in New England. The mill, the school, the church are planted after settlement is made in other places, and then not until the population will warrant their erection, and often not then. But here, under the auspices of the Society [the New England Emigrant Aid Company which settled rural people from the east], we have the mill, the receiving house, the school house, the church, and the Sabbath-School—all within the first three months of our prairie life. If I left my Eastern home with sighs for anything, they were sighs for the institutions, the society, and friends of the East. But, to my surprise, I find the very institutions . . . which I left behind, already planted and maturing in our midst.[16]

While the Lawrence settler expresses a settler colonial vision of the Kansas 'to come' that was imagined and promoted by the northern Abolitionists— and a lot rode on the back of the way in which the Kansas of the future was imagined (the US was ultimately thrown into a Civil War because of it)—it also defines its counterpoint: an unorganised migration devoid of any particular heterotopian charge. A displacement that is deprived of a sovereign capacity, the ability to establish permanent political orders, is not settler colonial.

As it is premised on a collective and permanent displacement, the settler crossing must be well prepared. Settler expeditions are very serious undertakings, where provision must be made to ensure that the settlers can sustain themselves. Thus, settlers must plan seriously for subsistence production and housing at the destination locale and en route. The Mormon trek across North America, for example, relied on *moving settlements* made up by some settlers who were left at strategic junctures in order to enable others to move and access supplies. While exploratory expeditions can travel relatively unencumbered, settler ones typically travel with women and children and, very often, with domestic animals. (On this, more to follow, but for the moment I should emphasise that husbandry, the careful management of *all* reproductive resources, does not get more concentrated than in the context of a settler expedition.) *Effective* settler crossings carry a resilient capacity to reproduce.

There is also a veritable archive of images pertaining to *failed* settler expeditions. The disastrous Scottish colony in Darien (1698–1700, also

56 Lorenzo Veracini

known as the 'Darien Disaster') constitutes a foundational example of how *not* to organise settler expeditions: an experience that still evokes a compound imaginary inclusive of tropical inaccessibility, disease, treacherous natives, and global financial upset.[17] Likewise, the Donner Party tragedy in 1846, when stranded settlers started eating each other when their attempt to reach California stalled, conveys images of ultimate disintegration of social cohesion—the very opposite of a capacity to transfer political orders. These experiences constitute dystopian examples of what settler-collective movements absolutely should *not* be; they are warnings and spectres haunting the imagination of the settler project.[18]

Finally, settler expeditions are armed. Admittedly, most other expeditions are armed too and often they are also remarkably violent. However, one thing a settler expedition must inevitably carry is a permanent self-defensive capacity. The Rhodesian settlers organised by Cecil Rhodes and the British South Africa Company, for example, were organised in a military column. They entered Mashonaland, established Fort Salisbury in 1890, claimed territory as 'conquest,' and allocated land and mining rights to themselves. The trekkers of the nineteenth century knew that their settler colonial expeditions had been successful because they arrived at the new place *and* because their claims were validated at the Battle of Blood River. As Mahmood Mamdani has fittingly noted, the settler is 'made by conquest, not just by immigration.'[19] The first without the latter, or vice versa, is not settler colonialism, and even the term 'pioneer,' a ubiquitous presence in the context of settler colonial displacements, descends directly from the language of military expeditions. Derived from the Old French term *paonier* for 'foot soldier,' it is also found as *peon* in Spanish, *pedone* in Italian, and *pawn* in English. The English usage dates from circa 1600, while the verb 'to pioneer' was first recorded in 1780.[20] A pioneer is literally a 'foot soldier who prepares the way for the army.' Figuratively, it refers to a 'person who goes first or does something first.' As well as being a military term, 'pioneer' carries a powerful sense of prophecy. A settler expedition is not a simple survey; it is the beginning of a permanent invasion.

RETURNS

Crossing an 'alien' expanse, however, is not the only crossing that the settler expedition needs to perform. The settler expeditions cross the borders of colonial subjection itself. Of course, this relates to the settlers only, and by definition excludes indigenous peoples. Establishing sovereign orders—what successful settler colonial expeditions essentially do—is necessarily premised on a double capacity: a capacity to escape the sovereignties that are entrenched in the locales the settlers are departing from, *and* a capacity to disavow existing ones in the new locales. Thus a triangular system of relationships inevitably characterises settler political orders. This is a dynamic system of relationships where both indigenous and metropolitan capacities are destined to eventually disappear and leave the settler one unchallenged. No wonder that a 'perfect' settler sovereignty has been convincingly seen, by Lisa Ford most notably, as fundamental to the global process of territorial sovereign formation: a development that clearly exceeds the limits of consolidating settler regimes at the peripheries of empire.[21]

Envisaging settlement outside the colonially sanctioned borders of the colonial polity, the limits defined by the Royal Proclamation of 1763 in North America, for example, or the 'Limits of Location' in Australia (the list of locales and trespasses could be easily extended), remains a crucial aspect of settler expeditions. Only a settler expedition can make a claim of localised sovereignty. If a colonial explorer claims land, it is on behalf of a distant sovereign, whereas the settler colonial expedition claims it on its own behalf. The Tasmanian settlers who abandoned the 'settled districts' and crossed Bass Strait to 'purchase' for themselves large tracts of what would become the colony of Victoria were recognising indigenous sovereign capacities *and* simultaneously and deliberately disregarding those of the British Crown.[22] The latter was displeased.

Bernard Bailyn famously called this sovereign-defying capacity a 'massive *Völkerwanderung*.' The territorial and demographic expansion of the North American colonies strained relations between societies on both sides of the Atlantic. In Bailyn's words,

> this massive *Völkerwanderung*, this surge of innumerable farming families from all over north America and from western Europe, couldn't be contained within the margins of the existing colonies, or even within the newly extended boundaries of permissible white settlements outside the established provinces. *Settlers defied all legal constraints.*[23]

The Dutch settlers in South Africa similarly escaped a consolidating colonial order, as did the Mormons in what was essentially a filibustering operation. Australia had its settler expeditions also. The squatter Horatio Wills, in leading his trek beyond the so-called Nineteen Counties (the demarcated limits of official settlement in New South Wales), asserted a notion of settler continental destiny in flagrant defiance of colonial law. He set out in 1839 with wife, son, drovers, shepherds, Aboriginal stockmen, 5,000 sheep and 500 cattle, travelling 'south in almost the fashion of the patriarchs of old.' He did not intend to return, and founded Lexington station in admiring and explicit reference to another settler crossing. He then waited for the sovereign to recognise his act.[24] It did.

Colonial orders catch up with the patterns of settlement—when they can. When they cannot, their attempts to regain the upper hand sometimes force settlers to truly cross the line and formally declare independence. Then it is war, but until then, by definition, and thanks to their mobility—that is, thanks to the capacity to set up settler expeditions—the settlers are on their

58   *Lorenzo Veracini*

own. At other times, it is the colonising cores that preempt settler preemption and throw entire regions 'open' for settlement under their guidance. But this approach, of course, is ultimately an acknowledgement of a settler ability to cross.[25] Thus, paradoxically, the settler expeditions into 'unknown' territory produce a return: a return to an (imaginary) age when sovereigns could be disregarded. It is not by chance that Bailyn needed a German term to describe the movement of settlers. He wanted to relate it to the movement of Teutons that had once shaped western European landscapes; he needed a term that would convey what he saw as a primordial drive. (Of course, Bailyn was only the last one to do so in a respected line of historians and cultural propagandists.)[26]

Because settler colonialism is premised on sovereign displacement, actually *getting* there and *staying* there are critical. It is not by chance that the age of the 'settler revolution,' as James Belich emphasises in *Replenishing the Earth*, is an outcome of the 'transport revolution.'[27] Until then, the areas that would be exploited by the 'great land rush' had been inaccessible.[28] The oxen-pulled wagon turns into the oxen-pulled plough, and it is these ruminants that are fundamental to two of the most crucial ceremonies of settler possession: a sovereign capacity to move to a new locale, and a capacity to perform a powerful title-generating spell, the mixing of one's labour with the land. (As Allan Greer has powerfully noted in the *American Historical Review*, ruminants and other animals are also crucial to the destruction of indigenous life-worlds, which in turn contributes to the viability of settler crossings.)[29]

But a foundational and sovereign displacement begs the question: displacing to where, exactly? This is another structuring distinction: explorers, by definition, move towards and through locales that are 'other.' Settlers are travelling towards what will become *their* country, a country that they will remake in the image of the old one. In other words, while the colonial expeditions travel in accordance with a register of difference that makes them move forward, the settler colonial expeditions travel in accordance with a register of sameness. Travelling towards sameness, however, can be construed as a return. The settler expeditions are thus premised on an intention to displace in order to return to a condition that they feel is now absent from the locales they are leaving. That settlers are carriers of capitalist modernity has been repeatedly emphasised. That they are also and simultaneously *returnees*, escaping that very same capitalist modernity and its consolidating sovereigns, should be also recognised.[30]

Historian Frederick Jackson Turner, for example, famously emphasised how it was a '*return* to primitive conditions' that enabled 'American social development' to continually begin 'over again on the frontier.'[31] If all the world had once been 'America,' and settlers take John Locke very seriously at all times—at least as seriously as Locke himself considered the question of colonising—the settlers that undertake their expeditions are also intent on travelling back in time (here 'America' should be understood not as the

Settler Colonial Expeditions 59

actual continent but as all the unappropriated 'New Worlds').[32] They move through space they define as 'not-yet-home,' a 'wilderness' they already perceive as it is to become, as the deliberate 'changes in the land' will make it: *like* the places they have left behind.[33] It is in this sense too, as they move towards a reproduction of the locales they have abandoned, settlers are constantly returning. The settler expedition sees itself travelling through time as well moving forward through space.

Like the land that settlers move through, the indigenous peoples they encounter are seen as essentially and already living in the past. Travelling through time towards an 'empty' locale in order to return to a putatively 'original' circumstance requires an enhanced capacity to disavow traditional owners. But settlers are legendary disavowers. Thus, unlike other expeditionary undertakings, the settler journeys are likely to refrain from making use of indigenous peoples and knowledge.[34] Yet again, the very idea of moving to a place that must be represented as 'empty,' even after its putative emptiness has been extensively disproven, is necessarily based on a developed array of disavowal techniques.

In the end, settler colonial expeditions do not establish what Richard White has called the 'middle ground,' a complex system of intercultural arrangements in which indigenous people retain power to ensure that newcomers adopt their cultural practices. If anything, they replace those practices.[35] Indeed, the concept of the middle ground is premised on expeditions of a completely different nature. The Canadian *coureur des bois* (runner of the woods), for example, excelled in a type of travel that involved a circular movement. Indigenous peoples and commodities were integrated into systems of international trade that allowed the development of hybrid forms of intercultural exchange. In contrast, and despite a pervasive official rhetoric of 'peaceful' settlement, the settler expeditions to the Canadian West were armed and relentlessly targeted a previously established indigenous-exogenous complex.[36]

It is the crossing that has established the settler-indigenous relation, but the settler is nonetheless ultimately bent on *returning* to the lack of relation that existed before that foundational moment. It is a manifestation of what Patrick Wolfe has characterised as the settler colonial 'logic of elimination,' and even if it is paradoxical, considering that it is the settler expedition that originally entered the indigenous space, the settler operates in the context of a genuine primal scene since he is deeply convinced that the indigenous person is ultimately the intruder.[37] Thus, the settler expedition moves through what can be described in psychoanalytic terms as a primal scene and then towards its re-enactment (of course, re-enactment is also a type of return).[38] As a number of scholars have perceptively noted, it is significant that the national park as a concept is an institution that developed in the settler societies. In this way, an original displacement ended up in its re-enactment within a socially constructed 'wilderness,' devoid of meaningful indigenous presence.[39] While recreational vehicles have recently celebrated

60 *Lorenzo Veracini*

their 100th anniversary, there is a direct link connecting the pioneer wagons and the twentieth-century vehicles that allowed citizens of settler nations to re-enact pioneering journeys. The fact that these vehicles provide access to national parks—artificial tracts of *terra nullius*—is indeed crucial.[40] But it exposes the significant difference separating settler expeditions and their re-enactment: the settler expeditions of the past travelled through someone else's land, whereas the settler re-enactors enter land that is unequivocally *theirs*.[41]

CONCLUSION

In this chapter I argued that colonial and settler colonial expeditions should be seen as structurally distinct undertakings.[42] While this distinction is often blurred in practice, the structuring differences are evident in three fundamental oppositions. The first relates to the system of reference on which different expeditions are premised: the colonial explorer reports back to an imperial metropole while the settler expedition does not. That is, the first type of expedition is premised on a system of reference that centres on colonising cores, while the other decentralises colonial hierarchies. The 'author-Explorer,' as Adriana Craciun notes in this volume, is a category characterised by 'the public designation of exploration as an idealized pursuit of disinterested knowledge.' The library is the essential institution for its consolidation and policing. The settler coloniser, in contrast, is a most acquisitive character. While the library is located in the metropole cores, the centralised land register that underpins the Torrens title system of land registration, another type of repository and a genuinely settler colonial invention, is located in the settler peripheries.

The second structuring difference in this typology is about which particular phase of a narrative comprised of departure, journey, and arrival is emphasised. Irrespective of whether he is anthropologically equipped to actually do so, the colonial explorer is focused on detecting and recording the peoples and places he encounters; he focuses on the middle segment of that narrative succession. The settler, on the contrary, is focused on his final destination: he displays a determination to disavow and dismiss the alien expanse he is traversing. The colonial explorer registers 'already-not-home' circumstances; the settler registers 'not-yet-home' ones. The value of this theoretical distinction is that it enables us to understand how, in practice, these two expeditionary modes overlap and inform each other.

Most crucially, while the colonial explorer moves in accordance with what could be defined as a fundamentally defining *animus returnandi*, the settler, as the very term indicates, expresses its very opposite. Let's call it *animus manendi*. Both expeditions move across space, but they do so in accordance with differing narrative structures. It is a circular *Odyssey* for the first category: a journey from 'home' to 'non-home' and back. In the second, it is a linear *Anabasis*, or an *Exodus*: a journey from 'non-home' to (new) 'home.' But there is a twist: the colonial explorer is a driver of a progressive type of colonial modernity, for even when he is returning he is moving forward. The settler expedition, on the contrary, moves forward towards a return as much as towards progressive modernity. In this sense, the settler explorer is driven by an *animus returnandi* of a different kind.

NOTES

1. Settler colonial studies has recently consolidated into an autonomous subfield of scholarly research, to which this is a contribution. On the development of settler colonial studies, see Lorenzo Veracini, 'Constructing "Settler Colonialism": Career of a Concept,' *Journal of Imperial and Commonwealth History* 41:2 (2013): 313–33.
2. Patrick Wolfe, 'Settler Colonialism and the Elimination of the Native,' *Journal of Genocide Research* 8:4 (2006): 388.
3. Quoted in Henry Nash Smith, *Virgin Land* (Cambridge, MA: Harvard University Press, (1950) 1970), 38.
4. It is not by chance, perhaps, that the image is routinely used in comparative works dealing with settler colonialism as a global phenomenon. See, for examples, Michael Adas, 'From Settler Colony to Global Hegemon: Integrating the Exceptionalist Narrative of the American Experience into World History,' *The American Historical Review* 106:5 (2001): 1692; and James Belich, *Replenishing the Earth* (Oxford: Oxford University Press, 2009), cover.
5. On *The Aeneid*'s importance in shaping US (and settler colonial) narratives, see Richard Waswo, *The Founding Legend of Western Civilization: From Virgil to Vietnam* (Hanover, NH: University Press of New England, 1997).
6. Australian settler and crosser-explorer Gregory Blaxland wrote about himself in the third person, a clear instance of settler distantiation. I am grateful to Martin Thomas for pointing this out. See Thomas, *The Artificial Horizon: Imagining the Blue Mountains* (Melbourne: Melbourne University Press, 2004). More generally, an awareness of how distantiation as a process is linked to settler colonial projects contributes to explaining recurring claims to exceptionalism. Self-reflection regarding the different settler colonial socio-political bodies routinely concludes that each constitutes an exceptional case. This is because they are originally postulated as an improved variant of the metropole and because they, unlike other colonies, constitute effectively sovereign polities. Moreover, these polities often represent themselves as positive variations of nearby neighbours (i.e., Canada vis-à-vis the US, Rhodesia vis-à-vis South Africa, New Zealand vis-à-vis Australia). Serially defined through a succession of negations, it is no surprise that they should routinely think of themselves as exceptional polities.
7. On settler ambivalence, see Bill Ashcroft, Gareth Griffiths, and Helen Tiffin, *The Empire Writes Back: Theory and Practice in Post-Colonial Literatures* (London: Routledge, 1989); Alan Lawson, 'Postcolonial Theory and the "Settler" Subject,' *Essays on Canadian Writing* 56 (1995): 20–36; Anna Johnston and Alan Lawson, 'Settler Colonies,' in *A Companion to Postcolonial Studies*, eds. Henry Schwarz and Sangeeta Ray (Boston: Blackwell, 2000), 360–76.
8. On this dynamic, see, for example, Paul Carter, *The Road to Botany Bay: An Exploration of Landscape and History* (Chicago, University of Chicago Press, 1987).
9. On the settler revolution, see Belich, *Replenishing the Earth*, especially 145–76.

62 *Lorenzo Veracini*

10. In *The Artificial Horizon*, Thomas focuses on the Blue Mountains crossing of 1813 and its importance in shaping the future imagination of Australia. It is significant that Wentworth was himself a member of the party that crossed the Blue Mountains. In a sense, the verse he wrote as *Australian poetry*, a crucial act of settler memorialization, was another act of crossing, irrespective of its quality.

11. Quoted in Benjamin F. Shearer, ed., *The Uniting States: The Story of Statehood for the Fifty United States* (Westport, CT: Greenwood Press, 2004), 438.

12. See Lorenzo Veracini, *Settler Colonialism: A Theoretical Overview* (Houndmills, UK: Palgrave Macmillan, 2010), 61–74.

13. On travel narratives as colonial texts (texts that are seen as specific instruments of colonial conquest, subjugation, and governance), see Steven Greenblatt, *Marvelous Possessions: The Wonder of the New World* (Chicago: University of Chicago Press, 1991); Mary Louise Pratt, *Imperial Eyes: Travel Writing and Transculturation* (London: Routledge, 1992); Nicholas Thomas, *Colonialism's Culture: Anthropology, Travel and Government* (Princeton, NJ: Princeton University Press, 1994).

14. Niall Ferguson, *Civilization: The West and the Rest* (New York: Penguin, 2011).

15. Mill quoted in Duncan Bell, 'John Stuart Mill on Colonies,' *Political Theory* 38:1 (2010): 36.

16. Quoted in Carter Goodrich and Sol Davison, 'The Wage-Earner in the Westward Movement, I,' *Political Science Quarterly* (1936): 102.

17. See J. Prebble, *Darien: The Scottish Dream of Empire* (Edinburgh, SCT: Birlinn, 2000); and A. Herman, *How the Scots Invented the Modern World* (New York: Three Rivers Press, 2001), especially 32–6.

18. See, for example, Kevin Starr, *Americans and the California Dream, 1850–1915* (New York: Oxford University Press, 1973), 126.

19. Mahmood Mamdani, 'When Does a Settler Become a Native? Reflections of the Colonial Roots of Citizenship in Equatorial and South Africa' (inaugural lecture as A C Jordan Professor of African Studies, Cape Town, ZA: University of Cape Town, Deptartment of Communication, 1998).

20. See 'pioneer,' OED Online, www.etymonline.com/index.php?term=pioneer, accessed 6 September 2013.

21. Lisa Ford, *Settler Sovereignty: Jurisdiction and Indigenous People in America and Australia, 1788–1836* (Cambridge, MA: Harvard University Press, 2010).

22. See, for example, Bain Attwood, *Possession: Batman's Treaty and the Matter of History* (Melbourne: Miegunyah Press, 2009).

23. Bernard Bailyn, *Voyagers to the West: A Passage in the Peopling of America on the Eve of the Revolution* (New York: Vintage Books, 1988), 20 (my emphasis).

24. See John Molony, *The Native Born: The First White Australians* (Melbourne: Melbourne University Press, 2000), 138.

25. Australian historian Alan Atkinson's analysis of the conquest of Australia emphasizes settler independence *since the beginning*: individuals and communities that had independently established themselves outside of the 'Limits of Location' 'had to be reconquered by the imperial state,' he concludes. But this is the point: it is a settler expedition that marks a settler sovereignty that is asserted *ex abrupto*. See Alan Atkinson, 'Conquest,' in *Australia's Empire*, eds. Deryck M. Schreuder and Stuart Ward (Oxford: Oxford University Press, 2008), 36.

26. On 'Teutomanias,' see Marilyn Lake, ' "Essentially Teutonic": E. A. Freeman, Liberal Race Historian; a Transnational Perspective,' in *Race, Nation and*

Empire: Making Histories, 1750 to the Present, eds. Catherine Hall and Keith McClelland (Manchester: Manchester University Press, 2010), 56–73.

27. Belich, *Replenishing the Earth*, 106–44.

28. See John C. Weaver, *The Great Land Rush and the Making of the Modern World, 1650–1900* (Montreal: McGill-Queen's University Press, 2003).

29. Allan Greer, 'Commons and Enclosure in the Colonization of North America,' *American Historical Review* 117:2 (2012): 365–86. On the various ceremonies of possession, see Patricia Seed, *Ceremonies of Possession in Europe's Conquest of the New World, 1492–1640* (Cambridge: Cambridge University Press, 1995).

30. See Gabriel Piterberg, *The Returns of Zionism* (London: Verso, 2008). Returning to the land as well as to Palestine, Zionism envisages a typically settler colonial form of displacement.

31. Quoted in John Mack Faragher, *Rereading Frederick Jackson Turner: The Significance of the Frontier in American History and Other Essays* (New York: Henry Holt and Company, 1994), 32 (my emphasis).

32. On the importance of Locke in shaping ideas about settler colonialism and, most importantly, on the fallacy of neo-Lockean arguments, see Greer, 'Commons and Enclosure,' 365–86. On Locke's thought as fundamentally shaped by the intention of justifying and facilitating the settler colonial project in America, see Barbara Arneil, *John Locke and America: The Defence of English Colonialism* (Oxford: Oxford University Press, 1996), especially 21–44.

33. William Cronon, *Changes in the Land: Indians, Colonists, and the Ecology of New England* (New York: Hill and Wang, 1983).

34. As Adriana Craciun has demonstrated, the 'author-Explorer' that emerged as a professional category in the nineteenth century relied systematically on indigenous knowledges (even if explorers generally preferred to disavow their reliance). See Craciun, this volume.

35. See Richard White, *The Middle Ground: Indians, Empires, and Republics in the Great Lakes Region, 1650–1815* (New York: Cambridge University Press, 1991), especially ix–xvi.

36. See, for example, D. N. Sprague, *Canada and the Métis, 1869–1885* (Waterloo, CAN: Wilfrid Laurier University Press, 1988).

37. See Wolfe, 'Settler Colonialism and the Elimination of the Native,' 387–409. On settler colonialism's 'primal scene,' see Veracini, 'Settler Collective, Founding Violence, Disavowal: The Settler Colonial Situation,' *Journal of Intercultural Studies* 29:4 (2008): 363–79.

38. On settler re-enactments, see Vanessa Agnew and Jonathan Lamb, eds., *Settler and Creole Re-Enactment* (Houndmills, UK: Palgrave Macmillan, 2009).

39. See Mark David Spence, *Dispossessing the Wilderness: Indian Removal and the Making of the National Parks* (New York: Oxford University Press, 1999); William Cronon, 'The Trouble with Wilderness; or, Getting Back to the Wrong Nature,' in *Un-common Ground: Rethinking the Human Place in Nature*, ed. William Cronon (New York: W. W. Norton and Company, 1996): 69–90; Tracey Banivanua-Mar, 'Carving Wilderness: Queensland's National Parks and the Unsettling of Emptied Lands, 1890–1910,' in *Making Settler Colonial Spaces*, eds. Tracey Banivanua-Mar and Penelope Edmonds (Houndmills: Palgrave Macmillan, 2010), 73–94.

40. Alex Calder, 'Reenactment and the Natural History of Settlement,' in *Settler and Creole Re-Enactment*, eds. Agnew and Lamb, 260.

41. See Stephen Turner, 'Reenacting Aotearoa, New Zealand,' in *Settler and Creole Re-Enactment*, eds. Agnew and Lamb, 245.

64 *Lorenzo Veracini*

42. Dane Kennedy has recently emphasized the role of local agents in shaping the nature and outcome of the exploratory expeditions that filled the world's last remaining 'blank spaces.' In his rendition, African and Australian expeditions emerge as quite different affairs. See Dane Kennedy, *The Last Blank Spaces: Exploring Africa and Australia* (Cambridge, MA: Harvard University Press, 2013).

4 The Expedition as a Cultural Form
On the Structure of Exploratory Journeys as Revealed by the Australian Explorations of Ludwig Leichhardt

Martin Thomas

'We're going to discover the North Pole.'
'Oh!' said Pooh again. 'What *is* the North Pole?' he asked.
'It's just a thing you discover,' said Christopher Robin carelessly, not being quite sure himself.
'Oh! I see,' said Pooh. 'Are bears any good at discovering it?'
'Of course they are. And Rabbit and Kanga and all of you. It's an Expedition. That's what an Expedition means. A long line of everybody . . . '

A. A. Milne, *Winnie-the-Pooh*, 1926

INTRODUCTION: TRAVELLING WITH LEICHHARDT

There is a vast gulf between the effects of expeditions on global history and what we know about them as micro-political entities. The lack of attention given to the constitution and generic features of expeditions is the matter that concerns me here. In thinking about this problem, it is useful to inquire how expeditions are composed, organized, structured, and financed. Why do they conform to certain rules and expectations? To what extent do they replicate, transform, or subvert the political institutions of the societies they in some way represent?

These sorts of questions pose a dual challenge, for the task of reckoning with the historical entity that is the exploratory expedition cannot be separated from the place of expeditions in the cultural imaginary—as the shenanigans of Christopher Robin and Pooh remind us. The playgrounds of empire must have bristled with expeditions kindred to that intrepid polar journey through the Hundred Acre Wood. That expeditions invite fantasy and role-play is no mere by-product of the culture of imperialism. Rather, it is a corollary of the effect of myth and fantasy in the conception and execution of exploratory journeys. The avowed mission of the explorer, as Thomas Mitchell explained when giving account of his first Australian expedition, was to spread 'the light of civilization over a portion of creation . . . where science might accomplish new and unthought-of discoveries.'[1] Yet the stimulus for his determinedly rational enterprise was the report of a mythical

66 *Martin Thomas*

river, said to flow northwest through the continent. The authority for the story was an escaped convict, subsequently recaptured, who 'had assumed the cloke [sic] and colour of the savage, that he might approach the dwellings of the colonists and steal from them with less danger of detection.'[2] The annals of exploration are littered with such rumours and 'mysterious tales,' as Mitchell calls them—a reminder that fantasy and discovery are dialectically related.

Because exploration straddles the realms of the actual and the imagined, the project of establishing a typology of the expedition must cast an especially wide survey. Even so eccentric a definition as Christopher Robin's 'long line of everybody,' can be treated as a piece in the puzzle; for if, as I think I can demonstrate, expeditions have an identifiable political structure, they might also have a particular physical shape. Consider a page, dated January 1847, from the field book of surveyor John F. Mann, a member of an expedition led by the Prussian explorer, Ludwig Leichhardt (1813–circa 1848) (Figure 4.1).[3] In this drawing, which records the measured stages of their progress while mapping impressionistically the features sighted to the right and left of their path, we can see how the linearity of the route informs the expedition's scopic processing of topography. The expeditionary trail forms a longitudinal ribbon through the notebook, bulldozing the contours like some highway of the future. In terms of expeditionary politics, these sketches mark a rare instance where Mann's outlook is in harmony with the expeditionary vision of his leader, Leichhardt, for whom the image of a lineal procession is connected with his highly developed sense of being

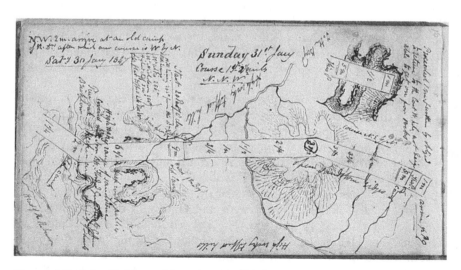

Figure 4.1 John F. Mann, Map showing progress of Ludwig Leichhardt's Swan River Expedition, 1847. By Permission of the Mitchell Library, State Library of New South Wales. (Call no. DLMS 178/2/19).

The Expedition as a Cultural Form 67

an 'actor in history.' A letter that Leichhardt wrote to Carl Schmalfuss, his brother-in-law in Prussia, makes this point rather well: 'As I stride onward behind my long file of horses and companions I can hardly control my feelings. For I can tell myself "This, at last, is the reward of your tenacity of purpose." '[4]

Like ships at sea (and it *was* at sea that many of the conventions for inland exploration were established), inland expeditionary journeys prefer linear trajectories.[5] They cut paths towards distant landmarks or they follow compass bearings. Hence the recurrence of lineal images in the discourse of exploration: the line is 'natural' to the expedition. This is evident not only in the way it moves, but in the way it establishes an order of precedence. Models of hierarchy, influenced by the military, shape the organizational structure of the expedition. Acknowledgment of these properties—the combined effect of physical shape and political structure—is a step towards addressing the question of *form* in relation to the expedition. Form is essential to the establishment of a typology, for the great proliferation of expeditions during the age of modern imperialism is evidence that expeditions are self-replicating phenomena. Exploration was of course an ongoing practice, not some assortment of extraordinary adventures and incidents. Expeditions provided the dominant model for co-ordinating and executing an exploratory journey. They are particular cultural formations, as distinctive to their epoch as the novel or the photograph.

To begin an exploration of the question of form, let us delve a little deeper into the aforementioned expedition, led by Ludwig Leichhardt.

Travellers Bound by Ritual

The expedition is travelling through forested country, now part of the state of Queensland. The date is January 1847 and Leichhardt's party, supposedly bound for the west coast of the continent, has departed the settled districts of the Darling Downs. At this stage they are headed on a roughly northward trajectory. Leichhardt, ubiquitously known as 'the Doctor' to his companions, is the initiator as well as the leader of this ambitious and ill-fated enterprise. Mann, who gets ever more disgruntled as the journey continues, will later publish a description of their progress.

> The Doctor as usual led the way mounted on his charger, compass in hand, closely followed by Perry, who led a quiet mule which carried the packs containing the most valuable articles, books, papers, sextant, powder, matches, cooking utensils, plate chest, etc.; then followed the mules, driven by Bœcking and myself; the cattle driven by Hely and Brown, and the rear was brought up by the sheep and the goats, driven by Bunce, Turnbull, and Wammai.[6]

Mann's narrative alludes to the differential power relationships inherent to this 'long line of everybody.' In a hierarchically organized company,

68 Martin Thomas

seniority is expressed through symbol. The compass in the leader's hand does more than direct their course; it denotes the scientific principles that at a deeper level steer the journey. Symbol operates in tandem with gesture, for this is a spectacle, a performance, to which the players themselves—and other auditors, usually unseen—bear witness. Although direct encounters with Aboriginal people were infrequent on this expedition, traces of them were seen and their presence felt. Mann tells us that 'the natives' are 'constantly on our tracks.'[7]

There are nine men in the procession, led at this moment by Leichhardt on his superior mount. He is followed by representatives of different social orders. Mann, who studied at Sandhurst, and Hely, the son of a wealthy pastoralist, rate as 'gentlemen.' Bunce is a botanical collector and Bœcking a tanner. John Perry, a saddler, and Henry Turnbull, a superintendent of livestock, are also among the party. Wammai and Harry Brown are Aboriginal men from districts now colonized.[8] Robbed of their ancestral country, they have become skilled riders and stockmen. They wear European dress and like their white companions, are volunteers on the expedition. While Brown, the elder of the two, is familiar with this section of the route—having travelled it with Leichhardt on a previous expedition two years ago—he and Wammai are, strictly speaking, strangers on this soil. The local indigenous languages are foreign to these men, since their homelands lie far to the south. Even so, with their superior bush skills and knowledge of Aboriginal diplomacy, they bring significant capital to the expedition—capital that yields both practical advantages and symbolic value. The presence of black men among a party of whites does not go unnoticed by the indigenous people.

Leichhardt's itinerant hierarchy is not restricted to the human contingent. Notionally under their charge is a large and unruly assortment of domesticated animals. Some, like their recalcitrant mules, are beasts of burden, but most of the livestock they intend to butcher and eat along the way. Of course, there are no women in the party; the penetration of 'new' country is a pointedly masculine affair. The gendering of the expedition accentuates one of the most distinctive features of the colony's demographic, where men predominate numerically (as well as politically and socially).[9] In its inclusions as well as its exclusions, the composition of the expedition gestures at the realpolitik of life in New South Wales. With weapons, instruments, implements, and subordinate animals, the expedition forms a microcosm of the colony that this journey will extend or replicate—or so the travellers like to think. For all the social, cultural, and linguistic differences between these expeditioners, the nine are heavily co-dependent. Before misfortune assailed them in the form of foul weather and disease, they felt a sense of corporate purpose. Early in the journey, they consolidated their fraternity in a ritual of their own devising. Mann tells of standing 'hand in hand around our small camp fire' and entering into 'a solemn compact to do all we possibly could to advance the expedition.'[10]

ON THE ECONOMIES OF EXPEDITIONS

No Tool of the Explorer

Like most cultural objects, expeditions are ciphers. They are *mythological*, in the sense defined by Roland Barthes.[11] Hierarchically organized according to the class, profession, and ethnicity of their participants, they serve as mechanisms for regulating power within a collective, the collectivity of which they then obscure. The leader's name, so often attached to that of the expedition, becomes synonymous with the discoveries and achievements of a party that included other Europeans and/or indigenous guides. As we will see, questions pertaining to Leichhardt's ownership of his expeditions, and the limited recognition afforded to his colleagues, had considerable impact on expeditionary politics, both within the colony and when the expedition was out in the field.

Recently, the historian of exploration Dane Kennedy, drawing on the observations of literary critic Simon Ryan concerning the 'univocal' qualities of exploration journals, wrote about the extraordinary limits that expedition leaders went to in suppressing the voices of deputies and other subordinates. He cites the example of the Australian explorer John Mc-Douall Stuart, who prohibited expedition members from keeping journals or even making notes during their travels.[12]

The subsumption of the many to the one is a key element of how expeditions function in the cultural economy. Expeditionary publications are conventionally ascribed to a single author, yet they result from group achievement. This aspect of the expedition is so thoroughly engrained in the discourse of exploration that even critical studies manage at times to skirt around it, as Kennedy's work reveals on occasion. His book, *The Last Blank Spaces* (2013), is a significant survey of imperial exploration in Africa and Australia. Of the explorer, he writes,

> the organizational framework for his errand in the wilderness was the expedition, another key term in the construction of exploration as a specialized enterprise. Every expedition was unique, but all of them shared certain characteristics: they were supported by institutional sponsors, such as government agencies and learned societies; they were supplied with instructions that outlined their operations and objectives; and they were structured with clear lines of command and defined duties. The Royal Geographical Society even prepared a kind of template for organizing expeditions and establishing their purposes, a document that went through multiple editions.[13]

To give even this much attention to the formal properties of expeditions is unorthodox and as far as it goes it is useful. Kennedy recognizes that expeditions are codified and rule-bound. He makes this point in a comparative

70 Martin Thomas

study that examines the development of imperial exploration across two continents in two key zones of British influence. In this way he opens up a typology of the explorer, and inevitably he reveals much about expeditions along the way. He demonstrates that the persona of the explorer is an evolving cultural construction, seeded in the soil of empire. But what limits his approach to the specific matter of the expedition is that he fails to establish that it, as much as the explorer, is a cultural and political formation that develops over time. In the passage quoted above, Kennedy treats the expedition as an almost preexistent entity that explorers could access at their convenience, much as they did their guns, pith helmets, and other goods and chattels of the trade.

Yet the strangely enduring phenomenon that is an exploratory expedition is no more a tool of the explorer than literature a tool of the writer, or theatre a tool of the actor. The expedition is the explorer's stage. As the forum that permits his coming-into-being, it necessarily predates him. In the wake of critics such as Paul Carter and Mary Louise Pratt, explorers' journals have become familiar sites of textual analysis and critique of empire. Theirs is an approach that spotlights the relationship between exploration and discursive production by a sole author.[14] The insights communicated by these critics, invaluable as they are, have deflected attention from the generic qualities of the expedition and the ways in which expeditionary travellers have strategically used this cultural phenomenon to their advantage. Leichhardt is a most interesting traveller to consider from this perspective. He had no official sponsor, government agency, or learned society behind him—despite many attempts to win support from such authorities. For example, Leichhardt in 1841 approached the Royal Geographical Society (RGS) executive in London with a proposal to explore inland Australia and 'spend with pleasure my unfortunately small fortune and even my life in such an expedition to which I have prepared myself these last 5 years.'[15] But as an unconnected alien in the British capital, he was given short shrift.

Being German, he lacked connections in the British imperial world, although eventually he won great distinction within it. Leichhardt led three Australian expeditions, none of which had instructions or directives, nor any mission prescribed by an external authority. Indeed, his journeys of discovery in Australia break nearly all the rules of expeditions outlined by Kennedy in the passage quoted above. Yet in a career with parallels to that of Henry Morton Stanley (who, as an illegitimate Welshman-turned-American, was much spurned by the geographical establishment), Leichhardt, through a process of self-invention, became one of the most celebrated figures in Australian exploration, the unevenness of his achievements notwithstanding. He led one expedition to the north coast of Australia in 1845–6 that was unexpectedly and triumphantly successful. His second, aimed at the west coast (which we have briefly visited), was shambolic, and eventually retreated without loss of life. Then, on his third expedition—again directed at Swan River Colony

The Expedition as a Cultural Form   71

on the west coast—Leichhardt and his party disappeared in circumstances that remain a mystery to this day. The last recorded sighting was in 1847 when they departed the colonized districts of southern Queensland.

On the Expeditionary Value of Disappearing

Beau Riffenburgh has observed that expeditionary failure, resulting in the death of the heroic explorer, was the fast trail to glory in British exploration.[16] In Australia, this was certainly the case. Like the disastrous attempt at a north–south crossing of the continent led by Burke and Wills a few years later (see Clarsen, this volume), Leichhardt's disappearance is a classic example of expeditionary catastrophe eclipsing the many explorations that proceeded without serious misadventure. As conjecture about Leichhardt's progress turned from concern to pessimism, and eventually despair, search parties scoured great tracts of country, finding only the most dubious traces of his passing.[17] As rumours churned through the colonies, and others lost their lives in search of him, Leichhardt made the not unusual transition from explorer to legend.

Even during his lifetime he was immensely famous, within and beyond New South Wales. The dress rehearsal for his ultimate disappearance had already taken place, and with it the beginnings of his great celebrity. He was thought to have died on his first expedition of 1844–6, a shoestring affair that managed, by the seat of its pants, to reach Port Essington, the isolated British garrison in what is now the Northern Territory of Australia. As it transpired, they reached their destination with only one loss of life, that of the naturalist, John Gilbert, who was fatally speared. From Port Essington a passing schooner took Leichhardt and his surviving companions to Sydney, where he had been given up for dead. Eulogies in his honour had already been written. Returned from the 'dead,' he became the toast of the town.

The path he had taken in establishing himself as an explorer—a route that bypassed the many gatekeepers who regulated the business of geographical discovery—is highly pertinent to this discussion because it tells us a great deal about the cultural form of the expedition and the possibilities it offered in terms of personal empowerment.

The Making of the Explorer

Felix Driver has much to say about expeditionary gatekeeping in *Geography Militant* (2001), his highly influential study of the RGS and cultures of exploration within the British Empire.[18] By lending, or refusing to lend, from its collection of precision instruments—unaffordable to most individuals— the society exerted considerable control over who could be recognized as a scientific traveller. RGS committee men assessed journals and field books of returned expeditions, ensuring that the 'proper' conventions for scientific data collection had been observed. Through its publications, lectures,

72 Martin Thomas

conferral of awards, and general mission of inculcating a geographical culture, the RGS exerted considerable power in establishing and policing the rules of engagement for explorers.

The rise of the explorer as a mythic hero in the culture of empire has many parallels in nineteenth-century modernity. In 1983, Eric Hobsbawm and Terence Ranger published *The Invention of Tradition*, a collection of essays that argued with humour and aplomb that one of the ways in which an industrializing world rooted itself in the newness of historical circumstance was to invoke past 'traditions' that were in reality very recent innovations.[19] In this vein, Adriana Craciun proposes that the flowering of the explorer involved a process of 'back-formation' whereby a 'supposed golden age of Elizabethan discovery' was 'idealized by the Victorian exploration industry.' Heroic travellers of the Enlightenment—Mungo Park and James Cook among them—were 'retrospectively referred to as Explorers,' despite never using that appellation about themselves (see Craciun, this volume). Remarkably, the *Oxford English Dictionary* (OED) dates the first usage of 'explorer,' in the modern sense of a scientific or imperial traveller, at 1812 (just one year before Leichhardt's birth).[20]

Brought up in modest circumstances in rural Prussia, Leichhardt was one of countless young men infected by the fast-growing cult of the explorer. Alexander von Humboldt, the pioneering naturalist of Latin and South America who set the prototype for scientific travel in the mid-nineteenth century, was his personal idol: 'The example that I have never forgotten.'[21] At considerable sacrifice, Leichhardt's family had sent their precocious son to university in Berlin, hoping he would acquire a respectable position in the civil service. But he became increasingly eager to win renown as a scientific adventurer. Giving up formal study, he began to kit himself with the intellectual and practical tools deemed necessary for a life of exploration. 'I'm setting my course myself, and shall be my own examiner,' he said in a letter to his father. 'The bigger the building the longer it takes to build. Great structures have taken centuries, and the Strassburg minster has never been completed.'[22] Like many expeditioners, for whom castle building is habitual, Leichhardt had a fondness for this sort of rhetorical extravagance, much to the irritation of his detractors (and to the delight of Patrick White, who used him as the model for the bathos-prone antihero of his 1957 novel *Voss*).

A Stranger in the Colony

In *A Swindler's Progress* (2009), the historian Kirsten McKenzie investigates the career of John Dow, a transported convict and confidence trickster, who obtained credit and in other ways defrauded the good burghers of colonial New South Wales by masquerading as the son of an English earl. McKenzie argues that stories such as Dow's have a wider relevance to scholars of the nineteenth century because they reveal deeper truths about the fluidity of

The Expedition as a Cultural Form   73

identity, engendered by imperialism, and the opportunities for mobility it presented. As an interpreter and exploiter of social expectations, the impostor could 'lay bare the assumptions of his own society.'[23] The Australian colonies were particularly conducive to social reinvention, given how many residents (including a multitude of former convicts) were trying to conceal the circumstances of their arrival. An element of pretence—essential to all class and caste systems—was especially pronounced in colonial society, given the amorphousness of class boundaries.

Leichhardt was not exactly an impostor, but he certainly bent the truth in order to establish himself as an explorer. Having failed to present himself for military service (after many attempts at getting an exemption on medical grounds), he was an outlaw in his own country. To obtain travel documents, he passed himself off as a native Englishman. A student by disposition, although no longer one in any formal sense, he not only attended lectures on anatomy in Paris, but went so far as to dissect corpses in the city morgue, pretending that he was enrolled for a medical degree. In reality, he had no degree in any discipline and certainly no claim to the title 'doctor,' first bestowed upon him in the colony by admirers of his erudition and subsequently used by the press.[24] He incorporated the honorific into his scientific persona, styling himself 'Dr. Ludwig Leichhardt' on the title page of his *Journal of an Overland Expedition* (1847).

Leichhardt's writings reveal other aspects of a shifting identity. He often wrote about his quest to win distinction for the British Empire, and the journals of his first two expeditions were written in English, rather than his native tongue. Leichhardt became an Anglophone and an Anglophile through his relationship with William Nicholson, an English medical student, whom he met in Berlin. A close bond developed between them, with Leichhardt assuming the role of mentor to his younger friend. Eventually they committed themselves 'to collaboration in a life of travel.'[25] Leichhardt was penniless, but Nicholson was a young man of means. The two began to cohabit and Nicholson paid all Leichhardt's expenses for a period of six years. Much conjecture about where they might explore preceded the decision to go to 'New Holland,' as Leichhardt still called it. Like Marlow in Conrad's *Heart of Darkness* (1899), the great blank expanses on maps of Australia lured him irresistibly. 'The interior, the heart of this dark continent, is my goal, and I will never relinquish the quest for it until I get there.'[26] But after all the planning and preparation, Leichhardt ended up sailing to the antipodes without his companion, arriving in Sydney in 1842. The biographer John Bailey suggests that it was pressure from Nicholson's siblings, increasingly appalled at his unorthodox friendship with the impoverished Prussian, that led to his decision—a monstrous blow to Leichhardt—to abandon all notions of exploration. Instead he would go to Edinburgh and practise as a physician.[27] In an expression of their friendship, which managed to survive this rupture, Nicholson supplied Leichhardt with a kit of travelling clothes, his ticket to Australia, and a loan of £200.

74 Martin Thomas

Meeting Thomas Mitchell

Leichhardt's inexperience and lack of contacts, and to some extent his ethnicity, must have counted against him when he joined the throng of supplicants seeking support from the RGS to embark on expeditions. In Sydney, however, he enjoyed a warm reception. He was one of many artists, intellectuals, and scientists—products of the elite educational system in Prussia and neighbouring states—who, for lack of German overseas territories in which to explore, travelled to locales of British colonization and made their mark.[28] Leichhardt's erudition and scientific curiosity won him many admirers in Sydney, where he gave public lectures and was welcomed into some of the better houses. Upon arrival in New South Wales, he presented a letter of introduction to the now Sir Thomas Mitchell, who had used his position as Surveyor General of New South Wales to establish a reputation as an inland explorer.[29] Leadership of three expeditions (and a goodly amount of lobbying in London) had won him his knighthood, although the extent to which exploration was part of the Surveyor General's job description was a matter of debate.

Even Mitchell, an imposing personality and one of the colony's most powerful officials, was obliged to fight long and hard to get permission to leave the busy Survey Office he headed in Sydney to lead protracted explorations. At the time of Leichhardt's visit he was trying to secure government support for his fourth major expedition, with Port Essington its destination. A problematic relationship with Governor Sir George Gipps, augmented by the financial restraints forced by the colony's first depression, counted against him. The idea that Leichhardt might accompany him to Port Essington in the capacity of naturalist was mooted, should the funding be approved. Leichhardt long remained hopeful that this would come to fruition. The fact that a collaboration was suggested, however tentatively, indicates that in the early days at least, Mitchell saw Leichhardt as too insignificant to be a possible rival. That was *not* the case in the southern winter of 1844, by which time Mitchell was awaiting permission from London to launch his proposed expedition. To his horror he learned that Leichhardt, having given up hope of ever being invited to explore through official channels, had rallied private funds and effectively appropriated his long-established scheme to make the first overland journey to Port Essington from the east coast.[30]

The superabundance of such stories in the history of exploration requires that the climate of competition among rivals be factored into the typology of the expedition. This might consist of competition between nations or companies (as in the early phases of maritime expansion), or between rival explorers (as in the races to the poles). Leichhardt's display of entrepreneurialism, which involved rallying financial and in-kind donations from settlers, is significant for what it reveals about the economic properties of expeditions. As Kennedy explains, the British government had only a faint interest in promoting or at least *financing* the exploration of Australia. His

The Expedition as a Cultural Form 75

book contains a table of 87 inland Australian expeditions mounted in the nineteenth century. Of these, only five received even partial financing from London.[31] That exploration was almost wholly the initiative of colonial interests (both government and private) prompts Kennedy's observation that there is a pressing need to 'decenter our understanding of exploration as an imperial enterprise.'[32] It also reveals fundamental differences between the way settler societies sought to extend their frontiers and thereby expand the polity, in contrast to other sites of imperial activity that were not predicated on the establishment of colonies (as was the case in much of Africa). The knowledge derived from exploratory forays in non-settler society situations was less concerned with the acquisition of land and more concerned with the advancement of trade and extraction of resources (see Veracini, this volume).

Following the Money

Earlier in this chapter I quoted from John Mann's description of Leichhardt and the team, marching northward with their truant menagerie of goats, sheep, mules, and cattle. They had with them an accumulation of food and other equipment. With its Aboriginal workers, the expedition exploited the labour of persons dispossessed by imperial expansion. Working together, the members of the party marshalled, ordered, and exploited the reserve of living capital on which their movement into uncharted territory depended.

In unpacking the reality that the expedition harboured a reserve of living capital, it makes sense to ask how that capital was accumulated. To trace the origins of an expedition's capital (monetary and otherwise) is to deal with the minutiae of how the journey is materially and culturally connected with its host society. In the case of Leichhardt, the financing of expeditions is doubly important for what it reveals about how outward expansion was driven from the colony. First, the almost permanent state of competition between persons aspiring to be explorers—a competition that necessarily extended to the problem of fundraising—emphasizes the inherently capitalist foundation of expeditionary activity. (That exploratory parties are referred to as *companies* is far from incidental.) Second, the fact that the desire to explore and expand was driven so heavily by colonists, often in defiance of their imperial masters, establishes the analytical value of tracing lines of investment when deciphering narratives of discovery. The capitalization of expeditions gives insight into the ways in which frontier societies channelled and made personal their expansionary desires and ambitions. Leichhardt's emergence as an explorer was contingent on his understanding of colonists' aspirations, which he manipulated astutely in resourcing his expeditions.

While there is much in Leichhardt's chequered history that points to appalling judgement in matters of leadership and choice of companions, it is important to understand that outside the confined sociality of the expedition, he was a popular and much-admired figure. Prior to his departure

76 Martin Thomas

for Port Essington, Leichhardt enjoyed a peripatetic existence around New South Wales. Unable to find employment or a place on an expedition, he journeyed extensively north of Sydney to Moreton Bay and beyond. Travelling the coastal ranges and settled districts further inland, he generated a modest income by gathering natural-history specimens that he sold to overseas collections. Conferring with settlers and stockmen, staying in fine homesteads or shepherds' huts, he played the role of freelance savant, liberally sharing his knowledge about botany, geology, or anything else. Willing to perform medical procedures in his guise as 'doctor,' he endeared himself to the colony, and in the process became attuned to the mood and sentiments of the rural population.

Leichhardt was a prolific letter writer and his correspondence reveals that he spoke at length to many people about his own dreams of visiting the interior. In the process, he synthesized their thoughts about what lay beyond the 'known' districts and who was best placed to try to get there. The territory within New South Wales that settlers were permitted to occupy was supposedly restricted to 19 so-called counties that the Surveyor General had famously depicted on a large map, the result of a trigonometrical survey that lasted several years.[33] But these 'Limits of Location,' as they were generally known, were a bureaucratic fantasy. Squatters had ventured far beyond the official limits, occupying land illegally, though in the well-founded hope that their claims would one day be legitimized. In sessions around the hearth or campfire, Leichhardt came to realize that Thomas Mitchell, his potential patron, was not popular among settlers. In a letter dated late 1842, Leichhardt wrote, 'although the colonists appreciate him as a surveyor, they certainly question his ability to find new country. The squatters have probably done more than he has, because they've pressed on, with their herds, far out beyond the farthest point reached by Mitchell.'[34] Ignoring evidence that many settlers had, on the contrary, *followed* Mitchell's wagon tracks, Leichhardt astutely developed expeditionary plans that spoke to the resentment towards government. Soon he was openly canvassing the idea of 'a squatting expedition into the interior.'[35]

The Squatting Expedition

In the same way that squatters colonized in defiance of external authorities, Leichhardt took ownership of the Port Essington journey, 'liberating' it from political squabbles and bureaucratic intransigence. The appeal of this strategy is evident in the announcement of the expedition, published by *The Australian* newspaper in July 1844. Leichhardt was lavishly praised for his resilience, intelligence, and selflessness, while the government—and by implication Mitchell—was ridiculed:

> Not accoutred from the public purse, not encumbered by a useless retinue of followers, but alone, or with one or two trusty friends . . . this resolute individual will, if his life be providentially spared, accomplish

The Expedition as a Cultural Form 77

single-handed, what many whom we are acquainted with declare to be impossible. Time will determine. In the mean while, making known this forthcoming adventure, we deem it only a duty to science to call upon such as may have it in their power to assist this interesting traveller in his bold enterprise.[36]

Significantly, the proprietor of *The Australian*, which published further stories that were headily pro-Leichhardt, was William Charles Wentworth, the Australian-born lawyer and politician who, as a young man in 1813, had participated in something of a 'squatting expedition' of his own by joining forces with the pastoralists Gregory Blaxland and William Lawson on a westward journey that opened a route from Sydney through the Blue Mountains. The governor, Lachlan Macquarie, had at the time displayed coolness towards this enterprise since he would have preferred that the boundaries of the then penal settlement remain curtailed.[37] In championing Leichhardt, *The Australian* insinuated that the qualities of grit and independence—ingrained in the colonists' self-image—were the essence of true expeditionary enterprise. This proved to be highly enabling for Leichhardt when donations not only of money, but provisions, livestock, and equipment, began to pour in. For a time, some actual squatters—members and employees of a grazing family named Russell—planned to accompany him to Port Essington, but they ultimately became suspicious of a man who 'crawls along with his compass and thingummies' and withdrew.[38] In addition to two Aboriginal participants (one was the aforementioned Harry Brown), Leichhardt ended up recruiting seven white men to the expedition, making a party of 10. (They were reduced to eight when two withdrew early in the journey.)

The Projecting Impulse
The preparedness of colonists to join the expedition, despite high risks and uncertain rewards, is a sign of the mutualism displayed by settler society in its embrace of Leichhardt. His expedition could never have made the faltering transition from dream to reality without volunteers and donors. The rush to assist is important for what it reveals about the structure and social significance of expeditions and how they connected with models of mercantile co-operation, dating from the early modern period, where involvement in a project or venture would be shared among subscribers or shareholders. In the seventeenth century these examples of co-operative enterprise were still sufficiently novel for Daniel Defoe to comment on them in 'Essay upon Projects' (1697). The 'prevaling [sic] Humour' of his epoch, he claimed, was 'the degree of Projecting and Inventing' in matters of business and 'Methods of Civil Polity.'[39] Subscription by diverse parties provided a mechanism for both taking risks and sharing them, which is why this method of fundraising was foundational to such commercial innovations as the insurance industry (allied as it was to shipping) and why it was the method of

78 Martin Thomas

capitalization employed by both the East India Company and the Hudson's Bay Company.[40] The latter, first known as the Company of Adventurers, is the world's oldest surviving capitalist institution. As scholars from the Smithsonian Institution have recently noted, its name and purpose suggest that the 'spirit of adventure is crucial, if not inherent to the operation of capitalism and its global expansion.'[41] Collective fundraising was used to finance expeditions from the time of the Enlightenment. The African Association, which funded numerous explorers of Africa, used a subscription model.[42] As expeditioners developed more sophisticated relationships with print and other media, the association between exploration and subscription developed in new directions. The National Geographical Society, which in the early twentieth century began its mutation from a somewhat crusty, learned society to media giant, is the outstanding example of this trend. Expeditions, carefully designed to provide maximum benefit in terms of content, were funded from subscriptions to *National Geographic Magazine*.[43] The funding of exploration reveals how socioeconomic practices, most familiar for their purely commercial applications, could be readily applied to the more extreme form of speculation required for the floating of an exploratory expedition.

With a host of minor parties claiming an interest in it, Leichhardt's Port Essington journey provided a focus for the hopes and sense of historical purpose felt by colonists. Here was an embodiment of their *projecting humour*, as Defoe might have put it. The progress of the fragile party through the wilderness signalled possibilities for prosperity, despite the readily acknowledged dangers. With a fast route to India among the mercantile fantasies abuzz in the colony, the press hinted at 'advantages to be extended to commerce' resulting from the journey.[44] These were additional to the anticipated discovery of land and perhaps other riches. While the 'shareholders' in Leichhardt's enterprise must have realized that personal pecuniary advantage was at best uncertain, the sense of ownership they felt in the 'squatting expedition' was itself a reward, and it created a sense of reciprocal obligation. Leichhardt never forgot his backers as he journeyed northward, bestowing toponyms in honour not of governors and peers, but storekeepers, farmers, and a host of friends and acquaintances who had contributed to the expedition or helped him in his rambles in the preceding years.[45] These tributes to sponsors are a further reminder of the hazy distinction between commercial and exploratory adventurism, exemplified in the well-established tradition, dating from the early seventeenth century, of financing books through subscription.[46] The publication of countless expeditionary journals was floated in exactly this way, resulting in the honour roll of aristocrats, savants, businessmen, and other philanthropists that forms the first item in so many accounts of expeditions. Leichhardt's *Journal of an Overland Expedition in Australia*, published by T. & W. Boone of London in 1847, is instructive for its non-conformity to this practice. His book had no subscribers, so it opens with a threefold dedication: first, to his friend (and financier) William

The Expedition as a Cultural Form 79

Nicholson; second, to his host and great supporter in Sydney, Robert Lynd; and third, 'to the Generous People of New South Wales.'[47]

Dividing the Spoils

For all New South Welshmen, generous and otherwise, who took interest in the first Leichhardt expedition, the ultimate reward was the return of the heroes. Church bells rang, bonfires blazed, and money poured into a testimonial fund, raised in appreciation of the discoveries made. Subscriptions from the public rapidly exceeded the considerable sum of £1,500. The ebullience of donors effectively shamed the New South Wales legislature into providing a further £1,000 in reward money from state coffers. In determining what share of the government money should go to the leader and what should go to members of the party, the governor determined that military conventions for sharing reward money should be followed, with the 'commander' receiving four to five times the amount of his officers, and token payments to lesser inferiors. Thus Leichhardt received £600 of the £1,000, while the remainder was distributed among the other returnees on a declining scale, according to social status. At the top were two 'gentlemen' participants who received £125 each and at the bottom were Charles Fisher and Harry Brown, the Aboriginal members of the party, who received just £25, to be held for them in trust.[48] The funds raised by public subscription were divided on the same formula. John Roper, one of the 'gentlemen' of the party, protested vociferously at these arrangements. But the Leichhardt euphoria was such that no one listened. Contributing to the Leichhardt fund was openly promoted as further investment in the common good of the colony. Biographer E. M. Webster explains that it was known from the outset 'that money given to Leichhardt would finance a new expedition, and this was dangled as "an inducement to the Colonists to subscribe liberally." '[49] Uninterested in pecuniary advantage, except as leverage for further exploration, Leichhardt did indeed devote the reward money to his next project, the east–west crossing.

In 1846, when Leichhardt mania was at its zenith, the explorer told his brother-in-law that 'everybody, from the poorest shepherd to the richest landowner, subscribed to the testimonial . . . and my name is a password to young Australians.'[50] The sense of communal involvement in the Leichhardt narrative is fully revealed in press coverage of the second expedition, which progressed through the settlements north of Sydney in 1847. In an astonishing display of empathy for the explorer and his party, a Hunter Valley journalist revealed the spectrum of hopes, fears, and aspirations engendered by the party's passage through the community:

> One cannot view the movements of this small party, this 'chosen few,' this 'band of brothers,' but with intense interest. To say only we wish them success, would be commonplace—the mere echo of the general feeling—the ardent desire of every intelligent being in the colony. But to

80 *Martin Thomas*

contemplate the general appearance of the party, the limit of their numbers . . . the vastness of their undertaking, the risks they are to run, the privations they must suffer, their personal qualifications, particularly the mild, gentlemanly demeanour of Dr. Leichhardt himself, his prepossessing manner, superior personal appearance, intelligent and commanding, with a total absence of vanity, common to superior minds; the pains and anxiety he exhibits in adjusting the most minute matter, and above all, the high moral responsibility he seems to feel as the leader of the party, impresses one with feelings of no common interest as to their ultimate fate. As we took a parting look, with deep concern and regret, of the intelligent and intrepid leader, the question naturally obtrudes itself on the mind—will this be the last time? Most seriously for his own sake, and that of his companions, we hope not![51]

Through monetary and other forms of investment, colonial society enabled the expeditionary journey, setting it on its way and maintaining an interest in it. Following the money is crucial to understanding how a polity empowers an expedition, and it helps elucidate how authority is channelled within the social microcosm that is an expedition in the field. These socioeconomic processes are highly informative for what they unveil about the making of explorers, and how heroic individuals attained prominence at the expense of the parties they led. The formula for dividing the wealth generated by Leichhardt's expedition—as naked a declaration as one could find of the comparative *worth* of participants—is crucial to any understanding of how social hierarchies are enforced in expeditionary enterprises. Two further facets of the expedition are made apparent by the link between money and power; both are essential to our typology.

The first concerns the devolution of power. The procession so plaintively described by the Hunter Valley journalist was two months further into its journey when, in an altercation that hinted at the eventual collapse of their relationship, Leichhardt impressed upon John Mann 'that he was my general officer, and I a private soldier.'[52] Undoubtedly, the talk of money can be heard in this assertion, for Leichhardt was no more a general than he was a doctor. (On this point: Mann and others had signed up for the expedition under the impression that 'the Doctor' was a qualified medico and well placed to care for them in the event of illness or injury. His lack of medical degree, and the fact he took almost no medical supplies on this journey across Australia, was a considerable blow to his authority.) That Leichhardt dubbed himself a 'general,' when he was in fact a wanted man in Prussia for refusing to serve in the army, is a strange lesson in the potential for role-play that becomes possible in an expeditionary hierarchy. Many years later when he published his damning account of the expedition, Mann would make much of Leichhardt's failure to serve his country. Mann himself was militarily born, bred, and educated; his father was a colonel and both grandfathers *were* generals.[53]

The Expedition as a Cultural Form 81

He was genealogically connected with the military hierarchy that Leichhardt presumed to invoke.

The poisonous relations that developed between the two men certainly contributed to the crumbling of Leichhardt's leadership as the expedition progressed. Mann considered Leichhardt guilty of hubris on a colossal scale, stemming from the adulation he received after the first expedition. In one of many altercations, Mann claims to have 'told him that he appeared to think that Australia was created especially for himself, but that he was quite mistaken if he supposed that he alone had the right to interest himself in the exploration of the country.'[54] While Mann's extreme criticisms have not gone uncontested in the highly polarized Leichhardt historiography, the theatre of disputation they reveal are relevant to our typology, especially since the self-inflation alleged by Mann is barely more excessive than the explorer's own rhapsodizing in the joy of conquest. 'No king could have been welcomed with greater gladness and deeper interest by a whole people,' wrote Leichhardt of his return to Sydney.[55] In the aftermath of that return, his journal was published in London, the RGS that had once spurned him awarded him its Patron's Medal, and even his great hero von Humboldt took interest in him, writing to the King of Prussia suggesting that his outlaw status be revoked.[56] The great reserve of economic and cultural capital pooled in Leichhardt's name was the basis of his license as an explorer. The accusations of hubris, and the excruciating demise of the second expedition, point to the explosive potential of this concentration of capital. When used with care, it can bring enormous power to the expeditionary leader. But such is the volatility of this capital that it endows an element of *instability* to the expedition as a cultural form.

A further facet of the expedition, revealed by financing, is to do with *replication*. The use of reward money from an earlier expedition to capitalize a new one points to a deeper trait, to do with seriality: expeditions beget new expeditions. Indeed, the generation of fresh adventure from the ashes of the old is as much a driver for exploration as those vague, if grandiose, imperatives to do with discovery and expansion. Every expedition exists in relationship to a greater set of other expeditions: past and future, real and imagined. That is why expeditions intrude on intellectual property as readily as they trespass on other people's territory. Leichhardt, as we know, appropriated Mitchell's notion of a Port Essington journey. Mann's recruitment as a 'private' in Leichhardt's party (although Mann preferred to think of himself as the 'engineer' and deputy) came about because Mann was preparing to launch a search party for the Prussian when his Port Essington expedition was thought to be lost. When Leichhardt truly disappeared, many others went in quest of him. Some made their own names as explorers, while others came a cropper. More lives were lost in search of Leichhardt than there were members of his third expedition. Even when the design life of the exploratory expedition was exhausted, the replication continued. The last person to die searching for Leichhardt was a bushman named Bryce Russell, who in 1937 took 20 camels and 34 gallons of water into the Simpson Desert (where Leichhardt is unlikely to have gone). He was never seen again.[57] In the cruel poetry of outback Australia, the disappearance of the searcher mirrors that of his quarry.

CODA

As we have seen, a pledge of fraternity marked the commencement of Leichhardt's second expedition. But as it progressed, the party became bonded in ways they could scarcely have imagined. The men became captive to the idiosyncratic circumstances of the journey's inception. The large and bizarre assortment of animals, largely donated by settlers, was too unruly for them to control. The imperative to discover new territory yielded to the necessity of searching, sometimes for days on end, for the cattle and goats that strayed at night in search of feed. To these frustrations can be added dramatic rainfalls, accompanied by disease. When the party were not hunting livestock they were paralyzed with fever and diarrhoea, as floodwaters collected around them. Tempers frayed, and they began to argue about the allocation of resources, especially food. In a classic bid for attention by a deputy (or in this case, a would-be deputy), Mann took to his sketchbook, drawing acerbic scenes of expedition life in which Leichhardt is depicted as a dictatorial clown (Figures 4.2 and 4.3). In one example he is seen using the prerogative of leadership to claim an unfair share of a small lizard that

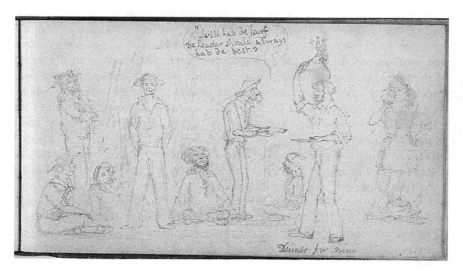

Figure 4.2 John F. Mann, 'Dinner for Nine,' 1846–7. By Permission of the Mitchell Library, State Library of New South Wales. (Call no. DLMS 178/2//51).

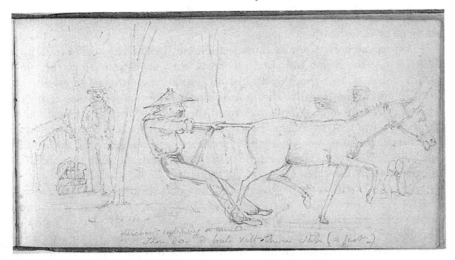

Figure 4.3 John F. Mann, 'Leichhardt catching a mule,' 1846–7. By Permission of the Mitchell Library, State Library of New South Wales. (Call no. DLMS 178/2//56).

was their dinner. Another bizarre drawing portrays his alleged incompetence in the handling of animals. Mann's journal gives gruelling account of these events. Titled *Eight Months with Dr. Leichhardt*, it was published more than 40 years after the journey and some Leichhardt scholars have denounced it as nothing more than malicious venom. Historian Dan Sprod describes Mann's account as a 'tirade,' claiming that he became 'more and more paranoid as he grew older, and that in the process he continuously tampered with his sources.'[58] Webster similarly suggests that much of it is fabrication—a post-expeditionary reimagining by a man who was delusional and embittered.

Yet for reasons not explained, both Webster and Sprod uncritically reproduce Mann's drawings in their publications.[59] They are, after all, the major visual evidence of the 1846–7 expedition. While Mann's manuscript journals, of which there are several versions in Sydney's Mitchell Library, *do* present evidential questions, since they seem to be copies by Mann of an earlier field book now lost or destroyed, there is little doubt that the drawings originate from the time of the expedition. They appear in a small notebook that also contains the maps recording the expedition's daily progress (see Figure 4.1). The calculations of distance, notations of compass bearings, and recording of identifiable landmarks in those maps make it extremely unlikely that the contents of this notebook were created after the event. That scholars apply a double standard in their approaches to written and visual evidence is unfortunately all too common. Here it is especially problematic because the message and tone of the drawings are essentially

84   Martin Thomas

consistent with the content of the written narrative, which Mann's critics claim to be inauthentic.

My purpose here is not to show that Mann, Leichhardt, or, indeed, anyone else left the more authentic record of the expedition. Since the nineteenth century, the Leichhardt historiography has lurched convulsively from hagiography to vilification, according to the temper of the moment. The most critical assessments date from the Second World War when anti-Teutonic sentiments were rife. I can but agree with some recent critics who lament the 'lasting "for or against" limitation to so much of the critical work on Leichhardt.'[60] It is a mighty distraction from the genuinely interesting themes raised by this man and his milieu.

Fortunately, the task of identifying the structural properties of expeditions does not require that we eliminate Mann as a figure of interest because he felt animus to his leader or because he copied and recopied documents in later years. The animus can be recognized as part of the internal political friction endemic to the political organization of an expedition; the copying of documents should be regarded not as perverse meddling with primary evidence, but as an extension of expeditionary record keeping, where copying, modification, and self-editing on the part of a diarist are the rule rather than the exception. The drawings, too, can be recognized for their political and performative dimension. Not only are they interpretations of moments in a journey, but their creation can be rated as events within it. Drawn, perhaps, in sight of fellow party members, or shown and laughed at while Leichhardt was out reconnoitring, they provided mirthful release from the confined social universe in which these men had become entrapped.

The project of defining and better understanding the cultural formation that is an expedition is still in its infancy. If the typology is to develop further, the Leichhardt story must ultimately be read in relation to a good many other expeditionary narratives. Even so, the trajectory he followed is instructive. The ties of connection he established in his accumulation and herding of expeditionary capital are revealing for what they say about colonial society and its acquisitive projection into 'unclaimed' territory. Leichhardt remained a focus of projective energy long after his disappearance. As he morphed from man to myth, accounts of the explorer's fate sprouted like exotic weeds. There were tales of mixed-race offspring sired by Leichhardt, rumour of a cave full of skeletons and surveying instruments, a report that Leichhardt was held prisoner in a secret desert community of black and white people, and another of an expedition survivor living as a slave to an Aboriginal tribe.[61] When Leichhardt set out for the last time in that 'long line of everybody,' he ensured that a multitude of people would, in the future, have some stake in his story and his memory. A martyr to science and empire, he became the sacrificial hero for a colonial society as it tried to find a foothold on foreign soil.

NOTES

1. T. L. Mitchell, *Three Expeditions Into the Interior of Eastern Australia, with Descriptions of the Recently Explored Region of Australia Felix, and of the Present Colony of New South Wales* (London: T. & W. Boone, 1838), 5.
2. Ibid., 1.
3. J. F. Mann, 'Sketch book 1846–7,' DLMS 178, Item 2, Mitchell Library, State Library of New South Wales.
4. Leichhardt to Carl Schmalfuss, 3 September 1844, in *The Letters of F. W. Ludwig Leichhardt*, vol. III, trans. and ed. M. Aurousseau (Cambridge: Cambridge University Press for the Hakluyt Society, 1968), 827.
5. On shipboard politics and naval discipline, see Greg Dening, *Mr Bligh's Bad Language: Passion, Power and Theatre on the Bounty* (Cambridge: Cambridge University Press, 1992). My thinking on the inland expedition is indebted to Dening. On linear trajectories and the influence of maritime models on terrestrial exploration, see Martin Thomas, *The Artificial Horizon: Imagining the Blue Mountains* (Carlton, AU: Melbourne University Press, 2003), 114–21 and Dane Kennedy, *The Last Blank Spaces: Exploring Africa and Australia* (Cambridge, MA: Harvard University Press, 2013), ch. 1.
6. J. F. Mann, *Eight Months with Dr. Leichhardt in the Years 1846–47* (Sydney: Turner & Henderson, 1888), 22.
7. Ibid., 70.
8. The Aboriginal men are said to have come from coastal areas north of Sydney: Brown from the Newcastle area and Wammai from Port Stephens. Biographical sketches of all expedition members appear in Dan Sprod, *Proud Intrepid Heart: Leichhardt's First Attempt to the Swan River 1846–1847* (Hobart, AU: Blubber Head Press, 1989), 67–115.
9. Males in colonial Australia outnumbered females by three to one in 1828 and by more than three to two in 1851. See Graeme Davison, 'Population,' in *The Oxford Companion to Australian History*, eds. Graeme Davison, John Hirst, and Stuart Macintyre (South Melbourne: Oxford University Press, 2001), 521.
10. Mann, *Eight Months with Dr. Leichhardt*, 14.
11. Roland Barthes, *Mythologies*, trans. Annette Lavers (London: Vintage, 2000).
12. Kennedy, *The Last Blank Spaces*, 251.
13. Ibid., 3.
14. Paul Carter, *The Road to Botany Bay: An Essay in Spatial History* (London: Faber and Faber, 1987) and Mary Louise Pratt, *Imperial Eyes: Travel Writing and Transculturation* (London: Routledge, 1992).
15. Leichhardt to Secretary RGS, 15 September 1841, in *The Letters of F. W. Ludwig Leichhardt*, vol. I, trans. and ed. M. Aurousseau, 384.
16. Beau Riffenburgh, *The Myth of the Explorer: The Press, Sensationalism, and Geographic Discovery* (Oxford: Oxford University Press, 1994), 6.
17. Darrell Lewis, *Where Is Dr Leichhardt? The Greatest Mystery in Australian History* (Clayton, AU: Monash University Publishing, 2013).
18. Felix Driver, *Geography Militant: Cultures of Exploration and Empire* (Oxford: Blackwell, 2001). See also Kennedy, *The Last Blank Spaces*.
19. Eric Hobsbawm and Terence Ranger, eds., *The Invention of Tradition* (Cambridge: Cambridge University Press, 1983).
20. Sir Robert Wilson, an army officer and colonial governor, is credited with this first modern usage when he wrote, 'the explorers enter, and immediately find themselves in a marble cave.' From 'explorer, n.,' OED Online, www.oed.com.rp.nla.gov.au/view/Entry/66670?redirectedFrom=explorer, accessed 8 October 2013.

86 Martin Thomas

21. Leichhardt to Carl Schmalfuss, 21 October 1847, in *The Letters of F. W. Ludwig Leichhardt*, vol. III, trans. and ed. M. Aurousseau, 963.
22. Leichhardt to Christian Leichhardt, 14 March 1836, in Ibid., vol. I, 29.
23. Kirsten McKenzie, *A Swindler's Progress: Nobles and Convicts in the Age of Liberty* (Sydney: New South Press, 2009), 295.
24. John Bailey, *Into the Unknown: The Tormented Life and Expeditions of Ludwig Leichhardt* (Sydney: Pan Macmillan, 2011), 55.
25. Leichhardt to H. Emrich, 18 January 1840, in *The Letters of F. W. Ludwig Leichhardt*, vol. I, trans. and ed. M. Aurousseau, 232.
26. Leichhardt to Carl Schmalfuss, 27 September 1841, in Ibid., vol. I, 392.
27. Bailey, *Into the Unknown*, 66.
28. Rod Home, *Science as a German Import to Nineteenth Century Australia*, Working Papers in Australian Studies (No. 104) (London: Sir Robert Menzies Centre for Australian Studies, 1995).
29. Significant works on Mitchell include William C. Foster, *Sir Thomas Livingston Mitchell and His World 1792–1855: Surveyor General of New South Wales 1828–1855* (Sydney: Institution of Surveyors NSW, 1985) and D.W.A. Baker, *The Civilised Surveyor: Thomas Mitchell and the Australian Aborigines* (Carlton South, AU: Melbourne University Press, 1997). For an account of the first three expeditions, see Mitchell, *Three Expeditions Into the Interior of Eastern Australia*.
30. My chronology of how Mitchell learned this news is from Foster, *Sir Thomas Livingston Mitchell and His World*, 371. Leichhardt did write to Mitchell on 24 July 1844 telling him of a plan to 'see how far I am able, with my limited means, to explore the country in the direction of the North West.' Expressing hope that approval for Mitchell's journey would be granted, and that they would 'meet in the Interior,' he did not specify that Port Essington was his objective. See M. Aurousseau, *The Letters of F. W. Ludwig Leichhardt*, vol. II, 780. It is possible—indeed likely—that Mitchell was already aware of the full scope of Leichhardt's plans, having read the newspaper report announcing Leichhardt's journey on 17 July 1844, discussed below.
31. Kennedy, *The Last Blank Spaces*, 100–1 and 271–4.
32. Ibid., 100.
33. Alan E. J. Andrews, *Major Mitchell's Map 1834: The Saga of the Survey of the Nineteen Counties* (Hobart, AU: Blubber Head Press, 1992).
34. Leichhardt to W. J. Little, 12 November 1842, in *The Letters of F. W. Ludwig Leichhardt*, vol. II, trans. and ed. M. Aurousseau, 591–2.
35. Leichhardt to Robert Lynd, 16 January 1843, Ibid., 623.
36. 'The Exploration of New Holland,' *The Australian*, 17 July 1844, 474.
37. Thomas, *The Artificial Horizon*, 41–57.
38. William Russell (writing in the guise of Bill Orton) cited in Bailey, *Into the Unknown*, 124.
39. Cited in Sarah L. C. Clapp, 'The Beginnings of Subscription Publication in the Seventeenth Century,' *Modern Philology* 29:2 (1931): 199.
40. Ibid., 200.
41. Joshua A. Bell, Alison K. Brown, and Robert. J Gordon, 'Expeditions, Their Films and Histories—an Introduction,' in *Recreating First Contact: Expeditions, Anthropology, and Popular Culture*, eds. Joshua A. Bell, Alison K. Brown, and Robert. J Gordon (Washington, DC: Smithsonian Institution Scholarly Press, 2013), 4. For discussion of expeditions in the context of twentieth-century capitalism in the US see Gregg Mitman and Paul Erickson, 'Latex and Blood: Science, Markets, and American Empire,' *Radical History Review* 107 (2010): 45–73.

The Expedition as a Cultural Form   87

42. William Sinclair, 'The African Association of 1788,' *Journal of the Royal African Society* 1:1 (1901): 146.
43. Mark Collins Jenkins, 'A Robinson Crusoe in Arnhem Land: Howell Walker, *National Geographic* and the Arnhem Land Expedition of 1948,' in *Exploring the Legacy of the 1948 Arnhem Land Expedition*, eds. Martin Thomas and Margo Neale (Canberra, AU: ANU E Press, 2011), 77–8.
44. 'Progress of Internal Discovery,' *The Australian*, 17 July 1844, 475.
45. P. R. Gordon, 'Origin of Leichhardt's Names of Rivers and Places,' *The Queenslander*, 1 November 1890, 835.
46. The earliest volume containing a list of subscribers dates from 1617. See Clapp, 'The Beginnings of Subscription Publication,' 205.
47. Ludwig Leichhardt, *Journal of an Overland Expedition in Australia from Moreton Bay to Port Essington, a Distance of Upwards of 3000 Miles, During the Years 1844–1845* (London: T. & W. Boone, 1847), i.
48. Bailey, *Into the Unknown*, 250.
49. E. M. Webster, *Whirlwinds in the Plain: Ludwig Leichhardt—Friends, Foes and History* (Carlton, AU: Melbourne University Press, 1980), 50.
50. Leichhardt to Carl Schmalfuss, 19 August 1846, in *The Letters of F. W. Ludwig Leichhardt*, vol. III, trans. and ed. M. Aurousseau, 900.
51. 'Raymond Terrace,' *Maitland Mercury & Hunter River General Advertiser*, 7 October 1846, 2.
52. Mann, *Eight Months with Dr. Leichhardt*, 13.
53. Peter Orlovich, 'Mann, John Frederick (1819–1907),' *Australian Dictionary of Biography*, National Centre of Biography, Australian National University, http://adb.anu.edu.au/biography/mann-john-frederick-4144/text6641, accessed 29 October 2013.
54. Mann, *Eight Months with Dr. Leichhardt*, 58.
55. Leichhardt to Carl Schmalfuss, 18 April 1846, in *The Letters of F. W. Ludwig Leichhardt*, vol. III, trans. and ed. M. Aurousseau, 856.
56. Webster, *Whirlwinds in the Plain*, 233.
57. Lewis, *Where Is Dr Leichhardt?*, 307–9.
58. Sprod, *Proud Intrepid Heart*, 89.
59. Another, more recent biographer repeats this inconsistency. See Hans Wilhelm Finger, *Ludwig Leichhardt: Lost in the Outback* (Dural, NSW: Rosenberg, 2013).
60. Andrew Hurley and Katrina Schlunke, 'Leichhardt After Leichhardt (Review Essay),' *Journal of Australian Studies* 37:4 (2013): 538.
61. These examples are drawn from Lewis, *Where Is Dr Leichhardt?*

5 The Theatre of Contact
Aborigines and Exploring Expeditions

Philip Jones

A re-examination of interactions between Australian expeditions and Aboriginal people reveals patterns and behaviours that may imbue those earliest meetings with a distinct character of mutual curiosity and a preparedness to engage, which was all too often erased from later encounters. This chapter proposes that 'mutual incomprehension and suspicion' did not necessarily underpin initial engagements between Australian exploring expeditions and Aboriginal people, challenging the recent proposition that these engagements are 'all but indistinguishable from . . . encounters with pastoralists, prospectors, and other agents of settler colonialism.'[1]

The immediacy of a naïve impact, unbiased by preconceptions or formed expectations, can cast light on something essential in the intersection of two quite different cultures: one stripped down to expeditionary mode—on the march, enquiring, recording, acquiring; the other reacting to strange, unprecedented incursions without notice—exposed, with its expectations often confounded, dazzled by new forms and new technologies, and yet retaining or falling back on ancient protocols.

For the purposes of the argument it is convenient at the outset to characterize the stance or nature of these two cultural groups, albeit in a reductive, simplistic way. Expressed in broad terms, the expeditionary Anglo-European culture came equipped with notions of the 'other' as essentially human cultures (in line with Enlightenment discourse), but incompletely realized—indeed, defined in terms of deficiencies of intelligence, technology, appreciation of a higher being, and so on. European expeditions were ready to treat the 'other' as a separable, classifiable form of humanity, not necessarily requiring integration. By contrast, Aboriginal cultures were distinguished by either their total socializing tendencies, requiring absorption of the 'other' within existing kinship structures as a matter of urgency (often 'recognizing' Europeans as their own dead returned as spirits) or as a necessary converse, repelling or ignoring strangers as inhuman, to be cast out and classified with their own demons.

Accepting this frame enables us to begin the process of describing and categorizing the main forms of behaviour and response when expeditions arrived in Aboriginal country for the first time. Of course it would be a

Aborigines and Exploring Expeditions 89

mistake to assume that this phenomenon of double response—the shock caused by the advent of strangers, followed by the shock of their reception—was purely a function of European contact. Despite the documented permeability of Aboriginal groups, we understand that the very definition of such groups rested upon their developed sense of themselves as 'men' and of other Aboriginal groups as ranging from peripheral strangers who could be accommodated within the social framework (marrying range), to exotic strangers, different in appearance, material culture, language, and customs, who might emerge periodically from 'beyond the pale.' Such strangers were regarded as human in form, but 'not men.' Inevitably this difference was marked and characterized by the charge of cannibalism. Several group names, such as the Lower Murray and Lakes group name 'Narrinyeri' ('We are men') and the north-east Arnhem Land 'Yolngu' ('men') imply this exclusivity in relation to neighbouring groups regarded, at best, with suspicion. Europeans did not have a monopoly on forms of racism or orientalism in Australia.

From the early eighteenth century, annual visits of Macassan trepang fleets to the northern coast provide the main exception—proof that familiarity can breed tolerance of a sort; but once again, in the historical traces relating to those two centuries of sustained contact (until the visits of the trepang fleets ceased in about 1908), we can see the same patterns of repulsion, confrontation, incorporation. And we should remember that the Macassans' contact with Aboriginal people was confined to the absolute edge of the continent and rarely involved the passage of strangers *through* Aboriginal country. Relationships between one local group and visiting Macassan crews, becoming familiar and known by sight and even by name, could develop over the years, gradually shifting the dynamic of encounter.

An awareness of the power of parochialism is important in our discussion, for Australia is distinctive in that most Aboriginal people had developed a mode of life that did not involve full-scale crossings or incursions from territory to territory. There were no outright grabs for territory; raiding parties existed, but these were for vengeance or for women, rather than for property or for land. Certainly, there was no expectation of losing land altogether, or of it being alienated from use. When visitors arrived, it was assumed that they came for social reasons; even if trade was the apparent or superficial goal, its transactions were socially derived and expressed, tangled closely with obligation and the governing principle of reciprocity. A casual observation by George Augustus Robinson in the journal of his expedition in the company of Aborigines from the Western Districts of Victoria provides a remarkable passing insight into the way encounters 'on the march' were marked. At Wannon Marsh in June 1841, Robinson observed an encounter between Mar.ke, an Aboriginal woman, who recognized one of his own 'native attendants.' Mar.ke 'took the kangaroo teeth ornaments that adorned his hair and reed necklace that adorned his neck and decorated her child therewith.' 'This,' Robinson wrote, 'was the custom of the natives when meeting with friends.'[2]

90   Philip Jones

But even if it was a revenge party arriving at a strange camp in the dead of night, we should remember that the motivating feud originated in personal and often banal entanglements between individual members of the two groups. The idea of a self-contained expedition of strangers (particularly strange white men) moving across the country without regard for social bonds and conventions was not readily comprehensible to the Aboriginal mind. Indeed, some of the conflict that arose in the course of early nineteenth-century expeditions such as those of Mitchell, Grey, Sturt, and Leichhardt can be traced to the affront implicit in the Europeans' decision to move the expedition on, rather than its initial appearance without invitation.

One constant factor distinguishes the early Australian exploring expeditions as extraordinary laboratories of contact: their transience in Aboriginal experience. This is what differentiates the phenomenon of the expedition from 'settler colonialism'—characterized by the permanent, ramifying presence of Europeans. Another key difference was the absence of European women on these early exploring expeditions, noticed immediately by Aboriginal people. It often provoked a particular response that baffled or intrigued European expedition members, but makes sense when interpreted against Aboriginal expectations and practices.

With these introductory remarks I suggest that almost all expeditionary journals may be analysed to reveal evidence for a set of behaviours and responses that may be compared with, or calibrated to, a set of ideal protocols of encounter. It is possible to speak of two principal modes of engagement. In practice, by considering a large number of explorers' accounts of first encounters, it is easy to see that these modes, and variations of them, were often confused and could easily overlap, with Aboriginal people switching from one to the other—almost in desperation in some circumstances—as they dealt with the apparition of strangers whose very presence tested all credibility.

Seen in this way, each expeditionary encounter plays out as a drama on a stage, in the sense first expounded by the anthropologist Erving Goffman. His redefinition of encounter as interaction and performance helped shift focus in studies of the frontier from one-dimensional 'representations of the Other,' or indeed, from standard characterizations of the colonizing, polarizing European, to the actual dynamics of colonial encounters as theatrical events enlivened by the agency of each troupe of actors—European and indigenous.[3] Goffman's analysis also provokes many further questions: How were these encounters activated or provoked, and why, and how did they unfold? Was there a pattern, an ideal, that was corrupted or subverted, and how did these encounters shift, gaining weight and bias over time? What was the role of gesture, of language, of artefacts, in forming these encounters? To what extent did Europeans or Aboriginal people engineer these changes? More than most others, the Goffmanian approach tends to yield satisfactory answers.

The approach also reminds us of a certain theatricality that enlivens and distinguishes these encounters. Certainly, many expedition journals accentuate this aspect, lingering particularly on those scenes in which the *dramatis personae* suddenly expanded to include Aboriginal players, and when our view of the stage offers a strange new perspective. Sensing this, several explorers, such as Mitchell, Sturt, Leichhardt, Giles, and Lindsay, often laid weight on these moments, expanding the seconds or minutes of encounter to the degree that they may be usefully analysed today. Other explorers—such as Warburton, Stuart, and, surprisingly, Edward Eyre—tended to paraphrase those moments and gloss over them, regarding them as distractions from their central preoccupation of exploration. But taken together, it is possible to distil the elements and to discern patterns and sequences, choreographies and ideal sets of events, and then also to understand how those encounters often lurched and went off the rails, with transgressions of protocol on each side.

Figure 5.1 Thomas Mitchell studying his map inside a 'temporary gunyah, or hut, set up for passing a night in the bush,' under the apparent protection of an Aboriginal man and one of the expedition's soldiers. Frontispiece of *Three Expeditions Into the Interior of Eastern Australia*, vol. 1, 1839. Engraving by G. Barnard from a drawing by T. Mitchell. By Permission of Barr Smith Library, University of Adelaide.

92 *Philip Jones*

These attempts at interpretation not only involve a search among the records for pattern and order but also entail an awareness of the random, uncontrolled potential of these frontier encounters. For if encountering groups shared enough in the way of conventions and protocols to steady an encounter and give it a base, this latitude soon reached its limit. As Frédéric Regard has written, 'with all the unpredictability of verbal and non-verbal interaction and communicational exchange, knowledge systems must have been challenged, frames of meaning-making disrupted, "representations" shattered, postures undermined, positions reversed and identities trans-formed.'[4] Indeed, the subject takes us into the heart of a debate over the extent to which we might impute the same standards of rationality to those groups encountering each other on remote frontiers—a debate most promi-nently associated with conflicting readings of the death of Captain James Cook by anthropologists Marshall Sahlins and Gananath Obeyesekere.[5]

OVERTURES AND CIRCUMSCRIPTION

A defining element of an expedition is its planned character, expressed most obviously in its confident listing of equipment and provisions, its division of duties among expedition members, and its defined objectives. Often enough, those objectives, and even provision lists including metal axes and knives, mirrors, cloth and tobacco, signal that 'encounters with the natives' were envisaged and accepted as integral to the expedition's key aims. These indi-cations also suggest that Europeans were confident enough to consider that they would be able to define those encounters on terms advantageous to themselves. In particular cases, that confidence extended further to the hope or expectation that indigenous people would be the beneficiaries. While early Australian expeditions rarely included missionaries, it is fair to say that the discourse relating to encounters between civilized men and savages also carried an obligation or duty to bring some form of enlightenment to the savages, often effected or enabled by the distribution of presents.

The early nineteenth-century surge in Australian exploration activity, first emanating from Sydney following the successful crossing of the Blue Mountains in 1813, coincided with the British government's formulation of articulated directions for exploring expeditions. These instructions inte-grated 'manners, customs and language' within the range of scientific facts and phenomena to be recorded by explorers, as in the following example:

Copy of Instructions from the Right Honourable the Secretary of State

Downing Street, April 18, 1816.

It is most desirable that any person travelling into the interior should keep a detailed Journal of his proceedings. In this Journal all observations and occur-rences of every kind, with all their circumstances, however minute, and however

Aborigines and Exploring Expeditions 93

familiar they may have been rendered by custom, should be carefully noted down; and it is also desirable that he should be as circumstantial as possible in describing the general appearance of the country, its surface, soil, animals, vegetables and minerals, every thing that relates to the population, the peculiar manners, customs, language, etc., of the individual natives, or the tribes of them that he may meet with . . .

The description, and characteristic difference, of the several people whom he may meet; the extent of the population, their occupation, and means of subsistence; whether chiefly, or to what extent, by fishing, hunting, or agriculture, and the principal objects of their several pursuits.

A circumstantial account of such articles, if any, as might be advantageously imported into Great Britain.

A vocabulary of the language spoken by the natives whom he may meet, using in the compilation of each the same English words.

If the people are sufficiently numerous to form tribes, it is important to ascertain their condition, and rules of the society; their genius and disposition; the nature of their amusements; their diseases and remedies, etc.; their objects of worship, religious ceremonies; and the influence of those ceremonies on their moral character and conduct.

(Signed) JOHN THOMAS CAMPBELL, Sec.[6]

By this time, it was already understood that such data would be gained at a price. An expedition's success would be measured partly by its capacity to negotiate its movement through country controlled, if not actually 'owned,' by ill-defined corporate groups of indigenous people, usually lacking identifiable leaders. Such negotiations would necessarily occur in polarized, fraught circumstances. This expectation solidified during the course of the nineteenth century, in step with the evolution of protocols of geographical observation and measurement. Here we meet a paradox; just as more experienced travellers inclined progressively towards open-mindedness about the world and its unpredictable, variable nature, an emerging rhetoric of exploration began to characterize and fix the indigenous subject as an undifferentiated savage. This rhetoric surfaces in a range of British colonialist and exploration literature—in books such as John Herschel's *Manual of Scientific Enquiry* (1849) or Francis Galton's widely read *Art of Travel* (1855), and popular tracts and lectures such as E. G. Wakefield's *A View of the Art of Colonization* (1849) and J. R. Seeley's *Expansion of England* (1883). Out of this discourse a harder, firmer view of 'the other' emerged, tending to predetermine the postures adopted by explorers in the field.

For their part, while Aboriginal people had no expectation whatsoever that they would meet Europeans, we know that they also carried with them a set of protocols and procedures, ordinarily employed when meeting 'stranger Aborigines.' With the unheralded appearance of expeditions in their territories these protocols and procedures needed to be deployed in an instant.

Three examples, each laden with drama, illustrate the precise moments of intersection between these protocols and European expeditionary practice,

94 *Philip Jones*

indicating how new and unprecedented cultural 'moments' might be generated. The first is taken from Ludwig Leichhardt's 1845 overland expedition from Moreton Bay to Port Essington. Leichhardt's journal contains the following entry, recorded 80 kilometres north of the site where the expedition's naturalist, John Gilbert, was speared near the Mitchell River a few days earlier:

> At dusk, when Charley brought in the horses, two of which we tethered near the camp, the form of a native glided like a ghost into our camp, and walked directly up to the fire. John, who saw him first, called out, "a Blackfellow! look there! a Blackfellow!" and every gun was ready. But the stranger was unarmed, and evidently unconscious of his position; for, when he saw himself suddenly surrounded by the horses and ourselves, he nimbly climbed a tree to its very summit, where he stood between some dry branches like a strange phantom or a statue. We called to him, and made signs for him to descend, but he not only remained silent, but motionless, notwithstanding all the signs and noise we made. We then discharged a gun, but it had not the intended effect of inducing him to speak or stir. At last I desired Charley to ascend the neighbouring tree, to show him that we could easily get at him if necessary. This plan was more successful; for no sooner were Charley's intentions perceived, than our friend gave the most evident proof of his being neither deaf nor dumb, by calling out most lustily . . . he did everything to make the silent forest re-echo with the wild sounds of his alarm; our horses, which were standing under the tree, became frightened, and those which were loose ran away. We were much afraid that his cooees would bring the whole tribe to his assistance, and every one eagerly proffered his advice.[7]

Here we see a lone Aboriginal man, who, having made the dreadful error of assuming that Leichhardt's campfire was that of his own people, was alarmed beyond all possibility of understanding his dilemma or negotiating his way through it. The Europeans and their animals could, under such circumstances, only be comprehended as devils. He had entered the nightmare zone of his people's worst fears and his behaviour reflected this.[8]

The second example is drawn from Thomas Mitchell's second exploring expedition, during 1835, as he followed the Bogan River downstream to its confluence with the Darling. It reveals an 'ideal encounter,' when each side had time and space to comprehend the other as human and even, in the Aboriginal case, as possibly related. The unfolding encounter was then choreographed on Aboriginal terms, and Mitchell's men saw every advantage in collaborating with this protocol:

> There, by their cooeys and their looks, they seemed to be very anxious about somebody in the bush beyond the Bogan. I expected to see their chief; at all events from these silent woods something was to emerge in

Figure 5.2 'First Meeting with the Chief of the Bogan Tribe' portrays an encounter between the explorer Thomas Mitchell and men of the Bogan River, conducted according to ideal protocols. Plate 12 of *Three Expeditions Into the Interior of Eastern Australia*, vol. 1, 1839. Engraving by G. Barnard from a drawing by T. Mitchell. By Permission of Barr Smith Library, University of Adelaide.

which my guides were evidently much interested, as they kept me waiting nearly an hour for the unseen genius of the wood.

At length a man of mild but pensive countenance, athletic form, and apparently about fifty years of age, came forth, leading a very fine boy, so dressed with green boughs that only his head and legs remained uncovered; a few emu-feathers being mixed with the wild locks of his hair. I received him in this appropriate costume, as a personification of the green bough, or emblem of peace.

One large feather decked the brow of the chief; which with his nose, was tinged with yellow ochre. Having presented the boy to me, he next advanced with much formality towards the camp, having Tackijally on his right, the boy walking between, and rather in advance of both, each having a hand on his shoulder.

The boy's face had a holiday look of gladness, but the chief remained so silent and serious, without however any symptoms of alarm, that my recollections of him then, and as he appeared next day, when better acquainted, are as of two distinct persons.

To this personage all the others paid the greatest deference, and it is worthy of remark that they always refused to tell his name, or that of several others, while those of some of the tribe were familiar in our

96 Philip Jones

mouths as household words. The boy, who was called Talambe Nadoo, was not his son; but he took particular care of him.[9]

These critical factors, allowing each side enough space and time to comprehend the other as human and responsive, were also in place during the early stages of Edmund Kennedy's ill-fated 1848 expedition from Rockingham Bay in Queensland. Here though, it was the Europeans who took control of an 'ideal' encounter, deploying gifts but preventing Aboriginal people from interpreting this overture as an invitation to closer, possibly risky contact:

> We found no difficulty in making them comprehend that we desired to be friendly with them, and they advanced towards us with green boughs in their hands, which they displayed as emblems of peace. We met them with our arms extended and our hands open, indicating that we had no implements of war with us. We made them a present of two circular tin plates, with Mr. Kennedy's initials stamped upon them, with chains to hang them round the neck; we also gave them a few fish-hooks, and they accepted our presents with great demonstrations of pleasure. We made signs for them to sit down about 200 yards from the spot where the horses and sheep were being landed, and marking a line upon the sand we made them understand that they were not to cross it to approach us. One of our party was placed amongst them to enforce this regulation, which he did with little difficulty, although they expressed great curiosity as to various articles brought on shore from the ship.[10]

Universal signals or protocols emerge from many of these descriptions; behaviours that might be recognized equally on the North American plains, in the Amazonian forests, or New Guinea highlands—the deployment of green foliage, the distribution of gifts, the tracing of a line or 'pale' around a camp. So also with the laying down of arms, as during John Oxley's 1817 expedition on the Lachlan:

> We had scarcely alighted from our horses, when natives were seen in considerable numbers on the other side of the river. I went down opposite to them, and after some little persuasion about twenty of them swam across, having their galengar or stone hatchet in one hand, which on their landing they threw at our feet, to show us that they were as much divested of arms as ourselves.[11]

Nonetheless, it is clear enough that as with so many other cultural characteristics in Aboriginal Australia, local variations might counterbalance these apparent congruities. The westward penetration of exploration expeditions from Sydney and Melbourne during the early nineteenth century provides sufficient data to test this proposition. Explorers moved from the tightly

Aborigines and Exploring Expeditions 97

bounded Aboriginal territories of the inland river systems of the Murray-Darling basin into open arid country where local groups ranged much more widely. Additionally, the Murray and Darling system provides a fascinating controlled study of expeditionary practice itself. These rivers offered logical corridors of movement for European explorers. They also supplied an Aboriginal precedent, for Aboriginal watercraft had always enabled strangers to appear unannounced from upstream, ready to negotiate their passage with local groups along the river systems. This fact may account for the relatively easy passage offered to Charles Sturt, and for his ready comprehension of clearly understood protocols.

Sturt and Mitchell each became accustomed to the appearance of significant old men who walked proprietorially into their camps and even spent evenings sleeping by the expedition campfires. Interestingly, the frontispiece to Mitchell's published journal of his first expedition depicts an example of this distinctive inversion, characteristic of that frontier in the brief period before the route became a forum for 'collisions' between Aboriginal people and Europeans overlanding sheep to Adelaide.[12] Those collisions appear to have been based as much on the Aboriginal desire for European sheep, metal, and other goods belonging to the overland parties, as on the European incursions through their lands. Here it is worth mentioning that as early as 1830 Sturt was encountering Aboriginal people who valued his commodities at least as much as the social exchange.

A key factor to be considered in evaluating these early frontier encounters is the presence of Aboriginal guides among expedition parties. Selected as much for their precocity as cultural brokers as for their skills as guides, these individuals were often torn between the great personal benefit and material rewards associated with being part of an expedition (successful or not) and their ambivalence at leaving behind the security of their own countries, languages, and kin. The effect of their presence within European expeditions upon encounters with 'stranger Aborigines' is not easy to gauge.

Sturt and Mitchell each had Aboriginal intermediaries. Sturt's diary offers remarkable insights into the dynamic operating between these men and stranger Aborigines, and between these men and his own party. During his 1844–5 inland expedition, which travelled northwest from the Murray-Darling Rivers into arid Central Australia, he was initially accompanied by Nadbuck and Toonda, two men from the vicinity of Rufus River. On the Darling itself, these men found themselves among Aboriginal groups that may have included their own distant relatives. That social proximity often represented a threat as well as a comfort, and resulted in a series of ambiguous, equivocal encounters in which Sturt's party were almost entangled. Nadbuck assumed the role of emissary with one group of stranger Aborigines on the Darling:

> They had a fine view of the drays as they descended a steep bank into it. These Natives have as many ceremonies as the Emperor of China,

98   *Philip Jones*

and it was really amusing to see old Nadbuck play the Courtier. I found him in the midst of the Tribe noticing all of them by turns. He then took hold of the hands of two of the old Men and walked away with them in deep and earnest conversation, and on his return to the Party said to me, "Bloody rogues that Fellow. Mind your Sheep tonight."[13]

Faced with this illustration of Nadbuck's propensity to play a double game, Sturt might equally have wondered how Nadbuck was representing the expedition party to the strangers. But Sturt's other guide, Toonda, went even further, advising him to treat one group of strangers on the Darling as mortal enemies:

I should before have mentioned that Toonda motioned to me to shoot the Natives, from what cause I cannot say but he was certainly greatly excited, and cramming his blanket into his mouth bit it violently.[14]

Toonda's behaviour is particularly interesting. As a 'Darling native,' he was approaching his own country. Although his relations with the Aboriginal people so far encountered had been friendly enough (if marked by aloofness), now he was among people who were known to him, not as close kin, but as people with whom he may have had contingent relationships involving risk and conflict, perhaps concerning trade or even marriage. In this sense, they were among the most potentially dangerous people in Toonda's social universe. He may already have been under some obligation to right a past wrong with them; failure to do so may have placed him in a difficult position with his own group upon his eventual return to his country. Such a circumstance would explain his exhortation to Sturt to 'shoot the Natives,' fulfiling his obligation while excusing himself from direct culpability. Other instances of Europeans on the frontier being enlisted by partisan Aboriginal groups to settle disputes have been recorded. The explorer and anthropologist Alfred Howitt was in Diyari country at Lake Hope in 1861. There a senior Diyari man, Jalina-piramurana, requested Howitt to 'go with him and kill all the "Kunabura-kana," that is, the men of Kunabura, who were "*Malingki kana*," that is, bad men.'[15]

As Sturt's party neared Toonda's own territory, his guide's behaviour towards the expedition party itself took a new turn. Sturt recorded this event without understanding its true significance:

The dogs killed a Kangaroo today, which was put on the Cart. When we arrived in Camp it was cut up and Jones came for one of the legs for the Dogs on which Toonda flew into a violent rage. [']Sheep yours['] said he [']kangaroo mine['], and he lifted his waddy at Jones as he was going away, but I gave him a sharp rebuke, but as it is[,] these people tho exceedingly fond of their children treat their wives & dogs most abominably.[16]

Aborigines and Exploring Expeditions   99

Sturt misinterpreted Toonda's anger and clearly had not learnt from the earlier incident involving Nadbuck. In the first place, now that Toonda was nearing his own country, he regarded all game killed in this vicinity as his own, over which he exerted primary rights. Sturt's sheep were distinguishable in this respect though, and in his expedition narrative Sturt pressed the point, refusing Toonda his usual share of a sheep killed for meat that evening on the grounds that 'according to his own shewing, he had no claim to any.' Toonda was 'astonished.'[17]

'OFTEN QUITE INEXPLICABLE': THREE FORMS OF REPULSION

If Aboriginal forms of response to European expeditions were rarely predictable at the time, they can be understood in hindsight. These responses ranged from outright and studied avoidance, first noted by Cook and by members of the First Fleet at Botany Bay and Port Jackson, to effusive hospitality, and apparently unprovoked violence. And while the analysis of such encounters may be partially successful today in uncovering a coherent logic or set of protocols underpinning these various reactions and responses, there is no doubt that nineteenth-century explorers found the matter baffling. Edward Eyre put it in these terms:

> The natives, generally, are a strange and singular race of people, and their customs and habits are often quite inexplicable to us. Sometimes, in barely passing through a country, we have them gathering from all quarters, and surrounding us, anxious and curious to observe our persons, or actions; at other times, we may remain in camp for weeks together without seeing a single native, though many may be in the neighbourhood; when they do come, too, they usually depart as suddenly as their visit had been unexpected.[18]

Charles Sturt had become familiar enough with Aboriginal meeting protocols on the Murray and Darling Rivers to expect similar codes of encounter in the arid interior. Instead he was soon frustrated by apparent inconsistency and resolved to discourage Aboriginal encounters of any sort. Other explorers, such as Ernest Giles or John McDouall Stuart, in Central Australia were met with apparently blatant hostility, which was answered in turn either with sustained fire, by Giles, or with cautious avoidance and restraint on the part of Stuart. In most cases explorers were left with little time to reflect on what had gone wrong, although several were sanguine enough about the generality of the reaction, rationalizing it simply in terms of their incursion into Aboriginal land.

The notion that hostility to the presence of explorers was a predictable, 'default' reaction on the part of Aborigines has been generally assumed by historians. As a result, little detailed analysis of frontier interactions has been undertaken. In fact, the evidence suggests that benign responses marked by curiosity, forms of hospitality, and exchange were even more characteristic of expeditionary encounters. In that light, it is worth attempting closer analysis of episodes of hostility, fear, and aversion. It becomes apparent that for a people whose menfolk were never unarmed and were always on their guard against attack, encounters with complete strangers carried the potential for hostility and violence. And yet such encounters were more normally channelled towards mediation through the series of protocols discussed above. If the immediacy or shock of encounter meant that those protocols were unavailable, hostility might indeed become the default reaction.

To take some of the most extreme and apparently inexplicable reactions on the colonial frontier—those moments of extreme fear and fright recorded in several exploration journals—it becomes clear that basic misapprehension was often a root cause. John Oxley's exploration journal provides at least three examples of these moments, in which the unprecedented appearance of Europeans occurred under such circumstances that Aboriginal people initially had no alternative but to perceive them as personified forms of their most extreme, nightmarish folk beliefs. Oxley's 1817 and 1818 accounts show how an apparently irredeemable situation could be unlocked, taking a turn towards creative accommodation in which

Figure 5.3 'Natives Robbing the Blacksmith, While the Old Men Chanted a Hymn or Song' shows the expeditionary party as a source of new commodities. Plate 15 of *Three Expeditions Into the Interior of Eastern Australia*, vol. 1, 1839. Engraving by G. Barnard from a drawing by T. Mitchell. By Permission of Barr Smith Library, University of Adelaide.

Aborigines and Exploring Expeditions 101

Aboriginal people and Europeans might collaborate. Revealingly, as in numerous similar circumstances, it was the deployment of objects—game and European axes in this instance—that shifted the encounter into a new mode, allowing Aboriginal people and Europeans to understand the other first as human, and second as individuals, even sharing allegiance towards a totemic bird, the emu.

> Hearing the noise of the stone-hatchet made by a native in climbing a tree, we stole silently upon him, and surprised him just as he was about to descend: he did not perceive us until we were immediately under the tree; his terror and astonishment were extreme. We used every friendly motion in our power to induce him to descend, but in vain: he kept calling loudly, as we supposed for some of his companions to come to his assistance; in the mean time he threw down to us the game he had procured (a ring-tailed opossum), making signs for us to take it up: in a short time another native came towards us, when the other descended from the tree. They trembled excessively, and, if the expression may be used, were absolutely intoxicated with fear, displayed in a thousand antic motions, convulsive laughing, and singular motions of the head. They were both youths not exceeding twenty years of age, of good countenance and figure . . . The man who had joined us, had three or four small opossums and a snake, which he laid upon the ground, and offered us. We led them to our tent, where their surprise at every thing they saw clearly showed that we were the first white men they had met with; they had however either heard of or seen tomahawks for upon giving one to one of them, he clasped it to his breast and demonstrated the greatest pleasure. After admiring it for some time they discovered the broad arrow, with which it was marked on both sides, the impression of which exactly resembles that made by the foot of the emu; it amused them extremely, and they frequently pointed to it and the emu skins which we had with us.[19]

In other instances there was simply no possibility of suppressing or dissipating this sense of fear. On 27 June 1818 Oxley happened upon a group of women and children:

> I returned to my party, and in company with them surprised the native camp; we found there eight women and twelve children, just on the point of departing with their infants in their cloaks on their backs: on seeing us, they seized each other by the hand, formed a circle, and threw themselves on the ground, with their heads and faces covered. Unwilling to add to their evident terror, we only remained a few minutes, during which time the children frequently peeped at us from beneath their clothes; indeed, they seemed more surprised than alarmed: the mothers kept uttering a low and mournful cry, as if entreating mercy.[20]

102   *Philip Jones*

But there were usually options of some kind, even *in extremis*, and even when flight was not possible. One option was a ritual display of hostility, such as Oxley observed during explorations in June 1818. His journal suggests that once this mode was entered, it could persist:

> One of the men, who was some distance ahead of the horses, saw a large party of the natives, who fled at his approach, and swam the river; there were upwards of twenty men, besides women and children: the moment they were safely across, they brandished their waddies and spears in token of defiance: this was the first time any of the natives were seen armed, or in any way hostilely inclined.

Then, the following day,

> as we were on the point of setting forward, a large party of natives made their appearance on the opposite side of the river: they set up a most hideous and discordant noise, making signs, as well as we could understand them, for us to depart and go down the river. After beating their spears and waddies together for about a quarter of an hour, accompanied by no friendly gestures, they went away up the river, while we pursued our course in an opposite direction.[21]

Another immediate reaction involved attempts to create a barrier of fire against exploration parties by setting grass or bushes alight. This reaction is documented in the exploration record on numerous occasions, particularly in northern Australia. It was often employed by Aboriginal women who carried fire-sticks during their daily rounds of food gathering, and while flushing out small game and lizards.

Aboriginal women's reaction to the expeditionary presence is a topic in its own right. Women were often kept apart from initial contacts between visiting Aboriginal groups, and this convention was certainly applied when European expedition parties were nearby. More than a hint of this reticence by Aboriginal women is contained in the following passage, taken from George B. Worgan's 1788 journal at Port Jackson:

> Captn Hunter, in one of his Excursions up the Harbour met with a Tribe of ye Natives, among whom, were a Number of these Warlike Eroes, and while One or two of ye Elderly Civilians advanced towards Him, these, stood at a Distance drawn up in somewhat a regular Disposition, each having a green Bough in his Hand (an Emblem of Peace among these People). Captain Hunter had invited them to come and take some Bawbles which he held out, but he refused to give them to the Old Men who had come up to Him, making Signs, that he wished to give them to the Women (whom, he saw a small distance behind the Warriors). The old Fellows finding he would not give the Presents to them, hollowed

to the Women in a stern Voice, on which, a young, attended by an old Woman (after being called to 3 or 4 times) came forth, but showed evident signs & Emotions of Shyness & Timidity in advancing to take the Presents from Capn Hunter's hand. They suffered (but not without trembling exceedingly), the Beads to be tied about their Necks & Wrists, this being done, they retired back behind the Guard.[22]

It seems that the sudden and inadvertent exposure of Aboriginal women to expedition parties produced more extreme reactions of fear than in the case of Aboriginal men. It appears that at least some ritual displays of male hostility, which halted expedition parties, were intended to alter their course so as to protect main camps in which women and children were located.

From the visits of early Dutch explorers onward, Aboriginal people invariably encountered European men, rather than women, in their meetings with expeditions. It has been observed that this presented Aborigines with a skewed view of European culture and society from the outset. This is true, but we should bear in mind that most groups of 'stranger Aborigines' encountered in pre-European Australia were also almost invariably male. Aboriginal men may have been most surprised to find European women among visitors to their country, although that assumption did not prevent Aboriginal people attempting to undress members of exploration parties in an effort to establish their sex beyond doubt, as occurred during Baudin's expedition to Tasmania in 1801.

Despite the ordinary reticence of Aboriginal women during their first encounters with Europeans, they were already accustomed to being 'deployed' in partnerships and strategic alignments within Aboriginal society itself, particularly in polygamous relationships organized by older men. Not surprisingly, Aboriginal women were offered to European explorers, under a range of circumstances. Sturt and Mitchell, and members of their expeditions, were each offered the services of Aboriginal women during their overnight camps; this probably represented an extension of the hospitality that Aboriginal hosts would ordinarily extend to visitors passing through their country. In other cases, as documented by Ernest Giles in Central Australia, it seems that women were deployed strategically as a means of gathering intelligence about the exploration parties, their assets, and their susceptibility to attack or robbery.

FROM 'STUDIED INDIFFERENCE' TO INCORPORATION

A final category of Aboriginal reaction to the unexpected appearance of European expedition parties can be described as that of 'studied indifference.' Europeans found this attitude difficult to understand, observing it among the very first reactions to the arrival of Cook's *Endeavour*, and then

104 *Philip Jones*

more particularly in the vicinity of Port Jackson during 1788. The master of the *Supply*, David Blackburn, described the phenomenon in a letter to his sister: 'They seem to have no Curiosity for they will scarce take off their observation from fishing in their Canoes whilst a Ship has Passed close by them in full sail.'[23] The botanist William Carron wrote in 1848, 'just as we were about to start this morning, two natives, carrying a bundle of reeds and a basket, passed within a short distance of our camp, and seemed to take no notice of us.'[24] There are many other examples in explorers' journals from across the country. The historian Alan Moorehead has suggested that Aboriginal people were simply unable to cope with the enormity of a new reality impinging on their own; 'the sight of the Endeavour meant nothing to these primitives because it was too strange, too monstrous, to be comprehended.'[25] Certainly, this explanation seems to accord with the fact that concepts of the 'dreaming,' peopled by a panoply of mythological ancestors, demons, and other apparitions, were employed often enough in daily life for Aboriginal people to interpret the presence of mounted horsemen, sailing ships, and strange animals as concomitant, if alien, elements of this strange spirit world, and that an appropriate response was to lower one's gaze and simply wait until the apparition removed itself. This appears to have been the strategy adopted by the unfortunate Aboriginal man who had wandered into Leichhardt's camp. By remaining absolutely immobile, he hoped that the nightmare scene around him would pass like a storm. Oxley's encounter with the tree-climbing possum hunter was similar. He also froze in the first instance. But when the apparitions did not disappear, both men entered a second phase of reaction, more characteristic of first encounters, in which they harangued the white men as if they were interlopers who would eventually turn tail. Only when that possibility was exhausted did the Aboriginal men cornered by Oxley entertain a third option, that of dealing directly with the Europeans as though they were, after all, human.

Encounters between Aboriginal people and European expeditions could progress or degenerate in this way, from one mode to another. Particular European expedition leaders such as Grey, Sturt, or Stuart seemed gifted with enough sensibility to perceive or manage these shifts. Explorers such as Mitchell were able to manage some encounters well, yet ruined other opportunities. Luck or happenstance played a role in almost all cases. Sufficient numbers of these encounters have been recorded in enough detail to point towards an ideal, in which Aboriginal people and Europeans were drawn together, initially by structured protocols, and then, often following an exchange of objects, into a form of engagement or mutual recognition. Indeed, the trajectory of pre-European Aboriginal encounters usually followed such a course, despite the apparent hostility of initial displays of anger between two groups of 'strangers.' This bias towards reconciliation can be detected in many exploration accounts of contact, and makes particular sense when it is remembered that for many Aboriginal groups the first Europeans were perceived as the ghosts of departed relatives in tangible

Aborigines and Exploring Expeditions 105

form. The experience of George Grey in Northwestern Australia during his 1837 expedition is particularly apposite here, for Grey was recognized in just this manner by an elderly woman:

> At last the old lady, emboldened by my submission, deliberately kissed me on each cheek, just in the manner a French woman would have done; she then cried a little more and, at length relieving me, assured me that I was the ghost of her son who had some time before been killed by a spear-wound in his breast. The younger female was my sister; but she, whether from motives of delicacy or from any imagined backwardness on my part, did not think proper to kiss me.
>
> My new mother expressed almost as much delight at my return to my family as my real mother would have done had I been unexpectedly restored to her. As soon as she left me my brothers and father (the old man who had previously been so frightened) came up and embraced me after their manner, that is, they threw their arms round my waist, placed their right knee against my right knee, and their breast against my breast, holding me in this way for several minutes. During the time that the ceremony lasted I, according to the native custom, preserved a grave and mournful expression of countenance.
>
> This belief, that white people are the souls of departed blacks, is by no means an uncommon superstition amongst them; they themselves, never having an idea of quitting their own land, cannot imagine others doing it; and thus, when they see white people suddenly appear in their country, and settling themselves down in particular spots, they imagine that they must have formed an attachment for this land in some other state of existence; and hence conclude the settlers were at one period black men, and their own relations. Likenesses either real or imagined complete the delusion; and from the manner of the old woman I have just alluded to, from her many tears, and from her warm caresses, I feel firmly convinced that she really believed I was her son, whose first thought upon his return to earth had been to re-visit his old mother, and bring her a present.[26]

For Aboriginal people whose experience of Europeans was confined to small groups passing through their country with no obvious intention to stay, and with no apparent family structures that might signal that intention more clearly, fraternization and incorporation were dominant and fruitful modes of interaction. This brought ready access to the extraordinary array of goods borne by Europeans, and it helped to guarantee their return. Of course, if Aboriginal people could predict the eventual consequences of this interaction, other modes of engagement might have been preferred, including hostility and outright violence. In the meantime, until the grim consequences of European contact emerged, the frontier remained a theatrical stage for interaction, characterized by a light, contingent character of

106 *Philip Jones*

chance, personality, and circumstance. One historical vignette, dating from John McDouall Stuart's final, successful crossing of the continent from 1861–2 conveys this sense of an incomplete but perfectable drama, quite at odds with received versions of the way frontier history played itself out. Attack Creek, near Tennant Creek, had been the scene of the affray that terminated Stuart's fourth expedition, and that looms large in many contemporary versions of frontier history as characteristic of the colonial period. But here is Auld's account of another encounter with Warramungu people at this place, just a few months later:

> At Attack Creek Thring and I were washing some of our scanty wardrobe, about 200 yards from camp, when suddenly a tall blackfellow made his appearance. He came up to us, and after talking and making signs he untied the lace of my boot. Then I made signs to him to take it off, which he did, and he gave a whistle. Next he took off the stocking, gave another whistle, and tried to peel off more. I made signs to him to replace them, which he did, doing up the lace and tying it in a bow the same as it was before. He seemed very much astonished at the whole process. We packed up our clothes, bade him a most polite good-day, and returned to camp.[27]

Perhaps the most remarkable aspect of this quotation, and of others that pepper the Australian exploration literature, is its matter-of-fact delivery. At this moment in frontier relations the idea that Aboriginal people and Europeans might go to lengths to explore or sample each other's worlds without undue prejudice remained feasible, even unremarkable.

NOTES

1. Dane Kennedy, *The Last Blank Spaces: Exploring Africa and Australia* (Cambridge, MA: Harvard University Press, 2013), 212.
2. George Augustus Robinson, *The Journals of George Augustus Robinson, Chief Protector, Port Phillip Aboriginal Protectorate*, vol. 2, ed. Ian D. Clark (Melbourne: Heritage Matters, 1998), entry for 6 June 1841.
3. Erving Goffman, *Encounters: Two Studies in the Sociology of Interaction* (Indianapolis: Bobbs-Merrill Company, 1961).
4. Frédéric Regard, ed., *British Narratives of Exploration: Case Studies of the Self and Other* (London: Pickering and Chatto, 2009), 4.
5. See, for example, Jerry D. Moore, 'Marshall Sahlins: Culture Matters,' in *Visions of Culture: An Introduction to Anthropological Theories and Theorists*, ed. Jerry D. Moore (Walnut Creek, CA: Altamira, 2009), 365–85.
6. John Oxley, *Journals of Two Expeditions Into the Interior of New South Wales, Undertaken by Order of the British Government in the Years 1817–18*, Appendix, Part I (London: John Murray, 1820), 360–1.
7. Ludwig Leichhardt, *Journal of an Overland Expedition in Australia from Moreton Bay to Port Essington, a Distance of Upwards of 3000 Miles, During the Years 1844–1845* (London: T. & W. Boone, 1847), 319–23.

Aborigines and Exploring Expeditions 107

8. On encountering John McDouall Stuart's 1858 expedition to the west of Lake Torrens, a similarly terrified Aboriginal man leapt up into a mulga tree: 'the poor fellow trembled from head to foot and could not utter a word.' John McDouall Stuart, 'Exploration in Australia,' *South Australian Parliamentary Paper*, no. 119 (1858).

9. T. L. Mitchell, 'Three Expeditions Into the Interior of Eastern Australia with Descriptions of the Recently Explored Region of Australia Felix, and of the Present Colony of New South Wales, vol. 1,' in *Journal of an Expedition Sent to Explore the Course of the River Darling, in 1835, by Order of the British Government*, 2nd rev. ed. (London: T. & W. Boone, 1839), 194.

10. William Carron, *Narrative of an Expedition, Undertaken Under the Direction of the Late Mr. Assistant Surveyor E. B. Kennedy, for the Exploration of the Country Lying Between Rockingham Bay and Cape York* (Sydney: Kemp and Fairfax, 1849), 3.

11. Oxley, *Journals*, Part I (25 April 1817), 8.

12. Mitchell, *Three Expeditions*, vol. 1 (1839), frontispiece.

13. Richard C. Davis, *The Central Australian Expedition, 1844–46: The Journals of Charles Sturt* (London: Hakluyt Society, 2002), 41–2.

14. Ibid., 42.

15. Alfred Howitt, *The Native Tribes of South-East Australia* (London: MacMillan, 1904), 299.

16. Davis, *The Central Australian Expedition*, 43.

17. Charles Sturt, *Narrative of an Expedition Into Central Australia Performed Under the Authority of Her Majesty's Government, During the Years 1844, 5, and 6: Together With a Notice of the Province of South Australia in 1847*, vol. 1 (London: T. & W. Boone, 1849), 112–3.

18. Edward Eyre, *Journals of Expeditions of Discovery Into Central Australia, and Overland from Adelaide to King George's Sound, in the Years 1840–1; Sent by the Colonists of South Australia, with the Sanction and Support of the Government: Including an Account of the Manners and Customs of the Aborigines and the State of their Relations with Europeans*, vol. 1 (London: T. & W. Boone, 1845), 318.

19. Oxley, *Journals*, Part I (14 August 1817), 171–2.

20. Oxley, *Journals*, Part II (27 June 1818), 236.

21. Oxley, *Journals*, Part II (17 & 18 June 1818), 224–6.

22. George B. Worgan, *Journal of a First Fleet Surgeon* (Sydney: Library Council of New South Wales, 1978), entry for 24 February 1788, 15.

23. Letter from David Blackburn to Margaret Blackburn, 15 November 1788, from HMS *Supply*, Sydney Cove, Port Jackson, N.S.W., David Blackburn Papers and Letters, ML MSS 6937/1/1, Mitchell Library, Sydney, AU.

24. Carron, *Narrative of an Expedition*, entry for 28 September 1848, 55.

25. Alan Moorehead, *The Fatal Impact: An Account of the Invasion of the South Pacific, 1767–1840* (New York: Harper & Row, 1966), 104.

26. George Grey, 'At Swan River,' chap. XIII in *Journals Of Two Expeditions Of Discovery In North-West and Western Australia, During The Years 1837, 1838, And 1839, Under The Authority Of Her Majesty's Government. Describing Many Newly Discovered, Important, And Fertile Districts, With Observations On The Moral And Physical Condition Of The Aboriginal Inhabitants, Etc. Etc.*, vol. 1 (London: T. & W. Boone, 1841), 301–3.

27. W. P. Auld, 'Through the Australian Continent: A Story of Stuart's Trip, –No. III,' *South Australian Register*, 5 February 1891, 6, http://nla.gov.au/nla.news-article48089336.

6 Expeditions, Encounters, and the Praxis of Seaborne Ethnography
The French Voyages of La Pérouse and Freycinet

Bronwen Douglas

Derived from the Latin *expeditio*, 'a voyage of war,' the word 'expedition' had roughly parallel usages in French and English from the fifteenth century. In English by the early seventeenth century, it might mean 'a journey, voyage, or excursion made for some definite purpose.' In French by 1835 it could specifically denote a 'maritime expedition.'[1] This chapter treats an expedition in this sense as an extended theatre for the enactment of diverse amalgams of preconception, expectation, precedent, instruction, and emotion in the experiential context of encounters with particular places and their human, faunal, and floral inhabitants. My discussion addresses one strand of a particular subset of maritime expeditions—those to the 'fifth part of the world,' or 'Oceania,' during the classic era of scientific voyaging from 1766 to 1840. The strand is encounters with indigenous people as inscribed in the specialised literary mode of seaborne ethnography, defined as the empirical observations and representations of human populations seen or met by sailors, naturalists, and artists.[2] My examples draw on written and visual materials generated by two French voyages: the ill-starred Enlightenment expedition of Jean-François de Galaup, comte de La Pérouse (1785–8), and the expedition led by Louis de Saulces de Freycinet (1817–20) at the dawn of the post-Napoleonic phase of scientific voyaging.

The chapter hinges on two entwined themes. One is the asymmetric status of human encounters in principle and praxis. The official instructions issued to captains and naturalists focus heavily on the physical, nautical, and natural sciences, with ethnographic enquiry only a minor concern. Questions of human relations are mostly limited to pragmatic injunctions to avoid conflict or inhumane treatment of local inhabitants in order to facilitate the critical replenishment of wood, water, and food supplies.[3] However, in practice, encounters with indigenous people during stopovers ashore were axial in voyagers' experience and figured largely in their representations, whether unpublished or published. The resultant empirical cornucopia of seaborne ethnography underpins my second, overarching theme: the significance of 'the expedition' as a key setting for the early production of knowledge about the populations of Oceania. Often produced for its own sake (the scientific motive), such knowledge provided precedents for subsequent travellers,

The Voyages of La Pérouse and Freycinet 109

served as a practical resource for colonisers, and was ultimately exploited by ethnohistorians. I conceive the creation of ethnographic knowledge as dialogic, since voyagers' representations were profoundly affected by indigenous agency during actual encounters.

Louis-Antoine de Bougainville's first French global circumnavigation on the frigate *Boudeuse* and the storeship *Etoile* during 1766–9 is commonly credited as the inaugural scientific voyage. Yet it is not among my case studies because it had no explicitly scientific goals beyond geographical reconnaissance, despite Bougainville's recruitment of the civilian naturalist Philibert Commerson. Bougainville's official instructions paraphrase his own proposal for such a voyage. With respect to the Pacific Ocean, they emphasise 'perfecting' knowledge of 'the lands lying between the Indies and the west coast of America' and acquiring possessions 'useful' to French commerce and navigation in a region where no European nation had either establishment or rights.[4] His narrative of the voyage is ethnographically very rich and earned him much popular acclaim, but little scientific acknowledgement.[5] Commerson's outstanding botanical collections remained virtually unknown and neither his shipboard journal nor his scattered ethnographic notes were published until the 1970s.[6] His only significant contemporary publication on the voyage is a notorious letter propagating the primitivist myth of the 'happy island' of Tahiti as a social and sexual paradise, the abode of 'natural man,' 'without vices, prejudices, needs, or dissensions,' who knew 'no other God but Love.'[7]

'SAD EXPERIENCE': LA PÉROUSE AND *'L'HOMME DE LA NATURE'*

The first explicitly scientific French voyage, that of La Pérouse on the frigates *Boussole* and *Astrolabe* during 1785–8, sailed with 17 'savants and artists,' among them the senior surgeon-anthropologist Claude-Nicolas Rollin and the portrait and landscape artist Gaspard Duché de Vancy. Unlike Bougainville, La Pérouse was if anything overburdened by directives, notably a 'Memoir from the King' at least partly composed by Louis XVI himself.[8] This five-part 'special instruction' comprises the proposed itinerary of the voyage; an outline of its political and commercial purpose, a set of scientific instructions, a section on 'conduct' towards 'savage peoples and the natives' of places visited, and a final section on measures to preserve the crews' health. Ethnography is a minor theme, though the second section includes an injunction to study *les mœurs et les usages* (the lifestyle and customs) and the 'distinctive character' of Pacific Islanders encountered. The scientific instructions mainly address the physical sciences requisite to a successful 'voyage of discovery,' intended to 'perfect geography and extend navigation.' But they conclude with brief nods to natural history and ethnography. The travellers were to observe the 'genius, character, lifestyle, customs, temperament, language, diet and number of inhabitants' at the various ports of

110   *Bronwen Douglas*

call and 'collect and classify' samples of their clothing and artefacts. The artists should draw their portraits and depict their 'dress, ceremonies, games, buildings, sailing vessels.' The fourth section enjoined that 'the natives' be treated with 'benevolence,' 'honest means,' 'good behaviour,' 'consideration,' 'mildness,' and 'humanity.' However, 'every precaution' consistent with prudence should be taken to maintain French 'superiority' against local weight of numbers. The use of force 'with the greatest moderation' was countenanced only to obtain desperately needed supplies or as a final defensive resort.

Among the appendices to the king's instructions are two documents explicitly directed to the savants: a *Mémoire* from the Académie des Sciences and a series of questions submitted by the Société de Médecine.[9] With respect to the study of man, both texts straddle the contemporary schism in natural history between traditional environmentalist and emergent innatist explanations for perceived collective human difference.[10] On the one hand, they endorse the methods and principles of the renowned French naturalist Georges-Louis Leclerc, comte de Buffon, who steadfastly attributed unstable human diversity to the varied impact of climate, milieu, and lifestyle on a single migrating species.[11] On the other, they advocate a broad program of physical anthropology grounded in comparative anatomy.[12] The *Mémoire* of the Académie des Sciences strongly emphasises the cosmographic and physical sciences. However, in two-and-a-half pages of the 23 devoted to anatomy and zoology, travellers are counselled to extend the comparison of the 'several varieties of the human species'—Buffon's innovation—beyond the usual description of 'external characters.' They should instead undertake 'anatomical' research into 'internal' variations in the 'form of the bones of the head' of representative corpses from 'nations' that obviously differed in facial or cranial shape from those of the 'temperate countries of Europe'— an allusion to Buffon's climate theory. The questions posed by the Société de Médecine are primarily medical, but begin with a general section on 'Structure of the human body, and functions of its organs,' which demands 'more exactitude' in the observation of human bodies in different countries. Specific attention should be paid to bodily proportions; skin colour; the 'particular form' of the head, skull, face, and hair; bodily 'deformation' and its likely origin in 'natural organization' or 'particular practices;' the 'comparative strength' of different groups, especially those who had not been 'weakened' by the *mollesse* (softness) induced in 'policed nations;' and the relationship of skin colour to that of the humours—as manifest in spermatic fluid, brain tissue, and blood—in different climates. These questions intersperse modern anatomical concerns with references to contemporary primitivist critique of civilisation, venerable humoral physiology, and climate theory.[13]

The demise of La Pérouse's expedition by shipwreck in 1788 limited its documentary legacy to those materials he dispatched to France during visits to Kamchatka and Botany Bay (Figure 6.1).[14] From an Oceanic perspective,

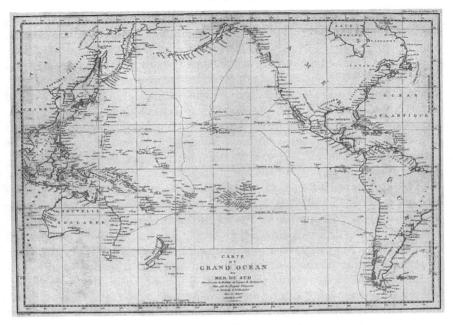

Figure 6.1 Pierre-François Tardieu, *Carte du grand océan ou mer du Sud dressée pour la Relation du voyage de découvertes faites par les frégates françaises la Boussole et l'Astrolabe dans les années 1785, 86, 87 et 88*, 1797, engraving. By Permission of David Rumsey Map Collection (image 3355003, www.davidrumsey.com).

the texts record fleeting encounters with the inhabitants of Rapa Nui (Easter Island), Maui (Hawaiian Islands), and Tutuila (Samoan Islands). In contemporary terms, this seaborne ethnography constituted an important body of anthropological knowledge about unfamiliar populations and their productions. In three memoirs appended to La Pérouse's published narrative, the surgeon Rollin addressed the questions posed by the Société de Médecine. Unable to respond with 'all the extent and precision' demanded with respect to the Easter Islanders and the Hawaiians of Maui, since he had spent only 'a few hours' ashore on both islands, he gave instead a 'succinct idea of the natives' and an overview of their diseases. Self-consciously ethnocentric, Rollin described a 'quite numerous' population in Easter Island in 1786, 'with a better share of grace and beauty than all those' he had since met, including the Hawaiians. 'The face' was no different from that of Europeans, apart from its 'tanned' colour. They generally appeared healthy. He admired the women's 'conformation,' 'polish,' 'grace,' and the 'mildness' and 'finesse' of their features that, skin tone aside, were 'beautiful' by European standards. Shifting momentarily from physical to behavioural traits, Rollin remarked that the men were eager to 'traffic' the women's 'favours' and to seize the strangers' property, especially their hats, mocking them in the process. He

112 *Bronwen Douglas*

commented briefly on their 'industry,' diet, and the great enigmatic statues or *moai* that remain the island's global signature.[15] His two other memoirs, on 'the Americans' and the inhabitants of the island of Sakhalin and the nearby East Asian mainland, show the benefit of longer stopovers since both texts end with a comparative table of bodily proportions. He listed precisely the places and latitudes where measurements were taken and outlined the method used. This anthropometric research, demanded by the Société de Médecine, inspired Rollin to an entirely Buffonian conclusion: 'There are differences in the constitution of these peoples that are developed or remarkably modified by climate, exercise, lifestyle, and even prejudices.'[16]

In contrast to Rollin's professional emphasis on physical anthropology, La Pérouse's narrative, based on his shipboard journal, interweaves geography, story, and ethnography. A chapter on Easter Island follows this classic trajectory: first, 'description of the island;' then, 'events that happened to us;' and finally, 'lifestyle and customs of the inhabitants.'[17] An enlightened believer in human progress, a practical sailor, and a realist, La Pérouse was a devotee neither of the contemporary philosophers' chimera—epitomised in Commerson's letter—of innately good and happy primitive man, uncorrupted by civilisation,[18] nor of the zoologists' emergent relegation of dehumanised, racialised man to the status of anatomical taxon within the animal series. The dominant theme of the Easter Island chapter is of honourable, civilised restraint confronted and exploited by hypocritical savage 'rapacity'— that is, indigenous agency. A landing party of about 70, protected by a small military detachment 'expressly forbidden to fire,' spent 'eight or ten hours' ashore, surrounded by several hundred unarmed Islanders, including many women. Even the soldiers on duty could not resist the coquetry of the women and, before long, most of the French party had lost their hats and handkerchiefs. Duché de Vancy's whimsical depiction of the scene, engraved for the *Atlas* of La Pérouse's *Voyage* (Figure 6.2), subverts the highly formalised genre of history painting by inserting vignettes of sly local agency: on the right, a man uses a stick to pilfer the hat of an officer who is measuring a *moai*, and, in the foreground, a man extracts a handkerchief from the pocket of another officer who is distracted by a woman.[19]

'Our mildness,' La Pérouse remarked ruefully, had only 'emboldened the thieves.' However, because the French stayed so briefly, they could afford to laugh at the Islanders' tricks, rather than chastise them. He added, perhaps prophetically, that during a longer visit such actions would need to be punished to avert the 'unfortunate consequences' of a policy of 'extreme' forbearance. Indigenous agency in Easter Island, the expedition's first Pacific landfall, confirmed La Pérouse's unsentimental rejection of primitivist enthusiasm for the *bon sauvage* (noble savage). No one who had read recent voyage narratives, he wrote ironically, could 'take the Indians of the South Sea for savages'; rather, they had 'made very great progress in civilization' and were as 'corrupt' as they could possibly be. The French had only come to Easter Island to do good—heaping the Islanders with gifts, sowing useful

Figure 6.2 François Godefroy after Gaspard Duché de Vancy, *Insulaires et monumens de l'île de Pâque*, 1797, engraving. By Permission of David Rumsey Map Collection (image 3355011, www.davidrumsey.com).

seeds in their gardens, giving them pigs, goats, and sheep, and asking nothing in exchange. Yet in return, he complained, these 'hypocrites' had robbed them of everything they could lay hands on while feigning welcome and then bombarded them with stones when they tried to retrieve a stolen grapnel.[20]

La Pérouse's narrative tracks his burgeoning disillusionment in the face of what he experienced as the 'crude,' 'barbaric' behaviour and 'wicked, deceitful' character of the 'man of nature'—these words encode the incomprehensible and often repugnant agency of indigenous people he encountered during the voyage. Resolutely empirical, he invoked the evidence of 30 years as a travelling 'witness' of the 'injustices and deception of these peoples' to fuel his anger with the 'fireside' philosophers who paint them as 'so good.'[21] La Pérouse's consistent use of the substantives Indian and Islander, rather than *sauvage*, was perhaps a protest at the pastoral implications of the philosophers' use of the latter term, with its etymology in the Latin *silva* (wood, forest, woodland). Almost every appearance of the word *sauvage* in La Pérouse's narrative is aimed at refuting the beguiling idea of the *bon sauvage*. His despair and fury reached a crescendo after 11 December 1787 when members of a vast crowd in the Samoan island of Tutuila (called 'Maouna' by La Pérouse) opportunistically attacked a French watering party and killed his friend Paul-Antoine Fleuriot de Langle, captain of the *Astrolabe*, and 11 companions. La Pérouse's distress is manifest in the structure of his narrative. The previously ordered sequence of representational modes is replaced by an untidy jumble of anecdote and reflection, embodying a heartfelt quest to assign blame for the tragedy.

The two chapters on Samoa written after the catastrophe are suffused with horror and regret—overtly so in La Pérouse's reconstruction of the killings and more obliquely in supposedly objective ethnographic and geographical passages, which punctuate his prose.[22] The relationship of nature to human nature—a contemporary preoccupation—is a recurrent trope in his narrative, intimating his ambivalence with respect to the agency of savages. At Lituya Bay in Southeast Alaska, he had damned country and people alike: 'Nature owes to such a frightful country inhabitants who differ so much from civilized peoples,' 'as crude and as barbaric as their soil is stony and uncultivated.'[23] Conversely, in Samoa he drew a stark verbal contrast between 'one of the finest countries in Nature' and 'these barbaric peoples' with their 'atrocious mores' who should have been the 'happiest denizens of the earth' but were instead 'ferocious beings.' Yet Nature had not deceived but left the 'imprint' of their 'ferocity' on these men's features as a warning that 'man living in anarchy in a nearly savage state is a more vicious being than the fiercest animals.'[24] No eyewitness drawing of the Samoan episode survived the final shipwreck. However, it was luridly portrayed in a work extrapolated from La Pérouse's narrative by the marine artist Nicolas-Marie Ozanne and engraved for the *Atlas* (Figure 6.3).[25] Ozanne visualised La Pérouse's contrast

Figure 6.3 François-Nicolas-Barthelemy Dequevauviller after Nicolas-Marie Ozanne, *Massacre de MM. de Langle, Lamanon et de dix autres individus des deux équipages*, 1797, engraving. By Permission of David Rumsey Map Collection (image 3355066, www.davidrumsey.com).

The Voyages of La Pérouse and Freycinet   115

between the civilised and the barbaric by juxtaposing the island's lush tropical beauty with the dark, angular savagery of the warriors in the foreground. The white, classical figures elegantly disposed at the extreme right and left of the engraving are perhaps an ironic salute to the myth of the *bon sauvage*, otherwise graphically discredited by the lethal violence depicted.[26]

At the start of his chapters on Samoa, La Pérouse speculated whether an attempted theft should not have been punished by 'an example of severity,' which would have 'shown them how much the force of our arms outstripped their individual strength.' He again justified his restraint by the intended brevity of the visit. In the event, only 24 hours were spent ashore.[27] The physical strength of the Samoans, a potent sign of their agency, was self-evident to the French and is a reiterated theme in the narrative. Yet it is rhetorically subsumed as a natural force rather than acknowledged as a tactical weapon. These Islanders were 'the tallest and best built' people they had met, with limbs of 'colossal proportions.' La Pérouse noted that the 'curiosity' of the savants to measure Samoan bodies ironically encouraged them 'to make frequent comparisons between their physical strength and ours,' always to French disadvantage. Perhaps, he agonised, their misfortunes were due to 'the idea of individual superiority which they took from these various tests.' He read on their faces a 'disdain' that only a demonstration of French arms on 'human victims' might have obliterated.[28]

La Pérouse's forlorn efforts to explain the massacre took European initiative for granted, even when it was misjudged. He blamed Fleuriot de Langle threefold: first, for his wilful insistence on sending the watering party ashore among these 'turbulent' Islanders in a reef-strewn bay out of range of the ships' guns; second, for his imprudence in landing at low tide, which grounded the ships' boats; and third, for his 'humanity' in failing to fire on the Islanders at the first sign of hostility—'he was victim of his humanity,' grieved La Pérouse. He questioned the wisdom of French 'moderation' and adherence to 'principles of mildness and patience,' which only emboldened 'these Indians' whom fear alone could curb. His 'sad experience' had shown that the man of nature was 'barbaric, wicked, and treacherous.' He castigated himself for ceding to Fleuriot de Langle's importunities, despite his own misgivings, and for his 'rigid' observance of the caveat on the use of force in his instructions.[29] In a bizarre inversion of responsibility, he directed much sharper rage at the philosophers who 'exalted the savages' than at 'the savages themselves.' The word *sauvage* now features regularly in his lexicon. He thus allowed these Indians no more than the reflex agency of savagery, was oblivious to the certainty that Islanders' actions always had strategic local dimensions, however inscrutable, and all but expunged the reported 30 or so Samoans who died when the French returned fire. Henceforth, as he wrote bitterly in one of his last letters, European navigators 'must regard the savages as enemies, undoubtedly very weak, whom it would be ignoble to attack without motive and barbaric to destroy, but whom one has the right to pre-empt when entitled to by just suspicions.'[30]

116   *Bronwen Douglas*

In the immediate aftermath of the disaster, La Pérouse admitted that their 'reflections' on the many examples of indigenous 'perfidy' in attacks on Europeans, culminating in their own 'atrocious' recent experience, had changed French modes of action with respect to Islanders. Henceforth, they forcefully punished the smallest thefts and 'injustices' and openly demonstrated the power of their arms to kill. At Botany Bay, he had a palisade built around the French camp as a 'necessary' protection against the inhabitants who, though 'very weak and few in number,' were 'very vicious, like all savages.'[31] Indigenous agency during a particular encounter thereby had an inadvertent but profound impact on the subsequent behaviour and representations of a particular European.

More than 50 years ago, Bernard Smith made the then fantastic suggestion that Pacific Islanders had actively contributed to the reshaping of imperial fictions. By killing 'the hero of empire' James Cook, the 'noble savage . . . transformed himself into "the inglorious native."' Smith further argued that 'the death of famous navigators' in Oceania during the late eighteenth century 'did much' to shift the weight of 'European thought' from sentimental approval of savages to disgust. The latter phraseology was (and remains) less contentious because the abstract noun death focuses human agency firmly in metropolitan thought, whereas the 'noble savage' himself is the subject of the first sentence.[32] I insist, however, that if 'the expedition' was a primary conduit channelling scientific and popular knowledge about Oceania into Europe, that knowledge was often generated in, and permeated by, indigenous presence.

'IF NOT INTIMATE, AT LEAST PEACEFUL': FREYCINET IN NEW HOLLAND

La Pérouse's instructions were repeated almost verbatim for the next two French expeditions dispatched to the Pacific: those of Joseph Antoine Bruni d'Entrecasteaux, sent in search of La Pérouse during 1791–4, and Nicolas Baudin, commissioned to explore Australian waters during 1800–4. They remained a ghostly template informing the instructions issued to Freycinet in 1817 when he resumed scientific voyaging for France on the corvette *Uranie*, after the long imperial hiatus. Freycinet had been a junior officer with Baudin and co-authored the official voyage narrative.[33] His ambiguous experience of encounters with Aboriginal people in southeast Van Diemen's Land (Tasmania) set a potent precedent for his future engagements with Indigenous Australians. Freycinet's savants included the naval surgeon-naturalists Jean-René Constant Quoy and Paul Gaimard, assigned to conduct zoological and anthropological research, while the artist Jacques Arago and the artistically talented midshipman Alphonse Pellion were responsible for graphic representation. Gaimard was also a keen linguistic researcher who collected local vocabularies whenever possible.[34]

The Voyages of La Pérouse and Freycinet 117

Freycinet's official instructions emphasise that 'questions relative to the shape of the earth and the theory of the magnet' constituted the main scientific objectives of the expedition. They were implemented during a three-year campaign that followed a mainly pelagic trajectory, with few ports of call. *Uranie* crossed a vast expanse of western and central Oceania but anchored only on the west coast of New Holland (Australia), at Timor and Waigeo (eastern Indonesia), and in Guam (Micronesia), the Hawaiian Islands, and Port Jackson (Sydney). The instructions reduce the study of man to the observation or measurement of seven physical qualities 'relative to the natural history of man,' listed in an attached note on the 'natural history of animals,' prepared for the voyage by the Académie des Sciences. The voyagers are enjoined to observe the inhabitants' height, strength, agility, and speed; the proportions of their head, skull, jaws, arms, and legs; the size of their facial angle; the colour of their skin; and the length, nature, and colour of their hair and beard.[35] The anatomical bias of this brief catalogue probably signifies the input of the renowned comparative anatomist Georges Cuvier who from 1800 to 1832 dominated the natural sciences in France, exercised great influence over the embryonic discipline of anthropology, and oversaw the professional instruction and assessment of the naturalists on scientific voyages. He was a prime mover in the emergent science of race that entrenched racial inequality as an immutable product of physical organisation.[36] Freycinet reiterated the tenor of his orders, with scant mention of people, in a brief letter to his officers on 'Observations to be made aboard,' written in October 1817 in the mid-Atlantic, en route to South America.[37]

The official instructions notwithstanding, the prevailing tone and content of the texts produced by this voyage are humanist and ethnographic. They are in keeping with another, personal set of instructions issued by Freycinet to his officers in Rio de Janeiro in December 1817: a 25-page table of 'observations and researches' to be made during stopovers on land. Freycinet's two directives to his officers differ remarkably. The later document is presented as a 'plan' to control the 'labyrinth of facts' that would confront them ashore. Its eight-page core—a 193-point schedule for 'Observations on the human species'—is bracketed by 147 items on the 'history,' 'general description,' and 'productions' of countries visited and 256 items on their 'industry,' 'commerce,' and 'government.' The central, anthropological section begins with just 19 questions on man's 'physical constitution' and 'physical qualities.' Expanding the desiderata of the Académie des Sciences, these initial questions echo contemporary racial discourse by camouflaging value-laden judgements as objective science. Were there 'different races of men, whether savage or civilized'? What was their origin? Were there 'mixed races'? Was there 'elegance in their forms'? Were they 'generally attractive or ugly'? What were the proportions of their head, skull, jaws, arms, legs, and facial angle and the colour and nature of their skin and hair? Was it possible to conduct dynamometric tests and what were the results?

118   *Bronwen Douglas*

The next 30 questions restate natural history's longstanding interest in the human life cycle and diseases. The final 144 questions in Freycinet's program for the study of man abandon 'Physical relations' to focus instead on 'Domestic' and 'Moral and social relations,' with an emphasis on religion.[38] In hindsight, the document might have been intended as a prospectus for Freycinet's three-volume official *Historique* of the voyage.[39]

The science of race always correlated and conflated the physical and moral characters of races.[40] Yet Freycinet's second letter strongly implies that he paid lip service to the demands of a static physical anthropology while emphasizing personal, social, and political dynamics, ethnographic description, and milieux. This implication is confirmed by the structure and content of his *Historique* that avowedly deals only 'in passing' with 'our scientific researches' and instead focuses 'with the greatest care' on the 'lifestyle and customs' of populations encountered, consigning their physical organisation to cursory prologues.[41] The vast bulk of the text comprises lengthy, ethnocentric, often essentialised consideration of the setting, social relations, history, languages, industry, commerce, politics, and so forth of places and people visited. Its imperialist connotations are patent. However, this work is far more an ethnography and a history than a racial study in the naturalists' sense of the term 'race.'

Consistent with this ethos, the naturalist Quoy prefaced his shipboard journal with two texts. One is a relativist dictum by the Scottish civic humanist William Robertson, who noted that everywhere that a traveller 'does not find the objects of pleasure and enjoyment he is accustomed to, he boldly pronounces that the people thus deprived must be barbarous and wretched.'[42] The second is Quoy's own profession of noble intent, echoing the royal instructions to La Pérouse and the enduring precedent set by Cook: 'I swear here that I prefer to lose my life than to keep it by killing unfortunates who are only barbarous by want of judgment and civilisation and cannot always work out our intentions in landing on their shores. Cook and his companions were pitiless in this respect.'[43] Before departing on the voyage, then, Quoy clearly acknowledged the common humanity of the 'natives' he expected to meet and attributed their behaviour to external circumstances or level of civilisation, rather than to their physical organisation. In other words, his agenda at this point was more Buffonian than Cuvierian.

Throughout the Oceanic campaign of the *Uranie*, the French enjoyed relatively friendly relations with the indigenous people they encountered. In September 1818, the expedition spent two weeks doing research on hydrography and natural history at the Baie des Chiens-marins (Shark Bay) on the 'desolate shores' of western New Holland.[44] French representations of a single, fleeting encounter with the local inhabitants on 15 September exemplify the mutual curiosity, caution, desire, and apprehension aroused. Just such an emotional amalgam was openly vented in the widely read travelogue of the artist Arago who described his reaction to news that 'the savages' had appeared. Avid to see them and certain of 'our superiority over them,' he nonetheless recognised the 'dangers' they posed. He was 'enchanted' by the hope of 'making friends with them' sufficiently to learn interesting details about their 'wretched existence' and to glean 'anecdotes' or 'grotesque and curious scenes' that would embellish his book with its atlas of plates. He sought to enhance the verisimilitude of his art by confirming 'the character of their physiognomy' and the 'marks' on their bodies.[45] Such more or less transient encounters were seedbeds of seaborne ethnography. The not inconsiderable attention paid to this meeting in the texts of Freycinet's voyage tallies with his ethnographic emphasis and expressed belief that the 'anecdotal part' of his narrative would 'doubtless appeal to the greatest number of readers.'[46]

Unlike several of his companions, Quoy personally saw no local people at Shark Bay. But his journal includes a three-page anecdotal and ethnographic segment on 'these poor inhabitants of this thankless land,' based on accounts by some of his shipmates who made 'if not intimate, at least peaceful' contact with a 'troop' of 15 'savages,' mostly men but with a few women and children.[47] Freycinet, who spied only a handful of men in the distance, published Pellion's eyewitness description of the encounter in his *Historique*. Arago gave another eyewitness account in his travelogue while his pencil drawing (Figure 6.4) was engraved for the *Atlas historique* of

Figure 6.4 Jacques Arago, *Première entrevue avec les sauvages*, 1927, collotype of pencil drawing. By permission of National Library of Australia (an11510415).

120 Bronwen Douglas

the voyage.[48] Pellion's report shows clearly that the Europeans' reactions or actions were largely dictated by the behaviour or demands of the indigenous men who had suddenly appeared on an escarpment behind the French camp and 'obviously' gestured to them to return to the ship. Remembering earlier voyagers' dire accounts of the inhabitants of 'this inhospitable land,' Pellion imagined he was about to confront 'audacious, cruel men.' But he quickly reassessed them as 'timid beings.' Nonetheless, the French remained constantly alert and tried various tactics to 'calm' and befriend their visitors. They made them laugh by dancing in a circle, proffered gifts, put down their arms, lay on the ground, and ignored them. However, the men refused to allow the sailors to come too close and insisted that gifts be left in the gap between the parties. Some items pleased them: a piece of tin plate that shone in the sun, a lump of lard that they intended not to eat but to rub on their bodies, a mirror, a pair of white drawers that they tore apart and divided amongst themselves, a brightly coloured scarf in return for which they gave Pellion a spear and another weapon. Even-handed Pellion admired their naturally musical whistling, their very expressive gestures, the 'good understanding' that seemed to reign amongst them, and the 'respect' they showed for a woman and child.[49]

Arago, who arrived late to this encounter, sensationalised the episode in sketch and word. Ironic and histrionic, he made himself the central figure and demeaned the indigenous protagonists. His drawing shows the artist playing the castanets as several naked men caper in 'so grotesque a manner, that we choked with laughter.' Meanwhile, another man strikes a spear with two sticks 'without keeping time or caring that he didn't.'[50] An officer proffers beads in one outstretched hand and with the other drapes a piece of cloth over the end of a spear, held at arm's length by another naked man. The entire scene is disingenuous. Arago's own text, as well as Pellion's, makes it clear that the castanet playing was peripheral. Pellion noted the rhythm with which the drummer accompanied the castanets and reported the dancing they inspired without derisive comment. Arago's visual trope of exchange at the end of a spear is absent from his written travelogue but became iconic. Although Quoy neither witnessed the action nor mentioned it in his journal, he much later made it racially emblematic of 'clearly the most degraded species on earth, at the last rung of humanity.'[51] Yet this method of transferring objects was only one of several modes of exchange described at the time by Pellion, who reflexively inverted the agency involved in a way unflattering to the French. 'On several occasions they threw us their spears, inviting us by gestures to attach our presents to them and send them back; at the same time they showed us how to do it. We did what they desired, no doubt awkwardly since they seemed to make fun of us.'[52]

Freycinet's *Historique* contains two chapters on Shark Bay. One is descriptive and anecdotal, including Pellion's account of the 'meeting with the savages.'[53] The other is a 17-page scientific overview with substantial sections on physics and geology, botany and zoology.[54] That a mere two pages are

The Voyages of La Pérouse and Freycinet   121

devoted to the 'Human species' epitomises the inconsequentiality of physical anthropology in the overall scheme of the narrative. Freycinet represented the 'sparse' population of Shark Bay in two different registers. He began with his own timeless, though not unfriendly, generalisation in the ethnographic present tense, taking stereotyped 'Negro' features as his yardstick: 'All the natives are of medium height,' with 'very thin' extremities, narrow shoulders, big head, large mouth, fine teeth, lively eyes, fairly long, black, 'lightly frizzy' hair, and 'features less flat than those of the Madagascan and Mozambican blacks.' He then cited Pellion's matter-of-fact eyewitness pen portraits of a 'single young woman' and 'several men,' 'whom we saw' at closer quarters. Pellion particularised them as individuals using the past tense but included the casual, essentialist judgement that 'these savages' were 'perhaps the most wretched beings in existence.'[55]

In contrast to Freycinet's *Historique*, anthropology's physicalist bent is signalled in another text of very different genre—Quoy and Gaimard's *Zoologie* of the voyage and its accompanying atlas of plates.[56] The 712 pages of text, prefaced by a brief chapter entitled 'On Man,'[57] were drafted by Quoy. The 96 engraved plates, of which only two represent human beings, were compiled by Gaimard. Both plates depict skulls plundered from indigenous graves in Waigeo, a large island off the western end of New Guinea.[58] The primary subject of the chapter 'On Man' is the skull, including the results of phrenological examination (see Kingston, this volume). Yet it lacks any craniometric comparison or any classification of the great range of human beings encountered during the voyage, many of whom were carefully measured and tested by Gaimard. He recorded the results in detail in his journal, with no comment or racial inference.[59] Instead, the chapter focuses on the cranial characters of the *Papous* (Papuans), people encountered in and around Waigeo. Moreover, the content of the chapter repeatedly strays into ethnographic territory. One such digression explains in Buffonian terms the 'state' of the inhabitants of Shark Bay. Though their 'development' and 'perfection' were blocked by what seemed to the French to be the 'most dreadful' soil, Quoy and Gaimard nonetheless saw their condition as far from 'that of the brutes,' since they possessed the (human) faculty of speech and were thus able 'to communicate their thoughts.'[60]

In writing about indigenous people met during his voyage with Freycinet, Quoy the naturalist adhered to Buffonian environmentalist rather than Cuvierian innatist explanations throughout his textual trajectory, from journal preface to published zoology. Such discursive consistency clearly owed much to Freycinet's influence and directives. Yet the maintenance of that humanist logic through the emotional vicissitudes of personal encounters is also testament to the range of prudent strategies adopted by local inhabitants to handle, welcome, exploit, or shun the ship's presence without recourse to overt menace or violence. Thus managed, Freycinet and his shipmates experienced and recorded their Oceanic encounters in largely positive terms. This is in sharp contrast to La Pérouse, whose experience of such

122   *Bronwen Douglas*

encounters was very different. An analogous contrast emerges in Quoy's writings about his subsequent voyage with Jules Dumont d'Urville during 1826–9. On this occasion, disturbing experience of indigenous agency during encounters provoked him to invert the causal relationship of environment and nature, and to engage fully with the science of race. In the process, he reconstituted indigenous Australians as 'a very distinct variety' of the 'black Race' of Oceania and 'one of the most degraded.'[61] But that is another story, told elsewhere.[62]

CONCLUSION

I conclude by returning explicitly to my umbrella theme: the significance of *the expedition* as a setting for the early creation of knowledge about Oceanic populations, which I call 'seaborne ethnography.' This rich corpus of constructed knowledge had linked intellectual and pragmatic impact. Heuristically, it generated questions for further investigation, providing empirical fodder for scholarly deduction in the natural history of man and ultimately the science of race. Politically, it supplied precedents that would guide or confound subsequent voyagers, together with practical information about places, resources, and human populations that influenced imperial decision-making. Intellectually, seaborne ethnography generated rich veins of written and visual materials that have been mined ever since by historians and ethnohistorians. In this vein, I have long professed two complementary principles: first, that contemporary Oceanic travel writing and art are infused with overt and inadvertent traces of indigenous presence or agency exercised during encounters; and second, that the empirical creation of such knowledge in situ was dialogic, rather than a linear process of European appropriation, production, and control.[63] Each principle is variously illustrated or borne out by the exemplary encounters investigated in this chapter.

Indigenous presence was more or less dissipated in the process of appropriation of voyage texts by metropolitan savants and policy-makers. Such texts nonetheless remain a crucial resource for ethnohistorical understanding of indigenous worlds, languages, and actions, and they provide a useful antidote to the teleological notion that modern ethnographic wisdom can be projected non-problematically onto the past. In contrast, ethnohistory draws with varying emphasis on the interplay of three strategies: deep immersion in the texts of encounter in the languages of their original inscription; an informed grasp, historical and ethnographic, of the shifting social and ontological contexts in which encounters took place; and cognizance of vernacular histories in a range of mediums, whether spoken, sung, danced, carved, or written. Each strategy throws light on the others. Through their interplay, the scientific maritime expedition is revealed as a crucial, if relatively ephemeral and shallow, contributor to the creation of such composite knowledge. Often situated at the dawn of Oceanic meetings

The Voyages of La Pérouse and Freycinet 123

with wider worlds, seaborne ethnography was written and drawn by dedicated, trained scientific observers who were strongly committed to empirical accuracy. Although ethnocentric and sometimes racialist, it retains heuristic significance as a reciprocal product of the encounters it inscribes, profoundly shaped by its genesis in praxis.

NOTES

1. Académie françoise, *Le dictionnaire de l'Académie françoise, dedié au roy* (Paris: Veuve de Jean Baptiste Coignard et Jean Baptiste Coignard, 1694), vol. 1, 417, http://gallica.bnf.fr/ark:/12148/bpt6k503971; Robert Estienne, *Dictionarium Latinogallicum* (Paris: Roberti Stephani, (1538) 1543), 270; Institut de France, *Dictionnaire de l'Académie française* (6th edition, Paris: Firmin Didot frères, 1835), vol. 1, 708, http://gallica.bnf.fr/ark:/12148/bpt6k50407h; 'expedition, n.,' Oxford University Press, *OED Online*, last modified June 2013, www.oed.com/view/Entry/66487?redirectedFrom=Expedition. This and all translations from French are my own.

2. I use 'ethnography' to mean the systematic study and description of particular human groups and 'anthropology' to mean physical anthropology, with growing connotation of the study of races. Both senses emerged in Europe in the late eighteenth century. See Han Vermeulen, 'The German Invention of *Völkerkunde*: Ethnological Discourse in Europe and Asia, 1740–1798,' in *The German Invention of Race*, ed. Sara Eigen and Mark Larrimore (Albany: State University of New York Press, 2006), 123–45; Raymond Williams, *Keywords: A Vocabulary of Culture and Society*, 2nd ed. (New York: Oxford University Press, (1976) 1985), 38–9.

3. For an overview of instructions issued to French Oceanic voyagers, see Hélène Blais, *Voyages au Grand Océan: géographies du Pacifique et colonisation 1815–1845* (Paris: Comité des travaux historiques et scientifiques, Ministère de l'Education nationale, de l'Enseignement supérieur et de la Recherche, 2005), 74–111.

4. Etienne Taillemite, ed., *Bougainville et ses compagnons autour du monde 1766–1769* (Paris: Imprimerie nationale, 1977), vol. 1, 22.

5. Louis-Antoine de Bougainville, *Voyage autour du monde par la frégate du roi la Boudeuse et la flûte l'Etoile en 1766, 1767, 1768 & 1769* (Paris: Saillant & Nyon, 1771).

6. Paulin Crassous, 'Lettres de Commerson, contenant un detail succinct de son voyage autour du globe, et précédées d'une notice de sa vie, de son caractere et de ses ouvrages,' *Décade philosophique, littéraire et politique* 29 (1798): 73. The most important of several disjointed Commerson manuscripts held in the Muséum national d'Histoire naturelle in Paris are published in Taillemite, *Bougainville*, vol. 2, 419–522.

7. Philibert Commerson, 'Sur la découverte de la nouvelle isle de Cythère ou Taïti,' *Mercure de France, dédié au roi. Par une société de gens de lettres*, November 1769:197–207. A manuscript of the letter is held in the Muséum national d'Histoire naturelle.

8. 'Mémoire du roi, pour servir d'instruction particulière au sieur de la Pérouse, capitaine de ses vaisseaux, commandant les frégates la Boussole et l'Astrolabe, 26 juin 1785,' in Jean-François de Galaup de La Pérouse, *Voyage de la Pérouse autour du monde . . .*, ed. Louis-Antoine Destouff de Milet-Mureau (Paris: Imprimerie de la République, 1797), vol. 1, 13–61; John Dunmore,

124   *Bronwen Douglas*

'Introduction,' in La Pérouse, *The Journal of Jean-François de Galaup de la Pérouse 1785–1788*, trans. and ed. John Dunmore (London: Hakluyt Society, 1994), xxiv.

9. 'Mémoire rédigé par l'Académie des Sciences, pour servir aux savans embarqués sous les ordres de M. de la Pérouse' and 'Questions proposées par la Société de Médecine, à MM. les voyageurs qui accompagnent M. de la Pérouse, lues dans la séance du 31 mai 1785,' in La Pérouse, *Voyage*, vol. 1, 157–96.

10. Bronwen Douglas, 'Climate to Crania: Science and the Racialization of Human Difference,' in *Foreign Bodies: Oceania and the Science of Race 1750–1940*, eds. Bronwen Douglas and Chris Ballard (Canberra, AU: ANU E Press, 2008), 33–96.

11. Buffon is cited first in the (non-alphabetical) list of authors on natural history carried by La Pérouse and is specifically recommended by the Académie as the best source of a necessary 'common method' for comparative anatomy (La Pérouse, *Voyage*, vol. 1, 167, 253). For his landmark works on human diversity, see Georges-Louis Leclerc de Buffon, 'Histoire naturelle de l'homme: variétés dans l'espèce humaine,' in *Histoire naturelle, générale et particulière* (Paris: Imprimerie royale, 1749), vol. 3, 371–530; *Servant de suite à l'histoire naturelle de l'homme*, in *Histoire naturelle, générale et particulière: supplément* (Paris: Imprimerie royale, 1777), vol. 4, 454–582. In the lead-up to the voyage, La Pérouse visited Buffon for advice on research to be undertaken in natural history (Dunmore, 'Introduction,' xxviii).

12. The growing emphasis on anatomy was perhaps influenced by the recent work of the German anatomist Samuel Thomas Soemmerring, *Über die körperliche Verschiedenheit des Mohren vom Europaer* (Mainz: s.n., 1784), 4, 24, who inferred from (very dubious) observation and experiment that 'the brain of a Moor [Negro] is smaller than that of a European' and that Africans therefore occupied 'a lower echelon at the throne of mankind.'

13. La Pérouse, *Voyage*, vol. 1, 165–8, 180–5.

14. The published voyage narrative (La Pérouse, *Voyage*, 2 vols.), with selected reports and correspondence and the Atlas du voyage, were edited by the army officer Milet-Mureau from La Pérouse's journal and papers, now in the Archives nationales de France (Marine 3 JJ 386–9). For a modern edition, see La Pérouse, *Le voyage de Lapérouse 1785–1788: récit et documents originaux*, eds. John Dunmore and Maurice de Brossard (Paris: Imprimerie nationale, 1985), 2 vols.

15. Claude-Nicolas Rollin, 'Mémoire ou dissertation sur les habitans des îles de Pâque et de Mowée,' in La Pérouse, *Voyage*, vol. 4, 8–11, 13.

16. Rollin, 'Mémoire physiologique et pathologique, sur les Américains'; 'Dissertation sur les habitans de l'île de Tchoka, et sur les Tartares orientaux,' in La Pérouse, *Voyage*, vol. 4, 59–60, 86.

17. La Pérouse, *Voyage*, vol. 2, 79–96.

18. Dunmore, 'Introduction,' lxxxviii, clvii–clviii; Catherine Gaziello, *L'expédition de Lapérouse 1785–1788: réplique française aux voyages de Cook* (Paris: Comité des travaux historiques et scientifiques, 1984), 234.

19. [La Pérouse], *Atlas du voyage de La Pérouse* ([Paris: Imprimerie de la République]), plate 11.

20. La Pérouse, *Voyage*, vol. 2, 83, 91–3, 96.

21. Ibid., 192–4.

22. Ibid., vol. 3, 186–241.

23. Ibid., vol. 2, 192.

24. Ibid., vol. 3, 190–1, 207, 225.

25. [La Pérouse], *Atlas*, plate 66.

The Voyages of La Pérouse and Freycinet 125

26. See Bernard Smith, *European Vision and the South Pacific 1768–1850: A Study in the History of Art and Ideas* (Oxford: Oxford University Press, (1960) 1969), 103–4.
27. La Pérouse, *Voyage*, vol. 3, 189, 207; vol. 4, 236.
28. Ibid., vol. 3, 189, 192, 194, 225–6, 231.
29. Ibid., 193–8, 204, 240–1; vol. 4, 239.
30. Ibid., vol. 4, 234, 239.
31. Ibid., vol. 3, 240–1; vol. 4, 239.
32. Smith, *European Vision*, 85–7, 99–105; see also Dunmore, 'Introduction,' ccvi.
33. François Péron and Louis de Freycinet, *Voyage de découvertes aux terres australes . . . sur les corvettes* le Géographe, le Naturaliste, *et la goëlette* le Casuarina, *pendant les années 1800, 1801, 1802, 1803 et 1804 . . . Historique* (Paris: Imprimerie impériale/Imprimerie royale, 1807–16), 2 vols.
34. Gaimard recorded vocabularies of the inhabitants of New Guinea and nearby islands, Guam and Timor, in his shipboard journal (Joseph-Paul Gaimard, 'Voyage physique dans l'hémisphère austral, et autour du monde . . . sur la corvette du Roi l'Uranie et la corvette de S.M. la Physicienne . . . pendant les années 1817, 1818, 1819 et 1820: Journal historique,' MN 1188, State Library of Western Australia, Perth, http://purl.slwa.wa.gov.au/slwa_b1745716_001).
35. [Ministre de la Marine] to Louis de Freycinet, [Instructions], [24 August 1817], BB⁴ 999:7-82v, Archives centrales de la Marine, Service historique de la Défense, Vincennes.
36. Douglas, 'Climate to Crania,' 40–1, 45–7, 53–61.
37. Louis de Freycinet, 'Observations à faire à bord. . . . à bord de la corvette l'Uranie, le 23 octobre 1817,' in 'Voyage de l'Uranie: plan général des travaux exécutés pendant le voyage autour du monde du Cap^ne. Louis de Freycinet,' MAR 5JJ 62ᴬ, Archives nationales, Paris.
38. Freycinet, 'Tableau des observations & des recherches à faire pendant les relâches. . . . Rade de Rio-Janeiro, le 28 décembre 1817,' in ibid. A minute in Freycinet's handwriting shows that he modelled the questionnaire on a volume in the *Statistique générale de la France* ([Freycinet], 'Analyse rapide de la Statistique du Depʳ. de Rhin et Moselle,' n.d., MAR 5 JJ 62ᴮ, Archives nationales, Paris; Philippe Boucquéau, *Mémoire statistique du Département de Rhin-et-Moselle, adressé au Ministre de l'Intérieur, d'après ses instructions* [Paris: Imprimerie de la République, 1803]). I thank Ralph Kingston for drawing my attention to this document that I had photographed in the Archives nationales but not read carefully.
39. Freycinet, *Voyage autour du monde, . . . exécuté sur les corvettes de S.M.* l'Uranie *et la* Physicienne, *pendant les années 1817, 1818, 1819 et 1820 . . . Historique* (Paris: Pillet aîné, 1825–39), 3 vols.
40. Claude Blanckaert, 'Code de la nature et loi de l'histoire: les appropriations naturalistes du "primitif contemporain" entre XVIIIᵉ et XIXᵉ siècles,' in *L'Autre: catalogue de l'exposition Muséum d'histoire naturelle du Havre, 21 mars—15 juin 2008,* eds. Gabrielle Baglione and Claude Blanckaert (Le Havre: Editions du Muséum du Havre, 2008), 14.
41. Freycinet, *Voyage*, vol. 1, ix.
42. Jean-René Constant Quoy, 'Corvette du roi l'Uranie: voyage autour du monde, pendant les années 1817, 1818, 1819, & 1820 . . . Tome 1ᵉʳ, Historique,' R-2520–11702, Archives centrales de la Marine, Service historique de la Défense, Rochefort, [i], paraphrasing William Robertson, *Histoire de l'Amérique*, 2nd ed. (Amsterdam: E. van Harrevelt, [1778] 1779), vol. 2, 179.
43. Quoy, 'Corvette du roi l'Uranie,' [ii].
44. Freycinet, *Voyage*, vol. 1, 448, 470, 487.

126   *Bronwen Douglas*

45. Jacques Arago, *Promenade autour du monde, pendant les années 1817, 1818, 1819 et 1820 sur les corvettes du roi l'Uranie et la Physicienne commandées par M. Freycinet . . .* (Paris: Leblanc, 1822), vol. 1, 264, 266.
46. Freycinet, 'Tableau'.
47. Pellion in Freycinet, *Voyage*, vol. 1, 453; Quoy, 'Corvette du roi l'Uranie,' 86–9.
48. Arago, *Promenade*, vol. 1, 263–9; Marie-Alexandre Duparc after Jacques Arago, 'N^{lle}. Hollande, Baie des Chiens-marins, Presqu'île Péron: entrevue avec les sauvages,' engraving, in Jacques Arago, Alphonse Pellion, et al., *Voyage autour du monde . . . sur les corvettes de S.M. l'Uranie et la Physicienne pendant les années 1817, 1818, 1819 et 1820. Atlas historique* (Paris: Pillet aîné, 1825), plate 12, National Library of Australia, http://nla.gov.au/nla.pic-an9031315.
49. Pellion in Freycinet, *Voyage*, vol. 1, 450–3.
50. Arago, *Promenade*, vol. 1, 267–8.
51. Quoy, 'Paul Gaimard,' n.d., 3, MS 2508, Médiathèque Michel-Crépeau, La Rochelle.
52. Pellion in Freycinet, *Voyage*, vol. 1, 452.
53. Freycinet, *Voyage*, vol. 1, 448–69, 729.
54. Freycinet, *Voyage*, vol. 1, 470–86.
55. Ibid., 480–1.
56. Jean-René Constant Quoy and Joseph-Paul Gaimard, *Voyage autour du monde . . . sur les corvettes de S.M. l'Uranie et la Physicienne, pendant les années 1817, 1818, 1819 et 1820 . . . Zoologie* (Paris: Pillet aîné, 1824); and *Histoire naturelle: zoologie. Planches* (Paris: Imprimerie en taille-douce de Langlois, 1824).
57. Quoy and Gaimard, 'De l'homme: observations sur la constitution physique des Papous,' in *Zoologie*, 1–11.
58. Quoy and Gaimard, *Planches* (Paris: Imprimerie en taille-douce de Langlois, 1824), plates 1, 2.
59. Gaimard, 'Voyage'.
60. Quoy and Gaimard, 'De l'homme,' 2.
61. Quoy and Gaimard, 'De l'homme,' in *Voyage de découvertes de l'Astrolabe exécuté . . . pendant les années 1826–1827–1828–1829 . . . Zoologie* (Paris: J. Tastu, 1930), vol. 1, 29, 40.
62. Bronwen Douglas, 'L'idée de "race" et l'expérience sur le terrain au XIXe siècle: science, action indigène et vacillations d'un naturaliste français en Océanie,' *Revue d'Histoire des Sciences humaines* 21: 175–209, doi: 10.3406/genes.1996.1390; *Science, Voyages, and Encounters in Oceania 1511–1850* (Basingstoke, UK: Palgrave Macmillan, 2014).
63. Bronwen Douglas, 'Art as Ethno-Historical Text: Science, Representation and Indigenous Presence in Eighteenth and Nineteenth Century Oceanic Voyage Literature,' in *Double Vision: Art Histories and Colonial Histories in the Pacific*, eds. Nicholas Thomas and Diane Losche (Cambridge: Cambridge University Press, 1999), 65–99; 'In the Event: Indigenous Countersigns and the Ethnohistory of Voyaging,' in *Oceanic Encounters: Exchange, Desire, Violence*, eds. Margaret Jolly, Serge Tcherkézoff, and Darrell Tryon (Canberra, AU: ANU E Press, 2009), 175–98; *Science, Voyages, and Encounters in Oceania*, ch. 1.

7 Armchair Expeditionaries
Voyages Into the French Musée de la Marine, 1828–78

Ralph Kingston

The displays in the Musée de la Marine au Louvre's salle La Pérouse were a mess. Contemporary accounts repeatedly refer not to an orderly collection but to a 'crowd of objects.' The *Magasin pittoresque* of 1847, for example, detailed drawers crammed with a mêlée of rings, necklaces, bracelets, shoes, weapons, musical instruments, fishing equipment, and totems. These ethnographic objects were interspersed with relief maps, ship models, and navigational instruments.[1] In 1827, when the French government proposed the conversion of part of the Louvre into a naval museum, its primary plan was to exhibit the latter category of objects: navigational equipment and model ships. The display only expanded to include native weapons, costumes, and everyday objects when the explorer Dumont d'Urville returned to France with the remains of eighteenth-century explorer La Pérouse's shipwreck in 1829. His and other explorers' trophies, as well as gifts and purchases from private collectors, expanded the museum's ethnographic collection, turning it into the eclectic jumble described by its visitors.[2]

Timothy Mitchell and others have argued that the 'carefully chaotic' nature of the imperial exhibition was a purposeful portrayal of the world's cultural and colonial order, rendered in 'objective' form. In the Egyptian exhibit in the 1889 Paris World Exhibition, not only were shops and stalls laid out in haphazard fashion in imitation of an oriental bazaar, but even the paint on the walls was made to look dirty.[3] The 'exotic' curiosities of the salle La Pérouse were also objects procured from supposedly more 'primitive' peoples and displayed chaotically.[4] The most eye-catching display in the Musée de la Marine was that of the 'savage' weapons crammed on the walls. Inevitably visitors went home with the memory of 'terrible war clubs' and 'poisoned arrows which make even the smallest wound mortally dangerous.'[5] These were artefacts whose killing power transgressed the norms of civilized Europe.

The 'primitive' nature of the Pacific, it could be argued, was further emphasized by the room's spatial relationship to the Louvre's Egyptian department founded at the same time. Indeed, visitors had to pass through the Egyptian display, past the imposing Great Sphinx of Tanis installed at its entrance in 1826, to visit the Musée de la Marine collections. The

Figure 7.1 View of the salle La Pérouse in the Musée de la Marine au Louvre, *Magasin pittoresque* (January 1847), 13. From collection of the author.

monumentality of the ancient Egyptian artefacts contrasted heavily with the piecemeal memorabilia collected by French voyagers in the Pacific. Both collections were self-conscious attempts to preserve original examples of lost or rapidly disappearing cultures.[6] Yet, while the Egyptian gallery was a vision of 'civilization' and order, the Marine collection presented only 'savagery' and disorder. One constructed a vision of homogeneity, the other a picture of extreme heterogeneity.

However, the Musée de la Marine was not without its own monumental aspect. The centrepiece of the salle La Pérouse celebrated an ongoing

Armchair Expeditionaries 129

tradition of French discovery. La Pérouse and his crew had disappeared without a trace, shipwrecked in 1787, and his fate was not officially known until Dumont d'Urville returned with debris from his ship in 1829. Towering over the artefacts, an obelisk erected in his memory—covered with the debris of his eighteenth-century sailing ship—was a reminder to Parisian audiences of France's past naval glories.[7] Accommodating the La Pérouse monument, the Musée de la Marine did more than just put the 'primitive' on display. Its ethnographic objects also served as proof of the 'virility of France and of its philosophic civilization' as well as a means to pique the emulation of naval officers and to engage them in scientific and artistic endeavours. As one commentator said, the ethnographic objects were a 'magical and prestigious *illustration*' of the romance of exploration—bringing to mind 'receptions by savage princes, the dances of the beautiful Islanders of the Pacific' and 'gusts of wind on far-away beaches.'[8]

Complicating the meaning of the museum display even further was the fact that, in its first decades of existence, it was not primarily ethnographic at all, but rather a collection of navigational instruments and model ships designed to educate visitors in hydraulics and the marine sciences. For example, this aspect of the museum was foremost in the mind of a visitor in 1849 who observed that 'one can, without leaving the rooms of this museum, take a complete course in naval construction, from the shipyard to the slipway . . . One can learn how [a ship] drifts, how to lay its sail, how to arrange its cargo in the hold.'[9] In the museum, navigational instruments and model ships sat beside native weapons, costumes, and everyday objects; a relief map and a plan of a Mandarin's mansion lay next to a collection of exotic bird feathers.[10] If the disorder of the ethnographic objects undermined the museum's more practical naval objectives, the side-by-side juxtaposition of European and non-European objects also destabilized its presentation of 'primitive' difference. The Musée de la Marine therefore resisted the sort of postcolonial analysis that one might apply to a later nineteenth-century ethnographic display. Instead, as I will argue, the museum to some extent replicated an 'expeditionary' culture of ethnographic comparison, distinct from and sometimes in opposition to metropolitan theories of racial difference.

OUT OF ORDER

To understand the Musée de la Marine, one must first understand the source—or, more accurately, the manufacture—of its confusion of objects. At the beginning, curators quite definitely intended to keep the ethnographic objects separate—in the final room of a seven-room sequence.[11] A lack of planning was therefore not responsible for the absence of coherent boundaries within the museum. However, it is also true that the curators were uniformly less concerned with the ethnographic than the marine collections. Most of the museum's funding went to building and repairing ship

Figure 7.2 View of salle La Pérouse in the Musée de la Marine au Louvre, *Magasin pittoresque* (January 1847), 12. From collection of the author.

models. As the collection of ethnographic objects grew in the museum's first half-decade, little was done to prevent the collapse of the spatial boundary between French maritime science and 'primitive' native artefacts. By 1839, just over a decade after the museum opened, Adolphe Caillé, a Ministry of War bureau chief, remarked that order 'hardly exists in the displays of naval arms and instruments.' As for the ethnographic collection, it was 'pell-mell, laid out without any natural or chronological order.'[12] Without anyone keeping a close eye on which object belonged where, artefacts that had arrived together had somehow moved apart.

Paris intellectuals were particularly displeased with how objects had floated around the Musée de la Marine. In making his comments, Caillé was echoing wider concerns in the Paris geographical community about the lack of a self-contained, organized ethnographic collection in the city, in which 'the diverse products of each single nation' could be studied separately. Already in 1831, the eminent metropolitan geographer, Edmé Jomard, had proposed to extract ethnographic artefacts from the Musée de la Marine to establish a separate 'geo-ethnographic' museum in the Bibliothèque nationale, where the objects would be viewed alongside maps and plans rather than among ship models and navigational instruments.[13] In that context, objects would be turned into texts, their inscriptions (if they had them) mined for geographic knowledge by scholars and experts. Meanwhile, as another metropolitan member of the Société de géographie noted, the materials from which objects were made would provide a useful insight into the physical geography of the places in which they were collected. This material information would complement descriptions of flora, fauna, soils, geology, and hydrography recorded by explorers and voyagers in their journals and travel accounts.[14]

For Jomard and his colleagues, the geographic origin of each object would determine its placement in the Bibliothèque nationale. This was a 'natural' order, the same natural order to which Caillé referred. Returning expeditionaries actually delivered objects to Paris in a way that confirmed the validity of the geographers' preferences. They catalogued and stored their finds in the order they were discovered and collected, island by island, encounter by encounter, ship by ship.[15] If arranged in the order they arrived in the museum, objects on display should have been a 'mirror of the exchange.'[16] The fact that the Musée de la Marine somehow departed from a strict geographical distribution of objects demonstrates that what was at work was more than just curator negligence. The objects had not moved themselves. The museum's 'disorder' had had to be manufactured.

TOUCHING OBJECTS

So what happened to the ethnographic collection between 1828 and 1839 to cause its disorganization? Who was moving objects about? The Musée de la Marine in its first decade of existence was a resource for naval officers first and foremost, and open to public access only secondarily.[17] Entry for the public was by means of a *laissez-passer* delivered by the Maison du Roi or the Ministry of Marine. Naval officers passing through Paris, however, were allowed simply to present their credentials and sign in. Even though the right to visit the museum was restricted, curators regularly found their ship models broken.[18] There was little to prevent this. The museum only purchased protective grilles for the ship models and La Pérouse's obelisk when the rooms were opened to the public in 1837. For the first few years of

132 Ralph Kingston

its existence, then, the behaviour of naval officers visiting the museum was governed only by their honour. There were no printed rules or regulations as to how they should treat the ethnographic objects. There were no standard expectations for visitor behaviour as the Musée de la Marine was one of the first public collections of its kind.

The unique status of the Musée de la Marine as a national collection (established inside the world's first national museum, the Louvre) set it apart from those put together by collectors of curiosities in the eighteenth century. There were many similarities, of course. The Musée de la Marine shared with the early modern cabinet of curiosity a tendency towards the eclectic. However, the cabinet of curiosity was typically an individual effort, expressive of the individual gentleman-scholar's intellectual disposition. While scholars worked with items in one another's collections—or benefited from the publication of information about specimens in text or image—the cabinet itself remained very much the property of the private individual (or corporation) and ordered according to his (or its) agenda.[19] While his act of donation to the Musée de la Marine served to underline Dumont d'Urville's success as a navigator and explorer, his ownership of the objects on display ended the moment they entered the museum.

The collection in the Musée de la Marine did not belong to anyone, but to everyone—to the nation. The emphasis in the post-Revolutionary Louvre was not on the rarity and curiosity of individual exhibits—on connoisseurship— but on the claim to represent the 'universality' of the arts and sciences. Its goal was to show how separate traditions were transcended by universal impulses. In the art galleries, old masters instructed a new generation of French artists, both professional and amateur, in the art of painting. Individual artists set up canvas and easels in order to emulate the genius of Leonardo da Vinci. The Musée de la Marine was expected to serve a similar purpose in terms of the individual's engagement with the nautical arts.[20]

At play here was not just a lack of museum etiquette, then. Naval officers had experience—they knew how to interact—with the other exhibits in the Musée de la Marine. Ship models in the period were used to consider design problems—issues of stability, hull design, and frictional drag—in a practical, hands-on fashion.[21] They introduced naval officers to the intimate workings of marine technologies—for example, the internal mechanism of a steam engine went on display in 1838.[22] The Musée de la Marine models included detail of the deck furnishings, masts, spars, and sometimes of the interior. Naval officers would hold, turn over, and examine them in order to learn their lines (and thus their capacity for carrying armaments), to assess their strengths and weaknesses, and to compare contemporary maritime architecture with that of the past.[23] The models were juxtaposed with other museum pieces, as a means to communicate other important naval lessons. Large history paintings illustrated particular engagements— tactical situations—in which ships similar to the models on display had taken part.[24]

Armchair Expeditionaries 133

The ethnographic collection was equally within the reach of the curious seaman. While many of the artefacts were kept in display cases, glass for these cases was not procured until late 1831, two to three years after naval officers had begun to visit the collection.[25] Locks were not fitted to cabinets until late 1833.[26] Iron grilles were added to distance people from models, objects, and paintings only in 1837.[27] Once objects were moved from one case to another, the lack of an integrated catalogue (the museum had only numbered acquisition lists) meant that it was difficult for curators to put them back in place. In any case, as one visitor noted, ushers in the museum were uniformly helpful but were woefully ignorant about the objects entrusted to their care.[28] The movement of ethnographic objects and their entry to the lives of contemporary Parisians reached its logical conclusion on 29 July 1830, when a crowd moving through the museum stole not only 26 navy swords and pikes and six small artillery pieces, but also 10 tomahawks, 20 lances, six bows, and 40 arrows.[29] Having used the lance he stole in the short-lived July Revolution, one insurrectionary was considerate enough to return it later that week.[30]

In 1876 the collection was catalogued so that the collections could be divided and moved, with the naval models going to the Musée de Saint-Germain-en-Laye and the anthropological artefacts to the Musée d'Ethnographie du Trocadéro. It was only then that the consequences of the objects 'floating' from one display to another became fully apparent. They no longer obeyed any geographic order. Objects that had arrived as part of a donation had long been separated from one other. A single display case contained objects from China, Fiji, New Zealand, and North America. A Buddha in marble sat between two Brazilian statuettes. Another Buddha had taken up position between two North American chiefs. The scholar charged with sorting the collections scoffed that these groupings seemed inspired by the fact that Europeans had decided to call cultures in both Asia and America 'Indian.'[31] Overall, he concluded, most ethnographic objects seemed to be arranged by size and colour. In terms of geography, this was ludicrous. What it meant in practice, however, was that models of canoes, tambourines, and tobacco sacks had been brought together for comparison.[32] These juxtapositions undermined geographical distinctions, but opened up different—ethnographic—comparisons. Visitors had redefined the purpose of the collection as they moved objects from table to table, from display case to display case.

Experts agreed that the museum was in a state of confusion, yet it was the juxtaposition of objects that fascinated visitors. French cannons lay next to Polynesian tomahawks, warships next to canoes, encouraging the visitor to accept the basic identity of these items. The writer Léon Gozlan, visiting in 1836, certainly felt the urge to move and compare objects: 'beside a tree trunk hollowed out by fire to make a boat, one imagines a pirogue excavated with an axe.'[33] For Gozlan also, a 'Patagonian god' was 'the twin of the god of the Brahmins.'[34]

134 *Ralph Kingston*

Despite criticism from outside, curators in the 1840s and 1850s seemed to accept that this was an acceptable way for visitors to 'read' the museum, to think about non-European objects. Even after a decision to (re-)separate ethnographic objects from the naval collections in 1850, the curators made a decision to allow the 'navigation of savage people' to remain part of the museum's marine display. Models of pirogues and French fishing boats continued to sit alongside one another, and alongside the models of vessels constructed in other European shipyards. This lack of a firm sense as to whether model canoes belonged to the museum's naval or ethnographic collections continued until at least the late nineteenth century.

This blurring of the boundaries between European and non-European objects was all the more potent because real pirogues were not put on display. The museum presented only models of pirogues manufactured by the Louvre *atelier* (normally to the scale of 6 cm:1 m). These, no less than the models of French ships, were objects intended to demonstrate design capacities. In fabricating the pirogues, museum modellers emphasized the detail of the outriggers that allowed them to be easily manoeuvred in shallow coastal waters. The curator Antoine Léon Morel-Fatio singled out a canoe from the Caroline Islands in Polynesia for praise in his 1853 Musée de la Marine catalogue, particularly for its capacity to tack. The model of the Carolinian pirogue was based on drawings made by François Pâris (later head curator of the museum), who was charged while a junior officer on an expedition led by Dumont d'Urville to sketch as many native vessels as he could.[35] Pâris's 1883 illustrated guide to the museum made prominent mention of the 'unique collection' of South Seas pirogue models on display beside Arab, Indian, Chinese, Japanese, and Malay vessels, and, of course, European war and merchant ships. These models showed the 'generalised use' of outriggers, 'of which one has never found any trace' in Europe.[36] Later in the guide, Pâris directly compared the Malaysian *bouanga* to the ancient Roman trireme. In the museum itself, Morel-Fatio's Carolinian pirogue was classified amongst the naval collection in 1850, but it ended up part of the ethnographic collection at some later stage. Even today, a French model of a Carolinian pirogue is preserved in the Musée du Quai Branly.[37]

The movement of objects—and the creation of new and 'unofficial' juxtapositions—determined the manner in which visitors experienced both marine and ethnographic objects in the Musée de la Marine.[38] The collection invited visitors to compare and contrast different cultures. Having toured the museum in the 1840s, Charles de Forster drew the following conclusions:

> All men are born with a penchant for destruction . . . in the state of nature like in the most advanced civilization, the first thing which preoccupies him is the means by which he can destroy. Bows, arrows, tomahawks or fighting axes, pikes, the savages have made them, chosen them, made them as murderous as possible . . . [and] here is a ship with

three decks, fitted out with 120 cannons; here is a frigate, there a corvette armed for war . . . Here are models of its weapons, its boarding
nets, axes and pikes.[39]

Forster also remarked that 'feathered ornaments, made with shells or with
the teeth of enemies, prove that women everywhere are flirts.'[40]

Instead of a common human penchant for warfare or coquetry, Léon
Gozlan saw evidence of universal artistic impulses. He noted that the objects

> of utility and of luxury employed by the people who our convenient
> erudition classifies under the universal denomination of 'savages' . . .
> possess, and the proof is under our eyes . . . a delicacy of work so great,
> so fine, and so patient that it is useless to compare them to the embroi-
> deries of Alençon or Malines . . . The savages have forged, without
> hammer and anvil, instruments which are indispensible to our civilized
> workers, elegant lances as flexible as they are strong. The arsenals at
> Toulon or Brest cannot offer their equal.

Putting French and native inventions side by side, Gozlan came to the
romantic conclusion that Pacific Islanders had developed the better of the
two civilizations. After all, who would swap a hammock made of rushes
and creepers, swaying gently in the breeze, for a bed of pine and a duck-
feather mattress?[41]

Gozlan and Forster arrived at very different interpretations. Yet the
museum in both cases inspired comparisons in which objects of French
manufacture were seen as part of the 'crowd of objects to which all [the
world's] peoples have contributed.'[42] Despite taking away different meanings, Gozlan and Forster approached the objects in a similar manner. The
lack of boundaries in the museum and the movement of objects from case
to case had undermined the 'otherness' of the Pacific Island artefacts.[43] Both
men saw Europeans and non-Europeans as driven by similar impulses.
Whatever their differences, they inhabited analogous social worlds.

CONTESTING THE METROPOLE

Visitors would not have been left with this impression had Edmé Jomard
and other Paris geographers been successful in the bid to create a 'geo-
ethnographic' museum in the Bibliothèque nationale. The divide between
the ideal meaning of the museum (in the minds of metropolitan experts) and
the actual meanings constructed and taken away by naval officers and other
visitors is part of a bigger story of tensions between scientists at home and
abroad. Much has been written about the difficulty of reconciling the knowledge generated by metropolitan 'centres of accumulation' with natural history in the field in the early nineteenth century.[44] 'Armchair' geographers

136 *Ralph Kingston*

and active voyagers also approached their subject in very different ways— one working from the study, collation, and comparison of sources in order to establish the 'relative position of places,' the other going out into the field to observe first hand.[45] Jomard's idea of geography was of a field that looked to fill holes in the empirical knowledge of places. In terms of geo-ethnography, this meant building up as full a picture as possible of a society in a specific place or within a particular region. In the naval museum, how-ever, visitors looked to compare and contrast different cultures (including their own) and, by doing so, to think about the relationship between natural and social phenomena. The informal classification of objects by genre first and species second in the Musée de la Marine suggests they thought that the forms of categorization used by natural historians were more useful for ethnographic objects than their geographic classification by place of origin.

The naval officers visiting the museum in its first decade, manufacturing disorder as they moved objects around, were to a large extent acting as they did when they were explorers. As French naval explorers in the Pacific sailed from island to island, their minds turned to exactly this sort of cross-cultural comparison. They observed the native cultures, asking detailed questions concerning the preparation of food, hunting and fishing methods, and, of course, questions of practical seafaring and the construction of pirogues. They asked the same questions in different places. It is hard not to imagine that they compared the answers when they returned to camp, or during long days spent cooped up on ship.

For instance, the crew of the *Uranie*, commanded by Louis de Freycinet, paid particular attention to the detail of boats and ships they encountered on their journey. They had been prepared in this regard. En route to the Pacific, Freycinet ordered his officers to construct a *pros volant* (a 'flying proa') following British navigator George Anson's description of those in the Mariana Islands. Anson had claimed that these sea-going boats could achieve a speed of nearly 20 miles per hour in a headwind. Freycinet's offic-ers failed to replicate that feat. Their boat, made of oak, was far too heavy, and all but impossible to sail. It ended up as firewood.[46] Nevertheless, the officers learned a valuable lesson in canoe construction, in particular about the importance of using the right materials. In 1818, at Rawak, off the island of Waigeo, the men of the *Uranie* were able to remark in detail on the design of dug-out canoes from Rawak as well as keel-built boats visit-ing from the nearby island of Pulau Gebe (a Moluccan 'spice island' and thriving Islamic settlement). In the official voyage memoir written after his return to Paris, Freycinet developed the point of comparison further by contrasting the Gebe keel-built boat to the vessels he had seen built at Kupang on the island of Timor, an important port and trading point dur-ing the Portuguese and Dutch colonial eras, and a long-established locus of Islamic trade.

Comparisons like this dictated the day-to-day decision making of the explorers. According to his voyage account, Freycinet explicitly avoided

Figure 7.3 Ambroise Louis Garneray, *Iles des Papous, vue du mouillage de l'Uranie sur l'île Rawak, dessiné par Garneray d'après A. Pellion*, 1822, engraving. By Permission of the National Library of Australia (nla.pic-an9031713).

Gebe, an island he knew was in regular contact with Europeans, in order to visit Rawak, 'an uninhabited island, in the neighborhood of a half savage people.'[47] However, while Freycinet's explorers went to Rawak looking for savagery, they left it with a 'very high idea of the intelligence and skill' of its boat-builders, who constructed their canoes with only a small axe and a large knife.[48] In the journals of Jean René Constant Quoy and Joseph Paul Gaimard, the expedition's medical officers and natural historians, one finds the same appreciation of the 'finesse' of the natives of Rawak. Gaimard was struck by their skill at fishing, noting the construction of their harpoons and their ability to cast and spear a fish from a distance of 10 to 12 feet. The island's fishermen were able to supply the ship abundantly during its stay at Rawak, with fish, turtles, and small birds, as well as fruit, which they exchanged mostly for European-manufactured knives.[49] Quoy also remarked on their fishing prowess, but was more interested in praising other forms of industry. 'Executed with very defective instruments,' he wrote, 'their work is long, tiresome, but also very delicate. I was struck to see the assembly of the windows in their tombs. A European carpenter could not produce better.'[50]

138 *Ralph Kingston*

At the same time as they were writing these words of praise, however, both Quoy and Gaimard were also making a very different set of observations, compiling extensive physical descriptions of the inhabitants of the islands. Metropolitan scientists had, since the Enlightenment, tasked voyagers with collecting physical and phrenological information about the native peoples they encountered. They sought this information explicitly in order to slot it into ethno-geographies, in order to map the races of the world (correlating the physical with the spatial was the main focus of what the early nineteenth century thought of as 'anthropology').[51] In the early nineteenth century, there was an increasing tendency towards polygenism, the idea that the races were created separately. European scientists increasingly believed in racial autochthony, in essential physical differences. The most famous and powerful natural historian of the day, Georges Cuvier, bought into the idea of separate and distinct human races; man had been made as a single species, but the races had divided irrevocably as a result of a global catastrophe 5,000 years previously. In his 'Note instructive sur les recherches à faire relativement aux différences anatomiques des diverses races d'hommes,' prepared for the Baudin expedition in 1800, Cuvier, drawing on the evidence of a small collection of human skulls collected by Johann Friedrich Blumenbach, argued (in opposition to Blumenbach's straightforwardly monogenist agenda) for the existence of at least three separate human races: the 'white' or 'Caucasian,' 'yellow' or 'Mongolian,' and 'black' or 'Ethiopian.' Asking that Baudin's scientists collect evidence to prove his theory, Cuvier provided detailed instructions on the best ways to sketch the heads of people encountered, as well as how to procure and preserve human skulls. His hope for the Baudin voyage was that it would bring back hard evidence on the racial identities of the indigenous inhabitants of South America, Australia, the islands of the Pacific, and the *Papous* (Papuans), the 'negro' inhabitants of New Guinea.[52]

Freycinet's plan for his voyage to the South Pacific in 1817 had begun with a decision to choose his entire scientific staff from among naval officers, and not to take civilian scientists on board. Unlike men appointed by the Muséum national d'histoire naturelle or the Observatoire, he could expect commissioned naval officers to follow orders. Keenly aware that their appointments had been made against the wishes of Cuvier and the Muséum national d'histoire naturelle, Quoy and Gaimard put considerable effort into following their scientific agendas.[53] At Rawak, they asked for and received permission from Freycinet to collect and take with them six skulls they had found arranged in front of an Islander's tomb. Gaimard also measured live human beings, including a visitor to Rawak from Gebe named Aïfola, noting his olive skin, smooth dark hair, flattened nose, scarred cheek, and prominent upper lip (covered by a light moustache). Gaimard also took a series of more 'scientific' dynamometric measurements of Aïfola and others. 20-year-old Aïfola was five-foot tall. The circumference of his head was two feet, one inch.[54] Gaimard remarked on the physical differences between

Armchair Expeditionaries 139

these Islanders and the 'negro' inhabitants of mainland New Guinea. Where one had olive skin, the other had black. Where one had straight hair, the other had 'frizzy.' Later, Gaimard recorded that the hair of inhabitants of Waigeo could be both 'frizzy, tousled' and 'straight and smooth.' Several of them had a physiognomy Gaimard described as 'lazy, stupid, and off-putting,' with large, flat noses, large lips, and black teeth. They were dressed in a simple loincloth, living in a state as far removed from European luxury as Gaimard could imagine.[55]

Quoy, conversely, found something 'agreeable' about their physiognomy, and even about their laughter. He described the inhabitants of Waigeo as medium height, sometimes well built but often spindly, and with light black skin. If he disagreed with Gaimard on skin colour, he agreed on hair types. Some Islanders had naturally 'bushy' hair. Others had 'flat, smooth, and very long hair which [they wore] falling down on their shoulders.' From this evidence, Quoy surmised that, even if there had been some intermarriage, the people of Rawak were essentially of a different race to the New Guinea mainlanders. Their noses were different, less flat than those of the 'African negro' race to whom he supposed the mainland New Guineans belonged.[56]

When presenting their observations of the people of Waigeo and Rawak to the National Institute in 1823, Quoy and Gaimard worked to smooth over the contradictions in their accounts. They agreed on a common set of observations. They solidified the idea that the 'Papuans' they had seen in Rawak and Waigeo were racially different from the people living on mainland New Guinea (who were, they noted, following Cuvier and others, '[physically] similar to the inhabitants of southern Africa'). Lacking the ability to create a single racial type using the 'plethora of nuances' they had observed at Rawak, however, they instead took the skulls they had collected to Franz-Joseph Gall for analysis. Quoy and Gaimard made the results of this examination central to their account, solving their racial profiling problem by emphasizing the importance of the shape of the skull over other physical factors. In later life, Quoy would declare Gall's theories a form of 'eccentricity,' not true science.[57] In 1823, however, he found use for Gall's analysis to comment on similarities between Papuan and African skulls, and differences with European skulls, helping his observations fit a Cuvierian framework.[58] Phrenology also excused him from providing 'detail about customs.' The report contained little of the information they had collected on the Islanders' social practices.[59] Committed to polygenism, Quoy in particular argued the right of metropolitan scientists to ignore the detail of observations made in the field. Only the metropolitan anthropologist could see past the 'fugitive' nuances of real life to 'obtain results,' and thereby draw clear lines between racial groups. In particular, commerce between peoples obscured the essential differences polygenists hoped to identify. Efforts to survey customs and analyse language groups were therefore doomed to give inconclusive results.[60]

140   Ralph Kingston

In the 1823 report, Gall's analysis 'proved' the aggressive nature of the Islanders of Rawak and Waigeo. Quoy and Gaimard concluded that they had an 'innate drive to steal,' a 'carnivorous instinct,' and a 'penchant for murder.' None of these observations appeared in their voyage journals. Conversely, according to Quoy's journal, the Islanders' engagement with their visitors failed at any stage to 'degenerate into trickery.' The inhabitants of Rawak were too timid, too afraid of the European visitors, in Quoy's opinion.[61] It was only in the concluding paragraph of their report that the authors hinted at the fact that their actual interactions conflicted with Gall's phrenology and its conclusions about the moral character of the Papuans. In a comment that directly contradicted the basic tenets of polygenism, Quoy and Gaimard argued that the Islanders 'only need to be exercised and developed to make them hold a distinguished rank among the numerous varieties of the human species.'[62] In 1826, a monogenist editor in the *Annales des sciences naturelles* would add to that paragraph, noting that this capacity for instruction was proof that the Papuans were not, as some naturalists had wrongly asserted, more like monkeys than [European] men.[63]

Therefore, both during expeditions and then back in the museum, naval officers who made comparisons between customs and objects found in multiple, different locations confronted the tenuous validity of the 'scientific' racial theories propounded in Parisian learned society. The comparison of peoples across the globe went against European scientists' basic belief in racial autochthony, essential differences, and the theories of polygenism. Voyager-naturalists like Quoy and Gaimard could 'prove' the validity of polygenism only by undermining the authority of fieldwork. Museum visitors equally encountered non-European cultures in a context that invited comparison. The patrons did not develop a single universally accepted interpretation as to how to compare cultures. Some came away from the collection of non-European artefacts with the idea that Pacific, Asian, or African peoples were comparatively savage. Others emerged with the sense that non-Europeans were comparatively advanced in their capacity for invention. What unified those who engaged with the objects in these settings was a sense that a comparison was possible. Housed in the Louvre, the Musée de la Marine's implicit invitation to its patrons to appraise, to decipher meaning, to appreciate sophistication (or decry its lack), meant that it was very much in tune with the larger institution. Although the ethnographic collection and the Egyptian department looked different, the challenges they posed were the same. The learned Frenchman was to appreciate the exquisite craft of ancient Egypt. He was also expected to read the presence of such monuments in Paris as a story about modern France.

All of this was informal. Comparative ethnography would emerge as an academic approach only in the early twentieth century, after it coalesced around the *mission civilisatrice*, the late nineteenth-century rationale for French imperial expansion on the grounds that it would spread civilization by creating conditions in which subject people could become French

Armchair Expeditionaries 141

(and embrace Republican democracy). The ethnographic collection in the Trocadéro, particularly after it was reorganized as the Musée de l'homme in 1938, worked explicitly to present this message. Anthropologist and curator Paul Rivet described the objects in his collection as 'instruments of colonial propaganda.' He organized them purposely by genre, displaying sets of weapons, musical instruments, or cooking utensils to illustrate the progress of non-European peoples in the development of key (French) civilized values: humanity and restraint, art and beauty, good taste, etc. His goal was to present 'humanity as an indivisible whole, in space and time.'[64] The only difference between Rivet's displays and the Musée de la Marine was its intentionality, and the fact that, in the twentieth century, French empire was not an aspiration but a fact. In the Musée de l'homme, unlike in the early nineteenth-century Musée de la Marine, therefore, French artefacts were not present. The power of European civilization was not in question; its exclusion underlined its position of authority.[65]

Although the Musée de la Marine does not represent a developed statement of the civilizing mission, it does offer us a means of understanding one of the ways in which eighteenth-century stadial theories of race retained their currency through the nineteenth century. In this form they remained available to colonial administrators from the 1870s until the 1890s. Martin Staum has argued that the official results of exploration in the period from 1820 until the 1840s served to confirm polygenist theories of race.[66] The scientists of the Institut de France had no interest in, and did not ask voyagers to collect, ethnographic objects. There was no place in the Muséum national d'histoire naturelle for the objects brought back. Rejected elsewhere, the objects found a home in the Musée de la Marine. Over the course of the rest of the nineteenth century, similar collections appeared in provincial public collections across France, as officers bequeathed objects to municipal libraries and museums in the towns in which they were born, or to which they retired. Like the 'disorganized' nature of the Musée de la Marine, the 'amateur' and 'local' nature of these collections may belie their considerable impact.

NOTES

1. 'Le Musée Naval du Louvre,' *Magasin pittoresque*, 1847, 11, 13.
2. The items brought back from the Pacific by official marine exploration expeditions were complemented by gifts made by explorers of Mexico, Greenland, and other 'far off and newly discovered places.' 'Musée de la Marine, au Louvre (Deuxième article),' *Magasin pittoresque*, 1838, 399. For lists of acquisitions, see EM4, Archives des musées nationaux (Louvre). For objects offered, see EM5, and for offers rejected, see EM7.
3. Timothy Mitchell, *Colonising Egypt* (Cambridge: Cambridge University Press, 1988), esp. 1, 6–7.
4. The display betrayed none of the moral difficulties involved in its acquisition. Some of the 'primitive' artefacts displayed by the museum were once upon a

142   *Ralph Kingston*

time simply some Islander's best utensils and plates. Dumont d'Urville identified two types of natives on his voyage—those willing to exchange food and artefacts for European goods, and those who 'stubbornly refused to exchange at any price.' At Vanikoro, for example, he contrasted the natives' 'duplicity' and 'insolent greed' with his own steadfast sense of fair play: *An Account of Two Volumes of Two Voyages to the South Seas by Captain Jules S-C Dumont d'Urville of the French Navy*, trans. and ed. Helen Rosenman, vol. 1 [Australia, New Zealand, Oceania, 1826–1829 in the corvette Astrolabe, 1826–9] (Honolulu: University of Hawaii Press, 1987), 210–5.

5. 'Musée de la Marine,' 399.
6. As noted in an 1827 report to the King, the Louvre collection would allow Frenchmen to justly 'appreciate the state of civilization of the ancient Egyptians, their morals, manners, religious ideas, degree of instruction, [and] progress in the arts . . . it is the same when it comes to the various monuments which allow us to understand the state of peoples . . . indigenous to the Americas, Africa, the Asian archipelago, and to Oceania, in particular those of the Southern Ocean up to the moment where European civilization, [by introducing] its own customs, replaced their primitive character.' Report to the King, 1827, (AN) O3/1420, Archives nationales, Paris. This and further translations from the French are by the author, unless stated otherwise.
7. J. A. Adolphe Caillé, *Considérations d'art et de politique à propos du Musée de la Marine au Louvre* (Paris: Dolin, 1839), 8.
8. Ibid., 119–20 (original italics).
9. Charles de Forster, *Quinze Ans à Paris (1832–1849). Paris et les Parisiens*, vol. 2 (Paris: Firmin Didot, 1849), 116–7.
10. 'Le Musée Naval du Louvre,' *Magasin pittoresque*, 1847, 13–14.
11. 'Note pour Chev. de Cailleux,' EM1, 1828, Archives des musées nationaux (Louvre). The British Museum collection was also established 'geographically' when a separate South Seas room opened in 1808.
12. Caillé, *Considérations*, 27. The reason for the disorder, according to Caillé, was that the museum was still 'an embryonic idea,' and thus had so far resisted cataloguing (14). He believed that everything ought to 'be in connection with the object which the museum was destined to glorify. Everything ought to be maritime in a Museum of the Marine' (19). Caillé's desire for a clear division of objects was the result of some social as well as intellectual anxiety. When working men came to the museum on Sundays, they gathered around the ship models, plans, and pictures of various French ports, and examples of other feats of French hydraulic engineering. His own preference was for the 'curiosities of far-away countries, loincloths, necklaces, bracelets, weapons, musical instruments and fishing tackle, savage fetishes, and the pyramid which rises up from the middle, the gloomy trophy on which is hung all that was left of the remains of the shipwreck of La Pérouse' (12). Having both sets of objects in the same room placed him shoulder to shoulder with his social inferiors. Caillé recommended that order should be re-imposed on the museum by devoting each room to a particular interest.
13. This museum, according to Jomard, would encourage others to go out and explore: E.T. Hamy, *Les Origines du musée d'ethnographie. Histoire et documents*, Publications du Musée d'Ethnographie 1 (Paris: Ernest Leroux, 1890), 91.
14. Férussac in Hamy, *Les Origines du musée d'ethnographie*, 161–2.
15. See, for example, the catalogue of objects from Dumont d'Urville's later voyage, organised geographically by island, which he added to the museum's collections in 1841: 'Note des objets provenant de la corvette la Zélée, mois de mars 1841' and 'Note des objets provenant de l'expédition de la corvette l'Astrolabe, mois d'avril 1841,' EM 4, Archives des musées nationaux (Louvre).

Armchair Expeditionaries 143

16. This term is used by Sylviane Jacquemin in *La découverte du paradis. Océanie, curieux, navigateurs et savants* (Paris: éditions d'art Somogy, 1997), 47.
17. The emphasis on the naval character of the museum is shown by the fact that, by law, only ex-naval officers could serve as head curator.
18. Zédé to the Director, 26 June 1834 and 10 April 1837, EM22, Archives des musées nationaux (Louvre).
19. As Horst Bredekamp has argued in *The Lure of Antiquity and the Cult of the Machine: The Kunstkammer and the Evolution of Nature, Art and Technology*, trans. Allison Brown (Princeton, NJ: Markus Weiner, 1995), the juxtaposition of objects in the cabinet of curiosity already facilitated the rise of new categories and classifications, and new theories of transformation—of evolution and revolution—in the realm of natural history. Yet, even when these cabinets were open to 'communities of users,' access remained limited to those who 'shared tacit codes of practice' and an obsessive concern that everyone should be on the same page: Ken Arnold, *Cabinets for the Curious: Looking Back at Early English Museums* (Aldershot, UK: Ashgate, 2006), 29.
20. On the modern universal survey museum and new installation practices, see especially Carol Duncan and Alan Wallach, 'The Universal Survey Museum,' *Art History* 3 (1980): 448–69. On the Revolutionary and nineteenth-century Louvre in particular, see Andrew McClellan, *Inventing the Louvre: Art, Politics, and the Origins of the Modern Museum in Eighteenth-Century Paris* (Berkeley: University of California Press, 1994). A classic nineteenth-century depiction of visitors copying old masters in the Louvre is Samuel F. B. Morse, *Gallery of the Louvre*, 1831–33. Oil on canvas. Daniel J. Terra Collection, 1992.51, Terra Foundation for American Art.
21. Simon Schaffer has described how ship models were used to train students in naval architecture in Britain in the Portsmouth School of Naval Architecture established after the Napoleonic Wars, 'Modèles normatifs et architecture navale dans un Etat militaro-fiscal,' *Réseaux* 18:102 (2000): 195–225, and 'Fish and Ships: Models in the Age of Reason,' in *Models: The Third Dimension of Science*, ed. Soraya de Chadarevian (Stanford: Stanford University Press, 2004), 71–105. See also Brian Lavery and Simon Stephens, *Ship Models: Their Purpose and Development From 1650 to the Present* (London: Zwemmer, 1995) on the historical development of ship models and the development of different types for different uses.
22. For the addition of the model of the steamship *Sphinx*, famous for its involvement in the conquest of Algiers, see Cailleux, directeur des Musées Royaux, to the intendant général de la Maison du Roi, 27 July 1837, EM22, Archives des musées nationaux (Louvre).
23. For example, the description of the 'Collection maritime d'un haut intérêt, composée de tous les instruments employés dans la navigation, et particulièrement de petits modèles exécutés avec autant de précision que de perfection, au moyen desquels on peut comprendre, et, pour ainsi dire, toucher du doigt les progrès accomplis par l'art nautique, depuis la pirogue faite d'un tronc d'arbre creusé jusqu'au vaisseau à trois ponts et au bateau [sic] à vapeur de six cents chevaux,' *Guide-François: Paris et ses environs* (Paris: Bureau des guides François, Dussacq, 1855), 55. In addition, educated commentators noticed a major difference between the models constructed during the time of Louis XIV and those constructed more recently. The former were highly decorative, designed to display the pomp and magnificence of the French navy, while the latter were constructed solely for the purposes for science and utility: *Annales maritimes et coloniales. 2ième partie. Sciences et arts*, 1 (1830): 186.

144 *Ralph Kingston*

24. The second of the museum modeled a French fleet between 1792 and 1814. On the walls of the same room were *tableaux* of engagements from the Revolutionary wars. See 'Note pour Chev. de Cailleux,' EM1 (1828), Archives des musées nationaux (Louvre).
25. Curator Pierre Zédé wrote to the Comte de Forbin in 1831 to inform him that the armoires were nearly finished and that that glass was being procured for them: 8 December 1831, EM1, Archives des musées nationaux (Louvre).
26. In 1834, the museum paid for 174 keyhole covers ('114 entrées de serrures à dauphins, 60 idem. à joncs unis'): Georges-Alphonse Jacob-Desmalter, 'Vitrine du musée dauphin,' in *Un âge d'or des arts décoratifs, 1814–1848: Galeries nationales du Grand Palais, Paris, 10 octobre–30 décembre 1991* (Paris: Réunion des musées nationaux, 1991), 168–70. What is pictured in the *Magasin pittoresque* is an entirely new set of display cases, constructed between 1834 and 1835. At this time, seven armoires were constructed specifically for ethnographic objects because the collection had outgrown its original accommodation. These plainer armoires, made by Jacques-Marie Renié, are now in the Département des objets d'art in the Louvre.
27. Cailleux, directeur des Musées Royaux, to the intendant général de la Maison du Roi, 28 December 1837, EM 22, Archives des musées nationaux (Louvre).
28. Léon Gozlan, 'Le Musée de Marine,' *L'Artiste: Journal de la littérature et des beaux-arts* 12 (1836): 201.
29. Alain Niderlinder, 'Le Musée de la Marine et ses collections, I,' *Neptunia* 194 (1994): 57.
30. Louis Rozet, *Chronique de juillet 1830* (Paris: T. Barrois et B. Duprat, 1832), 190.
31. The cataloguer, Emile Burnouf, later became very well known as a polygenist. He was also an early advocate of Aryanism, and had real intellectual differences with anyone classifying the cultures of ancient India as the same as 'primitive' North Americans.
32. Emile Burnouf, 'Note à consulter,' 15 November 1876, dossier 1, AN F/21/4483, Archives nationales, Paris.
33. Gozlan, 'Le Musée de Marine,' 201.
34. Ibid., 203.
35. On Dumont d'Urville's interest in native maritime architecture, see 'Voyage de *l'Astrolabe*, rapport lu à l'Académie royale des sciences par M. Dumont d'Urville,' *Nouvelles annales des voyages*, 42 (April–June 1829): 352. Pâris's drawing is reproduced in Dumont d'Urville, *Voyage de la corvette l'Astrolabe. Atlas historique* (Paris: J. Tastu, 1833).
36. Edmond Pâris, *Le Musée de Marine du Louvre. Histoire, description, construction, représentation statistique des navires à rames et à voiles, d'après les modèles et les dessins des galeries du Musée du Louvre* (Paris: J. Rothschild, 1883), 4–5.
37. 'Pirogue à balancier des îles Carolines,' 71.1894.34.32, Musée du Quai Branly.
38. Another example is Bayle St John, *The Louvre, or Biography of a Museum* (London: Chapman and Hall, 1855), 208–9. The British travel writer St John, visiting the museum in the early 1850s, commented that it was impossible not to consider, when moving through the museum, that 'the first elements of *all* commencing Art resemble one another in the most astonishing manner; and in the productions of tribes whose names one with difficulty remembers we find indications exactly resembling those met with in the primitive arts of the Etruscans, the Romans, etc.'
39. Forster, *Paris et les Parisiens*, 118.
40. Ibid., 117.

Armchair Expeditionaries 145

41. Gozlan, 'Le Musée de Marine,' 202.
42. Ibid., 203.
43. Like Caillé, Gozlan decried the difficulty of tracing the geographical origin of the objects in the collection. Yet, he did so with a very different purpose. The re-sorting of objects by location he called for was not an end in itself, but merely a means by which he could further 'pile up' more objects of similar natures—with similar uses—from different parts of the world (Ibid., 203). Gozlan was happy, therefore, to forgo the opportunity to move objects physically in order to expand the range of comparisons he could make mentally. In the meantime, however, other visitors were taking a more hands-on approach.
44. For example, Dorinda Outram, 'New Spaces of Natural History,' in *Cultures of Natural History*, eds. Nicholas Jardine, James A. Secord, and Emma C. Spary (Cambridge: Cambridge University Press, 1996), 249–65. Felix Driver, *Geography Militant: Cultures of Exploration and Empire* (Oxford: Wiley-Blackwell, 2001), 8–20 also draws on Outram's account to locate the difficulty in reconciling the knowledge generated by metropolitan 'centres of accumulation' and geography in the field in this period.
45. For one discussion of the tensions between 'armchair geographers' and 'explorers who travelled to the field' in Africa, see Lawrence Dritsas, 'Expeditionary Science: Conflicts of Method in Mid-Nineteenth-Century Geographical Discovery,' in *Geographies of Nineteenth-Century Science*, eds. David N. Livingstone and Charles W. J. Withers (Chicago: University of Chicago Press, 2011), 255–78
46. Jean René Constant Quoy, 'A. Amélie. Mars 1864,' MS 2507: 102, Médiathèque Michel Crépeau, La Rochelle. For the description used by Freycinet's men, see George Anson, *A Voyage Round the World: In the Years MDCCXL, I, II, III, IV*, 3rd ed., ed. Richard Walter (London: John and Paul Knapton, 1748), 453–8. Plate XXVII in the quarto edition of Anson's account illustrated this description with detailed figures of the boat's construction.
47. Jacques Arago, *Narrative of a Voyage Round the World, in the* Uranie *and* Physicienne *Corvettes, Commanded by Captain Freycinet, During the Years 1817, 1818, 1819, and 1820* (London: Treuttel and Wurtz, Treuttel, Jun. and Richter, 1823), 225.
48. Louis de Freycinet, *Voyage autour du monde, entrepris par ordre du roi . . . exécuté sur les corvettes de S.M. l'*Uranie *et la* Physicienne, *pendant les années 1817, 1818, 1819, et 1820* [Historique, II, première partie] (Paris: Pillet aîné, 1829), 60. In Freycinet's *Voyage*, objects also 'floated' from one account of encounter into another. The type of knife the crew had seen used to construct canoes was, in plate 46 (titled *Ile Rawak: Vue des Tombeaux Papouans*) of the expedition's *Atlas historique* (Paris: Pillet aîné, 1825), depicted in the hands of an Islander hacking open a coconut.
49. Joseph Paul Gaimard, 'Voyage physique dans l'hémisphère Austral, et autour du monde, exécuté sucessivement sur la corvette du roi l'Uranie et la corvette de S.M. la Physicienne, commandées par M. Louis de Freycinet. Journal historique,' ACC 3506A: 350, 361, Battye Library, State Library of Western Australia.
50. Jean René Constant Quoy, 'Voyage autour du monde pendant les années 1817, 1818, 1819 et 1820. Journal du chirurgien major Quoy. Historique,' 146, Service historique de la Défense, Rochefort.
51. Anthropology was, at this time, generally interested in phrenology; for example, in the *Société d'anthropologie* formed in 1832. It was heavily influenced by the medical revolution of the late eighteenth century and the belief in the interconnectedness of the physical and the moral: see Elizabeth A. Williams, *The Physical and the Moral: Anthropology, Physiology, and Philosophical*

146 *Ralph Kingston*

Medicine in France, 1750–1850 (Cambridge: Cambridge University Press, 1994), esp. 78–114. François Péron, a naturalist who sailed with Baudin, had been sponsored by the *Société des observateurs de l'homme*, and received Georges Cuvier's 'Instructive Note,' charging him to take note of the anatomical 'differences that characterise the races of the human species,' Bronwen Douglas, ' "Novus Orbis Australis": Oceania in the Science of Race, 1750–1850,' in *Foreign Bodies: Oceania and the Science of Race, 1750–1850*, eds. Bronwen Douglas and Chris Ballard (Canberra, AU: ANU E Press, 2008), 111.

52. Georges Cuvier, 'Instructions,' in Georges Hervé, 'A la recherche d'un manuscrit: Les instructions anthropologiques de G. Cuvier pour le voyage du 'Géographe' et du 'Naturaliste' aux Terres Australes,' *Revue de l'Ecole d'anthropologie de Paris* (1910): 305–6. For more on the instructions, see especially M. Bouteiller, 'La Société des observateurs de l'homme,' *Bulletins et Mémoires de la Société d'anthropologie de Paris* 7:5–6 (1956): 453; George W. Stocking, *Race Culture, and Evolution* (New York: Free Press, 1968), 29–31; and Bronwen Douglas, ' "Novus Orbis Australis",' 111–14. A separate set of instructions was given to Baudin's scientists by Joseph-Marie Gérando in 1800: *Considérations sur les diverses méthodes à suivre dans l'observation des peuples sauvages, par J.-M. Degérando* [Extrait des procès-verbaux des séances de la Société des observateurs de l'homme . . . 28 fructidor an 8] (n.p: n.d.). This pamphlet has been translated by F.C.T. Moore: *The Observation of Savage Peoples* (Berkeley: University of California Press, 1969).

53. According to François Grille, chef du bureau des sciences et des beaux-arts in the Ministry of Interior, at least 30 civilian scholars and artists asked to join the expedition, all with no success. In the wake of Freycinet's decision to appoint him over a museum candidate, Quoy had been afraid to present himself at the museum, to meet with Cuvier and Lamarck. According to Grille, 'Cuvier was, from the moment of [their] departure, very sour about Freycinet. He kept this grudge during the whole voyage,' François Grille, *Louis de Freycinet, sa vie de savant et de marin, ses voyages, ses ouvrages, ses lettres, son caractère et sa mort, avec des notes de Gabriel Lafond, membre de la Société de géographie* (Paris: Ledoyen, 1853), 11. On their return, Quoy and Gaimard surrendered their entire collection of specimens to the museum, which, as Quoy later remarked, was 'an act of generosity so rare that they knew to appreciate it,' Quoy, 'A Amélie. Mars 1864,' MS2507: 109, Médiathèque Michel Crépeau, La Rochelle. While Quoy was sanguine about turning over the fruits of his labour to Cuvier, Freycinet was not. He wrote to Quoy on 14 March 1822, complaining that Cuvier, in publishing an account of the new birds discovered by the Freycinet expedition, was stealing the 'flower of their work,' Freycinet to Quoy, 14 March 1822, MS2510, Médiathèque Michel Crépeau, La Rochelle.

54. Gaimard, 'Voyage physique dans l'hémisphère Austral,' 345–8.

55. Ibid., 362.

56. Quoy, 'Voyage autour du monde,' 141.

57. Both Quoy and Gaimard enjoyed a close relationship with Gall during the 1820s and 1830s, assisting with his demonstrations. They gifted him two of the skulls retrieved during their voyage. While Quoy ended up denouncing the 'fanaticism' and 'eccentricity' of Gall's theories, declaring phrenology a 'false science,' Gaimard seemingly did not break with phrenology, donating his skull to Gall when he died, Quoy, 'A Amélie. Mars 1864,' 135, 235.

58. As well as bringing the skulls to Gall, Quoy embarked on a careful reading of Gall's theories on the 'moral and intellectual functions of the brain.' His notes, carefully transcribed in the blank spaces of a small 1824 diary, are among his papers in MS 2507, Médiathèque Michel Crépeau, La Rochelle.

59. Quoy and Gaimard's report was published in an abridged version as 'Extrait d'un Mémoire sur la race d'hommes connus sous le nom de Papous, et particulièrement sur la conformation de leur crâne,' *Nouvelles annales des voyages* 19 (Paris: Gide fils, 1823): 115–27, and, unabridged, the next year in the official voyage memoir: Quoy and Gaimard, *Voyage autour du monde... exécuté sur les corvettes de S.M. l'Uranie et la Physicienne, pendant les années 1817, 1818, 1819, et 1820. Zoologie* (Paris: Pillet aîné, 1824), 1–11.

60. Quoy, 'Introduction,' MS 2507: 8, 39, Médiathèque Michel Crépeau, La Rochelle.

61. Quoy, 'Voyage autour du monde,' 141

62. Quoy and Gaimard's report is treated somewhat differently by Martin Staum in *Labelling People: French Scholars on Society, Race and Empire 1815–1848* (Montreal: McGill-Queen's University Press, 2003), 105–6. This treatment agrees more closely with that of Bronwen Douglas in ' "Novus Orbis Australis",' 117, while adding a more detailed account of Quoy and Gaimard's motivations. Douglas takes on Quoy's later polygenic writings on race more explicitly in 'L'idée de 'race' et l'expérience sur le terrain au XIXe siècle: science, action indigène et vacillations d'un naturaliste français en Océanie,' *Revue d'histoire des sciences humaines* 21 (2009): 175–209, noting both the disjuncture between Quoy's description of indigenous peoples and the actual experience of encounter, and the ways in which the racial theories brought by Europeans sometimes provoked indigenous reactions.

63. Quoy and Gaimard, 'Observations sur la constitution physique des Papous qui habitent les îles Rawak et Vaigiou,' *Annales des sciences naturelles, par MM. Audouin, Ad. Brongniart et Dumas* 7 (Paris: Grochard, 1826): 38.

64. In academia, Paul Rivet was one of the first anthropologists to question the use of visible physical properties to classify races, Alice Conklin, 'Science and Empire in Late Republican France,' *Osiris*, 2nd Series, 17 (2002): 255–90. This has caused some historians to assume that polygenist theories of race were uniformly accepted in France up to this point.

65. On the absence of western objects, see Zeynep Çelik, Displaying the Orient: Architecture of Islam at Nineteenth-Century World's Fairs (Berkeley: University of California Press, 1992), 189.

66. Staum, *Labelling People*, 103–17.

8 On Slippery Ice
Discovery, Imperium, and the Austro-Hungarian North Polar Expedition (1872–4)

Stephen A. Walsh

One of the most conventional narratives in expeditionary history involves the dispatch of a nationally conceived enterprise that plants a flag, draws a map, and acquires geographic knowledge, leading to territorial aggrandisement. However, this chain of events should not be viewed uncritically, for the connection between imperial iconography, cartographic inscription, and the actual expansion of empire is by no means unproblematic. This chapter examines a particularly fraught nexus of discovery and *imperium*: the First Austro-Hungarian North Polar Expedition (1872–4). More commonly known as the *Tegetthoff* Expedition (in reference to the name of the expedition's ship) or the Weyprecht-Payer Expedition (in honour of its two leaders: commander-at-sea Carl Weyprecht and commander-on-land Julius Payer), the expedition was celebrated for its 'discovery' of Franz Josef Land, the northernmost terrain in Eurasia. Today, Franz Josef Land appears on Google Earth as a small archipelago approximately 1,500 kilometres north of the Ural Mountains. This digital imaging, however, is only the most recent iteration of the long history of imaging and re-imaging Franz Josef Land, which forms the subject of this chapter.

This frigid and barren realm, home only to seals and polar bears, was named in honour of Franz Josef, ruler of the Habsburg Monarchy from 1848 to 1916.[1] On one level, both the expedition and the geography it delineated are steeped in the trappings of European imperialism. To the present day, the Habsburg sceptre is memorialised in the toponymy of the Arctic. Yet the 'discovery' of Franz Josef Land provided little in the way of imperial certainty. Its accomplishments were difficult to define and its effects were multivalent. After briefly discussing the key events in the chronology of the expedition, this chapter will demonstrate how, despite all its majestic rhetoric, the *Tegetthoff* Expedition and the discovery of Franz Josef Land proved too slippery for any one project, imperial or otherwise. I will then turn to the contested cartographic history of Franz Josef Land to examine how various professionals in the exploration business, in both the field and the study, used data and speculations about Franz Josef Land. There was no one 'discovery' of the area, but a complex series of interactions between various social, national, and professional groups, each with their own agendas.

On Slippery Ice   149

THE 'TERRORS OF ICE AND DARKNESS':
THE *TEGETTHOFF* EXPEDITION

Although hardly known in the English-speaking world, the *Tegetthoff* Expedition is among the most extraordinary narratives of endurance and accomplishment in the history of polar exploration.[2] The SMS *Admiral Tegetthoff* set sail from the North Sea port of Bremerhaven on 13 July 1872. The multinational expedition (including native speakers of German, Italian, Hungarian, Norwegian, and South Slavic dialects, later known as Croatian) had ambitious goals: to navigate the largely unknown waters between the Spitsbergen archipelago and the islands of Novaya Zemlya, and possibly sail the Northeast Passage. Additionally, it would perform an array of meteorological, geomagnetic, and hydrological observations. It was one of the most ambitious scientific programs ever proposed for a voyage of polar discovery.[3]

However, the expedition's geographic agenda was thwarted when the *Tegetthoff* became trapped in pack ice early in the autumn of 1872. For almost two years, the expedition was frozen in the boreal wastes of the Arctic. 'Frozen' in this Arctic environment, however, does not imply that their situation was static. Besides the vicissitudes of weather and encounters with polar bears, the tectonics of the ice were in constant flux, threatening to crush the ship. The shifting ice structure was due to the fact that the floes imprisoning the expedition were anything but stationary. The ice continued to drift north, taking the *Tegetthoff* in that direction. Over time, the ice conveyed the ship to one of the last significant discoveries of new land in the European age of exploration, which they christened 'Franz Josef Land' in November 1873. In spring the next year, Julius Payer, an experienced alpinist, surveyor, and veteran of an earlier Arctic expedition to the east coast of Greenland, led three sledge journeys into the interior of this unknown polar region.[4] During these excursions he made cartographic surveys and assigned place names to geographical features, including sighting the northernmost visible point of Franz Josef Land, supposedly the most northerly known point of land in the world, situated at latitude 83° north. Payer named it 'Cape Vienna.'

Knowing that a third winter would mean certain death, the expedition members abandoned the *Tegetthoff* in May 1874 and embarked on a gruelling southward trek across the polar ice, dragging heavy lifeboats and sledges in the hope of finding open sea. Progress was horribly slow over the jagged ice. It could take an entire day to cross a single fissure. Sometimes they appeared to make great progress, only to find that ice drift had resulted in a gain, rather than a loss, of latitude. But gradually things improved. Puddles in the ice became ponds; cracks became leads, the navigability of which incrementally grew, allowing respites on their boats before ice pressure would force the narrow channels shut. After a punishing 96-day trek across this oppressive terrain, they finally reached the open sea where, in

150 *Stephen A. Walsh*

a turn of fortune nearly as improbable, they found rescue in the form of a Russian fishing schooner, still at work in late August. Remarkably, every member of the expedition survived, save the machinist, Otto Krisch, who died of tuberculosis.

PLANTING A FLAG: EMPIRE AND NATION IN THE FAR NORTH

News of the expedition's rescue and its discovery of Franz Josef Land reached Europe in early September 1874, quickly sparking a polar craze in Austria. Weyprecht, Payer, and their fellow travellers received multitudinous honorary citizenships, society memberships, and medals of honour. Habsburg subjects cheered at marches dedicated to the explorers. They danced at 'North Pole balls,' wore 'Cape Vienna hats' and 'Weyprecht stockings,' drank 'Franz Josef Land beer,' and flocked to see amusing plays that were inexplicably set amidst glaciers.[5]

An example of graphic art from this period provides eloquent testimony to the craze for polar exploration motifs, triggered by the return of the *Tegetthoff* Expedition. 'North Polar Fashion' (Figure 8.1) is a cartoon, purporting to be an advertisement from a firm of clothiers, 'Polar Bear and Walrus.' Their premises were located at 'North Pole—Cape Vienna—83rd Parallel.' While it is unlikely that a reindeer head or enormous compass hat represented the height of Viennese fashion in the autumn of 1874, this cartoon suggests how thoroughly the discourse of polar exploration permeated popular culture. 'Our conversation has fallen completely under the freezing point,' as one contemporary Viennese journalist put it. 'The North Pole is the pole, around which . . . everything in Vienna revolves.'[6] That the capital was ablaze with talk of ice was not an inevitable outcome. Other expeditions of the period provoked nothing like this level of excitement, despite the *Tegetthoff* Expedition, for all its harrowing tales, having failed to accomplish its avowed aims.[7] So what explains this mass polar passion in Austria in the autumn of 1874?

Did this Arctic fervour have its basis in aspirations of imperialist expansion? In recent years, historians and geographers have probed the connection between geographic knowledge and territorial appropriation. Adopting Foucault's investigation of the relationship between power and knowledge, some scholars have argued that the practice of geography demonstrates 'the soaring proprietorial ambition of the European imperial mind.'[8]

Indeed, the discovery and reception of Franz Josef Land was conditioned by the specific local milieu of the Austro-Hungarian Empire, a polity that occupied a unique position in the broader framework of nineteenth-century global imperialism. A self-professed empire, the Habsburg Monarchy was both dynastic heir to the transcontinental dominions of Charles V and yet the only 'Great Power' in Europe without overseas colonies. Thus, imperial

Figure 8.1 'Nord Polar Moden.' *Der Floh*, 12 September, 1874. By permission of the Österreichische Nationalbibliothek (Austrian National Library).

152   Stephen A. Walsh

discourse did not necessarily match with formal imperialist political practice.[9] How different, then, were the terms in which Austrians construed their possession of Franz Josef Land, as opposed to more blatant instances of colonial expansion, such as British surveys of India or Russia's cartographic ventures on the Eurasian steppe?[10]

On the surface, the difference seems significant. In 1902, Emil Tietze, the president of the Austrian Kaiserlich-Königliche Geographische Gesellschaft (Imperial-Royal Geographical Society) claimed, 'when travellers from other lands, other nations, go abroad, very often they do so with distinct goals: to benefit, directly or indirectly, their homeland, be it in a political, colonial or commercial respect. The Austrian traveller, in general, has no other driving force than the love for research itself.'[11] In this reading, the Austro-Hungarian Empire's lack of colonies was a product of its putatively unique mission to advance the cause of an altruistic science. Only Austrian explorer-scientists could practise 'pure' science abroad. The efforts of other European powers were ignoble grabs for colonial domination.

In assessing the legitimacy of these claims, we should consider the argument of John Gallagher and Ronald Robinson, who said that to study only the 'formal' aspects of an empire would be akin to regarding an iceberg from only above the water line.[12] Historians such as Walter Sauer and Alison Frank have begun uncovering the Habsburg Monarchy's 'informal empire,' which they argue was directed at the commercial penetration of overseas territories, thus bypassing the need for political acquisition.[13] Austria was by no means a passive bystander to the imperialist project of the long nineteenth century.

In considering Austria's relationship with colonialism, we should bear in mind the argument of Felix Driver, who says of postcolonial critique that it 'has frequently given way to an essentialized model of "colonial discourse" which obscures the heterogeneous, contingent and conflictual character of imperial projects,' thus reducing complex texts or historical phenomena to a generalised imperial lust for power.[14] As Frank and Sauer have maintained, the Austrian imperial project centred on international commerce. However, Franz Josef Land—distant, barren, and inaccessible—offered few natural resources and no potential markets. Austria-Hungary's ambiguous standing as an 'empire' had a considerable bearing on how Austrian citizens, including members of the *Tegetthoff* Expedition, came to terms with Franz Josef Land.

Legally speaking, the Habsburg Monarchy did not annex Franz Josef Land. By the early nineteenth century, international consensus held that the mere 'symbolic' act of taking possession of a putatively empty and unclaimed geographic space through rituals of flag-raising and the like, was insufficient to vest a polity with ownership of the said terrain. The claimant needed to demonstrate occupation of, or effective administration over, the land in question in order to legally acquire it.[15] The Habsburg Monarchy took no such action in relation to Franz Josef Land, which hardly lent itself to the fulfillment of these conditions. Outside official circles, however,

On Slippery Ice 153

Austrian citizens did contemplate the appropriation of Franz Josef Land, albeit in an equivocal manner.

Payer's published narrative of the *Tegetthoff* Expedition endorsed the official lack of interest in annexation, while hinting that matters were not entirely clear-cut:

> With proud excitement, we planted Austria-Hungary's flag for the first time in the high north . . . But this was no legal act and it in no way portended taking possession of a land, as when Albuquerque or van Diemen unfurled the insignias of their fatherlands upon foreign soil, although we had gained this piece of cold, frozen earth with no less difficulty than they had acquired their paradises.[16]

Payer emphasised that his flag-planting ceremony on the top of the world was no petty attempt to gain territory for Austria. Yet his reference to Albuquerque and van Diemen suggests that it could well have been so. The practice was the same even if the function differed.

Other members of the *Tegetthoff* Expedition had less nuanced views concerning the place of the Austro-Hungarian flag in Franz Josef Land. On 3 November 1873, for example, the *Tegetthoff*'s ill-fated machinist recorded in his diary that 'Herr Payer, with the Austro-Hungarian flag in his hand, took possession of this land in the name of His Majesty the Emperor Franz Josef.'[17] The discourse of appropriation was in the air, as is demonstrated in an 1875 article from a popular journal. 'Modern science,' it proclaimed, 'celebrated a brilliant victory . . . when the Austro-Hungarian North Polar Expedition carried out the official act of the appropriation of Franz Josef Land.'[18] Here there is no sign of the qualification expressed by Payer. The symbolic import of the flag planted in frozen earth has shifted noticeably. For this author, the worth of Franz Josef Land lay in the fact that it was 'Austrians who took the first step upon that new land and it was the Austro-Hungarian flag that was first raised upon that virgin terrain of eternal ice.'[19] As previously noted, the flag ceremony had no legal bearing. Nevertheless, as this passage attests, legal realities and popular perceptions did not necessarily coincide. Tom Griffiths also notes how the polar regions can lend themselves to ambivalent flag-planting ceremonies and ambiguous geographic appropriation (see Griffiths, this volume).

Franz Josef Land could be appropriated symbolically, as is illustrated in popular art of the 1870s. A drawing captioned 'Payer und Weyprecht' (Figure 8.2) shows the double-headed eagle, symbol of the Austro-Hungarian Empire, flying above a frozen landscape with a medal inscribed 'Franz Josefs Land' in its talons. Below the eagle, the faces of Payer and Weyprecht are engraved into the ice that formed Franz Josef Land's defining landscape. The expedition leaders have become part of the topography, which shows how Austrian imaginations felt free to sculpt the very landscape in their own image. But to what end?

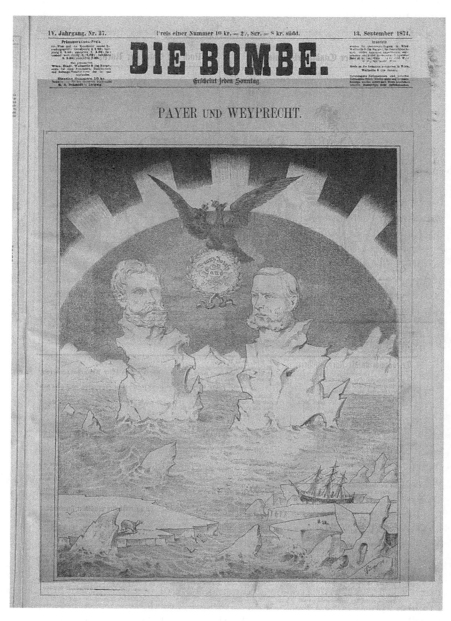

Figure 8.2 Anonymous artist, 'Payer und Weyprecht,' *Die Bombe*, 13 September 1874. By Permission of the Österreichische Nationalbibliothek (Austrian National Library).

On Slippery Ice   155

Michael Robinson, a scholar of American polar exploration, has shown that such was the publicity afforded to Arctic exploration that it came to be associated with the main social and political issues of the time—matters ostensibly far removed from the Far North.[20] Following this logic, Franz Josef Land could be regarded as an abstracted province or colony in the ideational landscape of the Austro-Hungarian Empire, where the problems of the monarchy could be addressed, both imaginatively and in terms of geopolitical practice.

Central Europe was coming to terms with tremendous changes in 1874. At centre stage was the question of Germany. As a consequence of the Habsburg Monarchy's military defeat by Prussia in 1866, Austria was toppled from its traditional position of influence in the German-speaking world. Under the leadership of Bismarck, conditions were created for the so-called 'unification of Germany' five years later, with the establishment of a state whose borders claimed to delimit the German nation, despite excluding the German-speaking citizens of Austria. That a Germany could exist in which Vienna, for centuries an epicentre of German culture and society, had no place was inconceivable for many Austrians. What did Austria's absence from Germany mean for its status as a Great Power? What did it mean for Austrians who also identified themselves as 'Germans'?[21]

The accomplishments of the *Tegetthoff* Expedition spoke to these concerns. One Viennese newspaper, for instance, found a counter-narrative to the legacy of 1866 in the discovery of Franz Josef Land. After the Austro-Prussian War, the journalist claimed, a number of Russian secondary school students sent a letter of thanks to Bismarck, in appreciation for how much his foreign and domestic policies had illuminated their understanding of Europe's political geography.[22] But did Bismarckian policies need to set the syllabus for European politics or geography? The author of this feuilleton proudly claimed that thanks to the discovery of Franz Josef Land, 'those unstudious Russian pupils have to learn more geography today, despite the facilitation of the German Chancellor, than they did in 1866.' All Bismarck had managed to accomplish, he argued, was to alter the fleeting borders of some states. The statesman's achievement was limited to changing the *political* description of the world, a transitory thing at best. But with the Habsburg flag planted into the frozen earth of Franz Josef Land, Austria had managed to remake the *physical* description of the planet—a permanent accomplishment. The article went on to place Weyprecht and Payer in the context of the British-dominated exploration of Africa. The author made it clear that the accomplishments of the *Tegetthoff* Expedition were best understood in light of the global stage of the British Empire—not the petty politics of Berlin. 'The newly discovered Franz Josef Land,' he crowed, 'is closer to the North Pole than any polar lands nominally subject to the British or Russian sceptre.'[23] By extension, Austria's discovery of Franz Josef Land could assure the monarchy's continued position in the first rank of global powers.

156   *Stephen A. Walsh*

For other advocates of exploration, Austria's polar accomplishments could ensure the Habsburg Monarchy's continued relevance in the German-speaking world. One journalist, basking in the international esteem lavished on the *Tegetthoff* Expedition upon its arrival in Hamburg—their first mainland European port—found the display of popular enthusiasm in that German city the cause of particular excitement.

> And if Austria is politically separated from Germany, language and science form an unbreakable bond. Hard-nosed Hamburg, which lives only for commerce, greets the polar explorers; their first greeting on German soil tells them how affinity for Austria is still alive.[24]

For this observer, Hamburg's enthusiastic reception of the expedition showed that even if Austria could no longer participate politically in 'Germany,' the practice of exploration and science provided avenues in which a larger 'Germany' that included Vienna could still exist as a field of cultural and intellectual activity. At stake here was how to define a national community. Reacting to the unification of Germany in 1871, the Austrian poet and playwright Franz Grillparzer famously opined, 'I am born a German, am I one still?'[25] Here, potentially, was a way to answer that question in the affirmative. Perhaps German language and culture could continue to define what 'Germany' meant, and not the recent changes in Central European political sovereignty.

Certainly, the leaders of the expedition were native German speakers.[26] But while many Austrian authors still clung to the idea of Germany as a cultural space that transcended political boundaries, others turned to the idea of the German nation as a unity of blood and spirit, and argued that the *Tegetthoff* Expedition was not an Austrian achievement at all, but a glorious accomplishment of German nationalism. As the Prussian geographer Julius Löwenberg proclaimed, it did not matter that the *Tegetthoff* Expedition served the Habsburg Monarchy. 'Whether the newly discovered land is christened Franz Josef or Wilhelm, or the oasis of an ice-rimmed promontory is named after Andrássy or Bismarck,' most important was that the expedition 'was inspired by Germans and accomplished by Germans in the German spirit.'[27] Such readings did not seek to put Vienna on parity with Berlin, but to exclude it entirely.

Such anti-Austrian sentiments, further exacerbated by the *Kulturkampf*, as Berlin's campaign to limit the power of the Catholic Church was known, made any association between the *Tegetthoff* and the broader German cultural space unacceptable to some German-speaking Austrians. As one Vienna-based clerical newspaper inveighed, 'if one tries to stamp "German" onto this Austrian enterprise, one should not forget for an instant that this is about an Austrian undertaking, that the expedition came about via Austrian property and blood, and also that "Mother Germania" played absolutely no role.'[28] Besides demonstrating how 'Germany' was a highly fluid concept

On Slippery Ice 157

at this time, these debates show how the expedition was used to support various—sometimes diametrically opposed—political visions.

Attempts to capitalise on the expedition were not only concerned with German nationalism. Its multinational character fuelled additional controversies to do with ownership. In 1893, the Dalmatian writer Petar Kuničić published a book, *Hrvati na Ledenom moru* (Croatians in the Icy Sea), based on Payer's narrative but incorporating the sailors of the *Tegetthoff* into the pantheon of Croatian national heroes.[29] Thirteen years later, at a meeting of the International Polar Commission, the Turin-based geographer Guido Cora appropriated the *Tegetthoff* as part of the heritage of Italian national polar exploration, by dint of those very sailors celebrated by Kunečić, although they had now become non-problematically Italian.[30] In the late 1920s, Mussolini's government went further and claimed sovereignty over Franz Josef Land on the basis of Italy's 1918 acquisition of Trieste, pointing out that the city (the main commercial harbour in the Habsburg Monarchy) had supplied the *Tegetthoff*.[31]

Nationally minded activists were not alone in seeking to appropriate the *Tegetthoff*. The multinational expedition could symbolise the diversity of the empire; the glory of their return became a focus of integrative patriotism for the entire monarchy. In the reading of one Habsburg loyalist, the brave explorers had only one motivation for their expedition: 'It was in praise of the fatherland to set sail . . . everything only in the interests and for the honour of the dear, beloved homeland!'[32] Unlike Germany, this homeland was distinctly multinational. At a banquet in Weyprecht's honour in Trieste, one attendee attested that, after a toast to the Emperor, an 'indescribable' level of enthusiasm prevailed. 'All of Austria seemed to be united in that room, ecstatic *Hochs* and *Evvivas* would not end, and stormy applause greeted the anthem [of the monarchy].'[33] For contemporary readers, the term 'all of Austria' directly highlighted the variegated nature of the Habsburg realms, not just the predominantly German-speaking areas that would become the Austrian Republic during 1918–19. The polity of that period included modern-day Hungary, Slovakia, the Czech Republic, Croatia, Slovenia, and significant parts of Poland, Ukraine, Romania, and Italy. With '*Hochs*' and '*Evvivas*,' typical celebratory exclamations in German and Italian, this observer chose to highlight multilingual support for the expedition, thus placing patriotism for the Austro-Hungarian Empire, with its 11 official languages, on centre stage.

Tensions between nationalism and internationalism continued for decades after the fall of the monarchy. Following Germany's annexation of Austria in 1938, the heroes of the *Tegetthoff* Expedition were incorporated into the Nazi pantheon of rugged Aryan heroes. A 1941 newspaper featured Julius Payer as part of a series titled 'Witnesses to Immortal German Culture.' Under the title 'Officer—Scientist—Artist,' Payer was portrayed in terms that drew from the familiar repertoire of tropes favoured by the Nazis: militarism, modern science, and romantic, Wagnerian art.[34] A year later, the

158   *Stephen A. Walsh*

Völkischer Beobachter, the central ideological organ of the National Socialists, commemorated the 100th anniversary of Payer's birth. Here, the multinational Austro-Hungarian North Polar Expedition, in a combination of virulent nationalism and Nazi *Führerprinzip* (leader principle), was reduced to 'the journey of two Germans, Weyprecht and Payer.'[35] Yet at the end of the Second World War, the same expedition provided rich material for a revived Republic of Austria, eager to distance itself from the recent excesses of German nationalism. In 1949 Vienna's Museum für Völkerkunde hosted an exhibition on the *Tegetthoff* Expedition. In stark contrast to the Nazi propaganda, the republic's Minister for Education claimed that commemoration of the expedition was 'Austria's honourable duty, and a welcome contribution to our national educational efforts . . . The scientific accomplishments of the Austrian polar explorers are today the common property of the educated world, not only . . . of every Austrian.'[36] Germany was again excluded from memorialisation of the *Tegetthoff* Expedition. Instead, it consolidated the vision of an Austria integrated into the international scientific community. Empire was inscribed into the very name of the Austro-Hungarian North Polar Expedition, yet the path from expedition to empire transported the heritage of that undertaking to a variety of contradictory destinations. Ultimately, most of the debate did not involve claims for imperialist expansion, but competing national and political projects for Central Europe; that is, agendas for the most part unrelated to the expedition itself. In fitting proportion to the number of disparate socio-political programs attached to the *Tegetthoff*, the expedition's primary accomplishment, the discovery of Franz Josef Land, also proved equivocal and became the fodder for further contradictory claims.

DRAWING A MAP: AMBIGUITIES OF DISCOVERY

An expedition's legitimacy rests primarily on its claim to having expanded knowledge. For the *Tegetthoff* Expedition, this claim depended, above all, on the discovery of Franz Josef Land. But what did they really discover? From one perspective, the discovery is well documented. The log of the SMS *Admiral Tegetthoff* records the precise moment: a little after two o'clock on the afternoon of 31 August 1873. With the lifting of a bank of fog that had obscured the horizon, boatswain Pietro Lusina, the sailor on watch, sighted land to the west-northwest, about 25 nautical miles from where the ship was frozen in the drifting ice. 'Because this land was completely unknown,' Weyprecht recorded, 'it was resolved by us to name it "Emperor Franz Josef's Land" on behalf of the entire crew.'[37] Despite the apparent certainties offered by this moment of 'discovery,' Franz Josef Land would continue to occupy a curiously indefinite position in the history of cartography. The fog had physically lifted, yet metaphorically it remained. The place name was established, but the place it referred to became the subject of considerable dispute. The discovery and naming of Franz Josef Land shows how mutable and yet persistent geographic 'knowledge' can be. Establishing the existence of something is tricky, but as the arguments concerning this mysterious tract of polar terrain reveal, establishing its non-existence can be even more difficult.

The aspect of Franz Josef Land that proved so tantalising to the geographic imagination was its unknown extent. This is revealed in a feuilleton titled 'Franz Josef Land and the North Pole Continent.' The unidentified author of this text hypothesised the existence of a massive Arctic continent. Greenland (the northern extent of which was then unexplored) was its western arm, Franz Josef Land its eastern. Perhaps this continent even stretched across the North Pole to 'Wrangel Land' (today's Wrangel Island) near the Bering Strait, the northern extremity of which was still undetermined.[38] Although it was too early to say with certainty, Franz Josef Land *could* have been part of an enormous polar continent.

Although Payer never claimed publicly to have discovered a continental landmass, his report to the Kaiserlich-Königliche Geographische Gesellschaft in Vienna emphasised that no boundaries to the new geography had been established. Franz Josef Land, he noted, appeared similar in geology to Greenland.[39] These affinities suggested a geographic link. In private correspondence, Payer was more forthright in his claims. Soon after his return to Europe, he wrote an excited letter to the geographer August Petermann, editor of *Petermanns Geographische Mittheilungen*, the most influential geographic publication in the German-speaking world.[40] Marked 'please burn,' Payer's missive implored Petermann to write to Emperor Franz Josef telling him that the land discovered 'is the most northern of the earth, [and] I, his subject, was the northernmost [person] since the creation of the world and say to him that Payer's tremendous discovery, that is his unprecedented sledge journeys, surpasses everything.'[41]

While decorum prevented Payer from articulating such bold claims in public, his map of Franz Josef Land could make similar assertions, albeit in a subtler manner.[42] Published by Petermann in October 1874 (Figure 8.3), the geography delineated by Payer in this chart is located within a waterway named Austria Sound. Payer travelled along this channel during his second sledge expedition, going as far north as Cape Fligely in Crown Prince Rudolf Land, at latitude 82° 5' north. His Franz Josef Land is dominated by two large landmasses on either side of Austria Sound: Wilczek Land, stretching out indeterminately to the east, and Zichy Land, its western extent unknown. In the north of Payer's map are terrains designated King Oscar Land and Petermann Land, offering further glimpses of a potentially vast polar landmass.[43]

What was the significance of these claimed discoveries for Payer? In his narrative of the expedition, the explorer recounted the mood on the ship in the days prior to the first sighting of Franz Josef Land. This occurred in August 1873, when it had become certain that they would have to spend

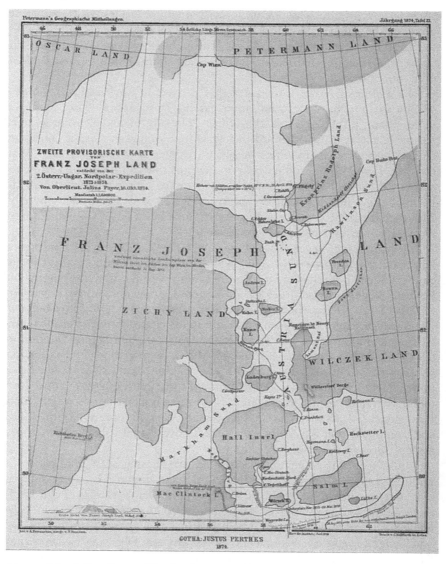

Figure 8.3 Julius Payer, 'Zweite Provisorische Karte von Franz Josef Land,' in *Petermanns Geographische Mittheilungen*, ed. August Petermann, 20 (1874), Table 23. By Permission of Harvard College Library, Cabot Science Library.

a second winter trapped in the ice. Payer was despondent, not because another dark and frozen winter loomed before him, but because he faced the prospect of returning home without concrete results. Everything changed with the appearance of a landmass through the fog.[44] Polar historians maintain that in the middle of the nineteenth century, explorers' claims for legitimacy were closely interwoven with the idea of scientific advancement. Mere adventure was typically deemed insufficient to warrant the risk and demands upon resources that an expedition entailed.[45] While in the twentieth century George Mallory could justify his yearning to scale Everest with the aphorism 'because it's there,' an explorer in the 1870s was expected not only to undergo arduous travel, but also to conduct scientific observations.[46] As Ferdinand Hochstetter, president of the Kaiserlich-Königliche Geographische Gesellschaft, told society members in January 1873, when the fate of the *Tegetthoff* was still unknown, participants in the expedition should be admired both 'for their heroic courage' and 'self-sacrifice for scientific goals.'[47] Enduring the forces of the Arctic was not on its own sufficient to win admiration, according to Hochstetter's criteria. While the naval officers on board the *Tegetthoff* had been conducting geomagnetic, meteorological, and hydrological observations during the ship's imprisonment in the ice, Payer's scientific contributions had hitherto been limited to drawing crustaceans, sea spiders, and other small specimens collected by Julius Kepes, the expedition's doctor.[48] His reputation as an explorer was dependent on geographical discovery.

Payer's map of Franz Josef Land does not explicitly claim that Franz Josef Land was continental, but it certainly suggests a vast expanse of land. As his correspondence with Petermann demonstrates, Payer was very concerned that his discovery be presented to the broader public as a major accomplishment. For this reason, size mattered.

Abroad, the geographic results of the *Tegetthoff* Expedition were acclaimed, even in the most authoritative geographic circles. In London, the Royal Geographical Society (RGS) awarded Weyprecht and Payer its two most prestigious medals—a rare instance of a single expedition receiving two of the society's awards. RGS president Henry Rawlinson exclaimed that the *Tegetthoff*'s achievements represented 'the most important geographical discovery of modern times.'[49] Payer's cartography had a lasting influence on Arctic exploration, contributing to a new consensus around polar geography. It became scientific orthodoxy that a shallow polar sea existed, containing either a substantial landmass or a series of islands extending north from Franz Josef Land.[50]

Meanwhile, the practice of Arctic exploration was changing in a way that put new emphasis on Franz Josef Land. In the latter decades of the nineteenth century, the popular concept of 'polar' became increasingly fixated on the two points at the extreme ends of the latitude scale. Reaching the North Pole became the sine qua non of Arctic exploration.[51] By the 1890s, many polar experts saw Franz Josef Land, with its unknown northern terrain, as the most promising route to the Pole. As the explorer Albert Hastings Markham argued, future Arctic expeditions 'should be directed to the little known Franz Josef Land, for it is in this direction that the greatest prospect, almost amounting to a certainty, of success will be obtained.'[52]

162 *Stephen A. Walsh*

Two expeditions in the mid-1890s emphasised the lack of knowledge concerning the newly discovered territory. The first attempt to reach the North Pole by way of Franz Josef Land was the British Jackson-Harmsworth Expedition (1894–7), which set off under the leadership of Frederick George Jackson. Their departure followed the commencement of Fridtjof Nansen's famous expedition aboard the *Fram*, an attempt to reach the Pole by deliberately freezing the ship into pack ice and drifting north with the current.[53] Neither expedition went according to plan. Jackson was thwarted by his inability to locate the northern parts of Franz Josef Land, as charted by Payer.[54] As for the Norwegians, the drift of the pack ice *did* take them to an unprecedented latitude, prompting Nansen and a companion to make a dash for the Pole. Forced back by the elements, they retreated in the direction of Franz Josef Land, desperately making their way south, sometimes via sledge over ice, through mixtures of snow and heavy slush, and sometimes via kayak between icebergs. However, like Jackson, they found no evidence of its northern reaches, including the alleged 'Petermann Land.' The impact was dire for the under-supplied Norwegians. Their survival was due to a most fortuitous coincidence when Nansen, entirely ignorant of Jackson's expedition, accidentally stumbled upon it, camped on Cape Flora in the southwest of Franz Josef Land.[55]

When the findings of these expeditions became known during 1895–7, Payer's claimed Franz Josef Land was seriously questioned. At a meeting of the RGS, Jackson's secretary, Arthur Montefiore, claimed that mountain ranges Payer alleged to have found could not be located, and several of the 'lands' on the Austrian's map were in fact small islands, if they existed at all. 'I believe I am justified in saying that . . . where *terra firma* has been placed [in several locations on Payer's map], there lies the salt of the sea.'[56] Nansen endorsed these views, announcing that he could not find any part of Franz Josef Land north of the 82nd parallel. Tellingly, he titled his map of the Arctic 'Preliminary Sketch Map of *the Group of Islands* Known as Franz Josef Land' (my emphasis).[57]

Although it was a blow to the reputation of Julius Payer, this reassessment of Franz Josef Land was more equivocal than might be expected. While the landmasses represented in Nansen and Jackson's maps are noticeably diminished, most of Payer's geographic assertions—even those that the English and Norwegian explorers pointedly looked for but failed to find (such as Petermann Land)—remained on the map. Practical considerations partially explain this. According to the logic of maritime cartography, an argument for the non-existence of a landmass requires a more exhaustive survey than does the argument for its existence. Furthermore, during his retreat to Franz Josef Land, Nansen's timepiece failed, making it impossible to determine longitude with any precision.[58] Without that reading, Nansen could not be absolutely certain where it was that he had been unable to find land.

That Franz Josef Land continued to survive, albeit ever more tenuously, in geographical science is due to the legitimising effect of cartographic

On Slippery Ice 163

representation. As the map theorist Christian Jacob has argued, a map is an archive of geographic data. That means it is far easier to add a name to a map than to remove one.[59] The highest authorities in geography had validated these constructions, and thus they lingered in Arctic cartography.

Consequently, there is no definite moment when we can say that Cape Vienna, for example—supposedly the northernmost known point in the world—was consigned to oblivion. Rather, it flickered in and out of cartography, gradually but inconsistently receding. Its fitful 'undiscovery,' for lack of a better term, was part of the complex series of negotiations that formed the ongoing re-conceptualisation of Franz Josef Land. Ralph Copeland, Astronomer Royal of Scotland, used Payer's notes to revise the Austrian's map and still found ample evidence to sanction the existence of its northern reaches in 1897. He even managed to discover new islands in Franz Josef Land, solely from Payer's data—a most striking example of discovery as process instead of event.[60] An expedition led by the Duke of Abruzzi to Franz Josef Land during 1899–1900 still hoped to find a route to the North Pole via Petermann Land.[61] The lingering state of ambiguity is encapsulated in a 1903 Austrian polar exploration treatise called *The North Pole Sphinx or Questions of Modern North Pole Research*. While admitting that Abruzzi had proven that Petermann Land did not exist, it nonetheless included a map on which it was featured.[62] An American expedition during 1903–5 failed in its attempt to reach the top of the world from Rudolf Land, and published a map that unequivocally denied the existence of any northern extent of Franz Josef Land. To drive the point home, it changed the name of every 'Land' to 'Island.'[63] So constrained a cartographic viewpoint did not gain currency and in 1914 a Russian expedition led by Georgii Sedov still felt the need to determine whether Petermann Land existed.[64] Despite significant evidence to the contrary, it seemed that the northern reaches of Franz Josef Land just had to exist, somehow. As late as 1931, during an Arctic journey by the airship *Graf Zeppelin*, a search was made for the northern reaches of Franz Josef Land.[65]

Just as the *Tegetthoff* Expedition was too slippery an entity for any singular imperial project or political interpretation, the 'knowledge' it produced proved liminal and contradictory. Like Cape Vienna, the coupling of discovery and empire at first seemed determinate. But it gradually vanished—a mirage of refraction in the polar fog.

CONCLUSION: EXPLORATION AS ART

Payer's later career is instructive for what it reveals about how expeditions and exploration were perceived and valued in the late nineteenth century. The explorer initially translated his Arctic experiences into significant social capital and prestige. During 1875–6 he wrote (and personally illustrated) his narrative of the *Tegetthoff* Expedition, which became one of the bestselling

164 *Stephen A. Walsh*

books in the history of the Habsburg Monarchy.[66] Soon an English translation (approved by Payer) appeared under the evocative title *New Lands in the Arctic Circle* (1876), casting appropriate emphasis on Payer's geographical ambitions.[67] The exploration historian Beau Riffenburgh has highlighted the tremendous success of *New Lands*, citing it as the first time the British and American reading public paid serious attention to an Arctic expedition from outside the English-speaking world.[68] In recognition of his Arctic achievements, Payer was elevated to the hereditary nobility in 1876.[69]

But these achievements belie a more complicated career. Little more than a month after the *Tegetthoff* Expedition's triumphant return to Vienna, Payer was denied promotion in the Austro-Hungarian army for reasons that remain unclear.[70] He angrily resigned his commission (later declaring himself a pacifist), and following the publication of his narrative, he left the Austro-Hungarian Empire for Frankfurt, Munich, and then Paris, where he pursued a moderately successful career as a historicist painter, specialising in massive, dramatic scenes of fierce polar bears, starvation amidst glaciers, impossible marches across the tundra, and ships frozen in unbreakable ice.[71] In 1890, he returned to Vienna, where he opened a painting school for young women.[72]

Five years later Payer began to plan a new expedition into the Arctic. The truth of the polar regions, he maintained, had been inadequately captured. To remedy this, he would lead a group of painters to Greenland. 'Would a discovery,' Payer asked, 'via the paintbrush be less glorious than the finding of new lands? To faithfully reproduce the natural phenomena of an unknown world in pictures, and thereby to serve art and science—would this not be worthy of recognition and support?'[73] As Adriana Craciun recounts, Payer was hardly the first Arctic traveller to aim at visually reproducing Greenland's natural phenomena (see Craciun, this volume). Historians of perception have argued for a growing alienation between scientific and artistic ways of seeing in the nineteenth century.[74] But according to Payer's plan, oil painting itself would become a domain of scientific discovery, rendering the artist as synthesis of explorer and scientist. Maps, as Payer knew well, could not *truly* represent a place. Questions of perspective, scale, and projection all reflect the fact that, ultimately, cartography can only act as a metaphor; we do not experience physical reality as a map. But the epistemic potential of expertly executed realistic portraiture held the promise of approximating reality. In the end, Payer was unable to secure sufficient funding to return to the Arctic, a circumstance that a prospective member of the expedition attributed to the fact that his plan did not involve an attempt to reach the Pole.[75] The failure to realise this enterprise was also coterminous with Jackson and Nansen's revisions of Franz Josef Land.

Responding to Montefiore in 1896, Payer acknowledged that his maps might contain imperfections, and that he expected future explorers to refine the cartography of Franz Josef Land. In other words, the construction of geographic knowledge was a process, not an event. At the same time he

On Slippery Ice 165

maintained that it 'may seem advisable to leave out all guesswork of the features of a country; but it does not seem to me desirable to recommend the discontinuance of this practice, as in that case, much of what is seen would also require to be left out.'[76] According to Payer, Franz Josef Land—and by extension, exploration—was not about establishing a set of facts, but rather a continually evolving process of speculation and interpretation. The work of the explorer-artist did not proceed to a finished, 'known' point, but remained open-ended. Discovery was a constant bustle of exploration, an expedition without end. Until debilitated by a stroke in 1912, Payer continued to formulate expeditionary projects, the last one being a plan to reach the North Pole by submarine.[77] Clearly, Payer's ways and means of discovery were malleable. The allure of charting the unknown endured.

NOTES

1. The state ruled by the Habsburg dynasty in the nineteenth century went by many names. Between 1804 and 1867, it was formally called the Austrian Empire, or Austria in common parlance. In 1867, the empire was divided into two entities (sharing sovereign, foreign ministry, and joint military forces), the smaller of which was the Kingdom of Hungary. The official name of the larger was 'The Kingdoms and Lands Represented in the Imperial Parliament' in Vienna, or, practically speaking, 'Austria.' The entire post-1867 polity was officially referred to as the Austro-Hungarian Empire or Austria-Hungary. 'Habsburg Monarchy' could refer to the state throughout the long nineteenth century. This chapter uses 'Austro-Hungarian Empire' and 'Habsburg Monarchy' interchangeably after 1867. In the context of relations within the German-speaking world, 'Austria' was the preferred term. This multiplicity of terminology reflects the heightened degree of political, national, and linguistic indeterminacy that was characteristic of the Habsburg realms. For adjectives, the cumbersome 'Austro-Hungarian' was usually used only in certain official situations, including naming polar expeditions. 'Austro-Hungarian' was never used to categorize personal citizenship or nationality. This chapter follows that usage, preferring 'Austrian.'
2. The Austrian novelist Christoph Ransmayr used the *Tegetthoff* narrative as a central aspect of his 1984 novel, *Die Schrecken des Eises und der Finsternis* (Vienna: Christian Brandstätter Verlag), later translated into English by John E. Woods as *The Terrors of Ice and Darkness* (London: Weidenfeld & Nicolson, 1991).
3. The *Tegetthoff* Expedition produced a wealth of narratives, published and otherwise, from expedition members and other polar enthusiasts. By far the most prominent was Julius Payer, *Die österreichisch-ungarische Nordpol-Expedition in den Jahren 1872–1874* (Vienna: A. Hölder, 1876). For a discussion of the various narratives of the expedition, see Frank Berger, 'Die Tagebücher der Expedition. Paralleltexte und Vergleich,' in *Eduard Ritter von Orel (1841–1892) und die österreichisch-ungarische Nordpolar-Expedition mit seinem Rückzugstagebuch von 1874*, eds. Enrico Mazzoli and Frank Berger (Trieste: Luglio Editore, 2010), 55–76. Mazzoli ably synthesizes the narratives of the expedition in *Dall'Adriatico ai Ghiacci. Ufficiali dell'Austria-Ungheria con i loro marinai istriani, fiumani e dalmati alla conquista dell'Artico* (Gorizia: Edizioni della Laguna, 2003).

166   Stephen A. Walsh

4. Payer's first polar expedition was the Second German North Polar Expedition (1869–70). See *Die zweite deutsche Nordpolarfahrt in den Jahren 1869 und 1870*, ed. Verein für die deutsche Nordpolarfahrt (Leipzig: F. A. Brockhaus, 1873).

5. For discussions of the reception of the *Tegetthoff* Expedition, see Johann Schimanski and Ulrike Spring, 'Polarwissenschaft & Kolonialismus in Österreich-Ungarn: Zur Rezeption der österreichisch-ungarischen Polarexpedition, 1872–1874,' *Wiener Zeitschrift zur Geschichte der Neuzeit* 9:2 (2009): 53–71 and 'A Black Rectangle Labelled "Polar Night": Imagining the Arctic After the Austro-Hungarian Expedition of 1872–1874,' in *Arctic Discourses*, eds. Ryall Anka, Johan Schimanski, and Henning Howlid Wærp (Newcastle upon Tyne: Cambridge Scholars Publishing, 2010), 19–42.

6. 'Brühwarmes vom Nordpol,' *Neues Fremden-Blatt*, 6 September 1874. This and all further translations are by the author.

7. For instance, compared to the *Tegetthoff*, the reception of the Second German North Polar Expedition was a relatively tame affair, despite the amazing survival of half of its members on an ice floe for 237 days after their ship had sunk. See *Zweihundert Tage im Packeis. Die authentischen Berichte der „Hansa"—Männer der deutschen Ostgrönland Expedition, 1869 bis 1870*, ed. Reinhard A. Krause (Hamburg: Ernst Kabel Verlag, 1997).

8. Michael J. Hefferman, 'Geography and Imperialism,' in *Sciences of the Earth: An Encyclopedia of Events, People & Phenomena, Volume I*, ed. Gregory A. Good (New York: Garland Publishing Inc., 1998), 237.

9. Whether the monarchy had a colonial relationship with certain peripheral provinces of its own is another question and subject to debate. See Evelyn Kolm, *Die Ambitionen Österreich-Ungarns im Zeitalter des Hochimperialismus* (Frankfurt-am-Main: Peter Lang, 2001); *Habsburg Postcolonial. Machtstrukturen und kollektives Gedächtnis*, eds. Johannes Feichtinger, Ursula Prutsch, and Moritz Csáky (Innsbruck: Studien Verlag, 2003); Andrea Komlosy, 'Innere Peripherien als Ersatz für Kolonien? Zentrenbildung und Peripherisierung in der Habsburgermonarchie,' in *Zentren, Peripherien und kollektive Identitäten in Österreich-Ungarn*, eds. Endre Hárs, Wolfgang Müller-Funk, Ursula Reber, and Clemens Ruthner (Tübingen: A. Francke Verlag, 2006), 55–78.

10. See Matthew Edney, *Mapping an Empire: The Construction of British India, 1765–1853* (Chicago: University of Chicago Press, 1997); Valerie Kivelson, *Cartographies of Tsardom: The Land and Its Meanings in Seventeenth-Century Russia* (Ithaca, NY: Cornell University Press, 2006).

11. As quoted by Walter Sauer, 'Jenseits der "Entdeckungsgeschichte": Forschungsergebnisse und Perspektiven,' in *k.u.k. kolonial. Habsburgermonarchie und europäische Herrschaft in Afrika*, ed. Walter Sauer (Vienna: Böhlau Verlag, 2002), 7.

12. John Gallagher and Ronald Robinson, 'The Imperialism of Free Trade,' *Economic History Review* 6:1 (1958): 1.

13. See Walter Sauer, 'Habsburg Colonial: Austria-Hungary's Role in European Overseas Expansion Reconsidered,' *Austrian Studies* 20 (2012): 5–23, and 'Jenseits der "Entdeckungsgeschichte"'; Alison Frank, 'The Children of the Desert and the Laws of the Sea: Austria, Great Britain, the Ottoman Empire, and the Mediterranean Slave Trade in the Nineteenth Century,' *American Historical Review* 117:3 (2012): 410–44 and 'Continental and Maritime Empires in an Age of Global Commerce,' *East European Politics and Societies* 25:4 (2011): 779–84.

14. Felix Driver, *Geography Militant: Cultures of Exploration and Empire* (Oxford: Blackwell, 2001), 7–8.

On Slippery Ice 167

15. James Simsarian, 'The Acquisition of Legal Title to Terra Nullius,' *Political Science Quarterly* 53:1 (1938): 111–28.
16. Payer, *Die österreichisch-ungarische Nordpol-Expedition*, 337. Afonso de Albuquerque (1453–1515) established Portugal's colonial empire in the Indian Ocean. Antonio van Diemen was Governor-General of the Dutch East Indies from 1636 to 1645.
17. Otto Krisch, *Das Tagebuch des Machinisten Otto Krisch*, ed. Egon Reinhardt (Graz: Leykam Verlag, 1973), 100.
18. 'Die Besitzergreifung des Franz-Josefs-Landes,' *Neue Illustrirte Zeitung*, 31 January 1875.
19. Ibid.
20. Michael F. Robinson, *The Coldest Crucible: Arctic Exploration and American Culture* (Chicago: University of Chicago Press, 2006), 3.
21. On the problems of defining the borders of 'German' history and Austria's role within it, see James Sheehan, 'What is German History? Reflections on the Role of the Nation in German History and Historiography,' *The Journal of Modern History* 53:1 (1981): 2–23; John W. Boyer, 'Some Reflections on the Problem of Austria, Germany and Mitteleuropa,' *Central European History* 22:3/4 (1989): 301–15.
22. 'Kap Wien,' *Fremden-Blatt*, 9 September 1874.
23. Ibid.
24. 'Die Ritter vom Norden,' *Neues Wiener Tagblatt*, 24 September 1874.
25. Franz Grillparzer, 'Auf des Dichters Porträtphotographie für das Album einer deutschen Fürstin,' *Grillparzers Sämmtliche Werke, Band I* (Stuttgart: Verlag der J. G. Cotta'schen Buchhandlung, 1878), 164.
26. Payer was born in Bohemia (roughly contiguous with the modern-day Czech Republic), a province of the Habsburg Monarchy, in a largely German-speaking area that in the 1930s became famous as the *Sudetenland*. Weyprecht was even born in Hesse, a territory outside the Habsburg Monarchy that would become part of the state called Germany in 1871.
27. Julius Löwenberg, *Die Entdeckungs- und Forschungsreisen in den beiden Polarzonen* (Leipzig, Prague, and Vienna: F. Tempsky, 1886), 97–8. Franz Josef and Wilhelm were the emperors of Austria and Germany, while Gyula Andrássy and Otto von Bismarck were the respective empires' foreign ministers.
28. *Das Vaterland*, 26 September 1874, http://anno.onb.ac.at/. Literature on the *Kulturkampf* is too vast to be recounted here. For examples see Jonathan Sperber, *Popular Catholicism in Nineteenth-Century Germany* (Princeton: Princeton University Press, 1984), 207–52; David Blackbourn, *Marpingen: Apparitions of the Virgin Mary in Nineteenth-Century Germany* (New York: Alfred A. Knopf, 1994).
29. Petar Kuničić, *Hrvati na Ledenom moru: Putovanje po sjeveru s hrvatskim mornarima* (Zagreb: Tisak i naklada knjižare Lav. Hartmana, 1893; reprint, Zagreb: Dom i Svijet, 1994). In 2004, the historian Ante Laušić published a 10-part retelling of the Croatian nationalist reading of the *Tegetthoff* based on the narrative of Kuničić in the popular newspaper *Slobodna Dalmacja*. See Ante Laušić, 'Hrvati na Sjevernom Ledenom moru 1872–1874' (Croatians on the Northern Icy Sea), *Slobodna Dalmacja*, 19–28 May 2004.
30. Mazzoli, *Dall'Adriatico ai Ghiacci*, 222–3.
31. Alexandr N. Krenke, 'Russian Research in Franz Josef Land,' in *Franz Josef Land*, ed. Susan Barr (Oslo: Norsk Polarinstitut, 1995), 134.
32. Hermann Quiquerez, *Österreich-Ungarn Hoch Oben im Norden! Geschichte der Österreich-Ungarischen Nordpol Expedition in den Jahren 1872–1874* (Vienna: Verlag von C. Stomp, 1878), 13–4.

168   Stephen A. Walsh

33. 'Das Banket zu Ehren Weyprechts,' *Triester Zeitung*, 13 October 1874.
34. 'Zeugen ewigen Deutschtums,' *Deutsches Volksblatt*, 11 July 1941.
35. 'Der Ruf des Nordens. Zum 100. Geburtstag Julius Payers am 1. September,' *Völkischer Beobachter*, 30 August 1942.
36. 'Zur Eröffnung der Payer-Weyprecht-Ausstellung,' *Das Kleine Volksblatt*, 18 December 1949.
37. Tagebuch des Schiffes, 'Admiral Tegetthoff,' 31 August 1873. Nachlaß Carl Weyprecht. Nr. 18, 354. Kriegsarchiv B/205. Österreichisches Staatsarchiv.
38. 'Franz Josephs-Land und der Nordpolkontinent,' *Neues Fremden-Blatt*, 18 September 1874.
39. Julius Payer, 'Österreichisch-ungarische Nordpol-Expedition: Berichte der Führer der Expedition,' *Mittheilungen der kaiserlichen und königlichen geographischen Gesellschaft in Wien* 17 (1874): 406, 410.
40. The exact title of Petermann's journal went through many permutations. The most common is *Petermanns Geographische Mittheilungen*.
41. Julius Payer to August Petermann, 23 September 1874. Historische Sammlung des Verlags Justus Perthes Gotha. Schriftleitung PGM 082/2 No. 301. Forschungsbibliothek Gotha.
42. For making political and social claims through cartography, see J. B. Harley, *The New Nature of Maps: Essays in the History of Cartography*, ed. Paul Laxton (Baltimore: The Johns Hopkins University Press, 2001).
43. Discussing Franz Josef Land's toponymy, Günther Hamann saw in it an object lesson on Austrian society of the 1870s, with an assortment of Austrian aristocrats and professors preserved in the ice of the Arctic. See Hamann, 'Das Zeitalter Franz Josefs im Spiegel der Topographie des Franz-Josefs-Landes,' in *Beiträge zur Allgemein Geschichte. Band IV*, eds. Hermann Wiesflecker and Othmar Pickl (Graz: Akademische Druck- und Verlagsanstalt, 1975), 139–51. However, fewer than half of the 90 place names Payer would eventually inscribe actually derive from people or places in the Habsburg Monarchy. Almost as many refer to prominent international figures in exploration and scientific research, the scientific elite who were essential to Payer's quest for legitimacy. On toponymy and exploration see Paul Carter, *The Road to Botany Bay: An Exploration of Landscape and History* (New York: Alfred A. Knopf, 1988).
44. Payer, *Die österreichisch-ungarische Nordpol-Expedition*, 136.
45. Robinson, *The Coldest Crucible*, 31–54. The first men to scale Mount Blanc, for example, received little credit for it due to their lack of scientific credentials. See Fergus Fleming, *Killing Dragons: The Conquest of the Alps* (London: Granta Books, 2000), 52–61.
46. The Mallory quotation comes from 'Climbing Mount Everest is Work for Supermen,' *The New York Times*, 18 March 1923. Adriana Craciun highlights another important aspect of the heroic Explorer's social construction, that of (perceived) authorship. See Craciun, this volume.
47. Ferdinand Hochstetter, 'Jahresbericht des Präsidenten der geographischen Gesellschaft für das Jahr 1872,' *Mittheilungen der kaiserlichen und königlichen geographischen Gesellschaft in Wien* 16 (1873): 16.
48. Camil Heller, 'Die Crustaceen, Pycnogoniden und Tunicaten der k.k. Österr.-Ung. Nordpol-Expedition' and Emil von Marenzeller, 'Die Coelenteraten, Echinodermen und Würmer der k.k. Österr.-Ung. Nordpol-Expedition,' in *Denkschriften der kaiserlichen Akademie der Wissenschaften, mathematisch-naturwissenschaftliche Classe* 35 (1878): 26, 357.
49. 'Presentation of the Royal and Other Awards,' *Journal of the Royal Geographical Society of London* 45 (1875): cix–cx.

On Slippery Ice 169

50. 'The North Polar Problem: Report of a Discussion at the Royal Geographical Society, 22 March 1897,' *The Geographical Journal* 9:5 (1897): 505.
51. Beau Riffenburgh, *The Myth of the Explorer: The Press, Sensationalism, and Geographic Discovery* (London: Bellhaven Press, 1993), 154–5.
52. Albert Markham, *Life of Sir John Franklin and the North-West Passage* (London: George Philip & Son, 1891), 312.
53. An idea, which Nansen acknowledged in a speech to the Austrian Geographical Society, had been inspired by the drift of the *Tegetthoff*. 'Festversammlung der k.k. Geographischen Gesellschaft in Wien zu Ehren Dr. Fritjof Nansen's,' *Mittheilungen der kaiserlichen und königlichen geographischen Gesellschaft in Wien* 41 (1898): 407.
54. Frederick G. Jackson, *A Thousand Days in the Arctic*, vol. 1 (London: Harper & Brothers, 1899), 260–4.
55. Ibid., vol. 2, 61–9.
56. Arthur Montefiore, 'A Note on the Geography of Franz Josef Land,' *The Geographical Journal* 3:6 (1894): 517.
57. Fridtjof Nansen, 'Some Results of the Norwegian Arctic Expedition, 1893–1896,' *The Geographical Journal* 9:5 (1897): 481–2. For his Franz Josef Land cartography, see *Preliminary Sketch Map of the Group of Islands Known as Franz Josef Land*, in *Farthest North: Being the Record of a Voyage of Exploration of the Ship "Fram" 1893–6 & of a Fifteen Months' Sleigh Journey by Dr. Nansen and Lieut. Johansen*, vol. 1, Fridtjof Nansen (London: Harper & Brothers, 1897).
58. Nansen, *Farthest North*, vol. 2, 397.
59. Jacob, *The Sovereign Map*, 211.
60. Ralph Copeland, 'On a Revised Map of Kaiser Franz Josef Land. Based on Oberlieutenant Payer's Original Survey,' *The Geographical Journal* 10:2 (1897): 180–91.
61. Susan Barr, 'The History of Western Activity in Franz Josef Land,' in *Franz Josef Land*, ed. Barr, 80.
62. Ferdinand Lupša, *Die Nordpolarsphinx oder Frage der modernen Polarforschung* (Ljubljana: Dragotin Hribar, 1903), 42, 58.
63. R. W. Porter and W. J. Peters, 'Map of Franz Josef Land Archipelago,' in *Fighting the Polar Ice*, Anthony Fiala (New York: Doubleday, Page & Co., 1906).
64. Vladimir Iulievich Vize, 'Kratkii istoricheskii obzor issledovaniia Zemli Frantsa Iosifa,' in *Zemlia Frantsa Iosifa*, (Moscow: Gosudarstvennoe Tekhnicheskoe Izdatel'stvo, 1930), 27.
65. 'Die Geheimnisse des Nordlandes. Das wissenschaftliche Ergebnis der Arktisfahrt des Graf Zeppelin [sic],' *Salzburger Chronik*, 18 August 1931.
66. Payer's *Die österreichisch-ungarische Nordpol Expedition* was first published in a series of 25 installments between October 1875 and June 1876. Thereafter, it was published as a single volume.
67. Julius Payer, *New Lands in the Arctic Circle: Narrative of the Discoveries of the Austrian Ship 'Tegetthoff' in the Years 1872–1874* (London: MacMillan and Co., 1876). By 1878, Payer's narrative had also been translated into Danish, Swedish, and French.
68. Riffenburgh, *The Myth of the Explorer*, 83.
69. Martin Müller, *Julius von Payer. Ein Bahnbrecher der Alpen- und Polarforschung und Maler der Polarwelt* (Stuttgart: Wissenschaftliche Verlagsgesellschaft, 1956), 160.
70. Payer's biographer attributes this to mysterious, untraceable doubts about his Franz Josef Land testimony in higher court and military circles. See Müller,

170 *Stephen A. Walsh*

Julius von Payer, 158–9. However, it is also noticeable that Payer's main patron within the government, General Franz Kuhn von Kuhnenfeld, had been ousted as war minister in the months before the rescue of the *Tegetthoff* Expedition. Johann Christoph Allmayer-Beck, 'Die Bewaffnete Macht in Staat und Gesellschaft,' in *Die Habsburgermonarchie, 1848–1918 Band V. Die Bewaffnete Macht*, eds. Adam Wandruszka and Peter Urbanitsch (Vienna: Verlag der Österreichishen Akademie der Wissenschaften, 1987), 107.

71. See Robert Doblhoff, 'Julius von Payer als Maler,' *Polarforschung* 3:21 (1951): 17–20.
72. Müller, *Julius von Payer*, 169.
73. Julius von Payer, 'Eine künstlerische Erforschung des Nordpols,' *Neue Freie Presse*, 4 January 1895, http://anno.onb.ac.at/.
74. Lorraine Daston and Peter Galison, *Objectivity* (New York: Zone Books, 2010), 246–51.
75. Müller, *Julius von Payer*, 175.
76. Julius von Payer, 'Correspondence—Payer's Map of Franz Josef Land,' *The Geographical Journal* 7: 1 (Jan. 1896): 105.
77. Müller, *Julius von Payer*, 180–1.

9 A Polar Drama
The Australasian Antarctic Expedition of 1911–14

Tom Griffiths

Expeditions are theatre—plays of power and possession performed for indigenous spectators, distant audiences back home, and even curious penguins in a howling wilderness. Theatricals have also been features of expedition culture, for they foster solidarity and co-operation among team members. Antarctic expeditions, which often drew on naval traditions, were especially devoted to dress-ups and high jinx as ways of maintaining morale through the long, dark polar winter.[1] The performance of *Cinderella* remains the centrepiece of the midwinter celebration in Australian Antarctic bases today.

There is a famous story of the director of the Australian Antarctic Division, Phillip Law, arriving at the sub-Antarctic Macquarie Island in 1950 to relieve a wintering party and finding everyone speaking to one another with theatrical nineteenth-century gentility. The men had survived the winter by repeatedly working through their small film collection, and the group's favourite was *Pride and Prejudice*. Once they tired of watching it, they turned down the volume and acted out the voices themselves. This ventriloquism easily tipped over into daily relations, and soon men were bowing and holding doors open for one another, and addressing their colleagues with sweet and elaborate civility. 'Such affability, such graciousness—you overwhelm me,' they could be heard saying to one another when passing the salt.[2]

In the spirit of Antarctic drama, I here offer a play of polar voices in six acts, accompanied by centennial reflections on the Australasian Antarctic Expedition (AAE) led by Douglas Mawson during 1911–14. The voices are those of the original expeditioners, words that I quarried from their diaries and letters when I was invited in January 2012 to assist the Australian government's centennial commemoration of the expedition's landing in Antarctica.[3] I joined the modern ship's company as a historian among scientists, and as functional expeditioners we created our own entertainment on board. So I performed an early version of this play on the voyage south, bracing myself against the swell of the ocean as I introduced the cast from a hundred years ago.

172   *Tom Griffiths*

ACT I: THE ADVENTURE

On a ship at sea on the Southern Ocean, December 1911

> BELGRAVE NINNIS: *I can hardly realise that I am absolutely off on a Polar Expedition. [Mawson is] a splendid fellow. He is quiet, and a scientist all over; also a gentleman, ditto. My respect for him increases daily . . . I am having the time of my life. I feel an object of envy to everyone . . . I cannot realise my luck; at times I lie awake simply hugging myself for joy . . . Here I am practically in my second childhood . . .*
>
> CHARLES LASERON: *It was with beating hearts, and a strange feeling of exaltation that we started on what will probably be the greatest adventure of our lives.*
>
> GEORGE DOVERS: *. . . everything is just ripping, we are landing in a place that will make the whole civilised world wonder . . . when I think of all the fellows slaving in offices in cities when there is all this beautiful God's world to explore & all its wonders to see, I pity them, this is living not merely existing . . .*
>
> DOUGLAS MAWSON: *It seemed to me that here was an opportunity to prove that the young men of a young country could rise to those traditions which have made the history of British Polar exploration one of triumphant endeavour as well as of tragic sacrifice. And so I was privileged to rally the 'sons of the younger son'.*

In late December 1911, Mawson and his men were leaning on the rails of the *Aurora* and excitedly scanning the horizon for their first sighting of ice.

ON DESERTS, RED AND WHITE

In the early twentieth century Antarctica became an additional site of European colonial rivalry, the place for one last burst of continental imperialist exploration, which had been such a trademark of the nineteenth century. The 'heroic era' of Antarctic exploration (1895–1917) was heroic because it was anachronistic before it began, its goal was as abstract as a pole, its central figures were romantic, manly, and flawed, its drama was moral (for it mattered not only what was done but how it was done), and its ideal was national honour. It was an early testing ground for the racial virtues of new nations such as Norway and Australia, and it was the site of Europe's last gasp before it tore itself apart in the Great War.

Douglas Mawson's account of the Australasian Antarctic Expedition of 1911–14, *The Home of the Blizzard*, was published in two volumes in early 1915, the year of the Australian and New Zealand Army Corps (ANZAC) landing at Gallipoli. It has often been claimed that the Australian nation was born in that year on that war-torn beach in Turkey on the other side

A Polar Drama   173

of the world. But the heroic landing a few years earlier at Cape Denison, Commonwealth Bay—a landing also 'hampered by adverse conditions,' a landing made by scientists rather than soldiers, and a landing in Australia's own region of the globe—deserves attention, for it was imbued with similar symbolism and sentiment. Both landings were self-conscious actions by a young country impatient to prove its racial vigour on the world stage. They were both deeds of a newly federated nation eager to rally the 'sons of the younger son' in the service of the British Empire.

But the AAE was also a distinctively Australian endeavour, driven by nationalism, a Southern Hemisphere sensibility about the need to know one's own backyard, and a keen sense of Australia's distinct geopolitical interests. In the two decades following Mawson's return, Australian scientists, politicians, and diplomats would exert strong pressure on Britain to secure sovereignty over the vast region of Antarctica south of Australia. In 1933 it led to the declaration of Australian Antarctic Territory (AAT) and the consolidation of a claim over more than 42 percent of the continent of ice. This assertive, confident Australian diplomacy exhibited no 'blind servility' to empire.[4] Rather, Australia acted on a clear conception of its distinctive outlook and material self-interest in Antarctic affairs.[5]

For Australians eager to assert a national identity and worried about the mental and physical effects of an urbanising population, the Antarctic frontier, like the outback, was a place of anxiety and opportunity. There were concerns about the organic vitality of the race (especially in a young nation founded as a penal colony) and the invigorating potential—and degenerative effects—of the frontier. As Brigid Hains has explored in her wonderful book, *The Ice and the Inland* (2002), the red heart and the white south provided vital, formative experiences of the frontier for a settler nation.[6] The harsh desert environments threatened regression and offered renewal.

To the invaders and colonisers of Aboriginal Australia, there was an attractive moral simplicity about colonising an uninhabited continent. Australia's Aboriginal lands had been appropriated under the doctrine of *terra nullius*, and a 'Great Australian Silence' grew up around the experience of frontier war and dispossession. So there was something redemptive about Antarctica's unalloyed whiteness. The cultural geographer Christy Collis reminds us that a shocking massacre of Aboriginal people took place at Coniston in Central Australia in 1928, just as another British, Australian, and New Zealand Antarctic expedition was preparing to go south to claim genuinely uninhabited lands.[7]

Sir MacPherson Robertson, businessman and confectioner (the maker of Cherry Ripe chocolates), donated £10,000 to those British, Australian, New Zealand Research Expeditions (BANZARE) during 1929–31. At the same time he sponsored a complete circuit around the Australian continent by truck (see Clarsen, this volume). Thus an entrepreneurial champion of racial whiteness, who dressed his workforce in white, conquered the Australian deserts, red and white, and had his name bestowed on a vast white sheet of Antarctic ice (Mac. Robertson Land). The ship of that expedition, the

Figure 9.1 'A turreted berg' as seen from the *Aurora*, circa 1913. Photograph by Frank Hurley. By Permission of National Library of Australia. (John George Hunter collection of photographs of Antarctica, nla.pic-an23323340.)

Discovery, sailed with a plain white flag, and a portrait of MacRobertson, as he liked to be known, stared down from the wall of the leader's cabin. Occupying that same cabin during 1929–31 was an older Douglas Mawson, consolidating the strategic work of his earlier expedition. He was securing for Australia a polar empire where any contests over ownership would be international, public, and honourable.

ACT II: THE ICE

Among icebergs off the coast of East Antarctica, late December 1911 and early January 1912

> FRANK HURLEY: *The first glimpse came one day when the breeze was blowing still and bleak from the south . . . Suddenly it grew calm . . . we felt like Argonauts whose quest had led to the World's brim. Slowly we crept on, filled with wonder and expectancy. The growl of surf, like*

*breakers grumbling on a reef, came to our ears. All hands mustered on
the fo'c'stle head and peered in the direction of the sound. Through a
rift we made out the glimmering sheen of a colossal berg.*

CHARLES HARRISSON: *The depth and purity of the colouring [is]
marvellous. I dashed down for my paint box and canvas . . . I was
doing what I never thought to, using pure cobalt and emerald green!*

PERCIVAL GRAY: *Everybody is delighted with the ice, personally it simply fascinates me . . . At present I am planning to spend most of the
rest of my life down here . . .*

But not everyone was delighted. Captain John King Davis expressed dis-
appointment at meeting the pack so far north, and now it was growing
heavier he was forced to follow the edge of it westward, looking for an
opening, a lead to the south. Every day was, as he put it, another *long
weary day coasting along the edge of the pack trying to get south, but
seldom making better than West.*

GRAY: *Still going west . . . Mawson is afraid of going into the pack
unnecessarily, as ships have been caught for a whole year in it before
now, and it would be a great farce if we came back without having
landed a party at all.*

By the night of 2 January, Mawson was in despair. His whole expedition
seemed in jeopardy, and he was facing personal failure and humilia-
tion. *Things looked so bad last night that I could do nothing but just
roll over and over on the settee on which I have been sleeping and
wish that I could fall into oblivion.*

Suddenly, at 6 a.m. on the third, they discovered a huge glacier tongue,
beyond which there seemed a clear passage south towards land. It was
a turning point for the expedition.

MAWSON: *Here within a gunshot is the greatest glacier tongue yet
known in the world—no human eyes have scanned it before ours.
What an exultation is ours—the feeling is magical . . . [we] literally
dance from sheer exultation—can you not feel it too as I write—the
quickening of the pulse, the awakening of the mind, the tension of
every fibre—and this is joy.*

GRAY: *Great happenings to-day. We have started the discoveries! . . .
They will have to be landed somewhere so the sooner we start about it
the better . . . I only trust that the show is not a failure.*

ON TIME AND ICE

In late 2011 another Australian ship, the *Aurora Australis*, was preparing to
sail south to commemorate Mawson's expedition. In Antarctica, you can't
just select a date, waltz in, and perform a ceremony. You have to submit
yourself to the control of the continent just as Mawson's men did; ice and
weather cannot be commanded. Antarctic logistics are ruled by what is
called 'the A-factor,' the destabilizing ingredient in all Antarctic planning.

176 *Tom Griffiths*

Uncertainty and waiting are the warp and weft of Antarctic history. The men of the Australasian Antarctic Expedition spent a lot of time waiting. Waiting for the wind to stop so they could work outside or hear themselves think; waiting agonisingly for the Far Eastern sledging party of Mawson, Belgrave Ninnis, and Xavier Mertz to return; waiting for the black speck of their ship, the *Aurora*, to appear on the horizon to take them home. They were not the first Australians in Antarctica—several, including Mawson himself, had participated in earlier expeditions—but this was the first Australian expedition and the first of any kind to set foot on the Antarctic continent directly south of the island continent.

In Antarctica, it can feel like time has not only skipped a beat, but has lost the beat altogether. Time there assumes different rhythms. There is the deeper pulse of the ice ages, the seamless months of eternal light or night, the transcendent other world of a blizzard, the breaking up of the sea ice, the exciting return of the Adélie penguins in spring, the schedule of the summer ships, and the intensity of the annual 'changeover' at Antarctic stations. A century might signify a hundred generations in Antarctica, or just one tick of the glacial clock.

It therefore seemed entirely appropriate that Antarctica itself should dictate the timing of the centennial visit to Mawson's Huts. Blizzards at Casey station in late December 2011 had delayed the schedule of our ship, the *Aurora Australis*. And there was an added complication. For possibly the first summer in a century, Commonwealth Bay was filled with ice.

Just to the east of the Bay there once existed the huge tongue of the Mertz Glacier (named after Xavier), the feature that had so thrilled Mawson on 3 January. That tongue of ice had seemed a constant attribute of the coastline, a geographical extravagance that was discernible on continental maps. But in February 2010 a huge iceberg from the Ross Ice Shelf—the size of the Australian Capital Territory and named B9B—collided with the Mertz Glacier tongue and sheered it off, sending it slowly spinning westwards. B9B itself became grounded about 25 kilometres offshore from Commonwealth Bay and corralled the sea ice near the coast. Cured hard by the wind and fastened to the land, the sea ice made it impossible for ships to reach Mawson's Huts in the 100th summer after the expedition's landing. But the Australian Antarctic Division was willing to await its moment. Equipped with three helicopters on board the *Aurora Australis*, it was determined to take on the A-factor.

The collision between B9B and the Mertz Glacier tongue initiated what the physical oceanographer on our ship, Steve Rintoul, called a 'natural experiment.' In the lee of the glacier tongue, furious katabatic winds funnelled down onto Commonwealth Bay and maintained a *polynya*, the beautiful Russian word for the belts of open water found within the ring of ice that surrounds Antarctica. The Mertz polynya, as one of the prime Antarctic sites of sea-ice production, releases salty, dense 'bottom water' that plunges to the ocean depths and drives the engine of ocean circulation. Was it the

Figure 9.2 The *Aurora Australis* off Commonwealth Bay with Iceberg B9B in the background, January 2012. Digital photograph by Tom Griffiths.

presence of the vast glacier tongue that made this polynya so active? What might now be the impact of the glacier's calving on salinity, circulation, and biodiversity? And how might it relate to a general trend—observed since the 1970s, possibly as a result of increased glacial meltwater—for Antarctic bottom water to become less salty and less dense?

In other words, how might global warming affect ocean circulation? It is ice cores from Antarctica, in which hundreds of thousands of years of climate history are embedded, that have delivered the sense of urgency we now feel about curbing greenhouse gas emissions. The continent has enabled us to travel through time to the atmosphere of Pleistocene Earth. Antarctica has become a luminous relic, a big white fossil, an archive of air.

ACT III: THE LANDING

> 67°south, 142° 40' east, on a rocky shoreline of East Antarctica, 8–19 January 1912
> Suddenly on 8 January 1912, following further days of hope, anxiety, and disappointment, the men of the AAE gained a clear prospect of accessible land.

GRAY: *Well, they really do seem to be making up their minds to land the first party at last . . . It has been a most beautiful day, brilliant sunshine, with the temperature above freezing . . . We are all waiting in great excitement for the boat to return.*

NINNIS: *We have just discovered what looks like a good landing place for our hut, and any minute we may receive the order to land stores that will see us working day and night until the ship leaves . . . This place has an extraordinary formation and I am already gripped thereby. Is so huge and white and quiet and . . . forbidding looking. . . I am enjoying myself more than I can possibly describe . . .Well now fare ye well. Welcome me with open arms if I return and weep over my distant and frozen corpse if I don't, and cast thoughts after me as I head my devious and crevasse ridden ways.*

MAWSON: *We were soon inside a beautiful, miniature harbour completely land-locked. The sun shone gloriously in a blue sky as we stepped ashore on a charming ice-quay—the first to set foot on the Antarctic continent between Cape Adare and Gaussberg, a distance of about 2000 miles.*

HURLEY: *Even the beauty of recent scenes waned before the glamour of this landing.*

But later that day, by the evening of 8 January, the true character of the place—its defining elemental essence—was revealing itself. Winds such as no one had ever known before were sweeping down onto the natural harbour they had found and forcing them to retreat to the ship, hoping that the anchor would hold. Great sheets of spray were being lifted off the water, covering everything on the ship in solid ice.

For two days the blizzard raged. Work began again on 11 January. They were sleeping on the ship and working on shore around the clock in shifts while the weather lasted, but as a storm brewed again on the evening of 12 January, Mawson and Frank Wild went ashore to join the five men working there and to sleep on the continent itself.

HARRISSON: *. . . we went up to Dr Mawson's tent. He had the Nansen cooker going preparing a meal. Meanwhile, we pitched a couple of the little sledging tents . . . unscrewed boxes and got out the Reindeer sleeping bags. Then a mug of hot soup was served round, most delicious! Followed by a mug of hot cocoa. And we turned in about 2 am. Great amusement over Hannam getting into his sleeping bag! . . . I snuggled into mine, fastened up all the toggles, and tired and cold, slept well. We did not wake until past noon—the day bright but blowing fresh.*

CECIL MADIGAN: *I was only conscious during about six hours of this day. We were all tired and there was nothing to do so we had a grand warm sleep.*

Thus began the Australian occupation of Antarctica.

The *Aurora* left Cape Denison on 19 January to establish the second, western base.

> FRANK WILD: *I for one could not help thinking that our goodbyes were to some of them forever. It is a fearful country where they are landed.*
> JOHN KING DAVIS: *They are a fine party of men but the country is a terrible one to spend a year in.*
> GRAY: *The whole thing impressed me very much, those 18 men on their little boat pulling away to their icy home.*

ON SOVEREIGNTY AND SCIENCE

By 16 January 1912, the men of the AAE were still waiting out storms and unloading stores. And this was the day, a hundred years afterwards, when we finally landed our own party. For five days we had waited on the edge of the sea ice 20 kilometres off Cape Denison for weather that would allow our helicopters to fly. That morning of the 16th, the cloud lifted and the white cliffs of East Antarctica sparkled in the sunlight. As we flew in we could see the exposed granites of the cape that had attracted Mawson, and beyond it, the white brow of the polar plateau climbing and receding into a pure infinity. Somewhere in the middle of this coastal patchwork of white ice, black rock, and aerial blue could be seen something else—at first I registered it as a different, surprising, organic colour, a pinpoint of warmth. It was the wind-bleached wood of a hut.

Mawson's book about this place is called *The Home of the Blizzard*, which honours (or laments) the ferocious katabatics that are the essence of this bay. But this was also the home of 18 men. This was their cosy, beloved refuge—and a century later it is still an inviting and reassuring presence. The swale in which it sits is also quite intimate, and the men made this their own, too, inscribing it with the daily religious duty of their scientific observations.

The low door of the hut had been dug clear of snow by our advance party. Appropriately, one bows to enter the darkness of this shrine. Inside on this calm day was the Antarctic silence. And there was also stillness. The air smelt musty and organic and the walls gleamed faintly, illuminated by the skylight. There were half-familiar shapes and structures to discern in the gloom: Frank Hurley's photographs reconstituted themselves before my eyes in ageing wood, metal, and paper. The old stove stands in one corner, the acetylene generator that produced lighting sits on a high beam, and all around the walls are the beds. The hut was insulated with a two-storey layer of people. I had walked into a boys' bunkroom! 18 men slept here top to toe for the first year, and it still feels private, intimate, domestic.

Outside the huts we gathered for a ceremony. In number we were similar to the party that landed here a hundred years ago. Surrounded by a voluntary audience of Adélies, Tony Fleming, the Director of the Australian Antarctic Division, read a statement by the Prime Minister of Australia,

Figure 9.3 Mawson's Huts, Commonwealth Bay, 2012. Digital photograph by Tom Griffiths.

Julia Gillard. The names of all the men of the AAE were read out and honoured: the 19 who served in Adélie Land (this included Sidney Jeffryes, who joined the six who stayed for the second year), the eight who established the Western Base, the five who maintained the station at Macquarie Island, and the men of the *Aurora*. Fleming spoke of the preeminence of science in the planning and practice of the AAE, and of the foundation it laid for the modern Antarctic Treaty System where science is so central: 'I am frequently asked: what is the enduring legacy of the Australasian Antarctic Expedition?' Fleming explained: 'My answer is unequivocal—an entire continent devoted to peace and science, where nations work together in a spirit of collaboration.'[8] The Australian flag was raised to applause from the people and squawks from the Adélies. I spoke briefly about the original landing and read some words from the diaries of the expeditioners.

A few years earlier, when writing a history of Antarctica called *Slicing the Silence* (2007), I made a bit of fun of proclamation ceremonies in front of audiences of Adélies on windy, remote Antarctic coastlines.[9] After all, claiming something as slippery as ice *is* laced with comedy, and narrow nationalism appears inapt on a continent of ice where humans are so marginal and vulnerable. Now, in January 2012, I was suddenly involved in the ritual myself . . .

While our ship was still in Antarctic waters, the Australian historian David Day wrote an opinion piece for the *Age* and the *Sydney Morning Herald* in which he questioned such expressions of patriotism in Antarctica.[10]

Entitled 'Antarctica is No Place for Politicking: Mawson's Expedition was About Territorial Gain, Not Science,' Day's essay was critical of the commemorative ceremony of 2012 that I have just described. He argued that it fell into a familiar pattern of Antarctic behaviour: 'From Mawson in 1912 to Monday's ceremony, it has all been done in the name of territorial acquisition and retention, with science acting as a cover.' Science, argued Day, was only 'the supposed purpose' of Mawson's Australasian Antarctic Expedition; its real aim was territorial acquisition and economic gain.

Why would Australians today raise the flag in this international place? There is no doubt that by doing so we were quietly affirming Australian sovereignty over 42 percent of Antarctica. Penguins are not the only creatures with a colony here. But the 2012 ceremony was carefully modest. No anthem was sung, no cheers called for, no proclamation made, no mention of 'territory' by the Prime Minister, and the emphasis of the speeches was on the science of the AAE and its continuities with the scientific priorities of the Treaty era. Attention was given to all the young men who were excited by this last frontier, not only Mawson. The two men who died were especially remembered. With typical Australian bashfulness at ceremonies, the formalities were completed quickly and simply. The real commemorative act, we felt, is in continuing to do science and history in Commonwealth Bay and Antarctica, and in helping researchers from other nations to do it too.

Figure 9.4 Mawson's Huts pictured on 16 January 2012, overlaid with a historic photo of the proclamation ceremony at the huts on 25 February 1912. Digital photograph by Karen Barlow.

182   *Tom Griffiths*

For Australians in Antarctica there is no more powerful word than 'Mawson.' Uttering it creates a significant space in the conversation. The thoughtful commemoration of Mawson and his legacy is a critical part of Australia's international obligation in Antarctica. Patriotism is not necessarily contrary to the spirit of the Antarctic Treaty. National endeavour is the means of contributing to the treaty system, and there is national pride in becoming an influential party to the Treaty. Quiet, reflective patriotism is the fabric of Antarctica's successful international governance.

How did the AAE expeditioners at the main base resolve the enduring Antarctic tension between politics and science? What priorities governed their behaviour in those first weeks after the landing and is it true to claim that 'science acted as a cover'? The landing of stores began on 8 January and after the ship was farewelled on 19 January, the huts were swiftly built between blizzards. No sooner had a 'House warming feast' been held on 30 January (not a flag ceremony as alleged by Day) than daily meteorological recording began. Ninnis and Mertz built two Stevenson screens to house the recording instruments, work began on the construction of the Absolute Magnetic Hut and Magnetograph House, a tide gauge was installed, and biological and geological monitoring and collecting was begun. Once the scientific infrastructure was in place, seals and penguins were butchered for winter stores of meat and blubber. Next the men began to prepare for their first exploratory sledging journeys; they were impatient to see where they were.

In late February, the dreadful winds were strengthening, the Antarctic cold deepening, and the days shortening. The poor weather delayed their sledging plans, so Mawson planned a ceremony instead. They had been six weeks at Cape Denison and finally they gave themselves a moment for ritual and reflection. But if the weather had been better, they would have been out and over the crest of the ice cap.

ACT IV: THE CEREMONY

Inside and beside the Main Hut, Cape Denison, Antarctica, 25 February 1912

FRANK STILLWELL: *Bickerton spent the afternoon erecting a 5' flag pole on top of the main hut and it gives a nice swanky appearance to the homestead. [6 February]*

MADIGAN: *[Mawson] wants to raise the flag tomorrow now we can be considered as residents here, having a house. This ought to be a fine little ceremony. [24 February]*

ARCHIE McLEAN: *This was the day of days in so far as the history of our stay in this place is concerned. We added to the British Dominions by taking possession in the name of George Vth of Adélie Land.*

A Polar Drama   183

MADIGAN: *This has been really like a Sunday, and the most pleasant day we have spent in Antarctica. The morning I attended the instruments and as soon as that was done, at 10.30, we had our first divine service in Antarctica. Mawson had the books on a cushion covered by a Commonwealth flag, the blue Australian ensign. We had enough hymn books supplemented by a few prayer books, including mine, to go round. The service was short and Mawson was rather nervous, but it was impressive and personally it was very comforting to me and I think to the others.*

STILLWELL: *The little organ was opened and I played the hymns. Playing was very poor and disgusted me properly. The service lasted a very short 1/2 hour after which Mawson proceeded to unfurl the flag from the small flagstaff. The wind was fierce and it felt like Antarctica as we stood bareheaded as the flag was unfurled. Mawson spoke of our right to do so because of our occupation for 1 month and because the French had only landed on an island for a few hours when they hoisted their flag. Hurley worked the cinematograph and took a photo.*

MADIGAN: *I reported a giant white petrel hovering about near the sea at the end of the West ridge and Bick and I were told off to try and shoot it as a specimen.*

NINNIS: *Simple as the ceremony was, it was impressive in its way. We have formally added our newly discovered land to the list of British possessions, and one more blot of red will be added to the map.*

McLEAN: *Dr Mawson wore an Australian flag and after tomato soup, mutton, vegetables, blanc manges, jellies, raspberries, cigars etc we had speeches to finish up a very historic evening.*

MADIGAN: *[Mawson] made a speech . . . He said we were snug and comfortable etc.; we were in a much worse place than any Antarctic expedition had ever landed in, the weather was far worse, it looked as if these winds were constant and sledging would be most difficult. No other expedition had been game to land here. Perhaps it was a terrible region; we were going to prove it. The meteorological results would be very valuable, the magnetic work, the biological work; but of more practical value at present was the geographical work, we must explore.*

ON THE SOUNDS OF SILENCE

American biologist David Campbell, in his lyrical book, *The Crystal Desert*, described terrestrial Antarctica as 'the antithesis of the Amazon . . . It is like the silence between movements of a symphony.'[11] It seems paradoxical that 'the home of the blizzard' should be renowned also for its silence. But silence is a period of non-wind, and the power of silence is heightened by the memory of the blizzard. It is the after-shock of wind that can give silence its resonance. Mawson remembered how at night 'one would involuntarily wake up if the wind died and be loth to sleep "for hunger of a sound."[12] Silence, then, is not just an absence; it has a texture and a timbre. It can roar in one's ears all on its own.

The Antarctic silence is also the space within which other, surprising sounds can be heard—the beating of one's heart, perhaps, or the thump of your pulse in your temples. It was said that Frank Wild had such a strong pulse and booming chest that if you happened to share a sleeping bag with him in Antarctica, you would be kept awake all night by the beating of his heart.

Antarctic history combines the vastly inanimate and the intensely intimate. You find yourself exposed both to elemental majesty and social claustrophobia. In Antarctica, it is dangerous to be alone. It is a continent that often draws people who seek solitude, only to condemn them to an intense human intimacy.

In the boys' bunkroom at Cape Denison, there was little privacy. Their only refuge, their sleeping bags, froze to the wall and had to be thawed nightly, and sometimes condensation produced 'small icebergs up to several pounds' in a bunk. The night watchman—and they each took their turn

Figure 9.5 'Midwinter Dinner, Adélie Land', with British flags hanging and an Australian flag wrapped around a post, 1911. Photograph by Frank Hurley. By Permission of Mitchell Library, State Library of New South Wales. (Home and Away 36708.)

A Polar Drama 185

in this role (it was also their chance to have a bath)—heard all the snoring, whistling, and 'talking in one's sleep, which is very common here.'[13] Soon the men began to have the same dreams, which were often of waiting, promise, and incompleteness. At work and over meals, 'fine old arguments' on social, political, and scientific subjects might last several days. A particularly heated debate concerned 'drunkenness versus sexual immorality.' In the depths of winter, they tried an experiment in thought transference and 'the result was *marvellous*.' They held hands in the semi-dark, looked into each other's eyes, made their minds a blank, and thought of a card—and it was drawn every time from a displayed hand of six.[14]

ACT V: THE WINTER

Inside the Main Hut, Cape Denison, Antarctica, Winter 1912

During dinner the Blizzard will render the usual accompaniments—'The Tempest,' 'For Ever and Ever,' etc.,—Mid-Winter Dinner Menu, 21 June 1912

NINNIS: *It really looks as if there must have been a large surplus of bad weather left over after all the land had been formed at the Creation, a surplus that appears to have been dumped down in this small area of Antarctica.*

MADIGAN: *. . . we have had three continuous months of the worst weather ever experienced on earth. For days it is only possible to crawl about outside.*

MAWSON: *The Hut has cracked from time to time; we begin to think of where we may seek refuge should it give way altogether . . . It is indeed difficult to understand how air can flow so swiftly . . . we have discussed the possibility of our roof bursting outwards . . . Imagine a hut with all in it suddenly blown away bodily into the sea.*

MADIGAN: *After some practice the members of the expedition were able to abandon crawling, and walked on their feet in these 90-mile torrents of air, 'leaning on the wind' . . . I found that in a 90-mile wind, if I faced it and kept the body straight, I could touch the ground in front by extending an arm.*

LASERON: *In the middle of lunch we all become aware of something strange. Our ear-drums commence to throb as with a great noise. Somebody speaks and his voice cracks like a whip on the stillness. For the wind has stopped, and, accustomed as we are to its howl, the silence can literally be felt.*

MADIGAN: *It was so calm we felt afraid to make a noise. I have read of this feeling, but never experienced it before.*

STILLWELL: *Following [Mid-Winter] dinner was song and gramophone and a little performance by McLean and Madigan of a Brutus-Cassius*

186 Tom Griffiths

> *scene out of Julius Caesar. Both were rigged in quite passable Roman Togas with rugs and butter cloth, and both were clean shaven. And indeed the whole was first class.*
>
> MERTZ: *Although I am uncertain about the present or the future and I know that Switzerland lies far away, I have never felt such satisfaction and peace in my life . . . Raving weather whips up my nerves and blood.*
>
> MAWSON: *I lecture staff in evening on value of work.*
>
> MADIGAN: *It is funny to hear the chaps talking, nearly everyone has a few words to say at times, in his sleep. From our corner came little whistles and sucking with the lips; it was Mertz or Ninnis calling dogs.*
>
> NINNIS: *From the creation, the silence here has been unbroken by man, and now we, a very prosaic crowd of fellows, are here for an infinitely small space of time, for a short time we shall litter the land with tins, scrap timber, refuse and impedimenta, for a short time we shall be travelling over the great plateau, trying to draw the veil from a fractional part of this unknown land; then the ship will return for us and we shall leave the place to its eternal silence and loneliness, a silence that may never again be broken by a human voice.*

ON SANITY AND SURVIVAL

1913 was the unexpected year. It was a year of trauma and waiting—and of nightmares more than dreams. On the first day of 1913, at the height of the Antarctic summer, Mawson and Mertz were sledging for their lives between two perilous glaciers in Adélie Land. Two-and-a-half weeks earlier, their companion, Ninnis, had been swallowed by the ice, taking practically all the food and the best dog team down with him. Mawson and Mertz turned desperately for home.[15]

Back at the coast, the ship *Aurora* had returned to Commonwealth Bay on 13 January 1913 to take home the men of the AAE. The *Aurora's* second officer, Percival Gray, was 'amazed at the change in some of these shore fellows when I saw them last night. A harder tougher looking crowd I never wish to see.'[16] Captain Davis anxiously awaited the return of all the men from their summer sledging trips so that he could sail west and pick up the other Antarctic shore party. 'There is still no sign of Mawson,' Davis wrote in his private journal on 22 January 1913.[17] The far eastern sledging party of Mawson, Ninnis, and Mertz was well overdue.

The last entry in Mertz's sledging diary was 1 January 1913, for in the following week he slipped quickly into convulsions, dementia, and death. On their race for survival back towards Cape Denison, Mawson and Mertz lost their hair and skin and suffered crippling stomach pains and dizziness, for they were unwittingly poisoning themselves by eating the livers of the

A Polar Drama   187

huskies they butchered and boiled. On 8 January Mawson solemnly buried Mertz and marked his grave. He still had more than 160 kilometres to go. On his lone trek back to Commonwealth Bay, Mawson fell down so many crevasses that he tied himself to his sledge with a rope ladder so that he could effect his own rescues. On 1 February he reached Aladdin's Cave, an excavated ice cavern just nine kilometres from the hut. For the next week high winds trapped him there.

At Commonwealth Bay, Captain Davis could wait no longer and had determined to leave by the end of January. But the same blizzard that delayed Mawson in the cave made it impossible for the shore party to approach the ship. When the wind finally relented on 8 February, Mawson was able to leave the cave and the shore party reached the vessel. Thus, as Mawson picked his way down the final, steep slippery slope to the hut, he glimpsed the *Aurora* steaming out of the bay for another whole year.

In this unwelcome second year, the lively, busy, hopeful community of the AAE had been reduced to a melancholy rump, afflicted by tension, heartache, and depression. An unaccustomed slackness settled on the hut. For a time after his ordeal, Mawson could do little but eat and sleep. He would follow people around the small interior, just to be near them. Mawson must have been haunted by questions about the loss of his companions. Had Ninnis broken through the lid of the crevasse because he was on foot and not on the sledge? Could Swiss ski champion Mertz have skied home himself? Why had they loaded most of the food on just one of the sledges? Would it have been safer to return along the coast, where there was also wildlife for food, rather than across the perilous inland glaciers? Looking back on 1913, Mawson confessed to his fiancée, Paquita Delprat, that 'most of my time during this winter was occupied in keeping myself and others sane.'[18]

In the first year Cecil Madigan and Frank Bickerton had shared their corner of the hut with Ninnis and Mertz. Now the corner was forlorn and those bunks were empty, even accusing. Bickerton sobbed under his blanket at night over the loss of his friends, and the men knew also by now that the katabatic winds that blasted their hut were the winds of Scott's death. As the polar night deepened, the new wireless operator, Sidney Jeffryes, slipped into madness.[19]

Jeffryes had begun the year well. He replaced Walter Hannam as wireless operator and soon established successful radio communication with Australia via the relay station at Macquarie Island. The AAE became the first Antarctic expedition to use this technology. We might say then, as curator Mark Pharaoh has suggested, that 1913 was the year the silence of Antarctica was broken.[20] During the early months of 1913, radio messages provided 'the real event of the day' and brought the outside world and loved ones closer. There was a constant battle to keep the wireless masts upright in the home of the blizzard. Jeffryes was the only newcomer in a small group of men that had already spent a year together, and his work

188   Tom Griffiths

further isolated him. He seldom went outside and often slept during the day, for his evenings were spent tuned to the wireless with his headset on, straining to hear signals, real or imagined. He was listening for voices in his head.

In early July, 'though curiously logical at times,' Jeffryes became paranoid, delusional, and violent, suspecting that his companions were plotting to murder him, believing that Mawson had cast 'a magnetic spell' on him, and threatening to expose these machinations to those at home. On 27 July, he tendered his 'resignation' from the expedition. Determined to isolate the madness in case it might catch, Mawson assembled his men around the table and publicly ridiculed Jeffryes with a carefully written speech. Jeffryes's madness waxed and waned, but the firearms were hidden and he had to be kept under constant watch. He was admitted to an asylum on his return to Australia.[21]

Jeffryes later claimed his own troubles had started when he defended Mawson from Madigan, who 'made a scurrilous insinuation against Mawson, with regard to Mertz.' Whatever we think of this testimony—the evidence of a madman—it does identify a likely taboo: a subject of disquiet in the polar night in a hut where Mertz's bunk lay empty and Mawson still lived.[22] Once suspicions had been voiced, there was no escaping them. They infiltrated the very fabric of the hut and, like ice in the crevices, set hard. Mawson did not eat Mertz. But there in the dark winter of 1913 it is reasonable to suggest that Mertz was eating away at Mawson.

Mawson—an Australian hero and icon in the making—was emaciated and broken as he faced this unexpected year of isolation, angst, and reflection. His men had always admired him for his energy and tenacity, for leading from the front, but he never commanded the kind of love or affection that Shackleton or Wild inspired. Mawson could be very demanding of his staff—he drove others as he drove himself—and he was sometimes sarcastic and lacked compassion and humour. But in this second year, he became a figure of disdain to some of his companions, especially Madigan and Bickerton.[23] Madigan had been understandably reluctant to stay another year—he had to defer his Rhodes Scholarship again—and during periods of depression he became deeply resentful of his leader. His diary remained private for a hundred years.

Among Madigan's grievances was the sense that Mawson spoke of Ninnis and Mertz in an offhand way. It may have been Mawson's way of coping with the tragedy. But even Paquita, Mawson's fiancée, wondered about the emotional depth of her beloved. 'It seems like writing to a wall,' Paquita declared to Mawson in September, 22 months into their separation. 'There is no reason why you shouldn't like me as much as before. But this everlasting silence is almost unbearable.' Paquita continued, 'I wonder why I feel so sad tonight. Am I afraid there is not room in your heart for the expedition and I? . . . Oh Douglas don't *don't* let Antarctica freeze you.'[24]

ACT VI: THE ASYLUM

Inside the Main Hut, Cape Denison, Antarctica, Winter 1913

Now is the winter of our discontent—Mid-Winter Dinner Menu, 21 June 1913

MADIGAN: *There is a curse on this place, I hate it, it is loathsome to me. I feel rotten today and have never had such gloomy thoughts. If it were not for two people who really love me I would as soon be at the bottom of a fathomless crevasse with my poor old Kamerad.*

McLEAN: *We have been listening to Doctor Mawson's terrible experiences piecemeal.*

MADIGAN: *I am afraid to write down what I think of Mawson now, my opinions have changed greatly . . . Bickerton and I agree in our opinions.*

One thing I can say, and am sure I will never go back on; and that is, that in this show it is Mawson first and the rest nowhere.

I don't know what the public will think of his sledge journey; he has sent messages which make him appear a hero.

His journey was a most unexpected failure, against every principle of sledging in this country.

MAWSON: *I may go off my rocker very soon.*

MADIGAN: *I did not record before, but I do now, that the way he talks of Ninnis and Mertz has disgusted us all from the first.*

From the day he came back my dislike for him has increased . . . His daily conversation is disgusting, and we are none of us too particular ordinarily. How an engaged man can talk incessantly as he does I cannot imagine. We pity the woman who has to live with him.

McLEAN: *It's very difficult to keep the diary going at times.*

MADIGAN: *Jeffryes has been becoming very peculiar of late. I think he is mentally deranged.*

JEFFRYES: *When I tell you that my reason, memory, and all my faculties of mind, are as good as ever they were; and yet I am insane, it will seem paradoxical, but it is really so.*

MADIGAN: *The poor wretch is hopelessly insane. He has been making some horrible noises in his bunk tonight . . .*

It is very unpleasant feeling his eye on you for minutes at a time, I must say. If you look back at him, he never looks away but keeps up a rigid stare. I tried the effect of looking calmly back for about half a minute some days ago and it disturbed him terribly, he wriggled and looked horrible so I gave it up; I thought at the time he thought he was being hypnotised.

JEFFRYES: *I am under a hypnotic spell which you [Mawson] have found it incumbent on you to place me under.*

MAWSON: *The accommodation houses are few and far between in the Antarctic and I am quite concerned that our tariff is too high to enable Jeffryes to remain at this admirable hostel. We are certainly prepared to let out an ice cave for his use on comparatively moderate terms.*

MADIGAN: *I feel years older after this experience. Bick and I both say we can't imagine ever feeling young or light-hearted or really happy again . . . and here we are, cooped up with a lunatic.*
McLEAN: *I'm afraid we think of nothing else but that ship.*
MADIGAN: *I often feel that the outer world is a dream, that this is the only life I know, I have become so used to it. It is hard to think of trees and grass.*
I had a dreadful dream last night, that dear old Mertz was back. I was looking at his happy, laughing face, and kept saying 'Is it really you, Xavier?' and felt full of joy, till his face started to fade away and I woke in tears.
MAWSON: *[Soon] the memories of the past were to fade into a dream—a nightmare?*

ON MEMORIALS AND LEGACIES

By mid-October 1913 the Adélie penguins had returned, the snow was thinning to icicles on the rocks and seabirds were again flying along the shoreline. At the end of November the men solemnly erected a cross on Azimuth Hill at Cape Denison in memory of their lost friends, Ninnis and Mertz. The cross honoured their 'supreme sacrifice . . . in the cause of science.'

In January 2012, after the commemorative ceremonies at the hut, I climbed Azimuth Hill where the memorial cross to Ninnis and Mertz still stands clearly on the skyline, surrounded by penguin colonies. Beyond it, the ice cliffs of Commonwealth Bay take your breath away. As I sat there among the nesting Adélies, gazing out across the sea ice to the tiny black dot on the horizon that was our ship, I was moved by this choice of words etched in wood that seems so emblematic of how the men of the expedition saw their endeavour. Their friends died not for 'the glory of empire' or for 'pride of nation'; they died in 'the cause of science.'

Douglas Mawson's Australasian Antarctic Expedition was strategically establishing 'residency'—their hut was significantly a 'homestead' and a 'house.' But they were also committed to exploration, to the detailed investigation of unknown territory and the comprehensive scientific measurement and assessment of as extensive an area as possible. Mawson employed more scientists, explored vastly more territory, compiled more data, and published more findings than any other Antarctic expedition of the 'heroic era.' The AAE, concludes polar historian Beau Riffenburgh in a recent scholarly study, 'became the model upon which many future expeditions in the Antarctic would be based' and 'helped establish the form that Antarctic science would eventually take.'[25]

Historian of science, Peder Roberts, argues for the value of attending to the routines and practices of an expedition's scientific life, and warns against

A Polar Drama 191

being too distracted by politics and personalities.[26] In the case of the AAE, he discerns a collective intellectual enterprise—of which Mawson was just one part—and a breadth of scientific networks within which the work of the young scientific team was embedded. Roberts hoped thus to reveal 'a history of a scientific expedition rather than an Antarctic adventure.' According to this view—which is consistent with what the experience of commemoration taught us—the character of an expedition can be found more truly in the fabric of its daily life than in its public tragedies and triumphs.

To the men of the expedition, science was no mere 'cover'—it was more vital even than ceremony for morale. It was science that justified their presence for at least a year on that remote, alien continent and that helped secure them to their windy place. These young men, mostly Australian, mostly in their 20s, mostly university-educated, were as eager as Mawson to *explore* and to apply their fresh scientific curiosity and training to new and challenging terrain. With their bodies and their minds they laboured towards understanding. Science was their daily discipline, their emotional anchorage, their intellectual sustenance—and perhaps it might keep them sane.

But it *was* also an adventure. Over 100 years ago, on that portentous day—8 January 1912, the day of the first landing of an Australian expedition on the great continent of Antarctica—what did our revered expeditioners do the moment they set foot on the ice? As Archie McLean recorded: *Mawson and Wild explored and the others had a snowball fight.*

NOTES

1. Elizabeth Leane, *Antarctica in Fiction: Imaginative Narratives of the Far South* (Cambridge: Cambridge University Press, 2012), 125.
2. Tim Bowden, *The Silence Calling: Australians in Antarctica 1947–1997: The ANARE Jubilee History* (Sydney: Allen & Unwin, 1997), 229.
3. The quotations that make up the six acts are drawn from the following diaries, letters, and books (in order of first appearance): Belgrave Ninnis, Correspondence 1911–12, Scott Polar Research Institute, Cambridge; Belgrave Ninnis, Diary, quoted in Beau Riffenburgh, *Aurora: Douglas Mawson and The Australasian Antarctic Expedition 1911–14* (Norwich, UK: The Erskine Press, 2011) and Riffenburgh, *Racing with Death: Douglas Mawson—Antarctic Explorer* (London: Bloomsbury, 2008); Charles Laseron, *South with Mawson* (Sydney: Australasian Publishing Company, 1947), 78; Charles Laseron, Diary, quoted in Peter FitzSimons, *Mawson and the Ice Men of the Heroic Age* (Sydney: William Heinemann, 2011), 354; George Dovers, Letter to Peg and family, 16 February 1912, quoted on Australian Antarctic Division 'Home of the Blizzard' website, http://mawsonshuts.antarctica.gov.au/, accessed 3 January 2012; Fred Jacka and Eleanor Jacka, eds., *Mawson's Antarctic Diaries* (Sydney: Allen & Unwin, 2008); Nancy Robinson Flannery, ed., *This Everlasting Silence: The Love Letters of Paquita Delprat and Douglas Mawson 1911–1914* (Melbourne: Melbourne University Press, 2000); Douglas Mawson, *The Home of the Blizzard: The Story of the Australasian Antarctic Expedition, 1911–1914*, first published in two volumes by William Heinemann in 1915,

192 *Tom Griffiths*

this edition a facsimile of the abridged popular edition of 1930 (Adelaide, AU: Wakefield Press, 1996); Douglas Mawson, undated pencilled speech in the hut, 1913, quoted in Philip Ayres, *Mawson: A Life* (Melbourne: Melbourne University Press, 1999), 90–2; Frank Hurley, *Argonauts of the South* (New York: G. P. Putnam's Sons, 1925), 40–1; Heather Rossiter, ed., *Mawson's Forgotten Men: The 1911–1913 Antarctic Diary of Charles Turnbull Harrisson* (Sydney: Pier 9, 2011); Percival Gray, Voyage Journals 1911–14, typescript copy, Australian Antarctic Division Library, Kingston, TAS; Captain John King Davis, Private Journal 1911–14, Davis Papers, Australian Manuscripts Collection, State Library of Victoria; Louise Crossley, ed., *Trial by Ice: The Antarctic Journals of John King Davis* (Norfolk: Bluntisham Books, Erskine Press, 1997); J. W. Madigan, ed., *Madigan's Account: The Mawson Expedition: The Antarctic Diaries of C. T. Madigan, 1911–1914* (Hobart: Wellington Bridge Press, 2012); Cecil T. Madigan, 'Tabulated and Reduced Records of the Cape Denison Station, Adélie Land,' in Australasian Antarctic Expedition 1911–14, *Scientific Reports* B: IV, Meteorology (Sydney: Alfred J. Kent, Government Printer, 1929), 20; Frank Wild, Letter, quoted in FitzSimons, *Mawson*, 414; Bernadette Hince, ed., *Still No Mawson: The Antarctic Diaries of Frank Stillwell* (Canberra, AU: Australian Academy of Science, 2012); Archibald McLean, Diaries 1911–14, Mitchell Collection, State Library of NSW, MLMSS 382/1, CY3805; Xavier Mertz, Diary, 26 May 1912, quoted in FitzSimons, *Mawson*, 492; and Sidney N. Jeffryes, Letter to Miss Eckford, July 1914, CY4164, Mitchell Library, Sydney.

4. The quoted phrase is from Klaus Dodds, *Geopolitics in Antarctica: Views From the Southern Oceanic Rim* (Chichester, UK: John Wiley & Sons in association with the Scott Polar Research Institute, University of Cambridge, 1997), 85.

5. Marie Kawaja, 'Politics and Diplomacy of the Australian Antarctic, 1901–1945' (PhD, Australian National University, 2010). See also Marie Kawaja and Tom Griffiths, ' "Our Great Frozen Neighbour": Australia and Antarctica Before the Treaty, 1880–1945,' in *Australia and the Antarctic Treaty System: 50 Years of Influence*, eds. Marcus Haward and Tom Griffiths (Sydney: UNSW Press, 2011), 9–47.

6. Brigid Hains, *The Ice and the Inland: Mawson, Flynn and the Myth of the Frontier* (Melbourne: Melbourne University Press, 2002).

7. Christy Collis, 'The Proclamation Island Moment: Making Antarctica Australian,' *Law Text Culture* 8 (2004): 39–56.

8. 'Dr Tony Fleming's address,' www.antarctica.gov.au/news/2012/antarctic-cente nary-celebrated-at-mawsons-home-of-the-blizzard/dr-tony-flemings-address.

9. Tom Griffiths, *Slicing the Silence: Voyaging to Antarctica* (Sydney: UNSW Press, 2007), especially ch. 6.

10. David Day, 'Antarctica is No Place for Politicking: Mawson's Expedition was About Territorial Gain, Not Science,' *Age* and *Sydney Morning Herald*, 19 January 2012.

11. David G. Campbell, *The Crystal Desert: Summers in Antarctica* (London: Minerva, 1993), 51.

12. Mawson, *The Home of the Blizzard*, 77.

13. Madigan, *Madigan's Account*, 3 July 1912.

14. Ibid., 25 June, 3 July, 29 August 1912.

15. Mawson, *The Home of the Blizzard*, chs. XII and XIII.

16. Gray, Voyage Journals, 14 January 1913.

17. Davis, Private Journal, 22 January 1913.

A Polar Drama 193

18. Mawson to Delprat, 26 December 1913, in Flannery, ed., *This Everlasting Silence*, 125.
19. My account of the hut in the winter of 1913 draws on Madigan, *Madigan's Account*; Mawson's letters to Delprat in Flannery, *This Everlasting Silence*; Stephen Haddelsey, *Born Adventurer: The Life of Frank Bickerton, Antarctic Pioneer* (Gloucestershire, UK: Sutton Publishing, 2005); Ayres, *Mawson: A Life*; FitzSimons, *Mawson*; and Riffenburgh, *Aurora*. An earlier version of this section appeared as Tom Griffiths, 'In Antarctica,' *Glorious Days: Australia 1913*, ed. Michelle Hetherington (Canberra, AU: National Museum of Australia Press, 2013), 15–21.
20. Mark Pharaoh, 'Mawson's Musings, and Morse Code: Antarctic Silence at the End of the "Heroic Era", and How it was Lost' (paper presented to the Antarctica: Music, Sound and Cultural Connections Conference, ANU School of Music, Canberra, AU, 27–29 June 2011).
21. I have based this account of Jeffryes's illness on Madigan's diary in *Madigan's Account* and on Ayres, *Mawson: A Life*, 89–95. Ayres reproduces a large part of Mawson's prepared speech.
22. Jeffryes, Letter to Miss Eckford.
23. See Madigan, *Madigan's Account* and Haddelsey, *Born Adventurer*, 60, 113, 119. For a severe assessment of Mawson's character, see Helen Rossiter, *Lady Spy, Gentleman Explorer: The Life of Herbert Dyce Murphy* (Paddington, UK: Jane Curry Publishing, 2004) and Helen Rossiter, 'Mawson's Forgotten Men Weathered it All, Only to be Frozen out of History,' *Australian*, 7 January 2012. Riffenburgh, *Aurora*, 388–9, provides an account of Mawson's correspondence with Sidney Jeffryes's sister in 1914 that does not reflect well on Mawson's care or compassion for an employee. Another example is the fact that Leslie Blake's scientific report on his original geological and survey work at Macquarie Island was published (after Blake died in the Great War) under Mawson's name alone. I am grateful to Dr Elizabeth Truswell, who shared this insight in a personal communication.
24. Delprat to Mawson, 21 September 1913, in Flannery, *This Everlasting Silence*, 102. It didn't help that Captain Davis failed to deliver the one letter Mawson had written to Paquita in that period.
25. Riffenburgh, *Aurora*, 426.
26. Peder Roberts, 'Specimens, Skins and Souvenirs: Rethinking the Australasian Antarctic Expedition' (Master of Arts thesis, School of History and Philosophy of Science, University of NSW, 2004).

10 The 1928 MacRobertson Round Australia Expedition
Colonial Adventuring in the Twentieth Century

Georgine Clarsen

The nineteenth century marked the high point of European exploratory expeditions in Australia. But they enjoyed a dynamic afterlife in twentieth-century national culture. Motorised overland journeys emerged as a new form of settler expedition that drew on familiar colonial tropes of land being won through arduous feats of exploration and travel across 'unknown' continents.[1] Twentieth-century expeditions continued to be framed as performances of gruelling mobility, involving geographical survey and cross-cultural encounter with native peoples. They were shaped, however, not so much by narratives of 'first' discovery or the imperatives of venture capitalism, but by the material, economic, and cultural transformations of global commodity capitalism, played out in a context where settler society was self-consciously defining its national formation and identity. This chapter explores one highly publicised truck expedition around the circumference of Australia in the late 1920s, a journey that projected the powers and pleasures of urban commodity culture into the 'vast spaces' of the outback. My discussion highlights the ways in which motorised expeditions functioned as an evolving constellation of material practices. These journeys presented new ways of moving across terrains to a mass audience. Enabled by new forms of sponsorship, they were performances that facilitated the display of highly gendered and racialised forms of subjectivity in a theatre constituted of settler landscapes.[2] To draw out some of the distinctive features of this expedition played out in a newly federated settler society, I end this chapter by comparing the Australian journey to an apparently similar, but quintessentially *colonial*, truck journey through Africa three years earlier.

The MacRobertson Round Australia Expedition began in April 1928 with a ritual drawn from the grand era of nineteenth-century exploration. Photographs and surviving film footage show a flurry of excitement around the Parliament of Victoria in Melbourne. The Governor-General, politicians, sponsors, and cheering onlookers waved farewell to 11 men who were setting out to circuit the Australian continent in two British trucks and an American touring car.[3] The trucks were painted in the colours of the primary sponsor's chocolate wrappers. Emblazoned in large letters were the words: 'MacRobertson's Round Australia Expedition,' 'Shell Oil and

Spirit,' 'Dunlop Tyres,' and 'All British Karrier Truck.' Maps of the continent, painted on the sides of the vehicles, illustrated their proposed route.

The party's ceremonial leave-taking alluded to an ill-fated cavalcade that had departed from Melbourne 68 years earlier. The trucks were named 'Burke' and 'Wills'—a reference to Robert O'Hara Burke and William John Wills, the leaders of Victoria's most famous exploring expedition. Organised by the Royal Society of Victoria, it involved 19 men, 23 horses, six wagonloads of equipment, and 26 camels. Their purpose was to make the first European crossing of the continent from south to north. Seven of the party perished and, of the four men who made it to the Gulf of Carpentaria, three died of starvation on the homeward journey, including both Burke and Wills. Six rescue parties and a commission of inquiry tried to discover their fate. The sufferings of the party generated enormous interest. A great many newspaper stories, books, sketches, sculptures, and paintings were devoted to the tragic events, and the expedition remains an iconic incident in national mythology.[4] Naming their prized trucks 'Burke' and 'Wills' was a declaration of the expense and ambition of the 1928 expedition, and at a time where old colonial rivalries still smouldered (the transition to nationhood notwithstanding) it marked the journey as a proudly Victorian enterprise. Unlike the original expedition, however, this new venture was not funded by public subscription or governmental support, but by the desire for publicity on the part of a flamboyant Melbourne businessman, the 'chocolate king'

Figure 10.1 Postcard of the Round Australia Expedition distributed on the journey, 1928. By permission of Geraldine Pratt of the Dunkerley family.

196 *Georgine Clarsen*

MacPherson Robertson. Well known as a public benefactor and nationalist, he was also Australia's wealthiest citizen.[5] For 'MacRobertson,' as he preferred to be known, this was an opportunity to put right the troubled story of Victorian exploration.

Cultural historian Tim Bonyhady argues that the interwar years saw a decrease in the power of the Burke and Wills legend.[6] New heroes, including the Anzac soldier and Antarctic explorer, were emerging at that time (see Griffiths, this volume). But the Burke and Wills expedition was far from forgotten. Romanticised accounts of the explorers' courage and endurance remained central in the teaching of history in schools, and burgeoning automobile ownership was turning explorer sites such as the 'Dig Tree,' an inscribed tree near where the expedition leaders died, into places of tourist pilgrimage. Arduous bicycle and automobile journeys around the outback had become the domain of solo adventurers like Francis Birtles and Ted Ryko, both of whom made a precarious living selling films, photographs, and stories about their travels in the footsteps of European pioneers.[7] In contrast to these one-man salutes to the history of exploration, MacRobertson, with his enormous wealth, could finance a collective expedition that integrated older cultural forms into new material practices. His expedition tells us much about settler Australian imperatives at that interwar moment.

MacRobertson's overlanding expeditioners were, like their nineteenth-century namesakes, 'provided and equipped in the most ample and liberal manner.'[8] The two six-wheel Karrier trucks, each weighing about seven tons when loaded, were outfitted at great expense. 'Wills' carried a 300-gallon fuel tank, spare parts, oil, tools, winching equipment, long mats to lay over soft ground, tinned food, ammunition, rifles, shot guns, and camping equipment. 'Burke' was fitted with a 100-gallon water tank and was wired for lights, sound, and vision. The inclusion of still cameras, cine-camera, film projector, gramophone player, record collection, floodlights, and generator made this homage to Victorian exploration a thoroughly twentieth-century affair. 'Burke' also carried the latest radio equipment, including long- and short-wave transmission and receiving sets, operated by George Flynn from Amalgamated Wireless Australasia (AWA).[9] Progress reports were transmitted to MacRobertson's Melbourne office and to a growing network of broadcast stations across Australia via AWA's experimental receiving station in Sydney.[10]

Bolted to the top of 'Burke' was a Giganticphone, a type of loudspeaker built by Marconiphone in London, which the party claimed could be heard two miles from the truck. The loudspeaker would signal their arrival as they approached settlements, and was also used to amplify radio programs and gramophone records. Floodlit dance parties and concerts were a feature of the expedition's visits to outback townships, as were movie screenings and public lectures. The expeditioners carried 12 hours of silent film, borrowed from the federal government's Development and Migration Commission, with titles like *His Majesty the Merino* and *Rice Growing in Australia*.[11]

They also carried American cowboy films, footage of MacRobertson demonstrating his daily exercise regime, and a documentary on his factory called *The Evolution of Chocolate*. Their cargo included a ton of Max-Mints, the newest MacRobertson product, to distribute on the way.

Like their nineteenth-century precursors, this expedition operated under instructions from their sponsors and was structured by clear lines of command with defined duties.[12] Two middle-aged men from Melbourne, associates of MacRobertson and also in the food business, led the expedition. William Dunkerley, director of the Melbourne Fresh Food and Ice Company, was head of the party.[13] Second-in-charge was J. A. Howlett, director of a wholesale butchery and a stock buyer at the Melbourne Meat Markets. The treasurer and secretary was H. Barker, an accountant in Dunkerley's office. Howlett and Barker acted as the expedition's 'diarists' and sent regular reports back to MacRobertson's Melbourne headquarters. The many press reports were based on these dispatches. Younger men, including Dunkerley's son Archibald (cameraman and Shell agent), made up the bulk of the crew. Archibald was already known as a record-breaking long-distance motorist. The team included mechanics, cooks, a 'general utility man,' and a surveyor. Flynn, the radio operator, was the only member of the team not from Melbourne.[14] 'All the party effect Khaki and their appearance is particularly smart,' according to a Queensland journalist.[15] In self-parody, the men photographed themselves in quasi-military formation at the edge of the Nullarbor Plain, preparing for the challenging terrain ahead.[16]

MacRobertson was a dapper, self-made businessman with a talent for product innovation and boundless energy for promotion.[17] Born on the

Figure 10.2 Night Camp Outside Port Augusta, South Australia, 1928, photograph. Courtesy of the University of Melbourne Archives. (Shell Company of Australia Collection, 2008.0045, file 13/20.)

198 *Georgine Clarsen*

Ballarat gold fields in 1859, he remained athletic until late in life. His success mirrored the rise of the Victorian colony as the home of Australian industry. From the second half of the nineteenth century, chocolate manufacture was frequently associated with utopian and temperance ideals. MacRobertson's paternalistic fiefdom in inner Melbourne was a settler colonial version of other 'factory-in-a-garden' chocolate empires, like those established by Cadbury, Rowntree, and Hershey.

MacRobertson steeped his narratives of success in the racialised imagery so characteristic of early twentieth-century Australian settlerism, building his public persona and promotional pitch around displays of exemplary whiteness, national vitality, and technological modernity.[18] He was an ardent advocate for the tariff protection of Australian industries, a key arm of the Australian industrial 'settlement,' closely tied to restrictive race-based immigration.[19] A depiction of his thriving business can be found in a self-published pamphlet authored by 'A White Australian.' A triumph of settler enterprise, MacRobertson is said to have supplanted 'the aboriginal firm of Jika Jika Brothers,' who foolishly 'let their broad acres go so cheap.'[20] MacRobertson dressed in immaculate white suits and hats and portrayed himself as a benevolent patriarch who presided over a city block of white-painted factories that he named 'the Great White City.' There he employed 'an army of white Australians,' dressed in white uniforms. A supporter of industrial arbitration, MacRobertson made it known that his employees received good wages and worked under fair conditions to supply 'energy-producing' confectionary to fellow 'white Australians.'[21]

The round Australia journey was first promoted as a 'positively audacious advertising scheme' and only slowly acquired the gravitas of an expedition of national importance.[22] The *Australasian Confectioner*, a manufacturers' journal that reported extensively on all MacRobertson's exploits, announced his aims: to advertise Max-Mints around the nation, to screen 'good' pictures and play the latest phonograph records to 'all and sundry' in 'wayback' places, to shoot moving pictures for city audiences, and to use radio technology to 'enable listeners-in throughout Australia to cross the enormous spaces by radio.'[23]

On setting out, the party travelled west from Melbourne and in each town they started up the music. 'Colonel Bogey' blared from the loudspeaker, bringing people into the streets to see what was going on and to hear about the trip. In Adelaide, expedition leader Dunkerley declared that his only orders were to give the people in the outback a 'good time with moving picture shows and wireless entertainments and make them remember MacRobertsons for the rest of their lives.'[24] But the promotion of confectionary began to take a lesser place as the travellers moved into areas of fragile settlement. When they reached territory that reduced their movement to a crawl, reports of the journey began to shift and MacRobertson's grand commercial stunt assumed broader meanings within a settler colonial sensibility.

MacRobertson Round Australia Expedition 199

When the expedition neared the Western Australian border on the Nullarbor Plain, the news stories disseminated by the marketing departments of its sponsors began to focus on the capacity of the trucks to operate in the 'unroaded regions of the outback.'[25] It was only two years since the first circuit of the continent by automobile—an event greeted with great acclaim—and the MacRobertson party was the first to take heavy vehicles across those same tracks.[26] British promotional campaigns cast Australian terrain as the antithesis of road conditions at home. For them, the outback provided an ideal test track for vehicles designed to operate in metropolitan conditions. Karrier Motors of Huddersfield produced a promotional booklet, declaring the expedition 'the greatest pioneering journey ever attempted with commercial motor vehicles' through a 'virgin' part of the empire. The trucks 'had to make their own tracks through, wild, undeveloped country, where outside mechanical assistance was unavailable.'[27] For British manufacturers, the antipodes served as an untouched place that was weak in its own meanings, except as an extreme location to demonstrate their products.

The crews sent out on these test runs knew how to take care of sponsors. They always spoke highly of the products and underplayed mechanical breakdowns. 'The trucks are running splendidly,' the trip's diarists took care to note.[28] William Dunkerley surely exaggerated when he declared that the six-wheel trucks 'ride like a limousine' and a pair of pliers left on a roof remained in position across the sandy track of the Coorong.[29] The expedition's cameraman was careful to record footage and still images of the trucks laboriously grinding across resistant landscapes and tackling apparently impossible conditions.[30]

By the time the party had reached the north of Western Australia the route consisted of a loose network of tracks that connected isolated settlements, pastoral stations, and deserted mines. The weight of the vehicles, struggling on ill-defined roads, began to test their mechanical limits. The men spent two days digging their trucks out of mud on the coast track near Pardoo Station, where the Great Sandy Desert meets the Indian Ocean. At Yallaroo, north of Broome, they spent a day covering just 15 miles, crawling through sand at a pace slower than a walk.[31] They cut down scrub and clumps of spinifex, and lay coconut matting and timber in front of the wheels to give them traction, unloading the trucks to get them across rivers. The first crossing of the Fitzroy River near Yeeda took two days, with rifles ready to shoot crocodiles. Donkey teams hauled them through the second crossing.[32] In Queensland they forded swollen rivers and creeks without bridges. Near Bowen the men had to dig under the railway bridge to make sufficient clearance.[33]

For the expeditioners, the effort of keeping the trucks moving around the periphery of the continent was not about testing products in a place that had little intrinsic meaning, as was the case for manufacturers in the metropole. These were places of tremendous significance to Australian settlers. Outback stories rendered them familiar, although presently they were 'wild,' 'empty,'

200 *Georgine Clarsen*

and 'underdeveloped.' These men saw remote territory with the eyes of tomorrow, as the places they were yet to become. So they made light of their trials in their reports, convinced that their very presence was a harbinger of the future. Sitting high in their trucks, this 'modern exploring party' of city men did not simply *see* the terrain around them; they were bringing it into being.[34] They shot footage of the long, slow donkey trains and camel teams that had delivered fuel to their advance supply dumps, revealing nostalgia for modes of transport they were making redundant. They carefully noted the extent of railway lines, port facilities, the beginnings of air transport, and emerging infrastructural systems to support future settlement and commerce. In news interviews they spoke of landscapes that were being remade by the arrival of new consumer products, new sounds, new people, and new stories.[35]

Colonial societies and settler colonial societies are both centrally organised around the making and unmaking of places by newcomers. But as Lorenzo Veracini has suggested, a particular quality of settler colonialism is its obsessive 'anticipatory geography.'[36] Settler narratives are built around imaginings of a wild and empty landscape that is 'waiting' to be brought to life by energetic and technologically enhanced newcomers who are able to realise its potential.[37] Even while honouring the achievements of 'pioneers,' the travel accounts of settlers are driven by a relentlessly progressive sensibility (see also Veracini, this volume).

The expeditioners' circuit of the continent, inscribed on the maps painted on their trucks, was an evocation of the nation's immense landed wealth. The long journey produced images of vast stretches of territory yet to be filled—and not just with sponsors' names and products, but with energetic and enterprising newcomers. As MacRobertson put it in the boosterist terms of a settler geographic imaginary,

> half of our Commonwealth remains unknown. One-third of our lands have not yet been sighted by white man. An unbroken area of one-and-a-half million square miles is devoid of the white man's habitation. The need is still great for Australians to know their own country.[38]

The expedition 'diarists' produced copy, published by newspapers around the continent, that aimed to 'stimulate interest in the vast potential wealth at present lying idle in the interior of this great continent' and 'completely disprove' the old belief in the 'vast waterless waste.'[39]

The travellers, with their proprietary vision, celebrated the ongoing transformation of unused spaces into assets for the new polity, offering an optimistic calculus of the agricultural potential of the landscape and its coming productivity. They noted irrigated gardens at cattle stations in the northern grassland country that produced fine vegetables, grapevines, watermelons, coconuts, and tropical fruits. When they reached the Queensland coast and it was clear they would return on schedule, their reports became energised

MacRobertson Round Australia Expedition 201

with success. The men found themselves celebrities in 'very fine and progressive towns.'[40] They were met on the outskirts by businessmen and escorted to civic receptions. Reporters interviewed them at length. Rotarians showed them the sights, organised dinners, and took them on tours of botanical gardens, water-supply works, sugar and banana plantations, refineries, abattoirs, butter factories, and distilleries. The men came away loudly supporting the need for subsidies to protect Queensland sugar production by white labour.[41]

From Brisbane they travelled the comparatively good roads to Sydney, reporting on the prosperous agricultural districts they passed. They stopped outside the new Parliament House in Canberra to be 'graciously received' by the Prime Minister and government officials, who came out for a 'personal inspection of the outfit.'[42] The final triumph was to arrive precisely at noon, loudspeaker blaring, on the steps of Parliament in Melbourne. With cameras whirring, they shook MacRobertson's hand five months to the minute after they had left, just as promised.

Sponsors largely managed the records of this trip and produced only admiring accounts. So it is not easy to get a sense of how the expedition was viewed by the residents of 'wayback' places. There are hints, however, that indicate just how incongruous and even surreal this party of city men appeared as they passed through remote settlements in trucks brightly painted in MacRobertson's gold and red. A correspondent to a remote Western Australian newspaper suggests how residents of a gold field ghost town of just 40 people viewed the travelling party:

> Last Friday no little sensation was caused in Marble Bar, and many curious people got up from their afternoon siesta, to take a peep at the cause of the noise of exhausts as two big yellow six-wheeled trucks came over the hill on the overland road into this little village of ours. Very shortly one could see men garbed in the unconventional attire (at least unconventional as far as we of the North are concerned) of riding breeches and top boots, which caused some of the local inhabitants to remark that the snakes must be bad where the travellers came from.
>
> However, it was learned that these people represented the famous MacRobertson of lolly, fame, who is financing the whole expedition . . .
>
> During the evening the hall was filled with as many residents as could be notified of the free picture show, rather a novelty here. The pictures were really good, and many will remember 'Buster and Tige' for a day or two. Another picture was how MacRobertson makes his lollies, and likewise his cash. A pleasant evening was spent, and many took home with them sample packets of Max-Mints, the gifts of the travellers.[43]

It is even harder to get a sense of how Aboriginal observers may have viewed the travellers, but we do know that the expeditioners cared very much about how Aboriginal people responded to them. Even before they

202 *Georgine Clarsen*

set off, the men were desperately seeking Aborigines. The Aborigines they sought, however, were 'primitives' in 'wayback' places and not to be found in Melbourne, on the way to Adelaide, or along the long-settled eastern coast. MacRobertson's publicist had promised to bring novel experiences to radio and cinema audiences of some 'weird chant' or native 'incantation received by a microphone in the isolated outskirts of Australia.'[44] He produced a lurid description of the anticipated footage, imagining the 'screams of laughter' from white cinema audiences at scenes of 'gaunt bewhiskered' natives enjoying a Max-Mint or sampling an Old Gold chocolate for the first time.[45] This play on primitivism and commodity consumption—used, for example in the 'Mine Tinkit They Fit' advertisements for Pelaco shirts, or the 'Lubra Kate' advertisements for motor oil—were fantasies of Aboriginal people as anomalous or mendicant outsiders, out of place in their own country.[46]

It was not until day 13, at Fowlers Bay in South Australia, that an encounter with Aborigines was noted. This occurred at a musical evening in their camp in the sand hills behind the settlement. From that day until they reached the Queensland coast, the men recorded many encounters with Aboriginal people. They brought home photographs and moving footage of unnamed Aborigines performing for the cameras, lined up in front of the trucks holding up boxes of Max-Mints, smiling, dancing, and placing a box through a hole in their ear lobe.

The expeditioners frequently reported that people travelled a hundred miles to attend their concerts and film screenings. Aborigines, mysteriously forewarned of their arrival, 'collected in large crowds,' listening intently to their programs and 'wondering where music came from.'[47] They told the press how 'Aboriginals dug one another in the ribs and rolled on the ground in sheer delight especially when any pictures depicting buck-jump riding were thrown on the screen.'[48] Their soundman enjoyed tricking Aboriginal audiences during film screenings, switching the microphone from music to the audience, 'hurling' their laughter back at them, 'fearfully intensified,' through the loudspeaker.[49] When they gave an Aboriginal man the microphone, the visitors enjoyed the joke that the 'natives' had mistaken his voice for an omnipotent being, apparently addressing them from space.[50]

For all of the travellers' protestations that this was a goodwill visit to bring joy and city amenities to the 'wayback' places—a term that suggested distance in time as well as space—their journey was a passage through places uneasily shared, where frontier killings were still occurring and recent dispossession a traumatic reality. From a settler's perspective, a fantasy of danger could heighten the drama. Newspapers noted that though the party travelled through some wild country, they did not keep guard and were never 'molested' by 'the blacks.'[51] But the apparent playfulness of the enterprise could have a sinister undertone, underscoring the ongoing power relations of dispossession and racial violence. At the Bovril Company's Victoria River Station, a huge pastoral enterprise, the expedition members encountered two other parties of overlanding motorists, also driving around the continent. They camped together among some fine gum trees, sheltering from the cold and dust blown up by the high wind. When the three groups went their separate ways next morning, the expeditioners took with them—yet also left behind—a record of this convivial campfire evening. With faux innocence, they had memorialised the spot by taking a photograph for their expedition album. A skull-and-crossbones can be seen above their chilling 'club' name, the Kandy Kids Klan, painted on a tree trunk.[52]

The expedition had set out with the fantasy that Aboriginal people were a disappearing remnant, overawed by modern technology and commercial products. Yet in the records there is suggestive evidence of interactions that were far more complex than the chorus of triumphalism would suggest. The Australia revealed is a hybrid and unsettled space. The men were hoping to observe primitive natives in their wild spaces—'specimens' as they were labelled in their photograph albums—but they encountered people who were observing them closely and actively incorporating settler imports into their lives. As they approached the Western Australian border, at Colona Station, the expeditioners were startled to find an Aboriginal man and woman driving an old Ford car. They stopped, spoke, and accepted a gift of Max-Mints.[53] During the second half of the 1920s, other travellers and missionaries had noted with surprise and misgiving that some Aboriginal men on the edge of the Nullarbor Plain were buying cars.[54]

As they moved through Western Australia and the Northern Territory, the expeditioners found that Aboriginal audiences were more than naïve and passive receivers of stories projected onto a screen. In Broome, for example, they screened a program for people who were already enthusiastic patrons of the outdoor Sun Cinema. They took a photograph that shows Aboriginal viewers in their usual place: segregated at the back of the theatre.[55] In remote settlements in the Northern Territory, Aboriginal audiences laughed uproariously at sequences that were not intended to be funny and added their own voiceovers, which the visitors were unable to understand. In Daly Waters, for example, a young man provided an amplified commentary in his indigenous language and ended the screening with a song.[56]

Aboriginal people were not just viewers of entertainment provided by the travellers. They performed for the visitors and their cameras: dancing; making fire; displaying skill with spear, boomerang, and rifle; hunting for dugong, crocodile, and buffalo. At Moola Bulla Station the visitors produced footage of the superb horsemanship of station hands whose laconic stylishness, and the pleasure they took in displaying their skill, is palpable. Far from finding the timeless 'real corroborees' they imagined when they left Melbourne, the expedition was presented with an extended dance performance that revealed an energetic appropriation of settler society's cultural forms.[57] In return for their film screening at Fitzroy Crossing, the managers of Gogo Station offered to get 'their blacks' to join with the 'Fitzroy tribes' to give an afternoon's entertainment in the form of 'a good corroboree.'

204 *Georgine Clarsen*

The expedition diary records that 'the natives took great pains and trouble to paint themselves up in a grotesque manner according to their various customs' and 'entered into the proceedings with much zest.'[58] The surviving film footage shows the expedition party sitting on the banks of the Fitzroy River. Alongside them are Aboriginal men whose backs are painted with motifs that look like knapsacks. They perform a comic corroboree that includes marching and saluting: a parody of the colonial expedition and the peculiarities of settler masculinity.[59]

Near the Victoria River in the Northern Territory, the men drove through a long stretch of 'high native wheat grass averaging six feet high and resembling to all appearances a cultivated field.' It made 'first class pasture land,' they quickly decided.[60] Across the savannah lands, they noted station hands burning the spinifex to bring on fresh grasses.[61] Among many descriptions of settler landscapes, these were brief hints that the terrain they were travelling through was Aboriginal country, shaped by indigenous horticultural practices.[62]

The distinctively settler colonial nature of the MacRobertson expedition is brought into focus by comparing it to an apparently similar African journey three years earlier. The Court Treatt Cape to Cairo Expedition shared much with MacRobertson's venture and was played out within similar mobility practices, modes of representation, and commercial imperatives. But it was conceived, conducted, and represented in rather different terms. The Court Treatt party drove two British-built Crossley trucks the length of the continent, never deviating from British territory and carefully adhering to an imagined 'all-red' route. This 'epic of travel, danger and adventure' through 'darkest Africa' was a quintessentially colonial journey linking the colonial periphery with the metropolitan centre.[63]

The leader was Major Chaplin Court Treatt, a celebrated English Flying Corps pilot in his mid-30s. His wife, Stella Court Treatt, was a South African of English descent who acted as second-in-command. The couple financed the journey themselves and hoped to recoup their costs through film distribution, sponsorships, and the sale of Stella Court Treatt's book, *Cape to Cairo: The Record of a Historic Motor Journey* (1927).[64] London's largest circulation newspaper, the *Daily Express*, held exclusive rights to their story and sent Canadian Fred C. Law as a special correspondent.[65] Photographer T. A. Glover recorded the journey in still and moving image. The resulting documentary, *From Cape to Cairo by Auto!*, was released in Britain and the United States in 1927.[66] Stella's teenage brother, Errol Hinds, acted as assistant mechanic. Julius Mapata from Nyasaland (Malawi), who reputedly spoke 32 native dialects, was a servant to the Court Treatts. Dubbed 'ambassador' to the many different ethnic and language groups they encountered, Mapata negotiated with the hundreds of African men whose labour they needed to keep the expedition moving. He also attended to more menial duties, such as buying provisions, setting up camps, and cooking for the party.[67]

MacRobertson Round Australia Expedition   205

Their 'dash from Capetown to Cairo,' as the *Express* first called it, was 'better equipped than any previous exploring expedition' and began in grand colonial style.[68] Glover's glamorous photographs and Court Treatt's determinedly upbeat book portrayed the party setting out in *sola topees* and tropical suits, with Jaeger blankets, gramophone and records, and folding camp chairs imprinted with the names of the 'explorers.' The 16 months that followed were of such astounding hardship that in the words of the *Express*, the 'dash' became the 'Great Trek.'[69] Dogged by mishap, they missed supply dumps, endured frequent breakdowns, lived on short rations, and were forced to jettison most of their equipment. In Rhodesia they were immobilised for months in mud. They were cold, hungry, ill, and tormented by scorpions and ants. Clothes and bedding became mildewed and they found themselves utterly dependent on the indigenous population to haul them through.[70] Further north in Sudan, they floundered in the fly- and mosquito-infested swamps. The local Governor ordered 'scores of reluctant Dinkas' to drag the trucks, carry timber, and build bridges across deep rivers.[71] They became lost in the deserts of southern Egypt and had to be rescued by government search parties before finally making it to Cairo.[72]

When they returned to London, the travellers were greeted with receptions, street parades, and an audience at Buckingham Palace. The *Daily Express* declared the journey a triumph of the British spirit and proof of the superiority of British engineering.[73] Of all of the party, Stella Court Treatt was the most celebrated. Photographed as a plucky and androgynous 'bright young thing' in safari outfits and bobbed hair, she was fêted as a new expression of femininity. Born and raised in South Africa, Stella's colonial background gave her an appealing vigour. But she was careful to position herself within the British nation in her narrative, creating a 'patriotic, Empire-supporting identity' in which she unquestioningly accepted British imperial authority.[74] Law's newspaper articles and Stella's own book traced her transformation from a frivolous young wife into a stylish and plucky 'African explorer' who had learned to make do without luxuries. Sharing the men's hardships, she had climbed waterfalls and shot wildlife with both camera and rifle. Lord Wakefield of the Castrol Oil Company announced at an Automobile Club reception that the expedition had 'set a new world record for endurance.' This younger generation showed the 'great courage which is the leading characteristic of our country' and proved that Britons had not become an anaemic nation, but still had 'iron in our blood.'[75]

Other assessments were less sanguine, with some critics describing the journey as a folly of British imperial arrogance and jingoism.[76] Even as it was happening, Court Treatt's forced co-option of massed African labour and his determination to drive overloaded, antiquated, and unsuitable vehicles along an impractical route through British territory was beginning to look outmoded and almost comic. As Elizabeth Collingham has argued in relation to the British Raj, such bald attempts to physically impose notions of race superiority were an ineffectual response to rising anti-colonial

Figure 10.3 *Crossing the Naam (Jur) River, South Sudan*, 1926, postcard. Original in author's possession.

sentiment. By the 1920s, even the British public was losing confidence in those anachronistic assumptions of imperial entitlement.[77] Like the Australian expeditioners, the Court Treatt party was attempting to revitalise an earlier style of colonial expedition for the motoring era, but they were drawing on a constellation of practices very different from those that drove the MacRobertson expedition.

These two journeys illustrate the ways in which settler societies and colonial societies are characterised by distinct practices and narratives that are centred around experiences of mobility (see Veracini, this volume). Although both forms of society overlap and share many features—indeed settler societies usually begin as colonies—there are important analytical distinctions between them.[78] Colonists typically remain a demographic minority whose key tasks are to extract wealth, harness indigenous labour, and create new markets in the service of the metropole. For colonists, the imagined end point of their mobilities, or 'home,' remains the metropolitan centre. Settlers, on the other hand, move onto other people's land with the intention of staying. Settlerism is not primarily about exploiting indigenous peoples or drawing them into an imperial economy, although indigenous labour is routinely co-opted by settlers and essential to their survival and prosperity. Stated in the baldest of terms, as the historian Patrick Wolfe has pointed out, settlers' collective task is to displace and replace indigenous people.[79] Settlers aim to create a sovereign polity that is avowedly better than both the indigenous one they seek to displace and their own society of origin. Through the movements of people, things, and ideas across contested territories, indigenous lands are transformed into settler places and settlers are remade into the 'new natives' who are legitimately at home in those landscapes.[80]

Those fundamental divergences between colonial and settler projects and the mobilities that characterise them help in teasing out some of the ways in which the MacRobertson and Court Treatt expeditions, for all their similarities, were very different enterprises. While both journeys were structured around ideas of technologically enhanced travel and financed by the commercial imperatives of commodity capitalism, the Court Treatt journey was primarily a venture of colonial extraction. Far from reinforcing the homeliness (actual or anticipated) of remote places in which travellers could dwell and broadcast their civility, this African expedition was represented as a battle to traverse exotic and hostile territory. Once they left South Africa, the Court Treatts were not at home, but outsiders always heading home. They carried 'Africa' back to Britain for domestic consumption, not as diamonds or gold, but as thrilling and marketable experiences: souvenirs, newspaper stories, a book, and a film.

Like the settler expeditioners, the colonial travellers pitted their trucks against resistant landscapes, not yet smoothed and tamed for motorised travel. But unlike the settlers, they also pitted themselves against recalcitrant 'natives,' who were indifferent and sometimes hostile to their adventure. These colonial expeditioners could not pretend to see empty landscapes. The Court Treatt party was obliged to recognise indigenous peoples as landowners and acknowledge that Africans possessed a degree of sovereign power over the lands they were traversing.[81] Indeed, frequently they held the key to moving across it.

In the Court Treatt journey, both obstacles—the terrain and the 'natives'— were represented as an exacting test of British engineering and character. But for all their arduous experiences, the thrust of their narrative was not primarily about the creation of new subjectivities. As Wakefield suggested when he welcomed them in London, their colonial identities were not so

208   *Georgine Clarsen*

much acquired in those encounters because they were already intrinsic to them. According to his wife's admiring account, the major's leadership qualities lay in his forceful assumption of command over the indigenous labour that propelled their homeward movement.[82] Stella's 'rebirth' into a new version of modern femininity, as she increasingly adopted masculine expressions of colonial subjectivity through the course of the journey, provided a drama of gendered transformation to their travel narrative.[83] Hers was an emerging subjectivity that was enacted primarily in relation to the men of the party. The men supported and encouraged her ambition to participate equally in their suffering and pleasures, and extended to her the masculine masquerade of British entitlement and race superiority.[84] Unquestioned was the expeditioners' right as privileged British subjects to visit spectacular landscapes, hunt leopards and elephants, and to command the indigenous labour that local officials provided. They made it their colonial duty to travel in a way that upheld British prestige and authority.

The social relations and imaginary geography invoked in the MacRobertson Round Australia Expedition were very different. Wherever they went, the MacRobertson team was always at home. Their travels served to generate new visions of productive landscapes and a unified, national life-in-the-making. They encountered Aboriginal landscapes aplenty, but they were shaped by cultural practices that outsiders could disregard or simply fail to discern. They also failed to acknowledge the 'emptiness' of the outback as an effect of dispossession and racial segregation.[85] Instead, the men carried with them all the urban assurance of a settler project successfully accomplished, even if it was not yet fully disseminated to isolated settlers in the 'wayback' places, whose modern civility was still to be established. Their circuit of the periphery, starting and ending in Melbourne, and threading together great cities and tiny settlements in 'isolated outskirts' across the 'vastness of the continent and its natural wilderness,' was a spectacle of national integration and progress, exemplified by the free entertainments and confectionary they distributed.[86]

Their settler narrative of travel, unlike the colonial one, carefully depicted their movement as entirely autonomous. Any indebtedness to indigenous people for their mobility was underplayed. Aboriginal people's role in building the tracks, hauling the vehicles across rivers, or transporting supplies to remote stations was not acknowledged. The expeditioners revelled in their gendered effort. The resistance of the landscape was a fitting challenge to their modern technology, masculine strength, and ingenuity. The film footage recorded the daily rhythms of a fraternal world of strenuous work, in which men and machines were joined in conquering remote territory, simultaneously demonstrating the power of their trucks and the vitality of settler society.

When their journey came to an end, the press presented their success as proof that settlers could now be at home in even the most inhospitable parts of the continent. Just outside of Melbourne, where the original Burke and Wills expedition had turned off the Sydney Road, newspapers reported that the returning party paused their battered trucks to remember the earlier expedition that had been 'thrown back in disaster by the untamed forces of the desert.' 'Burke and Wills Outdone,' the newspapers declared.[87] Their predecessors had been 'weakened by toil, emaciated by hunger and tortured by thirst,' the desert sun having sapped their 'lowered vitality.' But these modern expeditioners returned from an even longer journey 'chubby and rosy as from a prolonged picnic.' From the comfort of their trucks, they could 'mock mirages, where mirages had mocked Burke and Wills.' At night in the 'great solitude' they smoked by the campfire and listened to broadcasts of music or lectures from radio 3LO in Melbourne to a chorus of dingos or magpies.[88] No longer raw newcomers struggling to know and occupy the whole of Australia, the expeditioners exemplified a new race of Australian 'natives' who were at home in a united, continental landscape. These stories presented overlanders who were very different from their colonial predecessors. Fit national subjects, they were rightfully replacing the original natives, now barely surviving on the margins of white settlement.

But these triumphal stories reverberate through time in unexpected ways. Like the vehicular journey dubbed the Oxford and Cambridge Far Eastern Expedition (see Sobocinska, this volume), MacRobertson's expedition has been largely lost to settler memory. Yet the imperative to circle the continent for recreation and pleasure remains, as does enthusiasm for off-road 'bush bashing.'[89] More than a trace of the 1928 expedition survives in indigenous storytelling in the northwest, suggesting ways in which Aboriginal people produced their own meanings for these events, even when constrained by the power relations imposed by settler colonialism. In the award-winning musical *Bran Nue Dae* (1990), set in Broome during the 1960s (and since made into a feature film), MacRobertson's name was roundly satirised as an emblem of the random logic of settler practices.[90] Not Max-Mints, but MacRobertson's most enduring product, Cherry Ripe chocolate bars, were dispensed to Aboriginal children by Father Benedictus, the priest from the city mission, whose cassock was embroidered with shiny Cherry Ripe wrappers.[91] MacRobertson's products played an important part in the narrative, having an ambiguous role as objects of desire that nonetheless represented settler deception and oppression. In 1928 the expedition's brief was to make sure that MacRobertson's name would not be forgotten in the outback. Just how it would be recalled in indigenous storytelling, and the ways it would be received by Aboriginal and non-Aboriginal audiences six decades later, was something that neither MacRobertson nor his expeditioners could control.

ACKNOWLEDGMENTS

I acknowledge and thank Jeannine Baker for her research support in preparing this chapter.

210   Georgine Clarsen

NOTES

1. Dane Kennedy, *The Last Blank Spaces: Exploring Africa and Australia* (Cambridge, MA: Harvard University Press, 2013).
2. Felix Driver, *Geography Militant: Cultures of Exploration and Empire* (Oxford: Blackwell, 2001), 8.
3. Newsreel footage, 'Round Australia with the MacRobertson Expedition' (1928), NFSA Title No. 138660, Herschells Films Pty. Ltd., National Film and Sound Archive (NFSA). I am indebted to the Dunkerley family, especially Geraldine Pratt and Donald Dunkerley, for their help with this research.
4. Tim Bonyhady, *Burke & Wills: From Melbourne to Myth* (Balmain: Ell Press, 1991); www.burkeandwills.net.au/index.php.
5. George Taylor, *Making it Happen: The Rise of Sir MacPherson Robertson* (Melbourne: Robertson & Mullins, 1934); Jill Robertson, *MacRobertson: The Chocolate King* (Melbourne: Lothian, 2004). See also Griffiths, this volume.
6. Bonyhady, *Burke & Wills*, 287 ff.
7. 'Famous Tree,' *Adelaide Register*, 14 October 1925, 5, http://trove.nla.gov.au/ndp/del/article/64248240; Roslyn Poignant, 'Ryko's Photographs of the "Fort Dundas Riot": The Story so Far,' *Australian Aboriginal Studies* 2 (1996): 24–41; 'Overland by Motor: Birtles's Tour: Burke-Wills Route,' *Sydney Morning Herald*, 17 October 1912, 10, http://trove.nla.gov.au/ndp/del/article/15368028; Birtles' film, *Across Australia in the Track of Burke and Wills* (1915), has since been lost; Justine Greenwood, 'Driving Through History: The Car, the Open Road, and the Making of History Tourism in Australia,' *Journal of Tourism History* 3:1 (2011): 21–37.
8. www.burkeandwills.net.au/Commission_of_Enquiry/Report.htm, accessed 26 July 2013; 'Around Australia Expedition: The MacRobertson Enterprise,' *Adelaide Register*, 18 April 1928, 9, http://trove.nla.gov.au/ndp/del/article/57035091.
9. 'Round Australia by Motor: £3,000 Wireless Equipment,' *Home Journal*, 27 April 1928, 38; 'Around Australia: The MacRobertson Expedition,' *Townsville Daily Bulletin*, 1 August 1928, 4–5, http://trove.nla.gov.au/ndp/del/article/60227529.
10. 'Around Australia Expedition: Big MacRobertson Enterprise,' *Brisbane Courier*, 30 May 1928, 8, http://trove.nla.gov.au/ndp/del/article/21291785.
11. 'MacRobertson Publicity,' Correspondence files: CP211/2, 68/92, Development and Migration Commission, National Archives of Australia (NAA).
12. Kennedy, *The Last Blank Spaces*, 2.
13. '10,000 Mile Trek Around Australia,' *Royal Auto Journal*, 16 April 1928, 1; 'The MacRobertson Motor Expedition to Circle Australia,' *Adelaide Advertiser*, 18 April 1928, 14, http://trove.nla.gov.au/ndp/del/article/49372039.
14. Any private records left by members of the party are yet to come to light.
15. 'Eight Thousand Miles: MacRobertson Expedition Arrives in Rockhampton,' *Morning Bulletin* (Rockhampton), 6 August 1928, 7, http://trove.nla.gov.au/ndp/del/article/54632233.
16. 'Boys at Drill. Eucla SA' (1928), photograph album, B1.3/AL170, MacRobertson Collection, Royal Historical Society of Victoria (RHSV).
17. John Lack, 'Robertson, Sir Macpherson (1859–1945),' *Australian Dictionary of Biography*, National Centre of Biography, Australian National University, http://adb.anu.edu.au/biography/robertson-sir-macpherson-8237/text14421.
18. Advertisement, 'Onward and Upward: the Epic Story of MacRobertson,' *Melbourne Argus*, March 19, 1928, 22, http://trove.nla.gov.au/ndp/del/article/3918836; *A Young Man and a Nail Can: An Industrial Romance* (Melbourne: MacRobertson, 1921); Marilyn Lake and Henry Reynolds, *Drawing the Global Colour Line: White Men's Countries and the Question of Racial Equality* (Carlton, AU: Melbourne University Press, 2008).

MacRobertson Round Australia Expedition   211

19. On the Australian settlement, see special edition of the *Australian Journal of Political Science* 39:1 (2004).
20. 'A White Australian,' *A Great Australian Industry: The Rise and Progress of MacRobertson's* (1905), 1–3, printed brochure, MS001152, Box 261/5, RHSV.
21. Ibid., 2, 12.
22. 'A Tour of Australia: MacRobertson Moves,' *Adelaide Register*, 20 August 1927, 9, http://trove.nla.gov.au/ndp/del/article/55036051; 'MacRobertson Publicity,' Correspondence files, NAA: CP211/2, 68/92.
23. 'MacRobertson's Latest Enterprise: An Unusual Round Australia Venture,' *Australasian Confectioner*, 24 August 1927, 52; 'Cinema in the Wilds: Expedition on Modern Lines: Burke and Wills Coming,' *Daily News* (Perth), 27 April 1928, 2, http://trove.nla.gov.au/ndp/del/article/79491412.
24. *Adelaide Register*, 18 April 1928, 9.
25. 'Round Australia: MacRobertson Party's Progress from Melbourne to Perth,' *Argus*, 26 May 1928, 8, http://trove.nla.gov.au/ndp/del/article/3940839; 'MacRobertson Round Australia Expedition,' *The Woman*, 1 July 1938, 137; Clippings and typescript press releases in 'Motoring and Cycling Notes,' April 1928 to January 1929, Dunlop Rubber (Australia) Collection, 31/20/1, Noel Butlin Archives, Australian National University.
26. Georgine Clarsen, *Eat My Dust: Early Women Motorists* (Baltimore: Johns Hopkins University Press, 2008), 120–39.
27. *Karrier Gazette*, Special 'Around Australia' Issue (n.d.), MS1152, Box 261/4, RHSV.
28. *Diary of MacRobertson's Round Australia Expedition* (1928), n.p., Day 3, typescript, MS1152, Box 261/5, RHSV.
29. *Adelaide Register*, 18 April 1928, 9.
30. 'Across the Territory: Cold Winds and Alligators,' *Australasian Confectioner*, 28 July 1928, 70–3.
31. *Diary*, Day 53; 'Long Trip: MacRobertson Expedition,' *Brisbane Courier*, 16 August 1928, 3, http://trove.nla.gov.au/ndp/del/article/21317701.
32. *Diary*, Days 56–8 and Days 64–8.
33. *Diary*, Day 108.
34. *Brisbane Courier*, 30 May 1928, 8.
35. *Townsville Daily Bulletin*, 1 August 1928, 4–5; *Morning Bulletin* (Rockhampton), 6 August 1928, 7.
36. Lorenzo Veracini, 'The Imagined Geographies of Settler Colonialism,' in *Making Settler Colonial Space: Perspectives on Race, Place and Identity*, eds. Tracey Banivanua Mar and Penelope Edmonds (London: Palgrave Macmillan, 2010), 179–97.
37. Libby Robin, *How a Continent Created a Nation* (Sydney: UNSW Press, 2007); Michael Cathcart, *The Water Dreamers: The Remarkable History of Our Dry Continent* (Melbourne: Text Publishing, 2009).
38. 'Westward Ho: The MacRobertson Expedition: Overland Around Australia,' *Canberra Times*, 16 June 1928, 3, http://trove.nla.gov.au/ndp/del/article/1233480.
39. Ibid.
40. *Diary*, Day 125.
41. *Morning Bulletin* (Rockhampton), 6 August 1928, 7; 'Arrival at Brisbane: More than 8,000 Miles Covered,' *Australasian Confectioner*, 24 August 1928, 82–4.
42. *Diary*, Day 146.
43. 'Marble Bar News: A Surprise Party,' *Northern Times* (Carnarvon), 2 June 1928, 4, http://trove.nla.gov.au/ndp/del/article/74905926.
44. *Adelaide Register*, 20 August 1927, 9.

212   *Georgine Clarsen*

45. Ibid.; 'Max-Mints for Natives: MacRobertson Expedition Distributes Favors,' *Melbourne Herald*, 2 May 1928, clipping in Old Gold scrapbook, B1.3, RHSV.
46. Richard Broome, 'Mulga Fred (1874–1948),' *Australian Dictionary of Biography*, National Centre of Biography, Australian National University, http://adb.anu.edu.au/biography/mulga-fred-11194/text19953.
47. *Diary*, Day 46; *Townsville Daily Bulletin*, 1 August 1928, 4–5; 'MacRobertson Expedition: News from Broome,' *West Australian*, 14 June 1928, 7, http://trove.nla.gov.au/ndp/del/article/32118546>; 'Derby News,' *Northern Times* (Carnarvon), 23 June 1928, 4, http://trove.nla.gov.au/ndp/del/article/74906279>.
48. *Rockhampton Bulletin*, 6 August 1928, 7; 'Round Australia,' *Queenslander*, 23 August 1928, 21, http://trove.nla.gov.au/ndp/del/article/22952190.
49. *Townsville Daily Bulletin*, 1 August 1928, 4–5.
50. *Australian Confectioner*, 24 July 1928, 72; *Townsville Daily Bulletin*, 1 August 1928, 4–5.
51. *Queenslander*, 23 August 1928, 21.
52. 'Kandy Kids Klan,' photograph album, B1.3/AL173, RHSV; *Diary*, Day 77.
53. *Melbourne Argus*, 26 May 1928, 8; *Diary*, Day 15.
54. 'Native Australia,' *Sydney Morning Herald*, 11 July 1925, 9, http://trove.nla.gov.au/ndp/del/article/16221981; 'Aborigines Own Motor Cars,' *Adelaide Advertiser*, 18 November 1926, 16, http://trove.nla.gov.au/ndp/del/article/73652883.
55. 'Picture Show Given at Broome,' photograph album B1.3/AL170/161, RHSV.
56. *Diary*, Day 87.
57. Correspondence files, NAA: CP211/2, 68/92; *Adelaide Register*, 20 August 1927, 9; *Australasian Confectioner*, 24 August 1927, 52.
58. *Diary*, Days 65, 66, and 67.
59. Newsreel footage, NFSA Title No. 138660; 'Watching Corroboree,' 'Corroboree at Fitzroy Crossing,' and untitled photograph, photograph album B1.3/AL170/245, RHSV.
60. *Diary*, Day 78; *Australasian Confectioner*, 24 July 1928, 70.
61. *Diary*, Day 39.
62. Bill Gammage, *The Biggest Estate on Earth: How Aborigines Made Australia* (Sydney: Allen and Unwin, 2011).
63. *London Daily Express*, 25 November 1926, 1; Georgine Clarsen, 'Machines as the Measure of Women: Colonial Irony in a Cape-to-Cairo Journey,' *Journal of Transport History*, 29:1 (2008): 44–63; 'Crossley: The Court Treatt Cape to Cairo Expedition 1924–1926,' Malcolm Asquith, www.crossley-motors.org.uk/history/1920/court_treatt/cape_cairo_index.html.
64. Stella Court Treatt, *Cape to Cairo: The Record of a Historic Motor Journey* (London: George Harrap, 1927).
65. The *Daily Express* published more than 50 feature articles on the expedition as well as advertisements and letters from readers.
66. It seems that only a fragment of their film survives, held by British Pathé: 'From Cape to Cairo 1926,' *British Pathé*, www.britishpathe.com/video/from-cape-to-cairo.
67. *London Times*, 30 March 1926, 12d.
68. *Daily Express*, 29 August 1924, 1.
69. *Daily Express*, 11 February 1925, 1.
70. *Daily Express*, 11 June 1925, 11.
71. Court Treatt, *Cape to Cairo*, 176–220.
72. Ibid., 221–39.

73. *Daily Express*, 7 January 1926, 1.
74. Tal Zalmanovich, ' "Woman Pioneer of Empire": The Making of a Female Colonial Celebrity,' *Postcolonial Studies* 12:2 (2009): 193–210.
75. *Daily Express*, 10 February 1926, 1.
76. T. R. Nicholson, *Five Roads to Danger: The Adventure of Transcontinental Motoring* (London: Cassell, 1960), 63ff.
77. Elizabeth Collingham, *Imperial Bodies: The Physical Experience of the Raj, c. 1800–1947* (Cambridge: Polity, 2001), 10.
78. Lorenzo Veracini, *Settler Colonialism: A Theoretical Overview* (London: Palgrave, 2011); Georgine Clarsen and Lorenzo Veracini, 'Settler Colonial Automobilities: A Distinct Constellation of Automobile Cultures?,' *History Compass* 10:12 (2012): 889–900.
79. Patrick Wolfe, 'Settler Colonialism and the Logic of Elimination,' *Journal of Genocide Research* 8:4 (2006): 387–409.
80. Tracey Banivanua Mar and Penelope Edmonds, eds., *Making Settler Colonial Space: Perspectives on Race, Place and Identity* (London: Palgrave Macmillan, 2010), 1–19.
81. Kennedy, *The Last Blank Spaces*, 195ff.
82. Court Treatt, *Cape to Cairo*, 214–5.
83. Zalmanovich, 'Woman Pioneer of Empire,' 206–8.
84. Clarsen, 'Machines as the Measure,' 48–50.
85. Denis Byrne, 'Nervous Landscapes: Race and Space in Australia,' *Journal of Social Archaeology* 3:2 (2003), 169–93.
86. *Adelaide Register*, 20 August 1927, 9.
87. 'Burke and Wills Outdone,' *Adelaide Register*, 29 September 1928, 11, http://nla.gov.au/nla.news-page5116993; 'Successful Conclusion in Melbourne,' *Australian Confectioner,* 24 September 1928, 21–2.
88. 'Successful Conclusion in Melbourne,' *Australian Confectioner,* 24 September 1928, 21–2.
89. See Laina Hall, 'The "Zest of Adventure" in Australian Overland Narratives, 1920–2000,' *Journal of Tourism and Social Change* 4:2 (2006): 85–95; Catherine Simpson, 'Antipodean Automobility and Crash: Treachery, Trespass and Transformation of the Open Road,' *Australian Humanities Review* 39–40: (2006), www.australianhumanitiesreview.org/archive/Issue-September-2006/simpson.html; Delia Falconer, ' "The Poetry of the Earth is Never Dead": Australia's Road Writing,' *Journal of the Association for the Study of Australian Literature* (2009), Special Issue: Australian Literature in a Global World, www.nla.gov.au/openpublish/index.php/jasal/article/view/859/1749; Georgine Clarsen, 'Automobiles and Australian Modernisation: The Redex Around-Australia Trials of the 1950s,' *Australian Historical Studies* 41:3 (2010): 352–68; and Greenwood, 'Driving through History'.
90. Jimmy Chi and Kuckles, *Bran Nue Dae* (Sydney: Currency Press, 1991). For a clip of the stage production (Dir. Tom Zubrycki, 1991) see http://aso.gov.au/titles/documentaries/bran-nue-dae/clip2/. A feature film adaption, *Bran Nue Dae* (2010), was directed by Rachael Perkins. My thanks to Anna Haebich and Jimmy Chi for drawing my attention to the connection between MacRobertson and the stage production.
91. Cherry Ripe was acquired by Cadbury in the 1960s.

11 The Expedition's Afterlives
Echoes of Empire in Travel to Asia

Agnieszka Sobocinska

In 1955, six young men—five recent graduates from Cambridge and one Oxford undergraduate—decided to drive to Asia. Claiming that no one before had managed to motor overland between Europe and Singapore, they called themselves the Oxford and Cambridge Far Eastern Expedition (OCFEE). Having assumed this title, they carefully modelled their journey on an imperial mode of formal expeditionary travel. Yet, their journey did not discover any 'new' territory or further the cause of science and geography. What the expedition did explore, describe, and map was the path for a tourist track through the formerly colonised regions of Central, South, and Southeast Asia. Rather than adding to the annals of science, it served to plot a new product for a rapidly growing tourism industry. Aided by a skilful publicity campaign that influenced subsequent travellers, the expedition helped transmit a range of imperial routes, economies, and attitudes to the incipient culture of 'alternative' tourism in Asia. In so doing, OCFEE invoked an imperial mode of expeditionary travel that would provide a vehicle (both literal and symbolic) into postcolonial Asia at a key historical juncture: a moment when international tourism was booming and metropolitan attitudes towards the decolonising world were in the process of renegotiation.

Vernacular attitudes in the metropole often lagged behind the rapidly changing geopolitics of decolonisation. Mores and habits of mind that arose during colonial times continued to mark vernacular attitudes and popular culture even as decolonisation remade the world's political map. These attitudes functioned in dialectic with a popular culture that often perpetuated increasingly anachronistic assumptions. Developing the concept of 'internalised imperialism' put forward by D. M. Low, John M. Mackenzie has argued that popular culture encouraged 'an ingrained assurance of [the] inherent right to rule others' in a number of colonizing nations.[1] Mackenzie and others have isolated the role that travel and tourism played within this popular culture.[2] As Michael Kowalewski noted, travel literature helped ensure that 'the vestiges of imperialism continue to linger,' albeit 'less in the narrow sense of militant jingoism or explicit advocacy for annexing new territory than in a more ingrained and nebulous confidence about being culturally and racially superior.'[3]

Echoes of Empire in Travel to Asia   215

Building on previous scholarship, this volume argues that the imperial expedition was a significant cultural form that helped construct an imperial gaze while at the same time establishing routes for trade, settlement, and eventual colonisation. However, modes of travel that were less formal (and often more personal) also contributed to the internalisation of imperialism. As Hsu-Ming Teo notes, 'travel and travel writing played an important role in creating imperial consciousness among those Britons who stayed at home, acquainting them with the non-western world.'[4] The modes of imperial exploration and colonial travel—along with their cultures, assumptions, and mores—were also propagated through other cultural products, and their influence extended beyond Britain. Robert Dixon has argued that the colonial adventure novel, or 'ripping yarn,' encouraged popular admiration for the explorer/traveller in both England and Australia. Furthermore, he has linked this admiration with widespread support for empire at the peak of New Imperialism.[5] Read together, this scholarship establishes exploration and travel as key elements within the popular culture that buttressed imperialist assumptions across the British world at the height of empire.

These imperialist assumptions lingered even as decolonisation advanced. Scholars of the New Imperial history have argued that in order to understand the pervasiveness of imperialism's cultural residue, historians must make a 'detailed, contextual examination of the intellectual climates in which these attitudes developed.'[6] While tracing the intellectual and cultural genealogy of imperialism is certainly important, so too is a direct interrogation of the ways in which imperial mores were perpetuated after formal decolonisation. These continuities have begun to be probed in histories of vernacular culture and popular memory in the United Kingdom. Although the extent of popular support for empire has been much debated, recent work by Bill Schwarz clearly shows that many Britons upheld imperial values long after the sun had set on their empire.[7] As in the colonial era, these values were not limited to the political sphere, but also continued in vernacular and popular culture. Just as political attitudes did not undergo a dramatic schism to adjust to the reality of decolonisation, neither did a cultural revolution expel the broad range of popular productions that buttressed internalised imperialism. Colonial literature—particularly Kipling—continued to be read by young and old, and new cultural forms such as 'heritage' cinema encouraged colonial nostalgia decades after the overthrow of European imperialism.

Travel also played a part in perpetuating memories of empire. The twentieth century saw an unprecedented rise in mobility. The 1950s and 1960s brought a boom in the tourism industry. Twenty-five million people took an overseas trip in 1950; by 1961 this number had tripled to more than 75 million. A decade later the figure had soared to 175 million.[8] Tourism expanded most aggressively in Europe, but inroads were made across Asia too.[9] North Europeans and Americans accounted for much of the travelling population. Australians also became increasingly interested in overseas travel. In this context, a growing proportion of 'ordinary' people (neither politicians nor

216 *Agnieszka Sobocinska*

experts in relevant fields) learnt about the world through personal experience of foreign places and people.[10] As the number of travellers grew, their experiences were increasingly mediated by the culture of travel and tourism, developed through the interplay of the tourist industry and the ever-swelling cohort of travellers. As it became established and broadcast through travel literature and journalism, this culture came to shape visitors' preconceptions, experiences, and representations of racial and cultural Others.[11]

There is little doubt that contemporary travel culture bears some affinities with imperialism. As early as the 1970s, Dennison Nash argued that colonial inequalities—sociocultural as well as economic—were perpetuated through the context of travel and tourism.[12] Scholarship has also demonstrated strong resonances between tourism and imperialism in a number of tourism-dependent postcolonial nations.[13] The legacy of imperialism within contemporary tourism is all too clear at the upper end of the market. The colonial experience at Raffles Hotel in Singapore, the Imperial Hotel in New Delhi, or the Continental in Ho Chi Minh City is barely concealed; indeed, a crude form of imperial nostalgia (ironically, often supported by postcolonial governments through their tourism promotion boards) makes the link between contemporary mass tourism and colonialism distinct. Similarly, the great gulf in economic power between tourists and locals in destinations such as Cambodia and the Philippines has reconstructed colonial-era cleavages, encouraging behaviours (including sex tourism) that constitute a new iteration of the unequal power relations of colonialism.

While historians have shown the significance of the formal expedition to empire-building on the one hand, and identified the residue of imperialism in contemporary mass tourism in Asia on the other, the link between the two remains largely unexplored. How were colonial modes of travel, and the imperial attitudes that underpinned them, translated into decolonised spaces? This chapter argues that the culture of travel and tourism played a part in this transmission. It traces a genealogy of influence by plotting the ways in which an imperial mode of expeditionary travel inspired the Oxford and Cambridge Far Eastern Expedition, which in turn came to have an influence on 'alternative' travel culture via the overland Hippie Trail of the 1960s and 1970s. Offered as one case study in a broader tableau of reflections on the expedition, it suggests that travel and tourism played a part in the broader process by which colonial cultures and imperial attitudes were translated into the postcolonial context.[14]

RETRACING EMPIRE

The Oxford and Cambridge Far Eastern Expedition was the brainchild of Adrian Cowell and Tim Slessor, students at Saint Catharine's College, Cambridge. As the pair retold the story, a late-night drink turned to feverish conversation, and before long, the 'expedition was born.'[15] Cowell had

Echoes of Empire in Travel to Asia 217

previously served on the 'home team' of the Oxford and Cambridge Trans-African Expedition, a 40,000-kilometre tour of the 'Dark Continent' by Land Rover, which provided the immediate inspiration for OCFEE. Both Cowell and Slessor had prior connections with Asia and direct experience of life in imperial spaces. Cowell was born in China in 1934, when European and Japanese expansionism combined with civil instability to undermine national sovereignty; Slessor spent his compulsory national service in Malaya where anti-British sentiments had given rise to the bloody guerrilla warfare of the Malayan Emergency. Other Cambridge students on the expedition were Pat Murphy, who had read geography with Slessor, and Henry Nott, an agriculture student and secretary of the Cambridge University Auto Club. Antony Barrington-Brown, a photographer, was a recent science graduate. The only member to hail from Oxford University was Nigel Newbery, an undergraduate reading economics at Worcester College.

The Oxford and Cambridge Far Eastern Expedition was not supported by either of the universities after which it was named. The popular appeal of the intervarsity model was such that, with five Cambridge men already signed on, Cowell and Slessor advertised across all the Oxford colleges and 40 American universities to recruit their sixth member. Furthermore, they came to be regarded as 'the Expedition' only because they referred to themselves as such. The grandiose title was devised in the interest of public relations. Although none of them had been trained in marketing, the six young men had a genius for publicity. Indeed, half the team—Cowell, Barrington-Brown, and Slessor—were tasked with documenting and publicising the expedition's progress. Barrington-Brown took a slew of still photographs and films, some of which were broadcast on the BBC. Cowell was responsible for 'commercial blurb sheets' designed to elicit corporate sponsorship, and dispatched media articles to newspapers in England, Asia, and Australia. The most sustained effort came from Slessor, who wrote a popular book about the expedition, *First Overland*, published in the United Kingdom in 1957, and in Australia two years later.

First Overland made the claim that this journey was 'an Expedition.' Yet, Slessor did not define what this meant. Indeed, he had no need, since he took it for granted that the reader implicitly understood. Slessor's unquestioning faith that audiences would understand what he meant (which also extended to painting the words 'Oxford and Cambridge Far Eastern Expedition' on the doors of both Land Rovers) is revealing. By this time, the notion of the expedition had been recounted in so many adventure stories and *Boy's Own* annuals that it was a thoroughly recognisable entity within popular culture. Thus, there is no explanation why Slessor and Cowell decided that an expedition 'should consist of five or six people,' nor why they thought that it was not until they had arranged the delivery of their vehicles that they 'should really be able to call' themselves 'an Expedition.'[16] The journey itself appears to have been a curious fusion of a varsity camping trip, reliability trial, and publicity stunt. In fact, like many of its predecessors in expeditionary

218　*Agnieszka Sobocinska*

history, OCFEE was an expedition by self-proclamation. Their unshakeable self-belief—that they would be the first to perform the task that they set themselves, that their task was arduous enough to demand months of intense preparations and a devoted 'home team,' and that their goal was important enough to interest the public both at home and abroad—was sufficient to mandate the expeditionary label.

The group orchestrated a grand event to mark their departure from Hyde Park Corner in September 1955. A newsreel cameraman and numerous press photographers captured every last-minute adjustment and teary farewell. Interviews were given and everyone posed for the camera. In a jocular spirit, an unsuspecting policeman was asked to point out 'the way to Singapore.' After much fuss, and amidst cheers and waves, the expedition pulled away—and was promptly caught in heavy lunch-hour traffic. As they headed towards Westminster, their custom-fitted Land Rovers, painted in University colours and decorated with the expedition's proposed route, crawled amidst a sea of black Vauxhalls.

This vignette is revealing. Rather than embarking on something completely new, OCFEE was following well-worn tracks. Very little of the world had been left unexplored by 1955. Mount Everest had been conquered two years before. Expeditions to chart the ocean's depths and explore outer space—truly the final frontiers—were already underway. OCFEE's goal—to drive to Singapore—paled in comparison with these extraordinary feats. Furthermore, contrary to its pioneering claims, a number of hardy motorists *had* in fact already driven between Europe and Asia. Most famously, Australian Francis Birtles had coaxed an enormous Bean racing car from London to Melbourne in an epic 26,000-kilometre quest in 1928. Yet, OCFEE insisted that Birtles had in fact failed, as his car had been ferried for approximately 140 kilometres in Burma, at a point where roads did not exist.[17] With great pride, OCFEE boasted that they would conquer every kilometre on land. Of course, they had the advantage of nearly 30 years of automotive improvements to facilitate this: rather than a Bean, they had Land Rovers. Moreover, they could rely on infrastructure built during the Second World War, which included two major new roads connecting North India and Burma, constructed by the United States Army.

Despite—or perhaps because of—its relatively inconsequential aspirations, OCFEE's members insisted on its legitimacy as *an expedition*. The title of their account, *First Overland*, was clearly determined to stake a claim. In the preface to the 1959 Australian Readers' Book Club edition, author Tim Slessor insisted that 'whatever else the reader is tempted to think . . . we did not "gallivant." ' To further secure their image as genuine adventurers rather than mere vacationers, he took pains 'to point out that our complete journey (London-Singapore-London) led across twenty-one countries, and covered thirty-two thousand miles.'[18] *First Overland* also suggested that the journey had some claim to quasi-official status. The reader was advised that preparations had been based on the Royal Geographical Society's *Hints to*

Travellers, and their comprehensive stockpile of provisions was exhibited in photographs of the team and kit, arranged with military precision.[19] Slessor also insisted that OCFEE had the official support of the Royal Geographical Society (RGS), as they had received a £100 grant to conduct fieldwork on irrigation in post-partition Pakistan. There is no doubt that this fieldwork—presented to the RGS as the motivation for the journey—was an afterthought. As Slessor admitted, 'just why we should have had this intention is difficult to say,' but 'we were doing research because we wanted to—which is a pretty good reason.'[20] The scientific outcomes of the fieldwork (which mostly consisted of guided tours around farms, dams, and irrigation projects) remain unclear, and the £100 grant appears to have been little more than tokenistic. Nonetheless, one of the expedition's members, Patrick Murphy, did submit a report on the 'Partition of the Punjab and the Indus Basin Water Dispute,' along with a map outlining OCFEE's route, to the RGS library; and the RGS was regularly invoked to add gravitas to the trip as an expedition.

While the geographic or scientific justifications for an expedition were thin, OCFEE did make one important discovery: by making use of infrastructure established under British colonisation or under American modernisation projects, it was possible to drive overland between Europe and Asia with considerable ease, and even comfort. The expedition made frequent use of governmental, missionary, and commercial infrastructure that

Figure 11.1 The Oxford-Cambridge Far Eastern Expedition crew posing with equipment, 1955. Photograph by Antony Barrington-Brown. By permission of Chris Barrington-Brown.

220 *Agnieszka Sobocinska*

had been established under the British Empire across Iraq, Iran, Pakistan, India, Burma, and Malaya. They attended cocktail parties with ambassadors, visited tea plantations run by old colonial firms, had earnest discussions with missionary doctors, and became acquainted with every British club from Baghdad to Bangkok. In some ways, the expedition was a recreation of colonial-era tours of inspection. Yet this was an imperial tour made in postcolonial times. A wave of decolonisation had surged through the region. Iraq gained independence in 1932, England and the Soviet Union had withdrawn from Iran in 1946, India declared Independence in 1947, Burma became independent the following year. Negotiations concerning Malaya's forthcoming independence had commenced. The British clubs still stood, but their glory days had definitively passed. Yet, having been toasted by its former functionaries, the expedition represented the British Empire's legacy as a living one. Their imperial pride was tangible during a stop in New Delhi. Gazing at the architecture of the former imperial capital, Slessor insisted that 'our achievements were infinitely greater than some of our critics would have the world believe.' The British, he said, had 'left three things which the country might never have had without us . . . a common language, English . . . a single nation [and] a capital worthy of such a vast country.' All in all, Slessor declared New Delhi to be 'a permanent, and in many ways, worthy memorial to the British Raj.'[21]

While travellers had previously benefited from imperial institutions, OCFEE was pioneering in linking colonial and neo-imperial infrastructure, and using them both to its advantage. Economic historians including David Ekbladh and historians of US foreign policy such as Emily S. Rosenberg have argued that American power in the Middle East and Asia was established partly through international development and economic reconstruction regimes.[22] As Ekbladh notes, 'modernisation is deeply implicated in . . . the establishment of American global hegemony.'[23] This took place in the context of the Cold War, as strategic tensions between the Soviet Union and United States were played out in a battle for economic and political dominance in Asia and the Middle East.

OCFEE was, therefore, pioneering a path through nations and regions affected by colonialism, decolonisation, and the desire for neo-colonial dominance on the part of the postwar superpowers. The members of OCFEE warmly praised the benefits that American intervention brought to travellers in the Middle East and Asia. The most difficult section of the expedition's route, the pass between India and Burma, was made possible by a supply road cut into the jungle by US forces during the Battle of Burma in 1944. Furthermore, from the moment it crossed the Bosphorus, the expedition benefited from the United States's postwar investment in the Middle East: part of its push for strategic influence across the region in the context of the Cold War. Passing through Ankara, 'we travelled on the easy, rolling surface of a new strategic highway . . . the tyres hummed, the engine sang to itself, the speed went up to 60 m.p.h. and stayed there.'[24]

Echoes of Empire in Travel to Asia 221

They found the drive similarly comfortable across the Middle East, and right into India itself.

Despite publicising the benefits of modernity to travellers in the region, the expedition was ambivalent about the benefits that neo-imperial modernisation brought to local populations. OCFEE made no paeans to American developmentalism to match its ode to the British Empire. Indeed, *First Overland* drew a sharp contrast between the two Western hospitals operating in Iran, one run by the Church Missionary Society (CMS), the other built with US development money. While the CMS hospital was run down, it was manned by worthy missionaries 'who often work singly and with very little assistance' to provide aid that was 'practical and realistic.'[25] By way of contrast, the American hospital was 'interesting but disturbing': 'it is huge, and cost millions of dollars,' and so luxurious that 'there are only two other hospitals in the world like this—and they're in California.' However, *First Overland* reported that the hospital had been built in an impractical way (featuring, among other things, toilets that were unusable because they faced towards Mecca); moreover, it was impossibly expensive to maintain. Observing that the hospital only housed 23 patients when the expedition visited despite having capacity for 400, Slessor concluded that 'the Americans probably have a greater store of material knowledge than any other nation, but one suspects that their ideas of what to do with it sometimes lags behind.'[26]

A more fundamental critique of American intervention came in Slessor's observations about Nepal, which was only just setting out on its path to modernisation in 1955–6. OCFEE's members were delighted by the seemingly medieval nature of Kathmandu, a place where 'there is no industry, no rush, no neon signs, no cinemas.' While recognising that 'Nepal is one of the most backward countries in Asia,' Slessor admitted that 'one cannot help hoping that it stays that way.' It was with a tinge of regret, then, that he noted that 'well-intentioned advisers are flying in almost every plane with plans for Nepal's economic advancement.' Weighing up the impacts of modernisation, he wrote that 'one recognises that there may be much material justification for these plans, but one wonders whether these easy-going people will not lose immeasurably more than they will gain in the sudden acceleration to the nowhere-in-particular that the Western world so fondly calls progress.' By way of conclusion came the plea: 'Why not leave the backward, poor, illiterate, happy people of Nepal alone?'[27]

While they were ambivalent about American neo-imperialism, the members of the Oxford and Cambridge Far Eastern Expedition were nonetheless eager beneficiaries of the Western commercial networks established under colonialism and advanced by the postwar expansion of capitalism. The expedition was truly pioneering in the extent to which it integrated commercial interests into the narrative of their progress. While explorers had long relied on the support of wealthy patrons, OCFEE made the garnering of corporate support a fine art. Before setting off, the group's appointed 'publicity agent,' Adrian Cowell, sent off hundreds of press releases that asked corporations

222 Agnieszka Sobocinska

for support in exchange for advertising. Championing the possibilities of product placement—a truly modern twist to the notion of an expedition—the group claimed it would 'be particularly happy to carry any product which, due to its distinctive shape or colour—such as an electric razor or packet of soap-flakes—would be easy to incorporate and publicise in our TV film without actually mentioning its name.'[28] The response was enthusiastic, and by the time they set off, OCFEE had amassed 85 commercial sponsorships in cash and kind from corporations including British-American Tobacco, West Indian Sugar Producers Association, Imperial Tobacco, Nestle, Schweppes, and Mobil. Some of this corporate beneficence was truly spectacular. The Rover automotive company donated the two vehicles that made the journey possible. Fuel was provided, free of charge, by Mobil stations along the way. Companies also routinely offered accommodation and other hospitality. In return, OCFEE was bound to perform a number of publicity stunts. In India, they used an elephant to demonstrate the strength of a particular brand of plastic bucket. They conducted television interviews and wrote numerous newspaper articles praising the Anglo-Indian tea merchants, Brooke Bond. Crossing into Singapore, their many media commitments were co-ordinated by the Rover motor company. Even for OCFEE, there was no such thing as a free lunch.

The fact that OCFEE's route was punctuated by refills at Mobil service stations is revealing: by the 1950s, the sun never set on multinational corporate interests. Yet, there was also a direct link with empire: many of the commercial networks that supported OCFEE were largely imperial in both origin and nature. The legacy could be striking. In Pakistan, the expedition was welcomed by a Rover agent, 'one of those who other Pakistanis call a Muslim Englishman, a term which sums it up admirably.' With colonial-era swank, he erected a grand marquee to house the expedition, and staffed it with butlers who went so far as to serve breakfast in bed. In *First Overland*, this episode is recounted as marking the expedition's entry into 'the world of "Sahihibism."'[29] Slessor noted that, surrounded by so much swank, 'the "sahib" tag seemed quite the normal thing . . . although, bearded and dishevelled, we were never quite able to equate ourselves with the pukka sahibs of the days of the Raj.'[30] This passage captures something of the ambivalent and sometimes conflicting meanings that accompanied the expedition's progress. The immediate context for their journey, like the expeditionary mode itself, was clearly a legacy of empire; so much so that the expedition's members could will themselves to imagine they inhabited 'the world of Sahibism.' Yet, this was clearly at odds with the geopolitical reality of the nations they passed through: the days of the Raj and its 'pukka sahibs' were gone. The expedition found itself inhabiting a liminal sphere in which racial relations were in the process of being renegotiated, a sphere that encouraged travellers to imagine themselves within colonial frames, while simultaneously forcing them to recognise that doing so was an illusion sustained by little more than nostalgia.

A *BOYS' OWN* GUIDEBOOK

The expedition's account, *First Overland*, was a bestseller in both the United Kingdom and Australia, and much of its success came from the fact that it was an enjoyable and exciting read. Novels of colonial adventure remained wildly popular in both Britain and Australia in the postwar period.[31] *First Overland* blended elements of colonial adventure with another popular juvenile genre, the public school novel, while adding an undercurrent of self-knowing irony that made it appeal to an adult readership. The first line—'Yes, old boy'—set the scene, and the claim that the expedition 'began, like almost everything else at Cambridge, late at night over gas-ring coffee' introduced a chummy tone that continued throughout the narrative.[32] Once the expedition had left England's shores, the narrative conventions of the colonial adventure dominated, with OCFEE's progress marked by the dramatic anticipation of upcoming dangers. 'Much of the terrain east of Calcutta would be extremely difficult,' readers were advised early on, 'and this was, in fact one reason why no one else had ever made the journey—if it was possible at all.'[33] While such dramatisation situated *First Overland* firmly in the *Boys' Own* mould, the book departed from the generic script in significant ways. The self-conscious recognition of the fact that, as far as expeditions go, OCFEE's was a relatively minor achievement saw Slessor introduce a tone of lighthearted fun, which both exaggerated the anticipation of hardships and deftly handled the inevitable and repeated anticlimaxes. Dramatising the anticipation of danger and difficulty was clearly problematic in light of the relative ease with which the journey was actually made. Even in anticipation, Slessor knew that the greatest peril ahead was driving on roads reputedly unused for a decade, so that 'it seemed that they would be overgrown and derelict': hardly a claim to compete with the more thrilling dangers recorded in expeditionary history.[34] While Slessor worked hard to justify the journey as an official expedition, *First Overland* gently and knowingly mocked the colonial adventure genre by oscillating between earnest exposition and lighthearted irony. It poked fun at the genre of *Boy's Own* adventure even as it perpetuated it, updating the essentially colonial-era genre with a knowing sophistication that appealed to a modern, postwar readership. Closing the introductory section, Slessor earnestly concluded that 'the expedition was born,' before poking fun at himself by noting that 'these words are almost traditional to all expedition stories!'[35] Early on, Slessor explained that in his relentless quest for publicity, Adrian Cowell sold almost 80 articles detailing the expedition's progress to newspapers around the world. He bluntly stated that Cowell's success came about because he 'had a very fertile imagination, and could write wonderful letters about the terrors of the "burning sands and steaming jungles" that lay ahead.'[36] Such self-conscious humour punctuates the text. Attempts to keep teams of curious children away from the expedition's campsite were rendered into an ironic parody of colonial adventure: 'By 10.00 hours the enemy—as he now

224   *Agnieszka Sobocinska*

became—judged that all his ranks were massed ready for the Big Push. At first we managed to hold the position, but after two hours of sporadic skirmishing the infiltration of small boys was becoming too much.'[37] The wry tone, in which adventures were cloaked in playful irony, over-dramatisation, and anticlimax, created an air of lighthearted fun. Rather than undermining their achievement, however, this narrative strategy playfully integrated readers' sympathies with the expedition's aims, and so deftly elided questions about their actual claims to adventure. OCFEE was a thoroughly modern expedition, knowingly winking at readers as they went along. But this very irony allowed them to stake a claim to adventure—and its generic conventions—in spite of the relative ease and comfort of their journey. This interplay between colonial-era frames of reference and postcolonial experience was reflected in a text that crossed generic boundaries: part adventure novel, part political commentary, and part guidebook.

While the tone could be lighthearted, *First Overland* had a serious, even solemn, core. Rendered into 'adventure,' the Oxford and Cambridge Far Eastern expedition was represented as a final feat of authenticity in a rapidly modernising world. As Hsu-Ming Teo has noted,

> in the decades after decolonisation, an astonishing number of travel writers express a nostalgic sense of loss, not just of the Empire, but of the possibilities of 'real' travel and exploration that British imperial dominance over the world had made possible in the nineteenth century . . . when it was imaginatively possible to escape from the ubiquitous and monotonous culture of western modernity . . . when it was still possible to enact those adventure narratives.[38]

Some of OCFEE's irony was poignant, emphasising the fact that theirs was a final, almost desperate attempt to capture the spirit of true adventure in a rapidly modernising and mechanising world. The sense of loss was expressed through Slessor's depiction of mass tourism—and tourists. *First Overland* featured a number of set pieces in which the ignorance and stupidity of mass tourists was amply illustrated, and contrasted to the earnestness and 'authenticity' of the expedition's travels. At the Taj Mahal, Slessor was so moved that he proclaimed it 'the most wholly perfect building ever raised . . . one of the acknowledged wonders of the world.' Having established his refinement, Slessor admitted to feeling 'a little self-righteous indignation at the lack of taste' demonstrated by the American tourists he observed there, 'men and women wearing baseball caps [who] had come down from Delhi for the day to "do India."' As well as being loud, the tourists were ignorant ('Say boy, whatdya call this place?' one asks) and lazy ('that looks like too many steps for me'). They may have been wealthy, but they lacked refinement and soul; they were 'strung about with expensive cameras and exposure meters (none of which they knew how to use),' and which they had not bothered to set up properly. While this piece functioned on a number of

Echoes of Empire in Travel to Asia 225

levels, playing into established prejudices about English refinement versus American crassness, and upper-class sophistication versus the venality of bourgeois consumerism, it was directed most strongly at the emergent culture of mass tourism. The 1950s saw an unprecedented boom in the number of international travellers. The decade also saw the firming of stereotypes around the figure of the tourist. Slessor's passage contributed to the critique of mass tourism as a pointless, soulless activity, in which sights and sites were accumulated for prestige rather than for intellectual development and personal growth. As Slessor writes, 'one sadly expected that they would put yet one more tick against the lists of "musts" on their world itinerary . . . unaware that they had seen something perhaps even more remarkable than the Empire State Building.'[39] Implicit to such stereotypes was the contrasting image of a true 'traveller,' searching for the authentic, the genuine, and the profound. Here, the implied 'true' travellers are the OCFEE members themselves. As Dean MacCannell argued in *The Tourist*, the search for authenticity defined the mid-twentieth century tourist/ traveller dichotomy, and was revealing of a broader alienation from (post) modernity in the West.[40] By contrasting the expedition to mass tourism, *First Overland* made claim to a more authentic mode of travel defined by an ethos of true adventure.

Yet, perhaps the greatest irony lay in the fact that the expedition was not too far removed from the tourist industry at all. Where *First Overland* had opened with doubts as to whether a journey from London to Singapore was even possible, it closed with a series of instructional appendices that set out, in step-by-step instructions, how readers should prepare for a similar journey themselves. These short chapters provided medical advice, mechanical notes, details about navigation and routes, and photographic tips as well as notes about what to wear, what to eat, and how much money to take on the journey. In effect, they functioned as a mini-guidebook advising travellers on the roads to follow, and food, clothes, and equipment to pack. Presented as an appendix separated from the main text, these chapters recreate the anticlimax of the Expedition's progress. Where *First Overland* had begun in the mode of a *Boys' Own* adventure, it concluded as a tourist guidebook.

While geographical terrain may not have been defeated, a conceptual leap had surely been made. What the expedition explored was not new territory per se, but rather a new mode of travel. It revealed that by making use of the legacies of colonialism, such as high commissions, clubs, and commercial networks, along with the benefits of neo-imperialism—the infrastructure such as roads, airports, and hospitals that were built with US development funding—modern travellers could cross Asia in a way that was relatively comfortable while retaining the vestige of 'authenticity.' The OCFEE had discovered that ordinary people—students, even—could easily and comfortably travel across what had been previously imagined as dangerous or uncomfortable terrain, and they published step-by-step advice on

226   *Agnieszka Sobocinska*

how to do it. *First Overland* publicised this discovery to a mainstream audience who were beginning to turn their dreams of overseas travel into reality.

AN INSPIRING ADVENTURE

Largely because of their knack for self-promotion, the Oxford and Cambridge Far Eastern Expedition achieved widespread renown. Newspapers across the United Kingdom published dispatches from the route, and three films based on the expedition, introduced by David Attenborough, were screened as part of the BBC's *Traveller's Tales* series. The expedition's progress was also reported in Australia. The Melbourne *Argus* reported on their arrival at Singapore with the grandiose claim that theirs had been 'one of the most gruelling motor expeditions ever undertaken.'[41] Regional news outlets carried the story, with a newspaper in regional Victoria describing it with even more bombast as 'the most gruelling tour in modern history.'[42] Similarities in usage and tone suggest that these were among the 80 articles placed by Cowell. *First Overland* was an immediate success in the UK, where it was published by both George Harrap and the Companion Book Club in 1957. Its popularity extended beyond the British market, with publication by the Readers Book Club in Australia in 1959. OCFEE's claim to having pioneered overland motoring in Asia saw it enjoy a second wave of publicity during the London-Sydney Marathon, a 1968 car rally that drew a great deal of media and popular attention. In 2005, there were 50th-anniversary celebrations in Singapore that attracted hundreds of admirers and widespread media attention—a testimony to its long-term influence.[43]

Perhaps OCFEE's most significant legacy was its influence on the 'alternative' culture of travel and tourism that developed in Asia in its wake. The path 'pioneered' by the expedition, and outlined in the guidebook-appendix of *First Overland*, became the standard route of the famed 'Hippie Trail' that ran between Europe and Asia in the decades following OCFEE's journey. The first London-Calcutta tourist buses, operated by Indiaman tours, began to travel along the route popularised by the Oxford and Cambridge Expedition in 1957—the same year *First Overland* was published.[44] Before long, buses from corporations including Penn Overland, Magic Bus, Top Deck, Hughes Overland, and even Contiki were journeying towards the East, and they were joined by thousands of travellers in their own vehicles, hitchhiking or making their way on public transport. The Hippie Trail was at its peak from the mid-1960s to 1979, when the simultaneous collapse of Afghanistan into war and Iran into revolution forced its close. Although it is impossible to determine exactly how many people travelled the Hippie Trail, it is estimated that at least 100,000 (and probably many more) tourists from across Europe, North America, Australia, New Zealand, and Japan drove, rode, or hitched the path during the 15 or so years that it was accessible.[45]

Echoes of Empire in Travel to Asia 227

Travellers' attitudes are shaped by the culture of travel and tourism. Tourists tend to pay as much attention to each other as to the cultures and people they are visiting. Attitudes towards social and cultural Others are communicated within and between tourist groups, and signalled to novices through guidebooks, photographs, souvenirs, clothing, and other forms of representation. This applies both to mass tourists (usually defined as 'package tourists' and mainstream independent sightseers) and so-called 'alternative' travellers (including drifters, self-defined 'travellers,' and backpackers).[46] 'Alternative' travellers are often posited as being in the vanguard, creating travel cultures that are then subsumed into the mainstream; they are, in this way, particularly influential.[47] The strong travel culture that developed along the Hippie Trail—an in-group dynamic that shaped travellers' views of the people and places they saw along the way—was passed on to subsequent 'alternative' travellers. Its influence is still evident in the culture of contemporary backpacking in South and Southeast Asia.[48]

The Hippie Trail was a complex phenomenon with roots in the 1960s counterculture as well as Romantic ideas about the nature of travel and Orientalist assumptions about 'the East.' However, it must be noted that it was also indebted to the colonial past. Many young travellers were attracted to the Hippie Trail because of its promise of adventure, and they looked to colonial adventures for inspiration.[49] References to Rudyard Kipling's stories regularly appeared in the diaries, travel accounts, and subsequent recollections of Hippie Trail travellers. A number also made direct references to the Oxford and Cambridge Far Eastern Expedition and, particularly, to *First Overland*. The most influential of the Hippie Trail guidebooks, Tony Wheeler's *Across Asia on the Cheap* (first published in 1973), featured *First Overland* in its list of recommended reading. Describing it as 'a fascinating description' of overland travel, Wheeler made it directly relevant to subsequent travellers by noting that 'in general things have changed remarkably little . . . since that epic drive.'[50] Taking their markers from these influences, a number of travellers came to think of their own journeys as 'expeditions,' in the OCFEE model. An early report of the Indiaman tours insisted that theirs was 'an expedition rather than a tour in the normal sense.'[51] Mary Gage, who travelled overland with two small children in the early 1970s, was one of many to refer to her personal journey as 'our expedition.'[52]

The culture of the Hippie Trail mirrored some of OCFEE's modes and attitudes. Like its colonial-era predecessors, the expedition had no place for women; adventuring was strictly men's business. Women did not belong in the rough and ready culture of the road, and they had appeared in *First Overland* only as obliging hostesses who mothered the expedition's members during pit stops across Asia. They baked cakes and sticky puddings and mended worn clothes, but few remained on the page long enough to express an opinion. Premised on similar ideals of adventure, the culture of the Hippie Trail was also overwhelmingly masculine. One of the overlanders' mottoes was 'Leave the Chicks at Istanbul,' and it is difficult to find a female

228   *Agnieszka Sobocinska*

character either in iconic travel narratives such as Patrick Marham's *Road to Katmandu,* or in non-fiction accounts such as Richard Neville's *Play Power.* Even *Across Asia on the Cheap,* produced by Tony and Maureen Wheeler during their shared journey, appeared under Tony's name alone. Of course, many women did travel on the Hippie Trail. A small number even published their accounts.[53] However, they remained peripheral to the atmosphere of boys' own adventure that dominated the Hippie Trail, which was so ingrained that Neville, for example, addressed his readers as 'young man,' with little regard for the fact that women may have also been making the trip.[54]

The travel culture of the Hippie Trail also echoed OCFEE's conceit that theirs was the final flourish of adventure before modernity—and mass tourism—homogenised the world. As Neville put it, 'overlanders are anti-lemmings, scurrying across previously unexplored terrain as it slowly subsides into a deathly sea of uniformity;' they were making a 'final inspection of the bits between encroaching petrol stations, Wimpy bars and Hiltons.'[55] Perhaps unsurprisingly, strict codes separating 'authentic' from 'inauthentic' modes of experience developed on the trail, most often rendered into a division between the 'traveller' and the 'tourist.'[56] These codes demarcated the boundaries of the Hippie Trail's travel culture, determining insiders from outsiders by virtue of their clothes, vocabulary, experiences, and opinions.[57]

The complex performances that signified the division between 'travellers' and 'tourists' created a market for instructional literature, which could initiate novices into the travellers' culture, and so ease their entry into the in-group. Overland guidebooks taught aspiring travellers what was and was not considered 'authentic.' Claims to authenticity propelled a number of guidebook publishers and tour operators to great success. Partly because they helped confer status, guidebooks were also extremely influential in the formation of the culture of alternative travel. Gillian Kenny has found that Lonely Planet, founded by the Wheelers to publish *Across Asia on the Cheap,* helped to articulate a sense of identity for 'its' travellers.[58] Peter Welk has further shown that Lonely Planet had a formative influence in the development of 'alternative' and backpacking travel cultures.[59]

The Hippie Trail guidebooks—and Lonely Planet's in particular—are notable for their trademark tone, which echoes that of *First Overland* in being simultaneously authoritative and wry.[60] While insisting on the legitimacy of its claims to adventure, Lonely Planet also deployed self-conscious irony about the trail's status within the hierarchy of expedition and exploration. Lonely Planet insisted on 'getting down to the real nitty gritty of these countries,' and although the Wheelers had made their two overland trips in their own vehicles, they recommended public transport as 'the most genuine way of travel.' Nonetheless, the drive for authenticity was also gently mocked: Indian trains were 'a once only experience,' and half an hour 'reading about picking leeches off your ankles and living on cold rice' on the trekkers' bulletin board in Kathmandu 'will keep you in town.' Travellers were also

Echoes of Empire in Travel to Asia   229

warned that they would likely return home with 'Overlander Syndrome,' a tongue-in-cheek disorder with symptoms including 'a propensity for eastern clothing' (to which Wheeler added, 'don't worry, all factors of the syndrome are easily curable').[61] As with *First Overland*, over-dramatisation and anti-climax engendered a lightness of tone. While the 1979 version insisted that 'the Asian overland trip is still one of the great travel adventures,' earlier editions had referred to the 'overland travel game,' and noted a tendency amongst (other) alternative travel writers to be 'far too "aren't we something special." '[62] The tone of playful irony established by *First Overland*, in which authenticity and adventure were earnestly sought at the same time as its possibility was questioned, continued at the very heart of alternative travel discourse, and it had a similar effect. Only by self-consciously clouding it in knowing irony could Lonely Planet claim that overland and 'alternative' travel was truly an adventure—or expedition—despite its context of rapid modernisation and industrialisation.

THE EXPEDITION'S AFTERLIVES

This chapter unpicks one thread that bound travellers on the Hippie Trail to a broader colonial legacy. There are many more. It is not my intention to oversimplify the Hippie Trail, or to claim that it was influenced exclusively by OCFEE or the imperial expeditionary mode. Far from it: the Hippie Trail was an extremely complex social and cultural formation, which is yet to attract the range of critical scholarship it deserves. Although its origins in the 1960s counterculture have been well established, there has been scant recognition of the ways in which the colonial histories and neo-imperial contexts of the Middle East and South Asia also shaped the routes and cultures of the Hippie Trail.

The genealogy I have outlined here, from imperial exploration, through the translated mid-point of the Oxford and Cambridge Far Eastern Expedition and the Hippie Trail, to 'alternative' tourism in Asia, points to some of the enduring connections between tourism and imperialism. OCFEE was overtly modelled on imperial modes; it even came with the stamp of approval from the Royal Geographic Society. Its appropriation of the colonial adventure genre, its salute to *Boy's Own* expeditionary culture, and its evocation of the distinction between 'travellers' and 'tourists' positioned the overland trail as one of the last great adventures in a rapidly modernising world. The expedition's discovery that overland travel was both authentic and achievable helped lay the path for future travellers. From the mid-1960s, hundreds of thousands of Western youths followed OCFEE's tracks, collectively treading what one of its greatest evangelists, Tony Wheeler, called a 'groove worn across the map of Asia.'[63] The travel culture that sprang up along the Hippie Trail was influenced by the 1960s counterculture as well as Romantic and Orientalist ideas. Significantly, however, it also borrowed

230 Agnieszka Sobocinska

from the imperial expedition—as translated by the Oxford and Cambridge Far Eastern Expedition—in its route and its insistence on adventure, as well as its anti-tourist pretensions and gendered road culture. *First Overland* also provided a syntax and tone for Hippie Trail guidebooks, including Lonely Planet, which played a key role in establishing 'alternative' travel culture in Asia. In these ways, *First Overland* and the Hippie Trail functioned as the expedition's afterlives, ensuring that echoes of empire continue to be heard in guesthouses and backpacker cafes across Asia today.

NOTES

1. John M. Mackenzie, ed., *European Empires and the People: Popular Responses to Imperialism in France, Britain, the Netherlands, Belgium, Germany and Italy* (Manchester: Manchester University Press, 2011), 1.
2. John M. Mackenzie, 'Empires of Travel: British Guide Books and Cultural Imperialism in the 19th and 20th Centuries,' in *Histories of Tourism: Representation, Identity and Conflict*, ed. John Walton (Clevedon, NY: Channel View Publications, 2005).
3. Michael Kowalewski, 'Introduction: The Modern Literature of Travel,' in *Temperamental Journeys: Essays on the Modern Literature of Travel*, ed. Michael Kowalewski (Athens, GA: University of Georgia Press, 1992), 11.
4. Hsu-Ming Teo, 'Wandering in the Wake of Empire: British Travel and Tourism in the Post-Imperial World,' in *British Culture and the End of Empire*, ed. Stuart Ward (Manchester: Manchester University Press, 2001), 164.
5. Robert Dixon, *Writing the Colonial Adventure: Race, Gender and Nation in Anglo-Australian Popular Fiction, 1875–1914* (Cambridge: Cambridge University Press, 1995).
6. Morag Bell, Robin Butlin, and Michael Heffernan, eds., *Geography and Imperialism, 1820–1940* (Manchester: Manchester University Press, 1995), 2.
7. Bill Schwarz, *Memories of Empire, Volume 1: The White Man's World* (Oxford: Oxford University Press, 2011).
8. World Tourism Organization, *Yearbook of Tourism Statistics* (Madrid: WTO, 1997).
9. Tim Edensor, *Tourists at the Taj: Performance and Meaning at a Symbolic Site* (London: Routledge, 1998).
10. For an analysis of how tourism impacted on perceptions of otherness in the Australian-Asian context, see Agnieszka Sobocinska, *Visiting the Neighbours: Australians in Asia* (Sydney: University of New South Wales Press, 2014).
11. John Hutnyk, *The Rumour of Calcutta: Tourism, Charity and the Poverty of Representation* (London: Zed Books, 1996).
12. Dennison Nash, 'Tourism as a Form of Imperialism,' in *Hosts and Guests: The Anthropology of Tourism*, ed. Valene L. Smith (Oxford: Basil Blackwell, 1978), 33–48.
13. Malcolm Crick, 'Representations of International Tourism in the Social Sciences: Sun, Sights, Savings and Servility,' *Annual Review of Anthropology* 18 (1989): 307–44; Hutnyk, *The Rumour of Calcutta*; C. Michael Hall and Hazel Tucker, *Tourism and Postcolonialism: Contested Discourses, Identities and Representations* (London: Routledge, 2004); Peggy Teo and Sandra Leong, 'A Postcolonial Analysis of Backpacking,' *Annals of Tourism Research* 33, no. 1 (2006): 109–31.

Echoes of Empire in Travel to Asia   231

14. See also Sobocinska, 'The Language of Scars: Australian Prisoners of War and the Colonial Order,' *History Australia* 7:3 (2010): 58.1–58.19 and 'Hearts of Darkness, Hearts of Gold,' in *Australia's Asia: From Yellow Peril to Asian Century*, ed. David Walker and Agnieszka Sobocinska (Crawley, WA: UWA Press, 2012).
15. Tim Slessor, *First Overland: The Story of the Oxford and Cambridge Far Eastern Expedition* (London: Readers Book Club, 1959).
16. Slessor, *First Overland*, 12.
17. Ibid., 11.
18. Ibid., unpaginated preface.
19. Ibid., 12.
20. Ibid., 104.
21. Ibid., 126.
22. David Ekbladh, *The Great American Mission: Modernization and the Construction of an American World Order* (Princeton: Princeton University Press, 2011); Emily S. Rosenberg, *Spreading the American Dream: American Economic and Cultural Expansion, 1890–1945* (New York: Hill and Wang, 1982).
23. Ekbladh, *The Great American Mission*, 3.
24. Slessor, *First Overland*, 48.
25. Ibid., 87.
26. Ibid., 88.
27. Ibid., 136.
28. Ibid., 16–17.
29. Ibid.
30. Ibid., 107.
31. Dixon, *Writing the Colonial Adventure*.
32. Slessor, *First Overland*, 11.
33. Ibid.
34. Ibid., 11–12.
35. Ibid., 11.
36. Ibid., 16.
37. Ibid., 41–2.
38. Hsu-Ming Teo, 'Wandering in the Wake of Empire,' 172.
39. Ibid., 128–9.
40. Dean MacCannell, *The Tourist: A New Theory of the Leisure Class* (London: Macmillan, 1976).
41. '30,000 m. by Land Rover,' *The Argus*, 10 April 1956, 22.
42. 'A Grueling Tour,' *Healesville Guardian*, 31 March 1956, 4.
43. See 'From London to Singapore in 2 Land Rovers: First Overland,' Aural Asia, firstoverland.com, accessed 17 September 2012.
44. Rory Maclean, *Magic Bus: On the Hippie Trail from Istanbul to India* (London: Viking, 2006), 78.
45. No statistics separating 'alternative' from mainstream tourists have ever been kept. The estimate of at least 100,000 comes from the noticeable increase of travellers to India (one of the major destinations along the hippie trail) during the 1960s and 1970s. See Subas C. Kumar, 'The Tourism Industry in India: Economic Significance and Emerging Issues,' in *Tourism in India and India's Economic Development*, ed. Kartik C. Roy and Clement A. Tisdell (Commack, NY: Nova Science Publishers Inc., 1998).
46. Although the distinction is extremely problematic, travel cultures in Asia have been divided between 'mass' and 'alternative' since the 1960s, roughly following age-old elitist divisions between 'tourist' and 'traveller.'
47. Melvyn Pryer, 'The Traveller as a Destination Pioneer,' *Progress in Tourism and Hospitality Research* 3 (1997): 225–37.

232 Agnieszka Sobocinska

48. Sobocinska, ' "Hippie Sahibs": Colonial Cultures of Travel and the Hippie Trail,' *Journal of Colonialism and Colonial History* 15:2.
49. Ibid.
50. Tony Wheeler, *Across Asia on the Cheap: With 'Bad News' Supplement on Iran and Afghanistan*, 3rd ed. (South Yarra, AU: Lonely Planet, 1979).
51. 'By Indiaman to London,' *Australian Women's Weekly*, 18 December 1963, 12.
52. Mary Gage, *The Overlander's Handbook: A Guide for the Overland Adventurer to India and Beyond* (Perth: Id Publications, 1976), 1.
53. See, for example, Frances Letters, *The Surprising Asians: A Hitch-Hike Through Malaya, Thailand, Laos, Cambodia and South Vietnam* (Sydney: Angus & Robertson, 1968) and *People of Shiva: Encounters in India* (Sydney: Angus & Robertson, 1971).
54. Richard Neville, *Play Power* (London: Jonathan Cape, 1970), 203–4.
55. Ibid., 221–2.
56. Sobocinska, ' "Hippie Sahibs" '.
57. Ibid.
58. Gillian Kenny, ' "Our Travellers" out there on the Road: *Lonely Planet* and Its Readers, 1973–1981,' *Journal of Australian Studies* 72 (2002): 112.
59. Peter Welk, 'The Lonely Planet Myth: "Backpacker Bible" and "Travel Survival Kit",' in *Backpacker Tourism: Concepts and Profiles*, ed. Kevin Hannam and Irena Atelejevic (Clevedon, NY: Channel View Publications, 2008), 85.
60. Jon Krakauer, 'All They Really Wanted was to Travel a Little,' *Smithsonian*, no. 25 (1994): 132–44.
61. Wheeler, *Across Asia on the Cheap: A Complete Guide to Making the Overland Trip with Minimum Cost and Hassles*, 1st ed. (Sydney: Lonely Planet, 1973), 8, 12, 59.
62. Wheeler, *Across Asia on the Cheap* (1979), 1; Wheeler, *Across Asia on the Cheap* (1973), 3, 27.
63. Wheeler, *Across Asia on the Cheap* (1979), 1.

Contributors

Georgine Clarsen is Senior Lecturer in the History and Politics Program at the University of Wollongong. Her research interests include the history of gender and automobility, and settler colonial mobilities as a distinctive constellation of mobility practices. She is a founding associate editor of the journal *Transfers: Interdisciplinary Journal of Mobility Studies* (Berghahn Press). Her chapter in this volume was written as part of an Australian Research Council Discovery Project titled 'Mobile Modernities: "Around-Australia" automobile journeys, 1900–1955' (DP110101875).

Adriana Craciun is Professor of English at the University of California, Riverside, and Director of the university's Material Cultures of Knowledge multi-campus research group. She has published on exploration in relationship to book history in *Atlantic Studies, PMLA, Nineteenth-Century Literature* and *Interventions*, and is currently completing a new book titled *Northwest Passages: Arctic Disaster and the Cultures of Exploration*. With Luisa Calè she co-organized the series of international events, 'The Disorder of Things: Predisciplinarity and the Divisions of Knowledge, 1660–1850,' out of which developed *The Disorder of Things* special issue of *Eighteenth-Century Studies* (2011), in which her chapter in this collection was originally published.

Bronwen Douglas is Adjunct Senior Fellow in the School of Culture, History, and Language in the College of Asia and the Pacific at the Australian National University. A historian of the intersections of race, geography, and encounters in Oceania, she is author of *Across the Great Divide: Journeys in History and Anthropology* (1998) and *Science, Voyages, and Encounters in Oceania 1511–1850* (2014). She is co-editor of *Tattoo: Bodies, Art and Exchange in the Pacific and the West* (2005) and *Foreign Bodies: Oceania and the Science of Race 1750–1940* (2008).

234 Contributors

Tom Griffiths is W. K. Hancock Professor of History in the Research School of Social Sciences at the Australian National University (ANU). During the summer of 2002–3 he travelled to Antarctica as a Humanities Fellow with the Australian Antarctic Division, and in 2012 he was invited by the Australian Government to join the centennial voyage to Mawson's Huts. His books include *Slicing the Silence: Voyaging to Antarctica* (2007), co-winner of the Prime Minister's Prize for Australian History, and *Australia and the Antarctic Treaty System: 50 Years of Influence* (edited with Marcus Haward, 2011). He is Chair of the Editorial Board of the *Australian Dictionary of Biography*, a Professorial Associate of the National Museum of Australia, Director of the Centre for Environmental History at ANU, and a Fellow of the Australian Academy of the Humanities.

Philip Jones is Curator in the South Australian Museum's Department of Anthropology, where he has worked since 1984. He has undertaken fieldwork with Aboriginal people in Central Australia and published widely on material culture, frontier encounters, expeditions, Aboriginal art, art history, and the history of anthropology. He has curated more than 30 exhibitions on these subjects. His books include *Ochre and Rust: Artefacts and Encounters on Australian Frontiers* (2007), which won the 2008 Prime Minister's Literary Award for Non-Fiction.

Ralph Kingston held a British Academy Postdoctoral Fellowship prior to taking up an appointment at Auburn University in Alabama where he is now Associate Professor of History. He is the author of Bureaucrats and Bourgeois Society: Office Politics and Individual Credit, France 1789–1848 (2012).

Agnieszka Sobocinska is Deputy Director and Lecturer at the National Centre for Australian Studies at Monash University in Melbourne. She is a historian with research interests in Australia's relations with Asia, the history of travel and tourism, and the cultural history of foreign aid and international development. With David Walker, she is co-editor of *Australia's Asia: From Yellow Peril to Asian Century* (2012).

Martin Thomas is Associate Professor of History in the Research School of Social Sciences at the Australian National University and an Honorary Associate in the Conservatorium of Music, University of Sydney. His longstanding interest in narratives of exploration found an outlet in *The Artificial Horizon: Imagining the Blue Mountains* (2003), a study of landscape and the colonial imaginary. His other books include *The Many Worlds of R. H. Mathews: In search of an Australian anthropologist* (2011), winner of the National Biography Award of Australia. He is currently working on a film and a book about the American-Australian Scientific Expedition to Arnhem Land in 1948.

Lorenzo Veracini is Associate Professor at the Swinburne Institute for Social Research in Melbourne. His research focuses on the comparative history of colonial systems and settler colonialism. He is the author of *Israel and Settler Society* (2006), *Settler Colonialism: A Theoretical Overview* (2010), and *The Settler Colonial Present* (2014). He is managing editor of the journal *Settler Colonial Studies*.

Stephen A. Walsh is a historian of exploration and Central Europe. In 2014 he completed his PhD in Modern European History at Harvard University where his research was funded by the Minda de Gunzburg Center for European Studies.

Index

Page numbers in **bold** refer to figures.

Abolitionists 55
Adélie Land **184**, 186
Admiralty 8, 28–30, 41–2,
advertising 14, 195, 198–9, 202, 209,
214, 222
animals 68, 75, 82, 98–9, 101; totem
101
Arago, Jacques 116, 118–19, **119**, 120
Arctic Circle 35–6
'Armchair Expeditionaries' 10, 135
Arnhem Land 2, 4
Arnhem Land Expedition (American-
Australian Scientific Expedition
to Arnhem Land 1948) 1, **2**, 3,
3, 5, 7, **15**
art 119, 135, 164 ; cartoons 150, **151**,
popular culture 153, **154**
Australasian Antarctic Expedition (AAE
1911–14) 10–11, 171, 173, 176,
179, 181–2, 186–7, 190; impact
180–1, 183, 190; leadership
171, 174; objectives 172–3, 178,
191; publications 172, 179, 186;
weather 175–6, 179, 182–3, 187
Australian nationalism 173, 180, 182,
209
Austrian Imperial-Royal Geographical
Society (Kaiserlich-Königliche
Geographische Gesellschaft)
152, 159, 161
authorship 8, 25–9, 32, 36, 40–2, 69

Baffin Bay 30
Bailyn, Bernard 57–8
Barrow, John 28, 30, 38–9, 40
Bassett-Smith, Peter 6

Baudin, Nicolas 103, 116, 138
Bayly, C. A. 20
Billington, Brian **15**
Birtles, Francis 12
Bismarck, Otto von 155
Blaxland, Gregory 77
Bligh, William 21
Blitner, Gerald 6
Blue Mountains 53, 77, 92
Bougainville, Louis-Antoine de 109
Bouguer, Pierre 33–4, 36–8, 40
British Empire 5, 12, 205–6, 221
British Jackson-Harmsworth
Expedition (1894–7)
Bruni d'Entrecasteaux, Joseph-Antoine
116
Buffon, comte de 110, 112, 121
Bullock, William 41
Burke, Robert O'Hara 11, 71, 195–6

cabinets of curiosity 132
Caillé, Adolphe 130–1
cannibalism 55, 89
Cape Vienna 149, 163
capitalism 20, 75, 78, 207
Carter, Paul 17, 70
cartography 20, 149, 158–61, **160**,
162–3
ceremony 2–4, 93, 204; parody 204
Certeau, Michel de 42
climate change 177
Coleridge, Samuel Taylor 32
collecting 10, 17
commemoration 158, 175, 179–81,
181, 191
Commerson, Philibert 109, 112

238 *Index*

Commonwealth Bay 176, **177**, **180**, 181, 186–7, 190
Conrad, Joseph 73
convicts 72–3
Cook, James 14, 26–9, 43, 72, 92, 99, 103, 116, 118
Court Treatt Cape to Cairo Expedition (1925) 204–7, **206**; impact 205, 209; leadership 204; objectives 204; publications 204, 208
Cowell, Adrian 216–7, 223, 226
Croker, John Wilson 28
crossings 53–6, 58–9, 92
cultural brokage 4, 6
cultural imaginary 5
Cuvier, Georges 117, 121, 138–9

Dampier, William 26, 27, 43
decolonisation 13, 214–5, 220
Defoe, Daniel 77–8
Dening, Greg 21
De Quincey, Thomas 32
disease 68, 82, 186
displacement 58
'dreaming' 104
Driver, Felix 5, 71
Duché de Vancy, Gaspard 112, **113**
Dumont d'Urville, Jules 127, 129, 132, 134

Easter Island 111–12, **113**
East India Company 78
encounters 9, 15, 53, 59, 68, 88–93, **95**, 96–106, 108, **100**, 111, 115–16, 118–23, **119**, 201–3; asymmetry 108; cross-cultural 9, 15; early frontier 97; 'ideal' 94; interpersonal 4; protocols 9, 90, 99–100, 104; unpredictability 92, violence 21, 98, 113–15, 202
Enlightenment 14, 16, 26–7, 29, 32, 35, 40–1, 78, 88, 138
ethnography 108, 109, 112, 117–18, 121; objects 127–36, 140–1; seaborne 108, 111, 119, 122–3
etymology 18–20, 27, 56, 72, 108, 113
explorers 15, 17–20, 25–30, 37, 39–40, 42–3, 71–3, 96–7, 103, 156, 158–9, 161, 164–5; antagonism between 6; artist 164–5; as author 18 *see also* authorship; heroic 71–2; identity 26–8, 42; persona 70;

publishing 8; subject position 26, 29
European empires 10, 13, 20
European expansion 19
Everest ascent 13, 218
Expeditions: afterlives 229–30; as theatre 11 *see also* performance; form 5, 7, 65–8, 70–1, 74; imperial legacy 222, 225; intercultural nature 4; 'machines for producing discourse' 6, 16; naming 14; replication 65–8, 81; settler colonial 8, 51–3, 55–60, 204; settling *vs* discovering 9; terminology 13 *see also* etymology
Eyre, Edward 91

film 2, 194, 196, 200, 203, 218
finance 9, 74–5, 78–80, 196; donations 76; entrepreneurialism 74; private funds 74; sponsorship 12, 69, 70, 78, 194, 199, 197, 202, 204, 217, 221–2; subscription 77, 79
Forster, Charles de 134–5
Foucault, Michel 8, 25, 27, 150
Franz Josef Land 10, 148–50, 152–3, 155, 158–60, **160**, 161–5
Freycinet, Louis-Claude Desaulses de 9, 108, 116, 117–21, 136, 138
Friedrich, Caspar David 35, 41

Gage, Mary 227
Gaimard, Joseph Paul 137–40
gender 14, 68, 194, 208, 227–8; 'new femininity' 205, 208
geodetic expeditions 8, 35
Germany 155; culture 156; nationalism 156–8; unification 155–6
Giesecke, Karl Ludwig 39–40
gifts 120, 127, 209
Giles, Ernest 91, 99, 103
Gilpin, William 52–1
Goethe, Johann Wolfgang 32
Goffman, Erving 90
Gozlan, Léon 133, 135
Greenland **31**, 38–41
Grey, George 90, 104–5

Habsburg Monarchy 10, 148, 150, 152, 155–7, 164
Hakluyt, Richard 26
Hawaiian Islands 111

Index 239

Hearne, Samuel 27
heroes 16
Heyerdahl, Thor 15
Hillary, Edmund 13
'Hippie Trail' 12, 226–30
Hobsbawm, Eric 72
Hogg, James 32
Homer 52
Howard, Luke 36–8
Howitt, Alfred 98
Hudson's Bay Company 27, 78
human remains 4
Humboldt, Alexander von 32, 39, 72
Hurley, Frank **174**, 179, **184**

imperialism 5, 118, 122, 148, 150,
    152, 155, 158, 163, 172, 205–6,
    214–6, 230
indigenous agency 6, 9, 109, 112, 114,
    116, 122; story telling 209
indigenous people 9, 27, 59, 68–9,
    75, 77, 88–91, 93–100, **100**,
    108, 111–16, 118–23, 135–40,
    201–4, 207–9; in advertising
    202; cultures 88; dance 121,
    202–3 *see also* performance;
    in films 202; guides 97–8;
    languages 93, 97, 122, 139; land
    89; mediators 4; responses to
    expeditions 2–3; sovereignty 51,
    56–7, 207; 'studied indifference'
    103; women 102–3, 105,
    111–12

Jameson, Robert 39–40
Jeffryes, Sidney 11, 187–8
John Murray publisher 28, 40
Johnson, David H. 3
Jomard, Edmé 131, 135–6

Kennedy, Dane 5, 14, 21, 69–70, 74–5
Kennedy, Edmund 96
kinship 88, 97–8
Kipling, Rudyard 215, 227
Koerner, Lisbet 36

La Condamine, Charles Marie de 26,
    33, 35
La Pérouse, Comte de 9–10, 16, 27,
    108, 110–16, 118, 121, 129,
    131
Laing, John 30
Lawson, William 77
leadership 8, 17–18

Leichhardt, Ludwig 9, 14, 16,
    65–84, **66**, 90–1, 94,
    104; correspondence 76;
    historiography 84
Leichhardt Australian Expeditions (to
    Port Essington 1844–6; to Swan
    River 1846–7; to Swan River
    1848) 67–71, 75–84; impact
    78; leadership 68–9, 75, 81–2;
    masquerade 73, 80; objectives
    78; publications 78, 81
Lindsay, David 91
Linnaeus, Carl 35–6, 38, 40, 42
Lonely Planet Publications 12, 228–30
Louvre 127, 132, 134, 140
Luminous phenomena 31–8, **31**, **33**,
    41–3; illusion 34, 36–7

McCarthy, Frederick 6
McKenzie, Kirsten 72
MacLeod, Roy 11
Macquarie, Lachlan 77
Macquarie Island 171, 180, 187
MacRobertson Australia Expedition
    (MacRobertson Round Australia
    Expedition 1928) 11–12,
    194–204, **195**, **197**, 206–9;
    advertising 195, 198–9, 202,
    209; impact 199, 200, 202;
    leadership 197; objectives
    194–6; publications 197, 200
madness 11, 187–8
Mann, John F. 66–7, **66**, 68, 75, 80–4,
    82, **83**
Marham, Patrick 228
Maupertuis, Pierre-Louis 35–6, 42
Mawson, Douglas 7, 10–11, 171–6,
    179, 181–3, **180**, **181**, 186–8,
    190–1
media 2–4, 16, 196, 203, 218
memory 3, 6–7, 16, 21
Mertz, Xavier 176, 182, 186, 188,
    190
'middle ground' 59
missionaries 92
Mitchell, Thomas 20–21, 65–6, 74,
    76, 90–1, **91**, 94, **95**, 97, **100**,
    103–4
Mormons 55, 57
Mountford, Charles **2**, 6
Murphy, Pat 217
Musée de la Marine, 127–41, **128**,
    130; collection 130–3, 141;
    display 127, 129, 133–5, 141;

240 *Index*

foundation of 131, 140; visitors 132–5, 140
Muséum national d'histoire naturelle 138, 141
Mussolini 157
myth 13, 15, 65–6, 69, 72, 84, 109

National Geographical Society 1, 4, 78
National Geographic Magazine 2, 78
nationalism 11
naval models 21
Nazis 10, 157–8
neo-colonialism 220–1, 225, 229
Neville, Richard 228
Ninnis, Belgrave 176, 186–90
noble savage 112–13, 116
Norgay, Tenzig 13
Northwest Passage, 28, 30, **31**, 42

oral history 6
O'Reilly, Bernard 29–32, 34–9, 41, 43
outback Australia 173, 199, 201, 208
Oxford and Cambridge Far Eastern Expedition (OCFEE 1955) 12, 21, 209, 214, 216–30, **219**; humour 223; impact 214, 216, 219, 226–7; leadership 214, 216–7; members 217; objectives 214, 217–19; publications 217–18, 222–4, 226
Oxley, John 96, 100–2, 104

Park, Mungo 18–19, **18**, 43, 72
Parry, William 34, 39
Payer, Julius 10, 148–50, 153, **154**, 157–60, **160**, 161–5
Peillon, Auguste 116, 119–21, **137**
performance 16, 68, 70, 90–1, 105, 108, 194; indigenous people 203–4; masquerade 73; plays 150, 171
Phipps, Constantine 27–8
photography 2, 194, 203, 218
phrenology 121, 138–40
physical endurance 14
Pinkerton, John 32
Plato 35
polar craze 41, 150, **151**, 155
Port Essington 71, 74, 76–78, 94
Pratt, Marie Louise 70
propaganda 10, 141
Purchas, Samuel 26, 27,

Quoy, Jean-René Constant 116, 118–19, 121–2, 137–9

race 117–18, 122–3, 138–41, 173, 194, 208
racism 89
radio 196
Ranger, Terence 72
re-enactments 15–16, 59–60
record-keeping 29, 60, 69–71, 90, 104, 122, 131, 203; censorship 29, 69; diaries 97, 171, 200; drawings 82–4, **82**, **83**, **119**, 120; field books 71; journals 70–1, 91–2, 97, 100, 102, 104; log books 158
return 58–61; glory of 157
Riffenburgh, Beau 8, 164
rituals 2, 15, 103, 152–3, 182, 194–5
Robertson, MacPherson aka 'MacRobertson' 11, 14, 173, 196–8, 200–2, 209
Rollin, Claude-Nicolas 109, 111–12
Romanticism 25–6, 32, 229; idealism of 35
Ross, John 30, 39–40
Royal Dublin Society 32, 39–40, 42
Royal Geographical Society 5, 26, 69, 70–2, 74, 81, 161–2, 218–9, 229

Samoan Islands 111, **113**, 113–15
Schaffer, Simon 25
science 68, 71, 76, 117, 120, 138, 149, 152, 161, 182, 190–1, 219; instrumentation 68, 71; relevance to 1; *vs* politics 182
scientific travel 5, 71–2, 122
Scoresby, William 37–8, **37**, 40
Scott, Robert Falcon 11
settler colonialism 51–61, 90, 198, 204, 207–8; narratives 200
Setzler, Frank 4
Severin, Tim 15
Shackleton, Ernest 16
Shark Bay 118–21
silence 183–5, 187
Singapore 12
Slessor, Tim 12, 216–25
Smith, Bernard 116
Smithsonian Institution 1–2, 4
sovereignty 55–8 *see also* indigenous people
space travel 13
Specht, Raymond 6
'squatting expeditions' 9, 57, 76
Stuart, John McDouall 91, 99, 104, 106

Sturt, Charles 90–1, 97–9, 103–4
Szasz, Margaret Connell 4

technology 11, 14–15, 207
Tegetthoff Expedition (First Austro-Hungarian North Polar Expedition 1872–74) 10, 148–53, 155–9, 161, 163–4; impact 148–50, 152, 156, 158, 161; leadership 148, 153; objectives 148–9, 158; publications 149, 153, 157–9, 163–4; rescue 150
Teo, Hsu-Ming 215, 224
terra nullius 60, 173
territorial claims 11
Thomas, Martin 20
toponyms 18
tourism 12, 26, 214–6, 224–9; criticism 224–5; guide books 225–8
Treatt, Chaplin Court 204–5, 208
Treatt, Stella Court 204–5, 208

Ulloa, Antonio de, 32–4, **33**, 36, 38

vehicular expeditions 11–12, 194, 206, 208, 214, 217, 226
Veracini, Lorenzo 200
Virgil 53

Walker, Howell 6
Warburton, Peter Egerton 91
weather 68, 82, 149, 162, 175–6, 179, 182–3, 187
Wentworth, William Charles 53, 77
Weyprecht, Carl 10, 148, 150, 153, **154**, 157–8, 161
Weyprecht-Payer Expedition *see* *Tegetthof* Expedition
Wheeler, Maureen 228–9
Wheeler, Tony 228–9
White, Patrick 72
White, Richard 59
white Australia 198
Williams, Helen Maria 32
Wills, William John 11, 71, 195–6
women 68, 90, 119, 227–8
Worgan, George B. 102

Xenophon, 20, 52